Municipal Administration in Haryana: A Case Study of Performance of Municipal Council, Panchkula

Municipal Administration in Haryana: A Case Study of Performance of Municipal Council Panchkula (MCP)

Sanjeev Ranjan

KALPAZ

ISBN : 978-93-5128-103-0

Price : ₹ 1170

First Published, 2015

Published by

Kalpaz Publications
C-30, Satyawati Nagar
Delhi-110052, Ph. : 9212142040
E-mail: kalpaz@hotmail.com

Laser Typesetting : Future Computer, Delhi
Printed at : G. Print Process, Delhi

Cataloging in Publication Data—DK
Courtesy: D.K. Agencies (P) Ltd. <docinfo@dkagencies.com>

Ranjan, Sanjeev, author.
Municipal administration in Haryana : a case study of performance of Municipal Council Panchkula (MCP) / by Sanjeev Ranjan.
pages cm
Includes bibliographical references (pages).
ISBN 9789351281030

1. Panchkula (India) Municipal Council. 2. Panchkula (India)—Politics and government. I. Title.

DDC 352.160954558 23

Contents

Dedicated to Amar, Sanju,
My Dear Sister Mrs. Sangeeta Devi,
My son Gurdial Ranjan
& My father Sh. R.R. Ranjan,
My mother Late Smt. Prabha Devi.

(1950–2012)

Preface

I express my deep sense of gratitude to Prof. B.S. Ghuman, Professor, Department of Public Administration from whom I have learnt almost everything about how to write a book and due to his inspiration I could finally finish this work.

I express my heartful thanks to Professor Anil Monga, Dr. Akshat Mehta & Dr. Kuldeep Singh, Assistant Professor; Mr. Mritunjay Kumar, Assistant Archivist;

I am thankful to Dr. Rajiv Kumar, Assistant Professor and Dr. Balbir, Assistant Professor, Department of Evening Studies; Mr. Sartaj, Research Scholar, Department of Botany; Mr. Varinder Singh; Muhammad Saphik Alam and Amar Singh, Senior Assistant, DGP (Prisons Hqs, Pb), Chandigarh and Ravinder Prashar for helping me in my book work.

I am sincerely beholden to my father, Sh. Ramadhar Roy Ranjan and my uncle Sh. Sarwan Kumar and Sh. R.S. Prashar; my sister, Smt. Sangeeta Devi; my wife, Smt. Pooja Ranjan; my son, Gurdial Ranjan; and other family members for their love and affection. It is important to highlight the contribution of Sanju, who every time motivated me to write for subject.

My sincere thanks are also due to Prof. Keshav Malhotra, Chairman and Professor Sudhir Kumar, Department of Evening Studies-MDRC for invaluable guidance at every stage of its preparation.

I am also grateful to Ms. Manjeet Kaur, Baljeet Kaur and Rosy for their moral support in writing this book.

Last but not the least, I am immensely thankful to the Almighty and my mother Late Smt. Prabha Devi for continuously blessing me in this endeavour.

Dated:

Dr Sanjeev Ranjan

List of Tables

List of Figures

List of Matrices

List of Photographs

List of Annexures

Abbreviations

CCA	City Compensation Allowance
CSI	Chief Sanitary Inspector
DA	Dearness Allowance
DPC	District Planning Committee
EFC	Eleventh Finance Commission
EO	Executive Officer
HIPA	Haryana Institute of Public Administration
HMSIRCS	Haryana Municipal Services (Integration, Recruitment and Condition of Service) Rules
HPSC	Haryana Public Service Commission
HRA	House Rent Allowance
HUDA	Haryana Urban Development Authority
IMTs	Industrial Model Townships
JE	Junior Engineer
MCP	Municipal Council, Panchkula
ME	Municipal Engineer
MLA	Member of Legislative Assembly
MLC	Member of Legislative Council
MPC	Metropolitan Planning Committee
NDMA	National Disaster Management Authority
NITTR	National Institute of Technical Teacher Training and Research
NOC	No Objection Certificate
PDS	Park Development Society
PPP	Public Private Partnership
PRI	Panchyati Raj Institution
SC	Scheduled Caste
SI	Sanitary Inspector
SPSS	Statistical Package for Social Sciences
SSC	Staff Selection Commission
TA	Travel Allowance
ULB	Urban Local Bodies

1

Introduction

Local Government is the governance for local areas and Local Self Government is a people elected institution which is created for performing the basic functions of the local area. As a essential part of the governmental structure, it not only provides basic services (like roads, sanitation, streetlight, education, health etc.) and amenities to the citizens but also provides opportunity to them to take a part in decision making process in area of policy formulation and Implementation of Local affairs and ultimately plays vital role in development of nation through development of infrastructure physical as well as social in accordance to present needs, demands of beneficiaries, local issues and Public interests for these bodies are being encouraged to experiment with and introduce new practices and existing practices are being streamlined. Seeing above cited, there is need to define Local Government and Local Self Government. According to Oxford Dictionary the Government means the group of people who are responsible for controlling a county or state. Thus the form of government may be Central, State and Local government. Britannica (1974) defines it as, "Local Government means authority to determine and execute measures within a restricted area inside and smaller then the whole state". Lockard (1969) defines it "as a public organization, authorized to decide and administer a limited range of public policies within relatively small territory which is a sub-division of regional or government. Thus Local Government is the form of government which is at the bottom of pyramid of governmental guide, with the national government at the top and intermediate government i.e. state, regions and provinces and it manages its own affairs by the aid & abet of people of its locality.

Local Self Government

According to Gokhale (1972) Local Self Government is the government of a specified locality by the local people through the representatives elected by them.

Thus local self government is the body of primary elected people through the local citizen and it possesses a large amount of autonomy in its respective jurisdiction for performing its functions in better way. It may raise its revenue through local taxation and manages its spending with proper financial administration and systematic use of available personnel to provide basic services escorted by appropriate methods and techniques in its local jurisdiction.

Significance of Local Self Government

The Local Self Government and its effective working is rooted in its proper planning with bird eye view alongwith scientific assessment of available resources keeping in view of priority on the basis of direct and indirect impact for development of their affairs and coordinate activities to execute those plans and significance of Local Self Government may be given as below:

- Nursery of democracy
- Effective people participation
- Better planning and implementation
- Better Mobilization and distribution of local resources
- Effective reporting system
- Enhance economy
- Efficiency and effectiveness in basic services
- Adoption of new methods & techniques in its local affairs
- Forster Local Economic Development
- Facilitate experiment with and introduce new practices
- Provide foundation to other levels of the Government
- Proper inclusion of citizens, civil society and other stake holders in decision making process
- Basic services can not be left to the market making larger strata of the community be deprived. So, it is the body which come to the front in taking responsibility at its shoulder and assume citizens as clients rather than customers.

Thus, the significance of local self government can hardly be ignored for socio-economic development of country. With the enactment of the 74th Constitutional Amendment Act (1992), Urban Local Bodies have become a crucial third tier of government, after the centre and the states. The examples of Local Self Government particularly for urban areas are Municipal Corporation, Municipal Council, Nagar Panchayat etc. in India. In present scenario in India, due to the fact, where about 25% of total population where living in urban area in 1991 but it increased to about 27% in 2001 and further it has been increased to around 32% in 2011. It may be a fact for policy makers that by 2026, it is estimated that around 38.2% of the total population may be urban as per the proposed census. Other projections by the Mckinsey Global Institute is that by 2030 about 40% of the total population and by 2050 we have merely half of the total population as urban in India. In India the local Self Government has strengthen politically, now we have with roughly about 3.6 million directly elected representatives including about one million women. Further, the number of Local bodies in the country has increased to 2.4 Lakhs Units and it shows political upliftment through democracy.

Trends of Urban Population in India has been given below in table (1.1)

Table-1.1

Decadal Urban Growth in India between 1961 to 2011

Year	***Cities in India and its decadal growth***	***X***		***X***	***X***
	Total Population (in Millions)	Urban Population and its %	Decadal Growth in %	No. of cities
1961	439–23	78.93(17.97)	26.41	2365
1971	548–16	109.11(19.91)	38.23	2590
1981	683–33	159.46(23.24)	46.14	3378
1991	844–32	217.18(25.71)	36.47	3768
2001	1027–02	285.35(27-78)	31.13	5161
2011	1210–19	337.10(31.16)	31.80	7259

Source: Misra & Misra, Nagarlok, Jan-March, 2014

Above table depicts the facts about urban settlement. There were 17.97% urban population in India with decadal growth of only 26.41% and number of cities were 2365 in 1961. But it has drastically increased to 31.16%, 31.80% and 7259 for number of cities in 2011. So, one may conclude that percentage of urban population in total population has increased about two times in and no of cities has increased more than three times as compared since year 1961 to in the year 2011.

Above scene put high pressure on present infrastructure of particular local areas and the literature suggested that state of basic services like Water Supply, Sewage, Solid Waste Management and Urban Housing and Transport in Urban areas leaves much to be desired and following adverse factors also contribute for it, some of these are inadequate level of empowerment of Urban Local Bodies, lack of personnel with appropriate skill sets, Inadequate skill sets of personnel already deployed. Apart from this presently numerous issues of Urban Governance i.e. devolution of power, funds and functions, maintaining coordination with others related departments and Ministry particularly Centre as well as State Government, dilemma of autonomy, capacity building, how developed the confidence upon these institutions, are they capable in their affairs, how secure transparency, accountability through adopting of e-governance concept, explore new concepts and practices for generating finances for urban local self government. One of the important methods is being adopted recently as 'Pooled Finance Development Fund Scheme' and secure participation of citizens and other agencies (like NGOs, civil societies and academia) in better policy formulation and implementation.

For the purpose of understanding the dynamics of Urban Governance in the changed Scenario State has been taking a backseat in terms of providing number of Urban Services to the citizen's earlier and remaining occupied by the private sector. The steps have been taken place on the basis of Philosophy the State would play the role as a not only instrument but also promoter, facilitator and include itself in only core areas of the affairs and many times the competitor in the services market as well and Economic pressure complexities in one and other ways and new methods and technique like Public Private Partnership, contracting out, as recent development Public Public collaboration.

For the Census of India 2011, the definition of urban area is as follows;

1. All places with a municipality, corporation, cantonment board or notified town area committee, etc.
2. All other places which satisfied the following criteria:
   i) A minimum population of 5,000;
   ii) At least 75 per cent of the male main working population engaged in non-agricultural pursuits; and iii) A density of population of at least 400 persons per sq. km. The first category of urban units is known as Statutory Towns. These towns are notified under law by the concerned State/UT Government and have local bodies like municipal corporations, municipalities, municipal committees, etc. The second category of Towns is known as Census Town. These were identified on the basis of Census 2001 data. Others are:

Urban Agglomeration (UA): An urban agglomeration is a perpetual urban spread constituting a town and its adjoining outgrowths (OGs), or two or more physically adjoining of towns together with or without outgrowths of such towns. It must consist of at least a statutory town and its total population (i.e. all the constituents put together) should not be less than 20,000 as per the 2001 Census. And

Out Growths (OG): An Out Growth (OG) is a viable unit such as a village or a hamlet or an enumeration block made up of such village or hamlet and clearly identifiable in terms of its boundaries and location. Some of the examples are railway colony, university campus, port area, military camps, etc., which have come up near a statutory town outside its statutory limits but within the revenue limits of a village or villages contiguous to the town.

Out Growth possesses the urban features in terms of infrastructure and amenities such as concrete roads, electricity, taps, drainage system for disposal of waste water etc. educational institutions, post offices, medical facilities, banks etc. and physically contiguous with the core town of the UAs.

Thus, in 2011 census, cities have been classified in two categories i.e. statutory and census towns latter do not enjoy statutory municipal status as statutory and they are largely unregulated, lying outside the municipal governance and Tax net; Devoid of basic civic services and amenities as well as serve as potential sites for unplanned and slum-type growth in a form of as an Urban Agglomerations and Out Growths in cities and population of these settlement usually not in picture in formal way. Pattern of Urban cities in India is given below in table 1.2.

Table-1.2
Increase of Urban Cities between 2001-2011

Sr.No.	*Kinds of Town*	*No. of Town*		*Increased in Numbers between*	*Increased in percentage between*
		2001	*2011*	*2001–2011*	*2001–2011*
1	Statutory Towns	3799	4041	242	6.37
2	Census Town	1362	3894	2532	185.90
	Total	5161	7935	2774	53.74

Source: Census of India-2011

Above table depicts that there was a only 6.37% increase in statutory towns between 2001-2011 and huge 185.90 % increase in

Census towns, there were 1362 Census Towns in 2001 and it increased to 3894 in 2011. From this, it may be observed that policy was made for 242 but 2532 are expected to get benefit for this. The growth of Urban Agglomeration and out growths have been given in table 1.3 below:

Table-1.3
Growth of Urban Agglomerations and Out Growth between 2001-211

Sr.No.	*Kinds of Town Other Settlements*	*No. of Town 2001*	*2011*	*Increased in Numbers between 2001–2011*	*Increased in percentage between 2001–2011*
1	Urban Agglomerations	384	475	91	23.69
2	Out Growths	962	981	19	1.97
	Total	1346	1456	110	8.17

Source: Census of India-2011

In the 2011 Census, 475 places with 981 OGs have been identified as Urban Agglomerations as against (384) UAs with 962 (OGs) in 2001 Census. Thus, the decadal growth of UAs and OGs were 23.69% and 1.97% respectively between 2001-2011.

1.1 HISTORY OF URBAN LOCAL GOVERNMENT IN INDIA

In India the institution of urban local governments has been a phenomenon. The evolution of these local governments can be understood by studying the various phases that they have undergone ever since their conception and inception. These phases can broadly be divided under two heads:

I. The Pre-independence period during which municipalities were created to serve the imperial needs.
II. The Post-independence period during which attempts were made to turn them into self governing units.[1]

I. THE PRE-INDEPENDENCE PERIOD

The institution of urban local governments in India saw the first light of the day during the period of British rule. The municipal governments in India first came into being during the early 17th century with a view to serve the financial needs of the imperial government and reduce the heavy administration burden being petted on the district offices across the country. The establishment of Municipal Corporations in Madras and Bombay in 1687 and 1726 respectively, marked the beginning of the institutionalized local government in India. The British government however, belittled the significance of these institutions and considered them as merely income generating unit. The imposition of Local Taxation Act of 1801 and 1802 aimed at augmenting the imperial finances.[2]

Nevertheless, it was Lord Mayo's Resolution of 1870 on financial decentralization that paved for the significant and holistic development of local government institutions. Furthermore, Lord Ripon's Resolution of 1882 has always been hailed as the 'Magna Carta' of local self-government in India. He is also called the Father of local-self- government in India. In addition to this, the Royal Commission on Decentralization (1907) suggested the development of autonomous administrative units and recommended the strengthening of local government institutions by delegating more financial powers to them.[3]

Under the Diarchal System introduced by the Government of India Act of 1919, the local self-government was enlisted as a *transferred* subject. It was placed under the charge of an Indian Minister, and aimed at the empowerment of people. However, the paucity of funds and the indifferent attitude of British officials towards this cause became major impediments in the development of such local institutions.[4]

Under the Government of India Act 1935, the system of provincial autonomy was replaced by the Diarchal system. As a result, fresh legislations were enacted by various provincial governments. Besides, the financial position of the local bodies experienced slight improvement. But, these local bodies were confronted with an array of new problems as a result of the division of taxation between the local bodies and the provincial government.[5]

However, during the period that followed 1935, the local government institutions failed to serve their basic purpose and could not manifest themselves as efficient institutions of democracy. During the period ranging from 1938-1947, local governments underwent a massive transformation, and experienced various constructive changes with regards to their structure and functioning.[6]

Some of the prominent developments that took place during this period, have been summarized below:-

(a) Significant efforts were undertaken by a few of the Provinces to diagnose the prominent maladies responsible for the ill-health of local governments in India. The states of Uttar Pradesh and Bombay setup Committees in 1938 and 1939 respectively, to enquire into the affairs of their respective local authorities.

(b) De-officialisation of local councils was taken a step further by widening the franchise and the near – total abolition of the system of nomination. Urban bodies in this respect gained more than their rural counterparts.

(c) Separation of legislative and executive functions was introduced in larger urban local bodies. Executive functions were vested in a separate Executive Officer.

(d) The powers and functions of local authorities were increased significantly. However, a noteworthy point here is that the Local bodies, received a major setback with respect to their financial independence[7].

In the pre independence period, the municipalities were set up primarily to cater to the needs of the imperial governance in India. Thus as per the whims and fancies of the colonial matters, the municipal bodies were given limited powers, apart from a cosmetic financial standing and almost no democratic character.

II. POST-INDEPENDENCE ERA

The working of the local government institutions before independence left much to be desired and therefore, the Constitution makers incorporated Article 40, a provision which endowed these institutions with the much required authority.[8]

Despite the provisions contained in Article 40, the government of India constituted a number of committees and commissions from time to time to suggest significant remedial measures for improving the working of Urban Local Bodies. The Local Finance Enquiry Committee, was one such committee that was constituted in 1949 and presented its report in 1951. This committee advocated the expansion of the taxation sphere of urban bodies and suggested that the same can be done by way of allocating few more revenue generating taxes to them.[9]

While recommending the strengthening of the financial sphere, **the Taxation Enquiry Commission** (1953-54) advocated that the local institutions should be assigned the imposition and collection of certain taxes exclusively. [10]

The Committee on the **Training of Municipal Employees (1963)** emphasized on imparting training to the municipal personnel. For this, the committee recommended the setting up training institutions at the central and state levels.[11]

The Rural-Urban Relationship Committee (1963-66) recommended that the municipal administration should be set up in totality i.e. embracing all aspects of governance such as personnel, financial, planning etc. It also advocated for the setting up of separate town and village administrations.[12]

The Committee on **Service Condition of Municipal Employees (1965-1968)** recommended a state wise creation of separate cadre of municipal employees.[13]

The **National Commission on Urbanization** (1988) gave an away of wide ranging suggestions in order help revive and revitalize the urban governance.[14]

However, the suggestions given by these committees and commissions were not taken seriously and most of these remained buried in files and did not see the light of the day. In the 1980's, the need for giving a constitutional status of local bodies to bring uniformity in their structure and functions got momentum and as a result the 65th Constitutional Amendment Bill, called the *Nagar Palika Bill* was introduced in the Parliament in the year 1989. It was passed by the Lok Sabha but was defeated in the Rajya Sabha in October 1989. However in the year 1991, the Constitutional Amendment Bill concerning Urban Local Bodies was again introduced in the Lok Sabha. This time it was passed by the parliament in the year 1992 (with a few modifications) and became the 74th Constitutional Amendment Act; 1992. The basic provisions of this Act are summarized as follow:

1. **Setting up of Municipal Bodies**:- The 74th Constitutional Amendment Act, 1992, provided the setting up of the Urban Local Bodies on the basis of their population and density-i.e. (a) Nagar Panchayat for a transitional area; (b) Municipal Council for a smaller area; and (c) Municipal Corporation for a large area.
2. **Reservation of Seats:-**Article 243(T) deals with the reservation of seats for Schedule Caste (SC) and Schedule Tribes (ST) in municipal bodies in proportion to their population and 1/3rd of the seats are reserved for women including Schedule Caste and Schedule Tribe women.
3. **State Election Commission:** In the 74th Constitutional Amendment Act, 1992, Article 243 (Z) was inserted for the establishment of State Election Commission for superintendence, direction and conduct of elections of municipal bodies.
4. **State Finance Commission:-**Article 243(Y) dealt with the establishment of State Finance Commission to review the

financial position of the municipal bodies after every five years.

5. **District and Metropolitan Committees:-** The 74th Constitutional Amendment Act made a revolutionary step by providing the creation of District Planning Committee (DPC) and Metropolitan Planning Committee (MPC) along with Articles 243Z(D) and 243Z(E) to coordinate the plans framed by the various tiers of local bodies, both in the urban and rural areas.[15]

Development after 74th the Constitutional Amendment

Second ARC Report- 2007

In its 6th report, title 'Local Governance' gave manifold recommendations. Some of the recommendations were related at state level that Parliament may by law provide for Constitution of Legislative Council in each State, consisting of members elected by the local governments and on the other hand, at district level establishment of District Council with representation from both Urban and Rural areas and with other functions it may also examine report of audit committee about particular district at district level. Creation of separate standing committee in the State Legislature also for local bodies, this committee may function in the manner of Public Account Committee and multiple were related to Electoral reforms, State Finance Commission, Capacity Building, Methods for Provisions of Services (outsourcing, Contracting out, PPP), Training, Micro Level Planning through DPC & MPC, Accountability and Transparency, At District Level Audit Committee. So, the committee was recommended the creation of new deliberation house at the State level Legislative Council for Local Bodies at the district level District Council. Further, new institution on namely, separate Standing Committee for examination of Audit Report for entire local bodies in the State and Audit Committee for each district in particular state.[16]

All India Mayor Conference Chandigarh-2007

This conference was held in Chandigarh in 2007 and nearly about 150 delegates including 24 Mayors, 31 ex-Mayors, Deputy Mayors and Presidents of Municipal Councils from different parts of Country participated in this Conference. Various methods were highlighted in the conference for improvement of working conditions of urban local bodies, such as :

Bus Rapid Transit System,

Role of Local Self government in the way of governance,

And emphasis on larger public institutional alongwith matrix/ structure,

The various facts about Chandigarh were also magnified that Chandigarh was proclaimed as No.1 city in terms of cleanliness, sanitation, management. It was also miles ahead of all other 17 cities of India in all parameters in which the survey was undertaken by Org MARG in March, April-2007. It also came forth in conference that the MC Chandigarh has made a large number of achievements in Public Health, Sewerage, Storm Water, hygiene, sanitation and Horticulture. Apart from this the Chandigarh Municipal Corporation has also captured two prestigious awards. JNNURM Award for improvement in delivery of Municipal Services particularly in thie area of water supply and JNNURM award for improvement in delivery of Municipal services namely Sewerage and Drainage Coverage for 2007-08. Prof. B.S. Ghuman, who has participated in conference stresses State Government should be forced for devolution of powers. Other amenities have given weightage for great participation of women in local bodies. It also highlighted the various issues like; how to make city gender friendly, greening the city, proper solid waste management an answer to global warming, adopting E-Governance, increasing colonies & migrant population, development of urban infrastructure, Public- Private Partnership and bench marking through TWINNING.

This conference not only stressed upon new issues & challenges and highlighted various methods to tackle but also shows tantamount of present scenario.[17]

All India Mayor Conference at Bathinda- 2012

The conference was held in 2012 at Bathinda (Punjab) and it highlighted the conference highlighted to provide portable water and tackle sanitation problems with shortage of funds in the big cities of Punjab, the same problems are being faced by other States of India, like how to cope with the increasing burden of providing potable water and dealing with sanitation problems while there is perennial shortage of funds. The conference focused on, the problems of basic services are crucial in India, particularly in the area of proving portable water and dealing with sanitations. It was come up with fact about Mumbai that it was the largest civic body with its annual budget more than Rs.1000 crore and confirmed Surat City Municipal Corporation (SCMC) as 3rd the cleanest city in India and how it used method of brushing and scraping of 300 kms of roads on a daily basis at night and keep the city cleaned from dirt and garbage. However, the City with its population close to 4.6 million and only 1300 workers employed with the civic body. It also computerised water distribution and drainage system and having one of the best water treatment plants in the country. And conference favoured following advancement for improvements of Urban Local Bodies:

- Strong Mayor
- Five-year term for mayors
- Setting up of State Mayor-in-Councils, represented by the respective mayors of each state
- Setting up of the Indian Municipal Service (IMS) on the lines of the Indian Administrative Service (IAS)

Thus conference suggested contour of Policy and genuine certain facts in the tune of method and technology, which may be helpful in development in Urban Local Bodies.[18]

13th Finance Commission Report and Urban Local Bodies-2009

The finance commission has endorsed the service delivery strict with indicators or parameters as provided in (Simultaneous and Integrated Service Provisions) of Ministry of Urban Development for the Urban Local Bodies., It also spot lights the facts, which made it mandatory for all states to issue a gazette notification on current service levels and fix the target for improvement on annual basis. The main sources of increase in Income of all the categories of municipal bodies because of grants-in-aid not due to raising of revenue from their own resources. The Ministry of Urban Development has brought out the Handbook of Service Delivery Bench Marking which is prescribed universal service delivery benchmarks for some urban services. it mandatory to adopt the service level benchmarks by Urban Local Bodies across the country. It has also endorsed the indicators and made it mandatory for all the states to issue a gazette notification on current service levels and fix largest for improvement on annual basis.[19]

14th Finance Commission Report and Urban Local Bodies-2015

The commission was constituted by the President on January 2, 2013 under the chairmanship of Sh.Y.V. Reddy to give recommendations on specified aspects of Centre- State physical relation during 2015-2020. It submitted its report to the President on December 15, 2014 by covering all aspects of it mandate. The report of the commission will be covering the five year period commencing from April 1, 2015.

In this contest as per the enjoinder of 14th Finance Commission, Union Government has decided devolved much higher share of 42 % of unions net Tax receipts to the State earlier it was 32 %. The Commission has proposed grants in aid of revenues of States for revenue deficit local bodies and disaster management under article 275 of the Constitution of India. It has put up that local bodies should be required to spend the grants only on the basic services within the functions assigned to them and for the distribution of grants to states for local bodies 2011 population to be taken in consideration with weightage 90% for population and 10 % for on the basis of area. The purpose grants will be divided into two parts for rural bodies and urban local bodies on the bases of urban and rural population and worked out a total grant of Rs.2,87,436/- crore for the period of 2015-2020 for local bodies and it has been categoried as a basic grant and performance grant in the ratio of 80:20 with respect to Municipalities. It is weighty to mention here that the government has accepted above recommendations.[20]

India is a union of states. There are 28 states and 7 Union Territories. There are around 3700 urban local bodies with 100 corporations, 1500 municipal councils and 2100 Nagar Panchayats, besides 56 cantonment boards that are serving about 27 percent of the country's total population in 2001.

Municipal bodies have completed almost 20 years since the 74th Constitutional Amendment. Their performance across the country is mixed at the best. Due to general issues or challenges of urban local governance in India and particularly in Haryana. To do away with this lack or bring uniformity in the performance at national level in general and Haryana in particular, there is need to highlight few issues and challenges plaguing the functioning of urban local governance.

Issues of Urban Governance in India

Some of these issues in this regard as follows:

There are several issues of Indian Urban Local Governance which are related to participation, influence of social, economic and political factors in decision making.

Issues which affects its final outcome may include: Ignorance among members /authorities pertaining to different provisions of

Municipal Act; Dissatisfaction among members; Lack of transparency in sharing information; Unfair practices in the publicity of development works; Discrimination in the selection of contractors; Low level of services; Bias against maintenance of existing services and inefficiency in financial management, Lack of people participation in policy making and influence of social, economic and political factors in decision making process of authority of local government[21].

Inefficiency among urban local governments in the management of their finances, which affects adversely the efficient delivery of basic civic services. Some other issues are: deficiencies in the procedure for determining the cost of services; low cost recovery from taxes and non-taxes; high outstanding dues of previous years; high dependence on external sources of finance; etc. In addition to above, Induction Training Programmes for the employees, Lack of framework for Governance of Mega Cities, Strengthening of Ward Committees and Metropolitan Planning Committees (MPC), creation of separate Municipal Cadre, Setting-up of an Urban Service Regulator, Time Limit for disposal of various cases and use of IT and e-Governance tools in the working of urban local bodies may help achieve to goal[22]

Governance problems are also leaving a lot to be desired. Challenges to human resource capacity and management and unequal division of responsibilities between the councilors and officials. Complex Institutional and Legal framework which regulates the relations between State and Local governments. The State Government continue to exercise excessive controls over local Governments such as: providing their revenue sources and their by-laws.[23]

Issues of urban local government in India is prime concern regarding structural, procedural and behavioural reforms in urban local governance.[24]

Factors like how involve citizen's and civil society organisations in participation on affairs of urban governance by which transparency and accountability may be ensured and lastly but not least for the functional efficiency, privatization of some basic services and involvement of private sectors in service delivery through the various methods like contracting out and public private partnership.[25]

The mix bag results of municipal bodies necessitates examining the performance carefully and identifying the factors which result in good performance and also locate factors which cause poor performance. It is in this backdrop that the present study has been initiated.

1.2 HARYANA STATE – A Profile

Haryana is one of the leading states of North India. It is a small state that found a place on the country's map on 1st November, 1966. It is situated in the North West India and covers an area of 44212 square km, constituting 1.35% of the total geographical area of the country. It has 4 divisions which have been sub-divided into 19 Districts, 47 Sub-Divisions, 112 Tehsils/Sub-Tehsils, 116 Blocks, 6781 villages, 106 towns and 68 Municipalities.

As per the 2011 census, the population of the state was about 253.55 lakh constituting about 2.4% of the total population of the country. The population was found to grow by about 1.61% per annum. The percentage of urban and rural population worked out to be 32% and 68%, respectively.

Out of the total 19 districts, six have a high degree of urbanization and are situated in the north and the eastern part of the state. Panchkula, Faridabad and Gurgaon constitute the northern most part of Haryana and are famous for their educational and industrial activities. Panchkula has about 54.83 percent of urban population which makes it the third largest district in terms of urban population. Faridabad is on the top, in terms of urban population.[26]

1.3 URBAN LOCAL BODIES IN HARYANA

In Haryana, there are 68 Urban Local Bodies comprising 1 Municipal Corporation, 21 Municipal Councils and 46 Municipal committees (See Table 1.1).

Table 1.1
Urban Local Bodies in Haryana

Sr. No.	*Name of Urban Local Bodies*	*No*	*Population in Lakhs*	*Population in Percentage*
1.	Municipal Corporation	1	10.55	18.18
2.	Municipal Councils (Above 50,000 Population)	21	33.82	58.28
3.	Municipal Committees (below 50,000 Population)	46	13.66	23.54
4.	**Total**	**68**	**58.03**	**100.00**

Source: Report of Second State Finance Commission, Haryana.

As far as Municipal Councils in Haryana are concerned, Table 1.2 shows the range of population covered by the Municipal Councils along with the number of such councils.

Out of the total Municipal Councils, three councils including Panchkula, have a population in the range of 1.5 lakh to 2 lakhs (See Table 1.2).

Table 1.2
Municipal Councils in Haryana

	Range of Population	*Number of Municipal Council*
1.	Equal to 50,000 but less than 1,00,000	2
2.	Equal to 1,00,000 but less than 1,50,000	9
3.	Equal to 1,50,000 but less than 2,00,000	3
4.	2,00,000 and above	7
	Total	**21**

Source: Report of Second State Finance Commission Haryana.

In the light of the government of India's 74th Amendment Act, 1992, the government of Haryana, amended its Haryana Municipal Act in the year 1994. The Municipal bodies in Haryana have been functioning for the last eighteen years ever since this amendment but no significant effort has been made to evaluate the performance of these bodies.

The present study aims to examine the performance of the Municipal Council Panchkula with reference to select municipal services.

The Municipal Council Panchkula has been chosen considering the rapid urbanization that has taken place in Panchkula and the growing number of developmental activities being undertaken by the concerned administration.

MUNICIPAL COUNCIL, PANCHKULA

Municipal Council, Panchkula was established on 26th January, 2001 under the Haryana Municipal Act, 1973. It is divided into 31 wards. The wards include 28 sectors and 13 villages. Each ward is represented by a Municipal Councilor. In addition to this 1 Member of Parliament (MP) and 1 Member of Legislative Assembly (MLA) are also nominated to the Municipal Council. Panchkula has a total population of about 1,90,000, as per the census 2011.

The important functions performed by the Municipal Council, Panchkula include:

1. Sanitation;
2. Roads/Drains and Building Maintenance;
3. Street Lights;
4. License (grant of license, acceptance and acknowledgement of application and receipt of license fees);
5. No Objection Certificate (NOC for water supply/sewerage connection, NOC for electricity, NOC for registration of sale deeds);

6. Fire services;
7. Municipal Taxes;
8. Parks (Development of new parks, grass cutting, watering/ clearing etc.); and
9. Miscellaneous (Disposal of Complaints, Domicile, Resident, Caste Certificate Verification, Enquiries regarding supply of materials, tender of Municipal works).

However, in the 74th amendment ,there were provision of 18 subjects for the urban local bodies

1.4 REVIEW OF LITERATURE

A lot of literature on Municipalities is available. A brief account of the selected literature is as under:

Datta (1993)[27] in his study traces the past efforts at national-level municipal training in India and examines the working experience of its present institutional providers and the concerned sponsoring ministry. This is followed by an exploration of the emerging changes in the municipal environment and a much needed reorientation of the municipal training within the context of municipal development. He argues that the training in future, necessarily needs to be demand-driven rather than supply based as at present.

Mohanty (1993)[28] while evaluating Bhubaneshwar Municipality from the citizens' perspective, has commented that the municipal government's performance is far from satisfactory. He has suggested a reguola5r conduction of Municipal election as per the prescribed time schedule.

Sachdeva (1994)[29] has found the role of municipal governments to have increased enormously because of the promotion of grass-root democracy. His study revealed that the standard of civic amenities has continued to be disgusting due to a lack of capacity, expertise and financial resources. The credibility of the specialized agencies like water supply boards and improvement trusts was found to be massively eroded due to corruption in the system. Further, he has warned that the government control should not be so rigid so as to destroy the autonomy of the urban local bodies.

Misra (1995)[30] suggests a great potential in public and private partnership in the delivery of urban services. He calls for redefining the role and responsibility of the government. He suggests the privatization of select services such as public health, and public amenities in order to strengthen the financial provision of the Urban Local Bodies and provides effective and efficient delivery of services;

Chatterjee and **Ghosh** (2003)[31] in their study opine that the new challenges of globalization not only proved to the agrarian economy in the form of new compulsion of making the growth process self-sustaining and recombinant, but also new opportunities of decentralized decision-making by the participants of the growth process in different forms to help ameliorate the poverty of the under privileged without the tyranny of the inefficient bureaucracy raj in the name of management of poverty alleviation programmes in our rural economy.

Nahvi (2003)[32] analyse that the municipal corporations across the country have faced the burdens of increasing urbanisation on one hand and financial constraints on the other. He asserts that the municipal corporations today seem to be in a fix where 97.50 percent of their total income goes away to meet the staff expenses. He therefore, suggests that corporations contain their revenue budgets, increase tax collection and build up remunerative assets for income profits. However, this is possible only if the urban services network is diversified, becomes efficient, and is charged appropriately.

Sarda (2003)[33] in his study states that the local bodies, both rural and urban, do not have many sources of revenue and thus, mainly depend on the resources from state governments. As a result; these institutions of decentralised governance are under severe financial constraint. He therefore, suggests that the local bodies should have adequate revenue sources of their own for discharging their functions effectively, besides, having powers to take independent financial decisions to exploit the revenue sources assigned to them in a manner, most advantageous to them and therefore, utilize those revenues according to local priorities.

Singh (2003)[34] in his study stresses that the functioning of gram panchayats has suffered mainly due to the misutilisation of funds placed at their disposal beside, manpower corruption, unwanted delays, and the poor quality of goods and services. It is in this context that he calls for a need and significance of transparency in their functions. To ensure transparency, the measures that he has suggested include a convening of regular meetings of Gram Sabhas, generation of awareness, provision of equal opportunities, prior approval of development works, circulation of proceedings, wide publicity of programmes, involvement of reputed NGOs and a quintessential imbibing of democratic and moral values.

Bagchi and **Ghosh** (2004)[35] state that the loopholes in the present system of imposition and realisation of taxes, which are mostly attitudinal and psychological in nature are to be removed. They opine that utilizing of the sources assigned to them requires a strong political will to translate the 'potential into reality'.

Reddy and **Sreedevi** (2004)[36] found that with the passing of 73rd and 74th Constitutional Amendment Acts 1992, and consequently, the appointment of the State Finance Commission (SFC) to recommend financial transfers between the state and local bodies, there has been a renewed interest in the local bodies finance. According to him, the non- acceptance of (SFC) recommendations by the state government is further depleting the resource base of the Panchayati Raj Institution (PRI). Therefore ,the crude truth that unfolds itself here is that , though the constitution does not provide that all the recommendations of the Finance Commission should be accepted by the government, the Government of India has established an unsaid tradition of accepting all the recommendations of its Finance Commission. It will go a long way, if state government also follows the same tradition.

Heikkila (2007)[37] after analyzing data from a study of nine special districts in the state of Teaxas in order to assess the citizen participation in the performance management among the district of Teaxas. He suggests that although the district may not yet be in tune with the latest performance management trends, but they are making efforts to engage citizens in other ways and therefore, he suggests involvement of citizens as inputs, in the development of performance indicators and the monitoring performances.

Kundu (2007)[38] observes that the Haryana government is not serious about the timely constitution of the State Finance Commission and a prompt examination of its report. He opines that the government should constitute the commission well in time, at least before the commencement of the awarded period, so that the devolution of funds can be decided at on appropriate time. He further suggests that in case of rejection of recommendations, due reasons should be given, and also the progress report should be tabled before the state legislature. In addition to this, a District Annual Report having full details of the finances of local bodies should be published every year.

Palnitkar (2007)[39] in her study states that it is the urban local governments that are responsible for the delivery of civic services, mobilization of local resources giving coherent planning and to provide suitable quality of life for the city dwellers. According to her, the existing system of service delivery system of the urban local governments is not able to provide adequate services due to an expanding urban population. Moreover, their limited financial resources are not enough to cover the needed expansion of these services. In the light of this, there is a need to find alternate sources of service delivery and, one of the most viable options is to build up Public Private Partnership (PPP).

Sharma and **Sodhi** (2007)[40] are of the view that the role and performance of local bodies are judged by the silent observers of the civil society. The civil society constitutes the formal and informal actors involved in decision making and implementation of such decisions. They observe that despite numerous problems and challenges, civil society organizations are working incessantly to increase the participation and involvement of citizens in the affairs of local bodies in order to make them accountable, responsive, transparent, and citizen friendly. They have influenced the nature, working and range of functions undertaken by these bodies in an effective manner.

Handley (2008)[41] investigates the longitudinal political and administrative problems associated with federal local government relations. The findings demonstrate four primary challenges before the system of federal grants–in–aid that hinder the relationship of policy design at the federal level and policy implementation in local communities these challenges include: (i) The politics of decentralization, (ii) sub national capacity, (iii) program accountability and (iv) programme adaptability. A case study of the community development block grant, as assessed by the advisory commission on inter governmental relations and the general accounting officer since 1974 till now ,present was included to demonstrate the application of these problems within the system. The author states that although the 'evolution of devolution' could greatly benefit the recipients of public services at the local level, it often operated within an unorganized and ineffective system that public managers at all levels of government must continue to develop. The author suggests that the local government must actively participate in civic networks to communicate and learn from each other so as to strengthen the local capacity. Furthermore, the author states that the geographic and regional similarities must be emphasized so that the sharing of information is productive.

Sangwan (2008)[42] analyses the process of urbanization in Haryana. According to him, the pace of urbanisation has thus, been fast in the state as compared to India as a whole. He further analyses that the factors which gave an impetus to the growth of towns in Haryana were the increased agricultural production due to green revolution and expansion of agro-based as well as agro-oriented industries. The establishment of urban estates, residential, industrial and commercial, Industrial Model Townships (IMTs) by the urban development authority like HUDA, Housing Board were also other factors influencing the urbanization process.

Svara (2008)[43] puts forth his views regarding the scope of local government which is expanding rapidly. He asserts that there is a need to assess the impact of the expanding range of programs and services under the jurisdiction of a single government. He suggests the need for a better report card that measures how well a local government is meeting its performance goals, what are the benefits and costs of having services provided by the local government in control of the public schools, merging city and county functions and providing city and county services in a single consolidated government. Further, he also recommends that research is needed on the current nature of regional governance and changes that are occurring in regional policy making, regulation and structure. Underlying all these topics is the question of how new governance arrangements may impact local leadership and policy making, change the role of government in meeting public needs and delivering services, and affect accountability and democratic control.

Alok (2009)[44] opines that the task of restructuring public finance substantially depends upon the effective of streamlining the multiple channels of resource flow from the union to the local governments through the states. In the legal framework, the processes of fiscal devolution from states to the local governments take place through the State Finance Commissions. The role now for the thirteenth Finance Commission is to act as a path breaker in creating an enabling environment for fiscal decentralization at the sub-state level. Since, it is not mandatory that the transfer of funds to the local Governments should only be in the form of grants, therefore, he suggests that the local governments should be considered to get their share from the central divisible pool, along with the states. In this connection, fiscal transfers through Union Finance Commission have to play a critical role to augment resources of the local governments.

Singh (2009)[45] makes a commendable effort and ventured to convey the deeply felt performance impediments such as: job security; faulty staffing practices; poor motivation; role ambiguity; over centralization; multiple agencies; unprofessional management practices; red tapism and multiple window system; reluctance to dispose off old cases; trade unionism; delays; negativism; corruption; unresponsiveness; unaccountability; and politicization in their work environment. He is of the opinion that the performance problems listed above can not be fully eradicated but sincere attempts by all can definitely minimize them to a great extent. The management strategies such as: Computerized 'Human Resource Management System' at all levels; essential training for developing motivational skill at all levels; vesting adequate executive powers at all levels; greater coordination among various agencies; creating an office layout on the basis of 'time and motion' study; and a model code of conduct for the elected representatives, if applied would certainly enhance the effectiveness of administration in the government.

Vyasuly (2009)[46] reflects on some critical issues such as the functioning of local governments in India after the Constitutional Amendments of 1992. He tactfully argues that changing the law will not automatically change the way things are.

Argento, Grossi, Tagesson and Colin (2010)[47], they argue that in recent years, public service provisions are made through various forms of corporatization, public-public collaboration, public private partnership and contracting with the aim is to increase cooperation between public and private sector.

They addressed these matters with comparative reference to the experience in Italy and Sweden and highlighted the issues of ownership and significance of community in the management of public affairs.

On the basis of study, they discovered that the municipality had to play multiple role at the same time as purchaser, local regulator and shareholder, which may cause conflicts of interest especially in the areas of water, waste and transportation sectors.

They suggested that for greater efficiency in public service provision, with the effect being to dilute rather than eliminate public ownership.

Malik (2010)[48] argues that though urbanization is increasing globally, its ecological impact has not been very positive. Some of the obvious consequences include the problem of depletion of resources and the all prevailing pollution and climate change. He suggests that there should be a development strategy that meet the needs of present generation without compromising the needs of the future generations. He also recommends the adoption of the proper methods of Solid Waste Management(SWM) system. So that, the growth of sustainable cities in India can be promoted.

Ranjan (2010)[49] observes that after recognizing the growing importance of improving efficiency in the delivery of basic services in cities, the government of India has launched a series of initiatives aimed at enabling the urban local bodies to meet the unprecedented challenges that they face today. Apart from this, the Ministry of Urban Development has now adopted National Benchmarks in four key sectors of water supply, sewerage, solid waste management and storm water drainage. However, investments in the urban infrastructure have not always resulted in corresponding improvements in the levels of service delivery. Therefore, he suggests that a shift in focus towards service delivery and the hand book service level benchmarks shall provide a standardized framework for performance measurement in respect of service delivery system besides enabling the state level agencies and local level service providers to initiate a process of performance maintenance and evaluation system against agreed targets, thereby, finally resulting in an achievement of service level benchmarks identified in the handbook.

Singh (2010)[50] states that according to the Constitution's 74th Amendment Act, 1994; the tenure and responsibilities of Mayor or the Municipal Chairperson are left to be decided by the state governments. As a result, the variations are likely to be many. Therefore, what is required is that the urban local bodies elect their mayor or chairperson directly to make them more representative of the electorate in a city. In this case, the elected person would become more accountable and this accountability can be enhanced by the fact that having come to power by direct election, his position is secure for five year duration. However, on the other hands, the Second Administrative Reforms Commission has already dealt with concerns over abuse of authority by Mayors due to a fixed tenure.

I.I.P.O (2011)[51] finds that according to the Census 2011, 31.2% of the total Indian population lives in urban centers compared to 27.8% in 2001 and 25.5% in 1991.The number of towns in the country rose by about 53.74% in the last decade. Among the states, Haryana, Punjab, Uttrakhand, West Bengal and Manipur have seen faster urbanization than the rest of the country. Due to improper implementation of urban policies, due to an inadequacy of resources people have been getting used to a lower quality of life. The trend, if sustained, will redefine the political economy of the country, forcing a shift in public policy focus towards an urban India.

Jha and Kamthan (2012)[42] discussed the role of urban political leadership which though crucial, has lately undergone a tremendous expansion and change in the wake of globalisation and the 74th Amendment Act, 1992. The leader in this changing city scenario is meeting newer challenges every day. This success depends, to a great extent, upon a sound urban infrastructure, an efficient management of civic affairs and the over-all quality of life for the city-dwellers; all of which demand a highly efficient urban government or a high level of leadership skill in our local leadership today. A general decline is being witnessed in the quality of political leadership in the country and the local urban politics seems to be the worst victim of this phenomenon. As such the leader thus, not merely fall short of the expectations of their followers but are also not well-groomed to meet the constantly growing challenges of the present day urban government. Therefore, they suggest that we address these issues through sound governance.

Pandey (2012)[43] believes that India in the first decade of twenty first century is emerging as a positive force to trigger economic growth and is all set to undergo a rapid pace of urbanization during the next couple of decades. This growth definitely needs suitable and effective policies to ensure a balanced and inclusive urban growth across all the states. However, the systems and procedures to manage urban growth are relatively weak. This therefore, provides an impetus to firm up policies and strategies as was initiated in the year 1985. In the connection, the devolution of powers, funds and functions to urban local governments are critical for a pro poor, inclusive, environment friendly and citizen centric management system.

A.Narinder (2013)[52], he observed that the Census 2011, slums population figures were under estimated. The Census 2011 information that only 2613 towns out of 4041 statuary town reported slums implies that the remaining 1428 cities are slum free cities, which may not be true since there is a hardly any city in the country which is slum free. This under estimation can be corroborated by the fact that the committee on slum statistics/ Census setup by the Ministry of Housing and Urban Poverty Alleviation (MoHUPA) in 2007 was come up with higher slum population projection for the year 2011. The MoHUPA committee estimated the slum population to be 9.30 crore in 2011 and 10.46 crore in 2017 which are far higher than the slum population figures of 2011. Out total of 40,41 towns in India, 2613 are reported to have slums and 17.4 percent of the Urban households are located in Slum in 2011.

In his study, he reviewed the current status of slums, slum and housing policies over the years, emerging policy and approach of Rajiv Awas Youjna and indentified the issues and way forward for making Indian cities 'Slum Free'. According to him,the slum population in India was 52.37 million and constituted about 23.5 percent of the total Urban population. In Haryana, it was 33.07 and it was third in que of Indian States while Meghalaya was first with

41 percent followed by Maharashatra 33.3 percent as per 2001 census. In Haryana as per 2011 census, there were 75 reported slum towns, and these contain around 16.62 Lakhs population. He observed that there are several programmes conducting by the Government of India through Ministry of Urban Development for the improvement of conditions of people, who were lived in these areas. So, he suggested that, there must be effective implementation of slum free City Policy initiated by the Govt. through co-operation of Urban Local self Govt.

Document (2013)[53], Strategic Plan of Ministry of Urban Development for 2011-2016 made projection that there will be increase of 250-300 million population with present population in next two decades for the provisions in consonance of increase to enhancement basic infrastructure which ensures competitiveness and quality of basic services in cities, the scale of investment required would be of the order of nearly Rs. 50,00,000 crore over next two decades.

The document figures, the urban sector contributes around 62% - 63% of GDP which is likely to increase to 75% by 2021. Over 70% of new jobs will be largely generated in cities and ultimately it may provide employment to needy. And it stresses upon that though development is primarily a state subject, the Government of India needs to continue to play a catalytic role in provision of basic amenities, capacity building, policy formulation and bringing about convergence and synergies. So, the minister of Urban development should be paid a key facilitation of this process as efficient urbanization in the country would need closer cooperation between Union and States.

The document also highlights the States and cities than ever before and Ministry of Urban Development came with vision & objectives some of these facilitate creation of basic urban infrastructure relating to water supply, improvement in sanitation and urban transport service levels and coverage by 2017, making appropriate policy for efficient and inclusive Urban Governance with proper implementation, capacity building of key stake holders and facilitate planned development amongst are others.

The document also brings to the force that various challenges of Urban Government, the census of India has estimated that by 2026, urban population would rise to around 535 million or 38.2% of the population. However, India still has the second largest population in the world.

The State of basic services like water supply, sewage, solid waste Management and Urban housing and transport in Urban areas leaves much to be desired and Inadequate level of empowerment of Urban Local Bodies and lack of personnel with appropriate skill sets, Inadequate skill sets of personnel already deployed are the certain factors amongst more.

It also stresses upon broad strategy plan of the Ministry of Urban Development for the next five years for the development of urban areas and cope with new situations & problems, one of them is 'Pooled Finance Development Fund Scheme' to provide credit enhancement to ULBs to access marked borrowings based on their credit worthiness through State-Level Pooled Finance Mechanism and it may enhance investment capacity of these bodies, because, the fact is that the requirements of funds is much more than what can be made available through grants and from own resources, either taxes of Urban Local Bodies and non taxes and others are using of e-Governance methods in Government working.

Gurjant & Rajbans (2013)[54], they comment that the Government deals with citizen's, their needs and requirements tend to changing with time and this change may be coped with reforms only. In the case of local body ,it is closer to people than other levels of the Government. They observe that structural Human Resource and systems or procedural changes may be not only capable to foster the service delivery and ultimately it also will help in achieving the predetermined objectives of these bodies as a result facilitates citizen satisfaction.

In their study, they find that according to 74th amendment, there were 18 matters given to the urban local body. But only a small number of matters have actually been developed in most of states and ultimately it defeated the very purpose of the Act.

They communicate that the although Second Administrative Reforms Commission, 13th Finance Commission and High Powered Expert Committee (HPEC) report on Indian Urban Infrastructure and services for estimating the investment requirement for Urban Infrastructure Services have given lot of recommendations in the area of advancement of Local bodies, but some of the valuable recommendatio not been Implemented by the government with compatibility of need yet .

With the taking the states of Urban Governance with special reference of JNNURM, They suggest that agenda of reforms must be implemented with letter & spirit.

Jha (2013)[55], the author stresses that Local Self Government in India is the most prominent and eye-opening factor is a conspicuous mismatch between sources of revenue and devolved functions. So, he brings out it to make efforts, for the fiscal decentralisation for preventing tax exporting and facilitates funding at the margin through fiscal transfer from central as well as State Government, and this measure will not only promote accountability but also will be helpful for the decision makers to fully bears the cost of decisions taken by them in the area of service provisions. It requires adequate sources of revenue that must be in consonance with the range of functions devolved to the local Government.

Further, he opines that it may improve economy efficiency and accountability with increasing resource mobilization as well. And local govt will become capable of providing more equitable and efficient service delivery to the beneficiaries. But, fiscal decentralization may ensure through better financial regulation making by appropriate authority, prevent preparation of deficit budgets, prescribed accenting standard and effective tax administration system and procedures. However, there are risks of fiscal decentralization in relation with its proper design and implementation.

On the basis of the study, he endorses that proper devolution of funds with unisons of their respective functions from the concerned authority to the local self government and proper management of finance as well.

Khaiian (2013)[56], he states that there is inadequacy of infrastructural services in cities of India in terms of coverage, quantity, quality. In it he measured the gap between demand & supply of different infrastructural services but also examined the factors that explain the gap and he felt that inadequate access to infrastructure is a key constraint to the development of the cities. On the basis of examination of three services namely Water Supply, Sanitation, Sewerage and Solid Waste Management, he mentioned the condition of these services are not satisfactory in the Amritsar. Further, he suggested that making of appropriate policy and its implementation with well trained personnel and with the help of community participation the hurdles may be reduced and operation and maintenance of the infrastructural facilities will be improved and development of city may also be taken in planned manner.

Mahapatra (2013)[57] , he discloses that as an essential of government structure Local Self Government not only provides opportunity to the citizen's to take a part in decision making in area of policy formulation and Implementation of local affairs but also plays vital role in development of Nation through development of Infrastructure, physical as well as social in accordance to present needs, demands of beneficiaries, local issues and public interests. For this these bodies are being encouraged to experiment with and introduce new practices and existing practices are being streamlined.

Further, Local Self Government is the third level of Government Structure and provides root or base of the Central and State level. So, it has to work with close co-ordination with the various related ministries & department for the achieving of national goal.

In this study he colours that in India, the local Self Government has strengthed, we now have roughly about 3.6 million directly elected representatives including about one million women. Besides, this number of Local bodies in the country is increased to 2.4 Lakhs Units.

He zeroing down in accordance with 74th the Constitutional Amendment various, supportive provisions have been made for enhancement of urban local bodies but still several challenges are being faced by these institutions in the area of devolution of power, funds and functions. He is of the view that there is a need for, maintaining of proper Co-ordination and capacity building for managing their affairs in better way.

Malik & Kaur (2013)[58], they make out that Urbanization will help in Economic Growth & development because it has been presumed that in India an half of our population will have been living in Urban Centre within next three decades and it may also make complexity for the Urban Governance.

So, they highlight some of the emerging issues of Urban Governance, such as, how maintaining of interactive relationship between and within governments and non-governmental forces, seeking joint achievement in proper service delivery and proper distribution of collective benefit to the beneficiaries or stakeholders.

They not only hypothesize that the purpose of understanding the dynamic of Urban Governance in the changed Scenario, State has been taking a backseat in terms of providing number of Urban Services to the citizen's earlier and remaining occupied by the private sector but also widens about the steps those have been taken place on the basis of Philosophy, the State would play the role not only as an instrument but also promoter, facilitator and include itself in only core areas of the affairs and many times the competitor in the service market as well and Economic pressure grouping. But, this process presents very perplexing pictures of contrast and complexities in one and other ways.

Moreover, they stresse other issues like how government may be made participatory, transparent and accountable which may allocate developmental resources in appropriate manner and show responsiveness, consensus orientation, equity, effectiveness, efficiency and strategic vision with the quality of Governance. they further expand that in the process of Local Governance how these institution secure autonomy within the federal system, within the given structures the inclusion of citizens and civil society organization to be ensured the incorporation of private sector in essential Urban Services and Public Private Partnership for financial efficiency. He also believes that Structure initiated by 74th Institutional Amendment, which can be used for ensuring the participation of Civil Society groups, apart from the individual of Course in decision making processes of governance structures.

According to them it is glaring that neither the domain governments nor outside donor agencies have any faith and belief in the local urban bodies and they still rely on their own implementing agencies and bureaucratic machinery. So, this does not indicate well for the future of the Urban governance. On the basis of this, they beat the drum for if the charity is to begin at home, we shall have to create certain confidence levels, not only within the system as to these agencies, but also amongst the functionaries of these bodies as to their abilities to handle their affairs at these levels. they also presumes, beginning of this charity will as a challenge of 'democratic consolidation' process for India .

And they advise that ordinary people should be seen as citizen's, not clients and such a shift will help Urban governance institutions as institution of Local Self Government.

Misra & Misra (2014)[59], the Author stated that the various committees & commissions intuited and gave various recommendation for development of Local Self Government.

Despite plethora of recommendations made by several committees, the situation did not improve much owing to the magnitude of the problems created by rapid urbanisation, indifference of the state governments, lack of political will to initiate reforms and to enforce the recommendations and other major facts he highlighted indifference on the part of Local bodies to raise adequate resources to meet their needs. And acknowledge with the assistant of the fact that the rural population of India is urbanising and approximately one third of total population (377 million, 31.16.%) Lives in 7935 Cities. It is projected that by 2040 it will have the world's largest urban population and suggested implementation of recommendations.

A.Narinder (2013)[60], he observed that the Census 2011, slums population figures were under estimated. The Census 2011 information that only 2613 towns out of 4041 statuary town reported slums implies that the remaining 1428 cities are slum free cities, which may not be true since there is a hardly any city in the country which is slum free. This under estimation can be corroborated by the fact that the committee on slum statistics/ Census setup by the Ministry of Housing and Urban Poverty Alleviation (MoHUPA) in 2007 was come up with higher slum population projection for the year 2011. The MoHUPA committee estimated the slum population to be 9.30 crore in 2011 and 10.46 crore in 2017 which are far higher than the slum population figures of 2011. Out total of 40,41 towns in India, 2613 are reported to have slums and 17.4 percent of the Urban households are located in Slum in 2011.

In his study, he reviewed the current status of slums, slum and housing policies over the years, emerging policy and approach of Rajiv Awas Youjna and indentified the issues and way forward for making Indian cities 'Slum Free'. According to him,the slum population in India was 52.37 million and constituted about 23.5 percent of the total Urban population. In Haryana, it was 33.07 and it was third in que of Indian States while Meghalaya was first with 41 percent followed by Maharashatra 33.3 percent as per 2001 census. In Haryana as per 2011 census, there were 75 reported slum towns, and these contain around 16.62 Lakhs population. He observed that there are several programmes conducting by the Government of India through Ministry of Urban Development for the improvement of conditions of people, who were lived in these areas. So, he suggested that, there must be effective implementation of slum free City Policy initiated by the Govt. through co-operation of Urban Local self Govt.

Khaiian (2013)[61], he states that there is inadequacy of infrastructural services in cities of India in terms of coverage, quantity, quality. In it he measured the gap between demand & supply of different infrastructural services but also examined the factors that explain the gap and he felt that inadequate access to infrastructure is a key constraint to the development of the cities. On the basis of examination of three services namely Water Supply, Sanitation, Sewerage and Solid Waste Management, he mentioned the condition of these services are not satisfactory in the Amritsar. Further, he suggested that making of appropriate policy and its implementation with well trained personnel and with the help of community participation the hurdles may be reduced and operation and maintenance of the infrastructural facilities will be improved and development of city may also be taken in planned manner.

Sen (2014)[62], In her study she found that there were 5161 towns in 2001 and which increased to 7,935 in 2011. He observed on the basis of Census 2011 that the classification of the towns primarily in two categories i.e. statutory and census towns and these census towns do not enjoy statutory municipal status and as statutory so, they are largely unregulated, lying outside the municipal governance and Tax net; Bereft of basic civic services and amenities as well as serve as potential sites for unplanned and slum-type growth. And other as an Urban Agglomerations and out Growth's in cities, and population of these settlements.

She highlighted that rapid growth in the proportion of Urban population is exerting heavy pressure on the existing infrastructure and services and posing a serious challenge to the urban planners, policy makers and city mangers.

She not only noticed that the status of basic Urban services in India was not satisfactory and but also magnified only 80% of house hold having access to safe drinking water and 62 percentage of house hold having tap water from treated source, percentage of garbage collected disposed off daily in Urban areas are merely 70% to 90% in big cities and less than 50% in small cities share of Urban roads in total road network is only 9.0% and 92.7 % of households having access to electricity against the 100% Bench marks.

According to her the cities and towns in India were visibly deficient in the level of infrastructural development and in provisioning of quality services, So thus, the abysmal state of service delivery in the urban areas, India lags far behind in terms of ensuring coverage, accessibility, quality, reliability and effectiveness of major public services. The gap relates to long years of neglect of Urban planning and infrastructure coupled with overlapping of policy, regulation and operational roles, fragmentation and duplication of scheme, limited autonomy to Urban Local Bodies (ULBs), weak links with citizen's, lack of capacity, lack of incentives. Further, on the basis of MGI report (2010), he argued that there would be sharp deterioration in the quality of urban services in the Indian cities by 2030, and according to him this projection has been made keeping the view of current trends approaches of the city Governance.

She also found that weak institutional capabilities of the civic bodies with dwindling resource even in the post 74th amendment period severely restricted their potential to make provision for basic infrastructure and municipal services for its fast growing urban population. This requires greater need for appropriate governance mechanism curbing the situation.

A.Narinder (2014)[63], he remarked that the Decade of 2005-15 may be considered as watershed in the area of water supply and sanitation services in Indian cities. It was the National Urban Sanitation Policy-2008 that broadened the definition of sanitation and included sewerage, sanitation, solid waste management and storm water drainage. The Ministry of Urban Development brought out the Handbook of Service Delivery Bench Marking which prescribed universal service delivery benchmarks for these four sectors. The 12the Plan (2012-17) also called for spectral reforms in this for critical sectors in a big way while the 13th Finance Commission made it mandatory to for all the states to issue a gazette notification on current service levels and fix largest for improvement on annual basis.

On the basis of High Powered Expert Committee (HPEC) Report set up by the Ministry of Urban Development, (MOUD) Government of India, in 2011, he brought out only 21 percent of the waste water generated is treated, less than 30 percent of solid waste is segregated and scientific disposal of water is almost never practiced.

He also point up that the MoUD undertaken a pilot exercise in selected 28 cities, and around 1500 ULBs to assess the current service level in them against these bench marks. The data gave prominence to significant gaps in service delivery and the need for improving the performance of the sector in the coming year.

On the bases of Analysis of Census (2011) and NSS Data, 54th Round survey 1998-99 & 65th Round Survey 2008-09 Data on Current Service Levels- All India and States, he remarked that in Solid Waste Management Sector, the door to door collection or house hold coverage is found to be 48 percent collection efficiency, 75 percent and scientific fill around 8 percent. Thus, even after more than a decade of formulation of Solid Waste Management Rules compliance of the same by cities found to be poor.

He mentioned that the 12th Five Year Plan also emphasized the principle of Simultaneous and Integrated Service Provision (SISP) approach to covering road map for implementing service level benchmarks and suggested a method to formulating and implementing state and city sanitation plans as per National Urban Sanitation Policy for solid waste management and also, prepare implementable PPP Policy for cities.

Further, he made out the advisory Note of the MoUD (2012) on " Improving Urban water supply and sanitation services: The key principle of service delivery favours key role of local bodies in the area of sanitation and water supply for service provision, operation and maintenance either directly or by engaging PPPs, through establishment of Appropriate institutional and organizational framework. It also suggests that state should set up regulatory mechanism as an independent agency for setting standards, monitoring performance, and adjusting tariffs, etc.

Moreover, he highlighted that the 12th Plan working group on Industrial and Urban water supply and sanitation set up by the planning commission has suggested to build capacity of municipal officials and engineers to implement innovative and emerging technologies and approaches.

On the basic of above study, he suggested that for improving urban water supply and signification services, there is a need to constitute core teams in UBLs for each of the four sectors for formulating and implementing service delivery projects and an urgent need for states to establish and institutionalize the frame work with support from (MoUD) and other technical agencies.

Mishra & Mishra (2014)[64], in study they find that number of Urban Agglomerations/towns has grown from 1827 in 1901 to 7935 in 2011 . Number of population residing in urban areas has increased from 2.58 crore in 1901 to 37.7 crore in 2011. Increase in population of class-1 cities (cities with 1,00,000 population) during 2001-2011 from 394 to 468 house, 264.9 million persons constituting 70% of total population, 53 Million plus cities and density of Urban population is 382/sq.km. This proportion increased considerably as compared to 2001 census. According to Census-2011 for the first time India added more people to cities (91 million) than rural (90.4 million) areas. The decadal population growth rate for urban India is quite high compared to rural India (12.2%) leading to over congestion and heavy pressure on urban infrastructure and amenities. Decadal Growth between 2001-2011 in urban population is 31.8%. It is admitted that at present urbanization plays a catalytic role in maximizing economic productivity and integrating economy with global systems of production, consumption and distribution. It is estimated that Urban India contributes about 63 percent approximately in country's GDP Because as it attracts investment due to Infrastructural development.

They have also given the fact of 13th Finance Commission Report, according to the commission the main sources of increase in Income of all the categories of municipal bodies because of grants-in-aid not due to raising of revenue from their own resources.

U.B Singh (2014)[65], he examined that effective Solid Waste Management may be done through maintaining of waste hierarchy namely, Reduce, Reuse, Recycle and Recovery. The aim of the waste management is to extract the maximum practical benefits from products and to generate the minimum amount of waste.

He argued, that in India, under this approach focus is being given generally on the last phase, i.e Recovery of resources and as a result, leading to poor states of Solid Waste Management.

He also brought to that the force that Kanpur PPP Model and Role of Informal sector as giving the example of a non-governmental initiative as a Muskan Jyoti initiative started in a small segment of Lucknow city were good start in a big and small Urban Settlement and suggested for the need of common Waste Management Act for the country and a strategy to deal with this local problem and Waste Management should be treated in a holistic way and in planned manner, rather than opting for resource recovery and landfill of the residue was also part of his suggestion.

According to The World Bank Report-2014, Punjab (India) provides Water Supply 85%, Sewerage Cover 65% and with 65 % of Sewerage Treatment Plant Capacity of its urban population and it is merely 54.7 % and 50.49% and 58% respectively for all India level. Thus, the report gives prominence to Punjab as a top leading State in India for providing some of urban amenities such as, water supply sewerage and having sewerage treatment plant, **Aaj Samaj** (2015)[66].

1.5 INFERENCES FROM REVIEW OF LITER–ATURE

The review of literature clearly suggests that the poor performance of municipalities with regard to services is mainly due to a lack of financial resources. The administrative problems like lack of coordination, improper training, lack of transparency, prevalence of corruption and unwanted delays also contribute to the poor performance of the municipal bodies. The literature also reveals that a lack of functional autonomy and the absence of citizen participation adversely affect the performance of municipalities.Various issues and challenges have also been noticed.

1.6 INADEQUACIES OF EARLIER LITERATURE AND APPROACH FOR OVERCOMING THE INADEQUACIES

The review of literature reveals that most of the earlier studies have focused basically on one or two aspects of the urban local bodies at a time. For example the previous studies have focused either on the structural, procedural or the financial aspects, but none of the earlier works has attempted to study the overall performance of the urban local bodies by focusing on the delivery of essential municipal services from the citizens perspective. Besides, the previous studies have not made an attempt to assess the performance of local government on the basis of the established benchmarks for service delivery.

The present study aims to evaluate the overall performance of the urban local body, namely Municipal Council, Panchkula by covering organizational, financial and physical aspects related to select municipal services. In addition to this, the study also focuses on measuring the satisfaction level of citizens regarding the basic services being provided by the Municipal Council, Panchkula. Moreover, the present study also attempts to analyse the performance of MCP regarding service delivery on the basis of comparison with select benchmarks along with highlighting of Various issues and challenges of Urban Local Bodies .

1.7 OBJECTIVES OF THE STUDY

The objectives of the study are to:

1. examine the organizational structure of Municipal Council, Panchkula;
2. study the Personnel Administration of the Municipal Council, Panchkula;
3. review how efficiently the Municipal Council Panchkula is managing its finances;
4. analyze the physical performance of Municipal Council, Panchkula;
5. examine the level of satisfaction of citizens regarding basic services; and
6. suggest policy prescriptions for improving the performance of Municipal Council, Panchkula.

1.8 HYPOTHESES OF THE STUDY

In the present study, an attempt has been made to test the following hypotheses:

1. The organizational structure of Municipal Council, Panchkula is not conducive to performance.
2. The employees of Municipal Council, Panchkula are dissatisfied with the personnel policy of the Council.
3. The Municipal Council, Panchkula does not manage its financial resources properly.
4. The sources of income of MCP are inadequate resulting in its over dependence upon grants in aid.

5. The physical performance of Municipal Council Panchkula is not satisfactory.
6. Users of services of Municipal Council Panchkula are not satisfied with the quality of services.

1.9 RESEARCH METHODOLOGY

The study is based on both primary as well as secondary data. The primary data has been collected from 305 respondents spread over urban, rural and slum areas, through a structured questionnaire. The breakup of the respondents includes 200 from the urban areas, 80 from the rural areas and 25 from the slum areas who were chosen by through random sampling. Amongst the urban areas, the sectors in the city were grouped into three categories on the basis of their level of prosperity: (i) posh sector, (ii) other sectors, and (iii) villages and colonies. One sector from each was selected. On the other hand, villages were included in the sample on the basis of distance i.e. one village each in close proximity to Municipal Council, Panchkula and one Village each at maximum distance. In case of colonies, it was the biggest slum in the municipal area, namely Rajiv Colony that was included in the sample for study. The objective for collecting primary data in this regard was to assess the users satisfaction about the quality of services being provided by the MCP. In addition to the questionnaire, pictorial depictions, and content analysis of news reports were also employed. The primary data was also collected from 79 employees of MCP (58 Permanent and 21 Contractual) to assess their level of satisfaction regarding the personnel policy of MCP. In addition to this 16 councilors of MCP were also interviewed by means of a structured questionnaire. Observation was also used as a method of data collection during field visit to supplement the data collected with the help of questionnaires and interviews.

Apart from this , data from various officials of MCP, such as the President, and the former President was also contacted. Observation method was also used to supplement the data collected through various means as mentioned above.

The secondary data was collected from various sources which included Audit and Annual Reports of MCP, Citizen Charter, Municipal Act of Haryana 1973 and the official documents related to sanitation, parks, fire brigades, streetlights and roads of MCP. The secondary data was also collected from the official documents of Directorate of Urban Local Bodies Haryana, Directorate of Local Bodies Audit and Office of State Finance Commission, Haryana. The assessment of physical performance of MCP with regards to the select services was undertaken by comparing the existing position of MCP with regards to these services vis-à-vis the select parameters for the provision of these services.

The data thus, collected was analysed after classification, coding, editing, and tabulation by using SPSS package, and interpreted to test the hypotheses. Chi square was also used to check the association between select variables.

1.10 CHAPTERIZATION

The thesis has been organized into seven chapters.

I. Introduction.
This chapter deals in meaning and a brief history of urban local government in India alongside general issues and challenges followed by a description of the urban local bodies in Haryana. In addition to this, the chapter contains a review of literature, objectives and hypotheses of the study along with the research methodology and chapter scheme.

II. Organisational Structure of the Municipal Council, Panchkula.
This chapter describes the organizational structure of Municipal Council Panchkula including the composition, qualification, tenures and powers of its wings and offices.

III. Personnel Administration of the Municipal Council, Panchkula.
This chapter contains description of various components of personnel administration of Municipal Council, Panchkula including classification, recruitment, training, determination of pay, fringe benefits, leave system, conduct and discipline, service conditions and transfer system. It also provides empirical analysis of the employees' satisfaction about the components of the personnel administration.

IV. Financial Administration of the Municipal Council, Panchkula.
This chapter provides an overview of the municipal finance in India. It also discusses the statutory powers of taxation of municipality in Haryana. Besides this, the chapter analyses the performance of financial administration of Municipal Council, Panchkula with regards to the budgetary process, income, expenditure audit and accounts process. Apart from this, it also highlights the factors of efficient Financial administration.

V. The Performance of the Municipal Council Panchkula with special reference to select services.
This chapter analyses the physical performance of Municipal Council, Panchkula with special reference to select services on

the basis of a comparison with select benchmarks, assessment of government agencies, pictorial depiction, content analysis of news reports and data collected from the officials working in various branches of Municipal Council, Panchkula.

VI. Performance of the Municipal Council Panchkula from Citizens' Perspective.
This chapter contains an analysis of the primary data collected from 305 citizens residing in the MCP jurisdiction to assess their perception about the quality of service delivery for select services.

VII. Summary, Conclusions and Policy Prescriptions.
The last chapter contains summary, conclusion and policy prescriptions for improving the organisation and working of Municipal Council, Panchkula.**(Footnotes)**

REFERENCES

1. R. Argal, Municipal Government in India, Agarwal Press, Allahabad, 1960, p. 57.
2. S. R. Maheshwari, Local Government in India, Laxmi Narain Agarwal, Agra, 2011-12, pp.16-17.
3. Ibid., p. 61.
4. Ramesh K. Arora and Rajni Goyal, Indian Administration: Institutions and Issues, Wishwa Parkashan, New Delhi, 1977, p. 40.
5. Government of India, Report of Taxation Enquiry Commission, Vol. II, New Delhi, 1955.
6. Maheshwari, op. cit., p. 24.
7. *Ibid.* p.25.
8. D.D. Basu, Introduction to the Constitution of India, Wadhawa and Company Law, Agra, 2003, p. 158.
9. Government of India, Report of Local Finance Enquiry Committee, Vol. II, New Delhi, 1951.
10. Government of India, op. cit., 1955.
11. Government of India, Report of Committee on Training of Municipal Employee, New Delhi, 1963.
12. Government of India, Report of Rural Urban Relationship Committee, New Delhi, 1966.
13. Government of India, Report of Committee on Service Conditions of Employees, New Delhi, 1968.

14. Government of India, Report of National Commission on Urbanization, New Delhi, 1988.
15. P.M. Bakshi. The Bare Act of Indian Constitution, Universal Publication, New Delhi, 2010, pp. 112-113.
16. arc.gov.in
17. http://chandigarh.gov.in
18. www.tribuneindia.com/2012/20120912/battrib.htm
19. 13th finance Commission Report, Government of India-2009
20. www.finmin.nic.in
21. http://www.lse.ac.uk/resources/copyright.htm © LSE 2006
22. Manna Lal Meena, "Urban Governance in India: Urbanisation, Initiatives, Challenges and Futuristic Perspective", Nagarlok, Vol. XLIV, No2, April-June, 2012, pp. 79-80.
23. Inderjeet Singh Sodhi, "Evolution and Development of Local Government in Tanzania Issues and Challenges", Nagarlok,Vol. XLV, No 2, Apr-June, 2013, pp. 36-37.
24. Gurgant Singh and Rajbans Gill, "Status of Reforms in Urban Governance in India: An Overview", Nagarlok, Vol. XLV, No2, Apr-Jun, 2013, pp. 19-20.
25. Lokendra Malik and Avneet Kaur, "Urban Governance in India: An Analysis", Nagarlok, Vol. XLV, No 3, July-Sept., 2013, pp. 38-43.
26. Director of Census Operations Haryana, 2011.
27. Abhijit Datta, "National Level Municipal Training in India: Need Reorientation", Indian Journal of Public Administration, Vol. XXXIX No.4, October-December, 1993, pp. 652-662.
28. Bijoyini Mohanty, Municipal System in India: Citizen's Involvement, Ashish Publishing House, New Delhi, 1993.
29. P. Sachdeva, "Municipal Administration: The Punjab Scenario", Associated Publishing House, New Delhi, 1994.
30. Grish. K. Misra, "Public and Private Partnership", Quarterly Journal of Local Self Government, LXVII No.2, 1995, pp. 20-21.
31. Biswajit Chatterjee and Dilip Kumar Ghosh, "Globalisation and Decentralised Governance Reflection on Panchayats in India", Indian Journal of Public Administration, Vol. XLIX. No.2, April-June, 2003, pp. 129-146.
32. G.L. Nahvi, "Municipal Administration in Sri Nagar (J&K) A Review", Indian Journal of Public Administration, Vol. XLIX. No.2, April-June, 2003, pp. 187-200.

33. A. Sarda, "Financial Management for Decentralised Governance", Indian Journal of Public Administration, Vol. XLIX, No.4, Oct.-Dec. 2003, pp. 767-772.
34. Mohinder Singh, "Transparency in Functions: Vital for Gram Panchayats", Indian Journal of Public Administration, Vol. YLIX, No.4, Oct.-Dec., 2003, pp. 165-67.
35. Kanak Kanti Bagchi and Taran Kumar Ghosh, "Finance of Panchayats in West Bengal-New Areas of Resource Mobilisation", Indian Journal of Public Administration, Vol. L, No.3, July-September, 2004, pp. 777-791.
36. M. Gopinath Reddy and N. Sreedevi, "Local Finances in Andhara Pradesh: A Situational Analysis", Indian Journal of Public Administration, Vol.4, No.3, July-Sept., 2004, pp. 829-839.
37. Tanya Heikkila, "Citizen Involvement and Performance Management in Special Purpose Governments", Public Administration Review, March-April, 2007, pp. 238-249.
38. R.K.Kundu, "Urban local bodies and SFC in Haryana: Some Observation(s)", Nagarlok, Vol-XXXIX, No. 1, Jan.-Mar., 2008, pp. 18-23.
39. Sneha Palnitkar, "Public–private partnerships for urban service delivery system with special reference to solid waste management", Local Government Quarterly, July-Sept., 2007, pp. 48-91.
40. Ashok Sharma and Inderjeet Singh Sodhi, "Civil Society and the Governance of Local Bodies: Issues and Challenges", Nagarlok, Vol. XXXIX, No.2, April-June, 2007, pp. 18-19.
41. Donna Milam Handley, "Strengthening the inter governmental grant system-Long term Lessons for the federal – Local relationship", Public Administration Review, Jan.-Feb., 2008, pp. 126-136.
42. Randhir Singh Sangwan, "Urabanization in Haryana: The Emerging Trends", Nagarlok, Vol. XL April-June, 2008, pp. 20-21.
43. James H-Svara, "Strengthening Local Government Leadership and Performance: Reexamining and updating the winter commission Goals", Public Administration Review, Dec. 2008, pp. 37-49.
44. V .N Alok, "Share of Local Governments in the Union Divisible Pool: An Option Before the 13th Finance Commission", Indian Journal Of Public Administration, Vol. LV, No.1, January-March, 2009, pp.71-95.

45. Rajesh Singh, "Performance Impediments In Government: Some Suggestion For Reforms", Indian Journal Of Public Administration, Vol. LV, No.2, April-June, 2009, pp. 269-74.
46. Vinod Vyasuly, "The Functioning of Local Government in Federal System", Local Government Quarterly, jan.-mar., 2009, pp. 93-102.
47. Argento, Grossi, Tagesson and Colin, "The ' Externalization' of Local Public Service Delivery: Experience in Italy and Sweden", International Journal of Public Policy, Volumes, NO. 1, 2010. (PP 41 to 57,)
48. Lokendra Malik, "Solid Waste Management and Sustainable cities in India: A critique", Nagarlok, Vol. XLII Oct-Dec. 2010, No. 4, pp. 40-48.
49. Sanjeev Ranjan, "Service Level Benchmarking: An Initiative of the Ministry of Urban Development, Government of India", Nagarlok, Vol. XLII, No.1, Jan.- March 2010, pp. 1-10.
50. Sukhbir Singh, " Mayors: Looking Beyond Ceremonial Role", The Tribune, Nov. 27, 2010, p. 13.
51. The Indian Institute of Public Opinion, "Fresh Thrust to Urbanisation", Quarterly Economic Report, Vol.LIV, No .4 Oct.-Dec., 2011, pp. 7-9.
42. Rajani Ranjan Jha and Sarita Kamthan, "Leadership in Urban India: A case study of Allahabad in Uttar Pradesh", The Indian Journal of Public Administration, Vol. LVIII, No.2 April-June 2012, pp. 287 to 297.
43. K.K. Pandey, "Administration of Urban Development and Urban Service Delivery", Theme paper for the 56th Members' Annual Conference, Indian Institute of Public Administration, New Delhi, 2012.
52. A.Narender, "Towards Slum Free cities in India: Policies and Issues", Nagarlok, VOL. XXV Oct-Dec, 2013, No. 4, pp.13 to 38.
53. Document, "Ministry of Urban Development", Nagarlok, Vol. XLV April-June, 2013, No. 2, pp. 76-108.
54. Gurjant Singh and Rajbans Singh Gill, "States of Reforms in Urban Governance in India : An overview", Nagarlok, Vol. XLV Apr-Jan, 2013, No. 2, pp. 1-21.
55. Gangadhar Jha, "Fiscal decentralisation for strengthening Urban Local Government in India: Lessons From Practices in Developing and Transitional Economies", Indian Journal of Public Administration, Vol. LIX, No. 2, April-June, 2013, pp. 278-295.
56. Shubham S. Khailan, "Infrastructure Facilities in Growing cities : Case of Amritsasr City", Nagarlok, Vol.XXV Oct-Dec, 2013, pp. 76-88.

57. Biswajit Mahapatra, "Local Self Government and People's Empowerment: Challenges and Perspectives", Indian Journal of Public Administration, Vol. LIX, No. 4, Oct-Dec, 2013, pp. 804-811.
58. Lokendra Malik and Avneet Kaur, "Urban Government in India: An Analysis", Nagarlok, Vol. XLV July-Sept, 2013, No. 3, pp.35-45.
59. H.M. Mishra, "Frame Work and Perspective of Urban Governance in India and Madhya Pardesh. Changing Dynamics", Nagerlok, Vol. XLV No. 4 Oct-Dec, 2013, pp-1 to 11.
60. A.Narender, "Towards Slum Free cities in India: Policies and Issues", Nagarlok, VOL. XXV Oct-Dec, 2013, No. 4, pp.13 to 38.
61. Shubham S. Khailan, "Infrastructure Facilities in Growing cities : Case of Amritsasr City", Nagarlok, Vol.XXV Oct-Dec, 2013, pp. 76-88.
62. Payel Sen, "Dynamics' of Decentralized Governance in Urban India: Implications for inclusive city development", Nagarlok, Vol. LVI April-Jun, 2014- No.2, pp, 15-33.
63. A. Narender, "Urban water supply and sanitation in India: Emerging Simultaneous and Integrated Service Provision (SISP) Approach and the Need for Establishing Appropriate Institutional and organizational Framework", Nagarlok, Vol. XLVI April- June, 2014, NO. 2, pp, 15-67.
64. H.M.Mishra & Ajit Kumar Mishra, "Urban Development Dynamics challenges and way forward (A case study of Madhya Pradesh)", *Nagarlok*, VOL. XLVI NO. 1, Jan-March, 2014, pp. 1-15.
65. U.B Singh, "Managing Urban Waste in India: In search of a separate Act. and National strategy", Nagarlok, VOL. XLVI, No.1, Jan-March, 2014, pp 63-76.
66. Aaj Samaj, P-4, March 9, 2015.

2

Organisational Structure of the Municipal Council Panchkula

An organisation comprises a group of people working together, under formal and informal rules of behaviour, to achieve a common goal. Organisations are social units deliberately constructed and reconstructed to achieve specific goals.[1] At this point, it would be worthwhile to examine a few definitions of the term 'organisation'. According to Amitai Etzioni, "Organisations are social units or human groupings constructed or reconstructed to seek specific goals".[2] According to Harold Koontz and Heinz Weihrich, "An organisation applies formalised intentional structure of roles and positions".[3] According to Marx, "organisation is a structure developed for carrying out the tasks entrusted to the Chief Executive and his subordinates".[4]

From the above discussion, one may conclude that an organisation is not merely a structure but it also includes the human beings, who run this structure to achieve the predetermined goals.

2.1 Organisational Structure

An organisational structure defines how job tasks are formally divided, grouped and coordinated. An organisational structure is the established pattern of relationships among various components or parts of the organisation.[5]

According to Stoner, "Organisational structure indicates the organisation's hierarchy and authority structure, and shows its reporting relationships. It provides the stability and continuity that allow the organisation to survive the coming and going of individuals and co-ordinate its dealings with the environment.[6]

Thus, an organisation structure is the pattern of relationships among various components or parts of an organisation. It describes the relationships among various activities and positions. Since these positions are held by various persons, the structure is the relationships among people in the organisation.[7]

The statutory provisions related to the organisational set up of municipalities in Haryana are common which have been described as under with special reference to Municipal Council, Panchkula.

2.2 Classification and Constitution of Municipality

According to Section 2A of the Haryana Municipal Act, 1973 which governs the functioning of Municipalities in Haryana (here after to be referred as the Act), the following three classes of municipalities were constituted:

(1) "Municipal Committee" for a transitional area with a population of not more than fifty thousand;
(2) "Municipal Council" for a smaller urban area with a population exceeding fifty thousand but not exceeding three lakhs; and
(3) "Municipal Corporation" for a larger urban area with a population of three lakhs or more to be governed by a separate Act.

The Haryana Municipal Act, 1973 defines a "transitional area", "a smaller urban area" or "a larger urban area". These areas are defined by the state government on the basis of:

(1) The population of the area;
(2) The density of the population therein;
(3) The revenue generated for local administration;
(4) The percentage of employment in non-agricultural activity; and
(5) The economic importance or such other factors as the state government may consider.[8]

On the basis of the above classification, the state government set up a Municipal Council in Panchkula whose organisational structure has been discussed below.

2.3 Municipal Council Panchkula

The Haryana government had set up a Municipal Council in Panchkula district in the year 2001 as it was considered a smaller urban area with a population of about 1,52,000. The Municipal Council in Panchkula comprises of a deliberative wing, an executive wing and sub committees. The composition and functions of these wings of the Municipal Council have been discussed as under:

2.4 Organisational Structure of Municipal Council, Panchkula

The Municipal Council, Panchkula consists of:

1. Deliberative Wing;
2. Sub Committees; and
3. Executive Wing.

1). Deliberative Wing

The Deliberative Wing is the policy making wing of the Municipal Council which includes a President, Vice President and Councilors.

(a) ***President:*** The President occupies a pre-eminent position in the system of Municipal Government. He/she presides over the meetings of the Council and its Committees and, thereby, provides a coordinating link between the Council and Committees. He/she exercises control over the executive, personnel, financial and administrative matters. Furthermore, he/she is a channel of communication between the municipality and the outside agencies including the state government.

(b) ***Vice-president:*** The Vice-president assists the President. Whenever the President is absent, he/she does all the work of the President on his/her behalf.

(c) ***Councilors:*** Councilors are people's representatives. Most of them are elected directly by the people. However, some members are associated and nominated to the Council.

2.5 Composition of Deliberative Wing Of Municipal Council, Panchkula

The deliberative wing consists of the following categories of members/ councilors:

I. ***Directly Elected Members:*** Section 9 (1) of the Haryana Municipal Act provides that each municipality consists of such number of elected members as may be prescribed by rules but such number shall not be less than eleven. The Act further provides that the members are to be directly elected from the territorial constituencies constituted in the municipal area. Each municipal area is to be divided into territorial constituencies to be known as wards. The Municipal Council, Panchkula has been divided into 31 wards and there are 31 directly elected members.

II. ***Associate Members:*** They assist the council. They have a right to take part in the meetings of Municipality but can not vote.

III. ***Nominated Members:*** Section 9(3) of the Haryana Municipal Act, 1973 provides that in addition to the directly elected councilors elected from the territorial constituencies, the state government could nominate members to the Municipal Bodies. Apart from the elected members, following three categories of members were nominated as members in Municipal Council, Panchkula.

a. Not more than three persons having special knowledge or experience in municipal administration with right to vote;
b. Members of the House of People and the Legislative Assembly of the state, representing constituencies which comprised wholly or partly the municipal area; and
c. Members of the Council of States, registered as electors within the municipal area.

However, it is to be noted that the members mentioned at II and III above, did not have any right to contest for the election of President or referred to in points II and Vice-president of the Municipal Council, Panchkula.

Municipal Council, Panchkula consists of three nominated members.

2.6 Qualifications of Members

According to Section 13 (A) of the Act, the qualifications of members are as follows:

I. He/she must be of 21 years of age;
II. He/she must not be disqualified by or under any law made by the legislature of the State of Haryana for election in State; and
III. He/she must not have been convicted of specified offences.

Disqualification of Members

Further, Section 13 (A) of the Act provides that under the following circumstances, a person shall be disqualified/debarred from being chosen as and for being a member of a municipality:

I). If he is disqualified by or under any law for the time being in force for the purpose of election to the legislature of the State of Haryana.

II). If he is disqualified by or under any law made by the legislature of State of Haryana.

III). If he is convicted or has been convicted of an offence punishable under Section 29, 30 and 31 of the Haryana Municipal Corporation Act, 1994 (16 of 1994), the Prevention of Corruption Act, 1988 (49 of 1988) or the Prevention of Terrorism Act, 2002.

IV). A person having more than two children.

V). If any person furnishes a false caste certificate at the time of filing nomination, he/she shall be disqualified for a period of six years from contesting election to the municipality.

If any question arises as to whether a member of municipality has become subject to any of the disqualifications mentioned in sub section(1), the question is to be referred for the decision of such authority and in such manner as may be prescribed by rules.

2.7 Tenure of the Council

Article 243 of the 74th Constitutional Amendment Act of 1994, provides for a uniform tenure of five years for all categories of municipal bodies in the country.

Section 12 of the Haryana Municipal Act, provides a term of five years from the date of the First Meeting of the Municipality. However, it can be dissolved earlier under any law for the time being in force. The Act further provides that the municipality shall be given a reasonable opportunity of being heard before its dissolution. The Act further provides that an election to constitute a municipality must be completed:

a). Before the expiry of its duration of five years;

b). But when the remainder period for which dissolved municipality would have continued is less than six months, it shall not be necessary to hold any election for constituting the municipality for such period. A municipality constituted upon the dissolution before the expiration of their duration shall continue only for the remainder of period for which the dissolved municipality would have continued.

MCP had completed its five years tenure (2002-07) successfully and the new tenure (2008-2013) is nearing its completion.

2.8 Dissolution of Municipality

Section 254 of the Haryana Municipal Act provides that, the state government has the power to dissolve a municipality if in the opinion of the state government, it becomes:

a). Proves incompetent to perform, or
b). Persistently made defaults in the performance of duties imposed on it or by any other act; or
c). Exceeds or abuses its powers.

The Act further provides that before making a notification declaring the municipality to be dissolved, the matter must be inquired into by an officer not below the rank of an Assistant Commissioner appointed by the state government, and the municipality concerned must be given a reasonable opportunity of being heard.

Consequences of Dissolution of Municipality:

When a municipality is dissolved, the following consequences follow:

a). All powers and duties of the committee may, until the committee is reconstituted, be exercised and performed by such persons as the State government appoints in this behalf.
b). All property vested in the committee shall, until the Committee is reconstituted, remain vested in the state government.

2.9 Vacancy of Seats in the Municipality

There can be a vacancy of seats in the municipality under the following circumstances:

(1) ***By Resignation of a Member of Municipality:*** Section 13 of the Act provides that if a member of municipality wishes to resign his office, he/she shall submit an application in writing to the Deputy Commissioner.
(2) ***By Removal of a Member by the State Government:*** According to section 14 of the Act, the state government may, by notification, remove any member of the committee on the following grounds:

(1) Refusal to act or become incapable of acting;
(2) Having been declared bankrupt and insolvent;
(3) If he has been convicted by a criminal court;
(4) If he has been declared by notification to, be disqualified for employment in the public service;

(5) If he remains absent for more than two consecutive months from the meetings of the Committee without any reasonable cause;

(6) If he fails to pay any amount due from him to the Committee within three months of the service of notice making the claim. It shall be duty of the Chief Executive Officer, to serve such a notice at the earliest possible date after the amount has become due; and

(7) He has flagrantly abused his position as a member of the committee or has through his negligence or misconduct, been responsible for the loss, or misappropriation of any money or property of the committee.

According to Section 13 (A) of the Act, before removing a member, the matter must be inquired into by an officer, not below the rank of Commissioner appointed by the state government and the member concerned must be given a reasonable opportunity of being heard. A person removed under this section shall be disqualified for election for a period not exceeding six years.

Filling of Vacancies

Section 15 of the Act provides that whenever a vacancy occurs by death, resignation or removal of any member, the vacancy shall be filled within six months of the occurrence of such vacancy.

The Act further provides that every member elected or nominated to fill a casual vacancy shall be elected or nominated to serve for the remainder of his predecessor's term of office.

2.10 Reservation of Seats

According to Section 10 of the Act, reservation of seats for various categories is as under:

1. In case of Scheduled Castes (SC), the number of seats reserved for them shall bear, as nearly as may be, the same proportion to the number of seats to be filled by direct election in a municipality as the population of SC in the municipal area bear to the total population of that area.
2. For Women, one third of the total number of seats should be filled by direct election (including the number of seats for women belonging to the Scheduled Castes). In every municipality, such

seats may be allotted by rotation and by lots to different constituencies in the municipality.

3. For Backward Class, two seats shall be reserved in every municipality (constituencies having maximum population of persons belonging to backward classes).

2.11 Duties of Members of the Council

The duties of the members of the council include the following:

(1) policy making,
(2) passing the budget, and
(3) personnel matter i.e., appointment of class four employees.

Salary of Members of the Council

According to the Section 58 of the Act, the councilors are paid a fixed amount of salary with the sanction of the state government out of the municipal fund.

In MCP, councilors are paid Rs 1000 per month fixed Honarium and President is paid Rs 1500 every month.

2.12 Meetings of the Council

Section 25 of the Act provides that every municipality shall meet for the transaction of business, at least once in every month at such time as may, from time to time, be fixed by the law.

Types of Meetings: The meetings of the municipality are categorised into three types:

1). ***Ordinary Meetings:*** Any business may be transacted.

2). ***Special Meetings:*** At special meetings, that type business is to be transacted, which is specifically required by the Municipal Act, 1973, of Haryana for instance, a meeting called for considering the no confidence motion against the President and the Vice-President.

3). ***Extra Ordinary Meetings:*** The Act further provides that the President or in his absence, the Vice-president may, whenever he thinks fit, shall within a period of ten days from the date of receipt of a requisition signed by not less than one-fifth of the total number of members of the committee, convene either an ordinary or a special meeting. If the President or Vice-president fails to convene a meeting of the municipality within a period of

10 days from the date of receipt of such requisition, the members who sign the requisition may request the Deputy Commissioner to convene the meeting. The Deputy Commissioner on receipt of such request shall within a period of 10 days convene the meeting. A meeting convened by Deputy Commissioner shall be presided over by him, but without any right to vote.

Chairman of the Meeting

According to Section 28 of the Act every meeting of the municipality is usually presided over by the President or in his absence by a Vice-president or in the absence of both, by a member chosen by the council for this purpose.

Quorum of the Meeting

Section 27 of the Act provides that the quorum necessary for a special meeting is one-half of the number of the members of the committee actually serving at that time, but shall not be less than three. The quorum for an ordinary meeting can be decided /fixed by the municipality in accordance with the bye-laws but, in any case, it cannot be less than three.

Vote of Majority Decisive

According to Section 29 of the Act, normally all the decisions are taken by the majority of the votes of the members present and in case of equality of votes, the President of the meeting shall have a second or casting vote.

Record and Publication of Meetings

According to the Section 30 of the Act, the minutes of proceedings of each meeting are recorded in the proceeding book of the municipality and are signed by the Chairman and a copy of every resolution is forwarded within three days to the Deputy Commissioner. The recorded proceedings are normally open to the citizens inspection at any time without any charge.

Meetings Held in the MCP

Meetings held in MCP from year 2001 to 2010 have been given in Table 2.1.

Table 2.1
Meetings Held in Municipal Council, Panchkula

Years	*Meetings Held*
2002-2003	8
2003-2004	7
2004-2005	8
2005-2006	6
2006-2007	5
2007-2008	4
2008-2009	3
2009-2010	1

Source: Municipal Council, Panchkula.

A study of the meetings held in MCP reveals that in the year 2003, eight meetings were held, in 2004; seven meetings; in 2005, eight meetings; in 2006, six meetings; in 2007, five meetings; in 2008, four meetings; in 2009, three meetings were held; and in 2010 only one meeting was held. Thus, it is clear from the study that the meetings held in MCP were not regular or uniform in terms of their frequency of occurrence.

2.13 President and Vice-president

As mentioned earlier, Municipal Council, Panchkula has a President and a Vice-president. The President heads the Council and Vice-president assists him in performing different tasks. In the absence of the President, the Vice-president acts as the President of the Council.

A. Mode of Election of President and Vice-president

The mode of election of the President of a Municipal Council/ Committee is indirect in the State of Haryana. Section 18 of the Act provides that every Municipal Committee/Council shall from time to time elect one of its elected members to be the President and Vice-president. The office of the President in municipal council shall be reserved for Scheduled Caste, Backward Class and Women by rotation and by lots in the manner prescribed in Section 10(3) of the Act. It is pertinent to mention here that the Act bars nominated members namely Members of Parliament (MPs), Members of Legislative Assembly (MLAs), and Members of Legislative Council (MLCs) from contesting the election of President.

B. Term

The terms of the President and the Vice-president are for a period of five years or for the residue period of them office as a member, whichever is less. The Act provides that if the office of the President or the Vice-president is vacated during his tenure on account of death, resignation or no confidence motion, a fresh election for the remainder of the period shall be held from the same category.

C. Vacancies in the Office of President and Vice-president

The President and Vice-president can leave their seats by the following methods:

1. By resignation
2. By removal

a. By the Government
b. By the Council (By way of No Confidence Motion)

(1) ***By Resignation:*** The President or the Vice-President may resign from office by tendering resignation in writing, to the Deputy Commissioner.

(2) ***By Removal.***

(a) ***By the Government:*** Section 22 of the Act provides that the State government may at any time, by notification, remove a President or Vice President from his office on grounds of abuse of power or habitual failure to perform his duties.

(b) ***By the Council:*** Section 21 of the Act provides that a Motion of No Confidence against the President or the Vice-president may be made in accordance with the procedure laid down in the rules. A meeting for the consideration of no confidence motion can be convened by the Deputy Commissioner, or such other officer not below the rank of Assistant Commissioner, authorised by the Deputy Commissioner. The meeting of no confidence motion shall be presided over by the Deputy Commissioner or the officer authorised by him, but neither he nor such officer shall have the right to vote at such a meeting. Besides, a meeting of no confidence motion is carried with the support of not less than 2/3rd of the elected members of the municipality. If the motion is passed, the President or the Vice-president as the case may be, shall be deemed to have vacated his office.

D. Consequences of Vacancy of Seat of President and Vice-president

If a No Confidence Motion is passed against both the President and the Vice-President simultaneously, the Sub-Divisional Officer

(Civil) of the area in which the municipality is situated, or any other officer of the rank of Assistant Commissioner authorised by the Deputy Commissioner, shall henceforth exercise the powers and discharge the functions of the President till the election of a President is notified or a Vice-president elected.

E. Suspension of President or Vice-president

Section 22A of the Act provides that the Director Urban Development Department, Haryana, may suspend a President or a Vice-president under the following circumstances:

I A case against him in respect of any criminal offence is under investigation, enquiry or trial, if in the opinion of the Director the charge made or proceedings taken against him, are likely to embarrass him in the discharge of his duties.

II Where a case against him in respect of the grounds of removal mentioned under Section 22 is under enquiry, after giving him a reasonable opportunity of being heard.

The Act further provides that the suspension period shall not exceed six months from the date of issuance of the suspension order.

F. Salary of President

At present Rs 1500 per month honorarium is to be paid to President of MCP.

2.14 Powers of the President of Municipal Council Panchkula

As per Haryana Municipal Act, the powers of the President may be categorised under the following heads

(i) ***Legislative Powers:*** The legislative powers of the President are as follows:

As Presiding Officer: The president has to preside over all the meetings of the council. In that capacity, he exercises the following powers:

1. to convene ordinary as well as special meetings;
2. to maintain order and decorum in the meetings of the council;
3. to decide point of order;
4. to give rulings on all controversial matters in the meetings;
5. to maintain relevance in debates;
6. to regulate the conduct of business at such meetings;

7. to summon extra-ordinary meetings; and
8. to exercise a casting vote.

(ii) Executive Powers:

As per provisions in the Act, the President enjoys certain executive powers which are as follows:

1. He is responsible for giving timely replies to all government letters.
2. He exercises appointing and disciplinary powers over certain categories of municipal employees.
3. He may obtain additional powers from the Council.
4. He is responsible for issuing of tenders and signing of contracts.
5. He executes all the lawful resolutions of the Council.
6. He may supervise all the projects of the council.
7. He helps in preparing of agenda of Council.
8. He takes disciplinary action against those who break the law and bye laws of Council.
9. He may delegate some of the powers to another member in writing
10. He executes and implements all the decisions and directions of the Council.

(iii) Administrative Powers:

The President in the capacity of the Civic Chief has certain administrative powers which are as under:

1. He has the right to supervise and control all proceedings related to executive, administrative and financial matters of the council.
2. He hears appeals against disciplinary action taken by an Executive Officer.
3. He examines the reports submitted by the Public Works Department with regard to new building plans and may stop any unlawful and unauthorised construction.
4. He can issue general instructions and directions for the proper functioning of the administrative machinery.
5. He can inspect and supervise any work and property of the Municipality.
6. He is also responsible for the appointment of sub-committees and the division of work among members.

(iv) Emergency Powers:

An emergency may relate to imminent danger to public life and property. Such a situation cannot wait for discussions and decisions of the council.[8] Thus, to meet these emergent situations, the President has been empowered to authorise any expenditure on this count.

However, such an action has to get the approval of the Council in the forthcoming meeting of the Council.

The only limits are that the action should not contravene any standing order of the Council.[9]

According to Section 35 of the Act, the President of the Municipal Council, Panchkula, during the emergency is empowered to:

1. Incur any expenditure to meet any such situation.
2. Every such action shall be reported to the council at its next meeting.

He shall not act under this Section in contravention of any order of the council. No direction given under this section shall be questioned in any court, on the grounds that the case was not one of emergency.

(v) Financial Powers:

The financial powers of the President include preparation of the annual financial statement with the help of Secretary Accountant. Besides, it is also his statutory duty to publish the budget estimate and to see that provisions of the budget are being properly implemented. He also gets the accounts of the Municipal Council, Panchkula audited. He has an important role in the levy of new taxes and reduction current ones.

(vi) Miscellaneous Powers:

In addition, the President has the following miscellaneous powers:

1. Being a Chief and the first citizen of his city\town, he represents his city or town in all ceremonial functions.
2. The President prepares the Annual Administrative Report of the preceding year with the help of his staff and submits the same to the state government and the District Magistrate.

Apart from this, he not only participates in the discussions of the Council but also guides it in framing policies. He can initiate new measures and defend them and provide full political leadership to the Council.

Thus, the entire Municipal Council revolves around the President. He enjoys all the powers as long as he commands majority.

The powers of the President as depicted above, give him an enviable and exated position but in practice, he cannot make full utilisation of his powers, as in their exercise, he is to depend on majority support of the councilors of which he cannot be sure due to the vagaries of municipal politics.

This state of affairs has led to the Punjab Local Government (Urban) Enquiry Committee to remark, "constant endeavour groups seeking enlistment of support of members in dislodging the people in authority and the dual position of the President who has to supervise the day to day administration and has also to carry the majority with him, make the municipal administration more susceptible to extraneous influence and this in turn, sows the seeds of discord and constant party bickering".[10]

This state of affairs was very much present in Municipal Council, Panchkula, from May, 2003 to March 2008 as during this period the Municipal Council, Panchkula had four different Presidents for varying terms i.e., Mrs Seema Chaudhary for two years (12 May, 2003 to 12 April, 2005), Mr. Tarun Bhandari for nine months (17 June, 2005 to 15 February, 2006), Mrs Manvir Kaur Gill (22 May, 2006, to 19 September, 2007) for one year and four months, and Mrs Seema Chaudhary (1 October, 2007 to 6 March, 2008) for five months.

2) Sub-Committee

The second component of the organisational structure of Municipal Council, Panchkula is the Sub committee. The Sub-committee works on the same principles as that of municipality. Therefore, it is desirable to first look into the meaning, composition and functioning of the sub-committee system in general.

A Committee means, "A body to which some task has been referred or committed by some other person or body. It may be asked or required or permitted to carry out this task. But this is not all. The notion of a Sub-committee carries with it the idea of a body being in some manner or degree responsible or subordinate or answerable in the last resort to the body or person who set up or committed a power or duty to it. This is inherent in the notion of a Committee some idea of dependent status, in form at least; it lacks original jurisdiction. It acts on behalf of or with responsibility to another body".[11]

The municipal council is a legislative and executive body and is charged with the whole administration of the city. Since, the council meets only once a month, it is expected to delegate its functions for the running of the day to day administration to some of its officers or committees.[12]

The committee system has a long history behind it. In the nineteenth century, under the Town Improvement Act of 1872 and the District Municipalities Act of 1884, the local authorities were authorised to constitute vertical types of committees for particular subjects such as, committee for the management of schools, dispensaries, and other institutions maintained or aided by the local fund.[13]

The committee system in local governments is used for two separate interlocking purposes:

i). A sub committee may examine a matter; or thrash it out in detailed discussion.
ii). And so be able to make to the council a recommendation that is based on a more careful and prolonged examination than could be made in a Council meeting.

The above mentioned discussion reveals that the local self government has to perform multiple tasks to provide basic services to its citizens. Therefore, for a better specialised and efficient services, the creation of sub-committees according to the Act or bye law as a tool of efficient management device by the council, is an absolute necessity which may strengthen democracy with efficiency and may help the council to devote its concentration towards other major social services for the benefit of its citizens.

The sub-committees are of two kinds:

1. The Statutory.
2. The Non-Statutory.[15]

1). The Statutory:

The law statute may require the local authority to have a committee for some particular purposes, and may provide that the specified matters are to be referred to such a committee.[16] Thus, its creation, powers and functions are provided in the Municipal Act.

2). The Non-Statutory Committee:

The non-statutory committees are those which are created by the council itself under its bye laws. However, there is a special committee or *ad-hoc* committee also.[17] But a distinction has to be made between both special committees and *ad-hoc* committees which are appointed for a specific task and their existence is expected to terminate upon the completion of that task.

Composition of Sub-committees

There are two points here. The first is the constitution of each committee, that is to say, the requirement that is to have a prescribed number of members who are members of the council and so many co-opted members. The second is the selection of the people who are to serve on the committee.[18] Whether a committee should be large or small depends on the work it has to perform. If the committee is to be representative of different areas and have members with specialised knowledge and others with a wide range of experience in different ranges of life, it is apt to have a big committee. A committee must generally be large enough for the council to feel that all shades of opinion are reasonably represented. For co-opted members drawn to the committee, the idea allows men and women who can make a valuable contribution with their general ability or their special knowledge or position. Co-option is also a way of linking other bodies or organisations with the council.

Terms of Reference of Sub-committee

The terms of reference of the committee are contained in the Act and also by the resolution of the council by which the council establishes a committee, subject of course, to latter amending the resolution.

Method of Selection

There are two methods of selection. First is that the members may hold a private meeting, which is not technically a meeting of the authority. They discuss how the committees are to be filled and make a list, by agreement if possible, but otherwise, by voting. It is further settled that certain members will propose and second these names. Then when the items come up at the council meeting, someone is ready and proposes names, and the majority of councilors will support what they have in effect already settled in the private meeting.

The other method is to have a selection committee. The committee should be representative of the council, and contain leaders and most influential members. It makes a list of names for each committee, and these go to the council as recommendations or approval. This implies that if the councilors move an amendment in the council to add a name or remove a name, the council will not come to a decision until the matter has been referred to the selection committee.[19]

Selecting the Member of Sub-committee

In this regard there are two views. The members are selected annually or for the period of council. It is said that in authorities where the councilors hold office for five years, it would be quite feasible to appoint committees after the general election and let them hold office for five years. Where there are annual elections, a proportion of members of the council retire each year so that each year, the composition of the committee may change. There are, however, advantages in annual appointments. Some reshuffles are bound to be needed, and it is better to do that by a complete review each year than by bits and pieces. Although the Council appoints a person to a committee for a specific period, that does not bind the council. During the specific period, the council may resolve that a member of a committee ceases to be a member, and proceed to appoint someone else. The appointments are made by a resolution of the Council naming the individuals who are to serve for this purpose. For this, there is a need for preparation and selection of names which require reviewing the needs for all the committees. It is often like solving a complicated puzzle to find the right person or a member of the committee.[20]

Chairman of the Sub -committee

The Chairman of the committee is generally a senior or leading member of the committee who is selected by the committee itself or by the council.[21] Once elected, the Chairman often continues to be re-elected to this post. In some councils, committee Chairmen tends to retain their positions as long as they are in the council.

Reports of the Sub-committee

The report of each committee contains recommendations that are to be moved by its chairman to the council. The majority of the recommendations usually go through without any debate. Whenever there is a debate, the only provision of the law is that the Council proceeds by a majority of those present and voting, or manners/

methods that are provided by the Act or resolution by the council. In fact, the Chairman plays the main role in getting the report accepted. He is the committee spokesman and therefore, he/she must explain the reasons and present the arguments.[22]

The reports of the sub committees can be divided into two categories. First, the matters that have been referred to a committee for consideration and second, the matters where there has been a delegation of power. In the former instance, the committee recommends that the council should do something while in the latter, the committee has resolved (i.e. taken action) and reports what it has done.[23]

When the council is dealing with the recommendations from a committee, it always has a free hand. The council is in no way bound to follow the committee.

If there has been a delegation of power to a committee, the committee is empowered to act on behalf of the council, and the council is then informed about what the committee has done. If any objection is made by the council, it could record its view but this has no effect on what has been done. But for the future, the council can take steps to see that the same thing does not happen again. The council can give directions to its committee; alter the committee's terms of reference, which includes withdrawing the delegation of power or limiting it. But it is a complex task. The reason for this is that the delegation of power create agency. A master does not lose his own power to act because he authorises an agent to act. But the act of an agent counts as the act of master. If there can be only one act, then it is important to know who gets in first. In this case, the council having caught up its agent in time, can take the matter into its own hands.[24]

2.15 Municipal Sub-committees in Haryana and Municipal Council, Panchkula

The Haryana Municipal Business Bye Laws, 1981, provide that a Municipal Council may appoint the following sub committees to assist it in its administration:

1. Finance sub-committees;
2. Public Works and Building sub-committees;
3. Sanitation and Water Supply sub-committees; and
4. Special sub-committees

1). The Finance Sub-committee shall deal with

a. Preparation and submission of the budget estimates to the committee in time;

b. Monthly and Annual Account Statement;
c. Statement of grant/loans and advances;
d. Imposition, assessment and settlement of objections, collection and remission of taxes, rents, fees and settlements of objections thereto;
e. Acquisition, sale and lease of municipal properties;
f. Raising of loans;
g. Matters relating to schools, reading room, libraries, lighting and fire brigade; and
h. All the matters affecting the finances of Committees.

2). Public Works and Building Sub-committee

This committee shall enquire and report on all matters related to municipal works, maintenance and verification of municipal properties, roads and buildings under the control of the council. The sub-committee shall also deal with all cases of encroachment and projections. It may also consider town planning and building schemes and matters relating to the levy and recovery of development charges.

3). Sanitation Sub-committee

This sub-committee shall inquire and report on all matters related to sanitation, health, sewerage and water supply.

4). Special Sub-committee

In addition to the three sub-committees as mentioned above, the Haryana Municipal Bye Laws, 1981, also provide that the municipal council may appoint a special sub-committee consisting of one or more members of the committee to investigate and report on any matter not falling in the scope of the sub-committee or if so desired by the President, to advise or assist him in discharge of any of his duties.

Such special sub-committees shall cease to exist as soon as the matter has been disposed of by the committee.

A. Composition of Sub-committees

Each sub-committee shall consist of four members. The members of the sub-committees shall be elected at a general meeting of the municipal council/committee as soon as possible, after a new committee/council has been constituted. Elections shall be conducted through ballot and by single non-transferable vote.

The President or in his absence the Vice-president of the Council shall be the ex-officio member of all the sub-committees and shall have the right to vote.

B. Chairman and Secretary of Sub-committees

The President and in his absence the Vice-president and in the absence of both, a person elected by the member of the sub-committees shall take the chair.

The head of the committee concerned shall be the secretary of the sub-committees.

C. Term of a Member of Sub-committees

The term of the members of the sub-committees shall be one-year from the date of their election. A member elected to fill a casual vacancy holds office for the rest of the period of the term of members in whose place he is elected.

D. Removal of the Members

A member of the sub-committee shall be removed if he has absented himself without any reasonable cause from the three consecutive meetings of the sub-committees. A member may also be removed from a sub-committee by resolution of the committee passed by two-third majority of active members actively serving at that time.

E. Meeting of Sub-committees

Every sub-committee shall meet at least once a month or at such shorter period as the council or the sub-committee may decide.

Every sub-committee shall at its meeting, fix the date and time of the next meeting and a notice thereof, shall be sent by the secretary to all the members of the sub-committee. If any sub-committee fails to hold a meeting for a period of two months, the papers that should have been placed before it shall be put directly before the committee. The meetings of the sub-committee shall be convened by the secretary on a written requisition from the President and in his absence, from the Vice-president of the Council or of at least two members of the sub-committee at a time not less than twenty four hours, after the time when such requisition is delivered to the Secretary. Immediately on receipt of such requisition, the Secretary of the committee shall dispatch to all the members of the sub-committees, a notice of the meeting along with the note stating the business to be transacted.

F. Quorum

The quorum for a meeting of the sub-committee shall not be less than three members.

G. Procedure of Working of Sub-committee

The procedure of every sub-committee shall be conducted in accordance with the bye laws of the council. If on any matter, the sub-committee is equally divided the matter shall be decided by the casting vote of the Chairman of the meeting.

Sub-committees in Municipal Council, Panchkula

The Municipal Council, Panchkula has been given the discretion to appoint sub committees, though it has not felt it necessary to appoint them.

3). Executive Wing

The third component of the organisation structure of MCP is the Executive Wing. It is headed by an Executive Officer. He is to be the pivot of the Municipal Administration. The officer is of paramount importance for guiding controlling and coordinating the activities of all the officials. He is the Principal adviser and lieutenant of the President, who is the Political head of the Committee. [25]

He assists the President, who is the political head of the entire organisation. He is also responsible to the President for the discharge of his duties. All the members of the permanent establishment including the departmental heads, discharge their duties in subordination of the Executive Officer.

In the Municipality in which an executive officer has been appointed, the executive power for the purpose of carrying on the administration of the municipality is vested in him/her.[26]

2.16 Powers of Executive Officer of Municipal Council, Panchkula

The Executive Officer of the Municipal Council has been given executive, legislative, administrative, financial and miscellaneous powers and is discussed as under:

I. Executive Powers

The executive powers for carrying out the functions of the urban local self government are vested in the Executive Officer.

These are:

a). The enforcement of the provisions of the Act including the rules under it;

b). Appointments of certain categories of employees after consulting a Selection Board or Standing Committee (Promotion, Removal and Transfer);
c). Striking contract on behalf of the council;
d). Policy Initiation and preparation of memorandum and proposals (Extra ordinary Power);
e). Participation in the meetings;
f). Preparation of the Budget; and
g). Administrative functions (co-ordination, supervision and control).

II. Legislative Powers

The Executive Officers has the right to attend all the meetings of the municipality except a meeting convened for the purpose of considering the question of his suspension or removal and of any sub-committee, and also participate in discussion but he is not entitled to move any resolution or vote. Further, he is bound to attend any meeting of the Committee or of a sub committee when required to do so by the President. He provides the municipal council with any statement, account, report etc. as may be desired by it.

The executive power for the purpose of carrying out the administration of the municipality is vested in the hands of the Executive Officer and the Municipal Administration shall be under his direct control. As the chief executive of the municipality, he is responsible for executing the resolution of the council. He corresponds with the state government or (to the officer of the state government) on behalf of the committee. He is made responsible for seeing that the communication addressed through to the committee of the state government or their officers are dealt with promptly and efficiently. He places all the important correspondence between the Government and the Committee before the President and the Committee. It is also his duty to send copies of resolution of the committee to the Deputy Commissioner.

The executive officer has the power to issue certain notices, licenses, permits etc. on behalf of the municipality. He is expected to devote sufficient time in inspecting the municipal activities. He is responsible for the prompt disposal of audit objections and inspection notes of various administrative authorities.

III. Administrative Powers

He is the head of the municipal establishment. As such, all the municipal officials including the heads of the various departments and branches are subordinate to him. His powers over personnel entitle him to make appointments and dismiss or transfer employees carrying a certain salary. He possesses disciplinary powers over certain categories of employees as well. He may fine, withhold annual increments, censure, suspend or remove an employee carrying a certain salary. He also grants leave to the employees.

IV. Financial Powers

The executive officer is responsible for the preparation of the municipal budget and for its submission to the Municipal Committee.

The budget would be prepared by the Chief Executive Officer with the help and assistance of his department heads and their subordinates, under his supervision and direction of him. However, the Chief Executive Officer prepares the budget estimate on the basis of the discussion and decision which takes place in the meetings of the budget committee. However, any councilor has the right to make discussions with the Executive Officer and put forth suggestions to him regarding the budget estimates, before its presentation. Further, a councilor is entitled to put forward suggestions and amendments after the budget has been presented to the Committee. The Committee has the authority to fix general guidelines regarding the budget estimates. The Committee has power to make modifications and amendments in the budget if it thinks fit and necessary to do so. Through the budget, a chief executive accomplishes the dual tasks of participating in the policy making process and effecting supervision and control over the Municipal Administration.

The executive officer is also responsible for the execution of the budget. He is charged with the responsibilities of exercising all powers in relation to the collection of taxes, fees and licenses. It is he who has been given the responsibility of maintaining the municipal accounts, getting them properly audited and removal of audit objection. It is the duty of the Executive Officer to bring to the notice of the President, all cases of loss of municipal property, misappropriations and other financial losses incurred by the municipal council. In fact, he is to keep an eye on the expenditure and satisfy himself about the admissibility of the payments. He ensures that the municipal dues are received and credited to the municipal fund and all the money received for credit to the municipal fund is deposited daily as per law. He has also to ensure that all accounts registers and financial returns are kept up to date. Besides this, he also ensures that no municipal money is expended without the sanction of the municipality and that no payment is made except to a person entitled to receive it. He also has the power to sanction contingent expenditure up to a certain amount in any case at a time.

V. Miscellaneous Powers

In addition to the executive, legislative, administrative and financial powers, the executive officer also possesses certain miscellaneous powers, which are:

1. He is responsible for the management of fairs, places of amusement, gardens, parks, land and other immovable properties of the council.
2. He makes rounds in the city to inspect sanitation, octroi barriers, encroachments and municipal works.
3. He has the power to appear on behalf of the committee, in any court of law and to prosecute on its behalf any offender against the Act and rules and bye-laws.
4. He has the power to sanction the sale of trees, land produce, stores, sand and clay at the rate approved by the municipality.

2.17 Appointment of Municipal Executive

There are mainly six forms of municipal executives, namely: (1) The council as executive; (2) an executive committee appointed by the council; (3) an elected committee as an executive; (4) the elected mayor as an executive; (5) an executive officer appointed by the council; and (6) an executive officer appointed by the higher authority.[27]

The municipal executive under (6) above is an appointee of the higher authority, either the Central Government or where Federal Constitution is in force, the State Government.[28]

In India too, this system, though not in its pure form, is operative in some of its big cities where municipal corporations are in existence, and also in some of the municipalities.

A. Appointment

In municipalities in Haryana and also in Municipal Council, Panchkula the Chief Executive Officer is appointed by the State Government after consultation with Public Service Commission/Staff Selection Commission of Haryana.

B. Removal

The method of removal of an executive officer is closely connected with the mode of his appointment. The performance and effectiveness of a municipal executive as well as his behavioural pattern in relation to the various statutory bodies of the municipality, depends much on the methods of his removal.

In the Municipal Council, Panchkula, he can be removed by the State Government at any time after consultation with the Public Service Commission or Staff Selection Commission of Haryana, if the State Government is satisfied on a resolution passed by council or otherwise, that the Executive Officer is incapable of performing the duties of his office or has been guilty of any misconduct or neglect which renders his removal expedient.

C. Tenure

The Municipal Act of Haryana does not provide for a fixed term for the executive officer. In American cities where the council manager plan operates, the city manager is appointed for an indefinite period. The basic idea behind this is that a longer term provides a municipal executive with sufficient time to develop a rapport with his superiors as well as his subordinates. Further, this also helps in gaining the benefits of continuous service and experience.[29]

D. Salary

In Haryana, the salary and other allowances of the Executive Officer are fixed by the State Government from time to time and he is paid from the municipal council fund.

E. Leave

The Government has the right to grant him leave of absence. His application for leave is to be sent to the Department of Urban Local Bodies in Haryana, through the Deputy Commissioner.

2.18 Organisational Structure of Executive Wing of Municipal Council, Panchkula

In order to perform functions of the Municipal Council, Panchkula, the organisational structure of the Executive Wing of the Municipal Council Panchkula has been divided into various branches, each headed by an officer (See Figure 2.1). The details in this regard are as follows:

1. Engineering Branch

The overall responsibility of the engineering branch is the maintenance of buildings and parks, and is headed by a Municipal

Engineer. He is assisted by a Junior Engineer, a building inspector and a clerk. The statutory duties of the municipal engineer are as follows:

i). The Municipal Engineer is in charge of the Engineering and Building Branch. He is responsible for providing house connections with filtered water supply system, road lighting, water meters, municipal lands and properties, machinery, plants and stores and has to maintain stock register books laid down in the Municipal Accounts Code and the Municipal Works Rule.

ii). He is to ensure that all cases of unauthorised construction and encroachments are detected and reported in time for action.

2. Accounts Branch

The overall responsibility of the accounts branch is to prepare an account of income and expenditure and, is headed by an Accountant. He is assisted by a clerk and this branch reports directly to the secretary.

Figure 2.1

Organisational Structure Chart of MCP

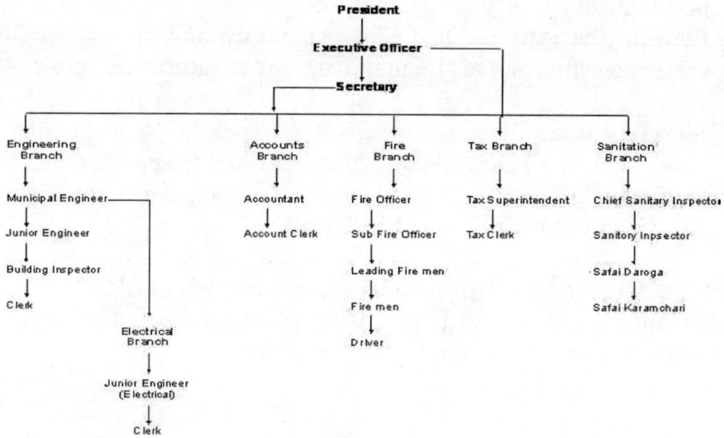

3. Fire Branch

The overall responsibility of the fire branch is fire prevention work in the city it is headed by a Chief Fire Officer and assisted by Sub Fire Officer (S.F.O), Leading Fire Men and Fire men. The statutory duties of a Chief Fire Officer are as follows:

He:

1. Gives approval to all commercial and residential buildings in their locality.

2. Takes account of all the fire related incidents in the locality and plans to prevent the same in future.
3. Plans to place proper infrastructure and manpower in place to tackle time related incidents in the locality.

4. Tax Branch

The overall responsibility of the tax branch is tax assessment, bill distribution and collection of taxes it is headed by a tax superintendent who is assisted by a tax clerk.

5. Sanitation Branch

The overall responsibility of the sanitation branch is the general cleanliness of the city. It is headed by a Chief Sanitary Inspector. He is assisted by a Sanitary Inspector, a Safai Daroga and a Safai worker. The statutory duties of a Chief Sanitary Inspector are as follows he:

1. Makes appropriate efforts for the cleanliness of the city.
2. Gathers necessary information regarding sanitation related problems of the city.
3. Puts in place the requisite infrastructure and manpower for better coordination of the management of sanitation services.

6. Electrical Branch

This branch is responsible for the overall lighting system of the jurisdiction of MCP and is headed by a Municipal Engineer and assisted by a Junior Engineer (Electrical).

2.19 Assessment of Organisational Structure of MCP

According to S. K. Bhatacharya, an organisational structure having the following features is conducive for performance:

i) Effective task allocation.
ii) Proper coordination.
iii) Proper supervision.
iv) Formation of smaller task groups.[30]

As mentioned above, in order to be conducive to performance, an organisational structure should have an effective task allocation. In case of MCP, it has been found that some of the branches have been allocated work, disproportionate to their capacity to perform. For example, the Engineering Branch of MCP has not only been assigned to look after the large area relating to roads (405 kilometers) in the MCP jurisdiction, but also has been allocated tasks related to the all around development and maintenance of around 200 parks.

Secondly, proper coordination is another significant determinant for the conducive performance of any organisation. The study shows that in MCP, there are cases of lack of coordination between the Deliberative Wing and the Executive Wing as well as between different branches of the MCP. For example, during the interview the Councilors revealed that the policies formulated by the Deliberative Wing are not properly executed by the MCP staff and due to weak coordination between both the wings. Furthermore, the study shows a lack of coordination between the Accounts Branch and the Engineering Branch with regard to payments to the contractors, particularly to the Park Development Societies.

The literature also shows that for conducive performance, a structure should facilitate supervision. In case of supervision, the study reveals that in MCP, there is a lack of proper supervision on the part of the Council due to inadequate number of Sanitary Inspectors and Junior Engineers for Sanitation and Electrical Branches respectively. In the case of sanitation services, the areas under MCP jurisdiction have been divided into two sanitary zones but in MCP a post of Sanitary Inspector is lying vacant. Further, only two Saffai Darogas have been assigned to supervise a large area i.e. 39.5 square kilometer area covering 1,90,000 population. Similarly, for street light, only one Junior Engineer has been assigned to look after as many as 10,000 street light points.

Formation of smaller task groups or sub-committees results in good organisational performance. The study suggests that MCP has failed to set-up sub-committees or smaller task groups. It is noteworthy to mention here that the Haryana Municipal Act, 1973 authorises urban local governments to constitute sub committees for effective functioning in different fields. However, MCP has not implemented this provision of the Act.

Thus, the evaluation of MCP on the basis of the above mentioned parameters suggests that the existing organisational structure of MCP is at variance with the organizational structure's conducive performance. In the light of this, the Hypothesis 1, namely, "The organisational structure of Municipal Council Panchkula is not conducive to performance" stands validated.

Concluding Observations

The study of the organisational structure of MCP shows that as per the Haryana Municipal Act, 1973 (HMA) the MCP has constituted its Deliberative Wing as well as the Executive Wing. However, it has not constituted any sub-committee which could have played an important role in improving the effectiveness and functioning of MCP. Further, the study found that there is a lack of proper coordination between both the Deliberative and the Executive Wings and also between its different branches and thus, results in poor performance. Moreover, in terms of task allocation, the study reveals that it has not been implemented in an effective manner as some branches of the MCP have been over burdened in contrast to others which have been allocated lesser tasks. Moreover, the structure has not been able to facilitate proper supervision. All these organisational inadequacies adversely affect the performance of MCP.

REFERENCES

1. Gregory Moor Head, Ricky W. Griffin, *Organisational: Behaviour Managing People and Organization*, Biztantra, New Delhi, 2009, p. 421.
2. Amitai Etzioni, *Modern Organisation*, N. J. Prentice-Hall Inc., Englewood Cliff, N.J, 1964, p. 3.
3. Harold Koontz and Heinz Wihrich, *Essentials of Management,* Tata McGraw Hill Publishing Company Ltd., New Delhi, 2001, p. 134.
4. F. M. Marx (Ed.), *Elements of Public Administration*, Prentice Hall of India, New Delhi, 1968, p. 140.
5. L. M Prasad, *Principles and Practices of Management*, Sultan Chand and Sons, New Delhi, 2004, p. 305.
6. S.S. Khanka, Organisational Behaviour (Test and Cases), S. Chand and Company Ltd., New Delhi, *2010, p. 300.*
7. Prasad, *op. cit.*, p. 484.
8. *Haryana Municipal Act*, 1973, p. 24.
9. Sahib Singh Bhayana, *Local Government in India*, New Academic Publishing Co., Jalandhar, 1989, p. 200.
10. *Ibid.*, p. 201.
11. S.S Dhaliwal, *Municipal Administration*, Deep and Deep Publications Pvt. Ltd., Rajauri Garden, New Delhi, 1990, p. 30.
12. Samuel Humes and Eileen M. Martin, *The structure of local government through out the world,* The Haguemartinus Nijhoff, Netherlands, 1956, p. 93.
13. R. Argal, *Municipal Government in India*, Agarwal Press Allahabad, 1960, p. 89.

14. A. Avasthi and Lakshmi Narain, *Municipal Administration in India*, Agarwal, Agra, 1980, p. 65.
15. Argal, *op. cit.*, p. 90.
16. *Ibid.*, p. 92.
17. Humes and. Martin *op.cit.*, pp. 94-96.
18. R.M. Jackson, *The Machinery of Local Government*, Macmillan and Co. Ltd, New York, 1959, p. 64.
19. *Ibid.*, p. 68.
20. *Ibid.*, p. 67.
21. Humes and Martin, *op. cit.*, p. 95.
22. Jackson, *op.cit.*, p. 87.
23. *Ibid.*, p. 88.
24. *Ibid.*, pp. 89-90.
25. Mahadeo Prasad Sharma, *Local self government and finance in Uttar Pradesh*, Kitab Mahal, Allahabad, 1954, p.56.
26. Ratan Lal Khanna, *Power, Function, Duty: Local Government in Punjab*, The English Book Shop-Book Seller and Publishers, Chandigarh, 1972, p.42.
27. Humes and Martin, *op. cit.*, pp. 119-143.
28. William A Robson, *Great Cities of the World*, George Allen and Unwin Ltd, London, 1972, p. 48.
29. Charles R. Adrian, *Governing Urban America*, Charles Press McGraw-Hill Book Company, 1977, p. 345.
30. S. K. Bhattacharya, *Achieving Managerial Excellence Insight from Indian Organization*, Macmilan India Ltd., New Delhi, 1989, pp. 67-76.

3

Personnel Administration of the Municipal Council Panchkula

The art of managing men or mob is a very important and challenging job; important because it is a job, not of managing 'men', but of administering a social system. The management of men is a challenging task because of the dynamic nature of the people involved in any particular group or activity. It is in fact, a universal truth that no two persons are similar in mental abilities, traditions, sentiments and behaviour. They differ widely, and are subject to many and varied influences. All the people in a group or team are responsive; they feel, think and act. Therefore, they can't be operated like machines or shifted and altered like a template in a room layout. They therefore, need a tactful handling by management personnel. If the manpower is properly utilised, it may prove a dynamic motivational and guiding force for the running of an enterprise at its optimum. Besides, it may also work as an elixir for maximum individual and group satisfaction in relation to the work performed.[1]

3.1 Meaning of Personnel Administration

Personnel administration is that branch of Public Administration which can help an organisation in the management of personnel resources with the use of well thought out principles, practices and rationalised techniques in selecting, retaining and developing personnel, for the fulfillment of organisational objectives, systematically and scientifically. It is the art and science of planning, organising, implementing and evaluating the personnel resources in any organisation to ensure their best use for the achievement of the objectives, goals and targets of an organisation.[2]

According to Thomas G. Spates, "Personnel administration is a code of the ways of organising and treating individuals at work so that they will each get the greatest possible realisation of their intrinsic abilities, thus attaining maximum efficiency for themselves and their group, and thereby giving to enterprise of which they are a part its determining competitive advantage and its optimum results".[3]

Jucious has defined Personnel Administration as "the field of management which has to do with planning, organising, directing and controlling various operative functions of procuring, developing, maintaining and utilising a labour force, such that (a) the objectives, for which the company is established are attained economically and effectively; (b) the objectives of all levels of personnel are served to highest possible degree; and (c) the objectives of the community are duly considered and served."[4]

Public personnel administration is more than a series of steps of organisational constructs. It is more than recruitment, hiring, retention, job analysis, evaluation and promotion. It is cluster of activities that are changing and evolving with some activities changing more rapidly than others.[5]

3.2 Municipal Personnel Administration

The problems of urban living are increasing and becoming complex. The number of specialties in urban government is likely to grow in future. The cost of local self-government is mounting because of the extension of municipal activities to new areas. Therefore, a sound and systematic personnel administration structure has to be built up by the local self-governing institutions.[6]

In order to provide efficient services to the citizens, municipalities require an administrative framework based upon alert and committed personnel, particularly at the cutting edge of the administration. This would enhance the organisation's image in the public eye. Therefore, an efficient administrative, professional and technical staff at the municipal level is the first requirement for an effective municipal government[7].[7]

As local government is the responsibility of the State, under the Constitution, personnel practices at the municipal level manifest wide inter-state variations. It is possible, however, to group them under the following three types of personnel systems:

1. ***Separate Personnel System:*** In this system, each local government appoints and administers its own personnel. They are not automatically transferable to another jurisdiction of other bodies. By and large, this is the most prevalent practice of organising municipal service.[8]

   However, the State Government exercises control over certain personnel matters such as appointments at the higher management level and disciplinary action related to them, the creation of posts and imposing a limit of establishment expenditure. It is inherent in the term 'self-government' that the municipal government should enjoy an authority to recruit and control its personnel. The personnel so recruited and controlled, is apt to develop undivided loyalty to the local government and besides, would be held accountable to it. A separate personnel system has been in vogue in many countries such as the United States, Britain and Japan.[9] However, this system has not proved to be successful in India because of the following reasons:

I. Local government is too small in size and its financial resources are inadequate to employ a really competent staff.

II Widespread favouritism and nepotism in procedure involving selection, appointment and promotion, etc.

III Employee stagnation due to limited promotional opportunities.

2. ***Unified Personnel System:*** A unified local government personnel system is the one in which some or all categories of personnel of municipal government constitute a single career service for the entire state. The state government administers and controls the service. Employees are transferable between local governments only and as such, they spend their entire service career in the municipal administration. The state government constitutes the statewide services. The authority to make appointments, promotions, transfers and dismissals vests with the state government. The recruitment at the top cadres is often made by public service commission as or by bodies especially set up by the state government.

   Unified municipal cadre often includes executive officers, revenue officers, accountants, etc.

3. ***Integrated Personnel System:*** In this system, there is no distinction between the state civil service and the municipal service. The personnel of the state government and that of the local government form part of the same service.

Transfers are possible not only between local governments but between the various departments of the state government. Thus, the officials have vertical as well as horizontal mobility. In practice, the integrated personnel system is only restricted to the meaning of posts at the higher levels of technical departments in the municipal administration.

However, no state has adopted one single type of personnel system to the total exclusion of the other types. The pattern followed by and large, is a combination of the three personnel systems. Where a separate personnel system exists, some heads of the technical department may be on deputation from the state services, whereas the rest of the employees belong to the local body.

Where unified personnel system exists, the state government officials are deputed to head the technical departments of the Municipal body. However, the lower level Class III and Class IV employees of these municipal bodies belong to a separated personnel system.

The first and second Conference of the Local Self-government Ministers held in 1948 and 1954, made recommendations for the creation of a unified personnel system. It was recommended in 1948 that, "In view of the fact that the provincial cadre will facilitate recruitment of suitable personnel from a wide field and provide a more efficient and contended service, this conference is of the opinion that there should be provincial cadre for the higher executive and technical staff employed by local bodies.[10] The Taxation Enquiry Commission (1953-54) also favored the same.[11] The Central Council of Local Self- government also lent its support to this proposal in the years 1956, 1959 and 1960. In 1963, the Central Council of Local Slf-government as well as the Fourth Conference of Ministers of Town and Country Planning requested all the State Governments to provincialise administrative, health, engineering and town planning services of the municipalities in the interest of better and more efficient administration".[12] Similarly, the Rural Urban Relationship Committee had also carefully examined the entire question of Municipal personnel, and suggested a unified cadre for the administrative services and an integrated cadre for the technical services.[13]

The Committee on the Service Conditions of Municipal Employees, set up in 1965 by the Central Council of Local Self-government examined the issue of Integrated Personnel System for local governments. It was felt that "while in the initial stages, the state governments may take recourse to unified or integrated cadres for various categories of services in the light of the circumstances prevailing in each state, the ultimate objective should be to integrate municipal services with corresponding categories of state services in order to ensure that the personnel available for municipal employment would have the desired competence and prestige, enjoying appropriate conditions of service".[14]

3.3 PERSONNEL ADMINISTRATION OF MUNICIPAL COUNCIL, PANCHKULA

As far as the Municipal Council, Panchkula is concerned, the unified personnel system is adopted by it. Table 3.1 shows the staff position in MCP.

Table 3.1
Staff Position in 2002-03 and 2009-2010 in Municipal Council, Panchkula

Sr. No.	*Branch Name and Name of Post*	*2002-03*			*Change of Post in (2009-10)*
	General Administration	Sanctioned Post	Filled post	Vacant post	
1.	Executive Officer	1	1	...	
2.	Secretary	1	1	...	
3.	Superintendent	1	...	1	
4.	Assistant	2	1	1	
5.	Steno-Type	2	...	2	
6.	Clerk (Computer)	3	...	3	
7.	Driver	3	2	1	
8.	Store Keeper	1	1	...	
9.	Peon	2	2	...	
	Total	**16**	**8**	**8**	No change
	Accounts Branch				
1.	Accountant	1	1	...	
2.	Clerk	3	3	...	
3.	Cashier	1	...	1	
	Total	**5**	**4**	**1**	
	Tax Branch				
1.	Superintendent	1	1	...	
2.	Tax-Collector	2	2	...	
3.	Clerk	1	1	...	
	Total	**4**	**4**		No change
	Sanitation Branch				
1.	C.S.I.	1	1	...	
2.	Safai Daroga	1	1	...	
3.	Safai Worker	10 (Working as peon)	10	...	
4.	Sanitary Inspector	1		1	
	Total	**13**	**12**	**1**	No change
	Electrical Branch				
1.	Junior Engineer	1	1	...	

2.	Clerk	1	1	...	
3.	Electric Worker	-	-	...	
	Total	**2**	**2**		
	Fire Brigade				
1.	Fire Station Officer	1	1	...	
2.	Assist. F.S.O.	1	...	1	
3.	Leading Firemen	9	7	2	
4.	Driver	9	2	7	
5.	Firemen	16 +10	4	12	10
6.	Peon	1	1	...	
	Total	**47**	**25**	**22**	10 posts increase
	Engineering Branch				
1.	Municipal	1	1	...	
2.	Junior Engineer	1	3 for 2 days	...	
3.	Work Inspector	1	.....	1	
4.	Clerk	1	1	...	
5.	Steno-Typist	1	...	1	
	Total	**5**	**3**	**2**	No change
	Building Branch				
1.	Assistant Town Planner	1	....	1	
2.	Building Inspector	2	....	2	
3.	Clerk	1	....	1	
4.	Patwari	1	....	1	
	Total	**5**		**5**	No change
	Public Health Branch				
1	S.D.O.	1		1	
2.	Junior Engineer	5	...	5	
3.	Clerk	1	...	1	
	Total	**7**		**7**	
	TOTAL	104	48	46	48 + 10 = 58

Source: Establishment Branch of MCP.

Table 3.1 depicts that in the General Administration Branch, there are 16 sanctioned posts, out of which only 8 were filled while in the Accounts Branch, out of five sanctioned posts only one post was vacant. Besides, it was found that in the Tax and Electrical Branches, all the sanctioned posts were filled and there were no vacant posts in these branches. It is relevant to mention here that there is no sanctioned post of Electrical Worker in MCP and it has been providing these services through the contracting-out mode.

As far as the Sanitation Branch of the MCP is concerned, out of the total 13 sanctioned posts all the posts have been filled except that of the Sanitary Inspector. However, the *safai* workers are performing the peon functions and the sanitation work is being undertaken by means of contracting-out process.

In the Engineering Branch, there were five sanctioned posts, out of which three were filled and the remaining two have been vacant for a long period. It can be seen from the Table 3.1 that 22 posts out of 47 sanctioned posts in the Fire Brigade Branch were found unfilled. However, MCP contracted out some parts of fire services like the recruitment of fire men and it was only in 2007 that 15 fire men were provided by the contractor.

In the Building Branch there were five sanctioned posts and all remained vacant for a long period. In public health branch, there were seven sanctioned posts and all posts have remained vacant for a considerable period.

The analysis of Table 3.1 reveals that over a period of seven years between 2002-03 to 2009-10, no posts have been added and very few have been filled in case of MCP. In case of sanctioned posts, in the period mentioned above no change has been observed. However, in case of filled posts, the numbers of posts have witnessed a nominal increase of 10 from 48 in 2002-03 to 58 in 2009-10, as 10 fire men were recruited in 2010.

It can therefore, be concluded that a number of posts in different branches were not filled, since as out of 104 sanctioned posts in the MCP, about 44.2 per cent posts were lying vacant.

The MCP has failed to develop an appropriate personnel policy to recruit employees for its various branches and this certainly affects the performance of MCP till this date.

In order to assess the satisfaction level of the employees of MCP with regard to the personnel policy, two interview schedules were administered to 58 permanent employees and 21 contractual employees.

Profiles of the Respondents belong to the Permanent Employees Category

The profile of the respondents belonging to the Permanent Employees category has been described below on the basis of gender, education, age and designation:

(1) ***Gender:*** Out of total 58 respondents, 54 were males and four were females respondents.

(2) ***Education:*** On the basis of education, nine were illiterate, seven were below matric and 42 were matric and above.

(3) ***Age:*** On the basis of age of the respondents, seven respondents were below 30 years, 23 respondents between the age group of 30 to 60 years, 23 respondents between the age group of 40 to 50 years and five respondents of 50 years and above in age.

(4) Designation: On the basis of designation, there four were Grade A employees, five Grade B, 16 Grade C and 33 Grade D employees (For details see Table 3.2).

Table 3.2
Category-wise Number of Respondents

Category	*Sub category*	*Number of Respondents*
Gender	Male	54
	Female	4
Education	Illiterate	9
	Below Matric	7
	Matric and above	42
Age	Below 30	7
	30 to 40	23
	40 to 50	23
	50 and above	5
Grade	A	4
	B	5
	C	16
	D	33

Source: Field Survey.

Profile of the Respondents belonging to the Contractual Employees Category: The profile of the respondents belonging to the Contractual Employees Category has been described below on the basis of gender, education and age:

(1) ***Gender:*** Out of 21 respondents, 19 were males and two mere females respondents.

(2) ***Education:*** Five were below matric and 16 were matric and above.

(3) ***Age:*** 13 were below 30 years and eight between the age group of 30 to 40 years (For details see Table 3.3).

Table 3.3
Category-wise Number of Respondents

Category	*Sub category*	*Number of Respondents*
Gender	Male	19
	Female	2
Education	Illiterate	0
	Below Matric	5
	Matric and above	16
Age	Below 30	13
	30 to 40	8

Source: Field Survey.

The responses were sought about the classification system, recruitment, pay policy, leave system, transfer policy, service conditions, conduct and discipline and management employee relations. The description of the components of personnel policy alongwith the response of permanent as well as contractual employees is presented subsequently, in this chapter.

3.4 Classification

A systematic classification of jobs is one of the most essential features of an effective Personnel System. Classification of jobs is no more regarded as an organizational necessity but as a functional necessity.

W. F. Willoughby has rightly said, "Classification and standardisation of public employment constitutes, indeed the starting point or the basis upon which the whole personnel structure must rest".[15]

According to F. M. Marx, "The purpose of classification is to group position that have similar duties and qualifications so that they may be conveniently treated jointly for all management requirement i.e. recruitment, compensation, budgeting, training and organisational planning".[16]

Thus, a judicious classification system helps in sorting out the questions of pay, lines of promotion, duties and responsibilities. Dr Herman Finer is of the view that, "Upon proper classification, depends the efficiency of recruitment, the possibility of creating a rational promotion system and the equitable treatment of people working in different departments".[17]

A classification of positions refers to the grouping of positions into classes on the basis of their duties and qualification requirements. The personnel agency cannot perform its functions properly unless the job titles and definitions describe the duties and responsibilities of various positions and indicate the qualifications necessary to fill them. The classification system also makes it possible to divide uniform work standards for the various levels so that control over the productivity of the personnel is more effective.

3.5 Classification in Municipal Council, Panchkula

Under Section-38 (1) of the Haryana Municipal Act, 1973, the State Government has the power to constitute municipal services at various levels concerned with the affairs of the municipalities:

1 At the State level, it has power to constitute Haryana Municipal State Level Services of Executive Officers, Municipal Engineers, Health Officers and the Secretaries.

2 At District level, Haryana Municipal District Level Services has been constituted in connection with the affairs of the municipalities.[18]

At present, there are following categories of municipal services in Haryana:

1. Haryana Municipal State Level Services of Executive Officers, municipal engineers, health officers and the secretaries [at present the total number of services in this category vide appendix 'A' of Haryana Municipal Services (Integration, Recruitment and Condition of Service) HMSIRCS Rules, 1982 are 10].
2. Haryana Municipal District Level Services [at present the total number of services in this category vide appendix 'A' of HMSIRCS Rules are 68].
3. Regulation of Service of Municipal Employees in Haryana. Section 38 (3) of the Haryana Municipal Act, 1973, provides that State Government shall have the power:
   a. To determine the strength of municipal services constituted under Section 38 (1) and their cadre.
   b. To determine the strength and categories of personnel required by each municipality.
   c. To make rules related to recruitment, pay, transfer and other conditions of services of personnel appointed to the said services.
4. Haryana Municipal *Safai Majdoor* Service of a Municipal Committee:
   Haryana Municipal *Safai Majdoor* Service Rules, 1976, governs this service. Municipal Committee, from time to time with the approval of the Deputy Commissioner shall determine the number of posts in the service.[19]

The employees of Municipal Council, Panchkula, belong to either of the above mentioned categories of municipal services. The details of which are given in Table 3.4.

Table 3.4
Personnel Belonging to Haryana Municipal State Level Services

Sr. No.	*Name of the Post*	*Class of the Post*
1	Executive Officer	Class II
2	Secretaries	Class II
3	Superintendents (Office)	Class III
4	Superintendents (Tax and Octroi)	Class III
5	Accountants	Class III
6	Chief Sanitary Inspectors	Class II
7	Fire Station Officers	Class III
8	Engineers	Class III
9	Work Inspector (Technical)	Class III
10	Sanitary Inspector	Class III
11	Sub-Fire Officer	Class III
12	Assistant Fire Brigade	Class III
13	Leading Fire Men	Class III and Class IV
14	Fire Men	Class III
15	Peon cum Chowkidar	Class IV
16	Clerks	Class III
17	Fire Brigade Driver	Class III
18	Driver	Class III
19	Office Assistant	Class III
20	Superintendent	Class III
21	Patwari	Class III
22	Assistant Town Planner	ClassII
23	Bhawan Nirman Nirikshak	Class III
24	Sub-Divisional Engineer	Class III
25	Junior Engineer	Class III
26	Safai Worker	Class IV

Source: Establishment Branch of Municipal Council, Panchkula.

Table 3.4 depicts that the employees of MCP belong to class II, class III and class IV services. The table shows that there are four class-II posts, 19 class III and two class IV posts in the MCP. However, some of the senior level officials like executive officers receive pay band I salary, equivalent to that of class I officers of the State Government.

3.6 Employees' Satisfaction About Classification System

Responses of Permanent Employees

As far as the classification system is concerned, out of the sample respondents, 66 per cent employees were either dissatisfied or highly dissatisfied and remaining 34 per cent were indifferent. The level of satisfaction further has been examined on the basis of gender, education, age and designation. The responses of respondents have been given in Table 3.5.

Table 3.5
Satisfaction with Classification System
(Figures in Parenthesis Represent Percentages)

		Highly Satisfied	*Satisfied*	*Indifferent*	*Dissatisfied*	*Highly Dissatisfied*
Gender	Male	0	0	19(35.2%)	31(57.4%)	4(7.4%)
	Female	0	0	1(25.0%)	3(75.0%)	0
Education	Illiterate	0	0	6(66.7%)	3(33.3%)	0
	Below matric	0	0	1(14.3%)	5(71.4%)	1(14.3%)
	Matric and above	0	0	13(31.0%)	26(61.9%)	3(7.1%)
Age	Below30	0	0	5(71.4%)	2(28.6%)	0
	30 to 40	0	0	7(30.4%)	15(65.2%)	1(4.3%)
	40 to 50	0	0	8(34.8%)	12(52.2%)	3(13.0%)
	50 and above	0	0	0	5(100.0%)	0
Grade	A	0	0	1(25.0%)	2(50.0%)	1(25.0%)
	B	0	0	1(20.0%)	3(60.0%)	1(20.0%)
	C	0	0	3(18.8%)	13(81.2%)	0
	D	0	0	15(45.5%)	16(48.5)	2(6.1%)

Source: Field Survey.

Out of the total male respondents, 35.2 per cent were indifferent, 57.4 per cent dissatisfied and remaining 7.4 per cent were highly dissatisfied. In the case of females, 25.0 per cent were indifferent and remaining 75.0 per cent opined dissatisfaction with the classification system.

The analysis on the basis of education reveals that among the illiterates, 66.7 per cent were indifferent and 33.3 per cent were dissatisfied. In the case of below matric, 14.3 per cent were indifferent, 71.4 per cent were dissatisfied and the remaining 14.3 per cent were highly dissatisfied. Around 31.0 per cent above matric respondents were indifferent, 61.9 per cent dissatisfied and remaining 7.1 per cent were highly dissatisfied about the classification.

On the basis of age, out of the total employees having an age below 30 years, 71.4 per cent were indifferent and 28.6 per cent dissatisfied. Out of the total employees between the age group of 30 to 40 years, 30.4 per cent were indifferent, 65.2 per cent were dissatisfied and remaining 4.3 per cent were highly dissatisfied. In the case of employees in the age group of 40 to 50 years, 34.8 per cent were indifferent, 52.2 per cent were dissatisfied and remaining 13.0 per cent were highly dissatisfied. Out of the total employees having an age above 50 years all expressed dissatisfaction with the classification system.

On the basis of grade, out of the total employees of Grade A, 25.0 per cent were indifferent, 50.0 per cent were dissatisfied and the remaining 25.0 per cent opined highly dissatisfied. In the Gradc B category, 20.0 per cent were indifferent, 60.0 per cent were dissatisfied and the remaining 20.0 per cent expressed high dissatisfaction. In the Grade C category, 18.8 were indifferent and remaining 81.2 opined dissatisfaction. In the case of Grade D employees, 45.5 per cent were indifferent, 48.5 per cent reported dissatisfaction and remaining 6.1 per cent were highly dissatisfied about classification.

On the basis of the foregoing analysis, it can be concluded that a large number of employees of MCP are either dissatisfied or highly dissatisfied with the classification system.

3.7 Recritment

The recruitment constitutes the corner stone of the whole personnel structure.[20]

Recruitment determines the tone and caliber of public services upon which the nature and the degree of usefulness of administrative machinery to the service of which human elements are dedicated.[21]

Recruitment is a process of searching for prospective suitable employees and stimulating them to apply for jobs in the organisations. It may be taken in a positive way as it stimulates the candidates to apply for the job. A sound policy in regards to recruitment is of utmost importance in order to get competent staff employed. As municipal administration is close to the public in their respective locality, it can inspire respect and confidence only if competent and efficient employees man it. The basic elements of such policy include or should include the following:

a. Discovery and cultivation of the employment markets for posts in public services;
b. Use of attractive recruitment literature and publicity;
c. Use of scientific tests for determining abilities of candidates;
d. Tapping capable candidates from within the services;
e. Placement programme which assign right man to the right job; and
f. A follow up probationary programme as an integral part of the recruitment policy.[22]

The basic problems of recruitment in local government in India are the following:

a. Multiplicity of recruiting agency for local authorities.
b. Non-availability of highly trained and technical staff.
c. Excessive interference by politicians in appointments because of the nature of local laws, which require the local authorities to recruit the employees themselves.
d. Local employment opportunities are non-competitive because of low salaries, which affect the quality of recruited personnel and hinders excessive turnover.
e. Fewer chances for in-service training to facilitate progressive promotion policies.[23]

3.8 Recruitment in Municipal Council, Panchkula

Chapter III of Section 38 (1) of the Haryana Municipal Act, 1973 provides that recruitment to Haryana Municipal State Level Services and Haryana Municipal services shall be made by the State Government. Further, Section 38(3)(C) of the Act also empowers the Directors and Deputy Commissioner to make recruitment to these services on the behalf of the Government. The recruitment process for these services is regulated by HMSIRCS Rules, 1982. The Rule I of Municipal Rules, 1982 provides that, except the executive officer, the recruitment to various services shall be made in the following manner:

1. In case where the initial pay of the post is Rs 700 and above (pre-revised), recruitment shall be made on the recommendation of Haryana Public Service Commission (HPSC).
2. In case where the initial pay of the post is Rs 400 or more but less than Rs 700 (pre-revised), recruitment shall be made on the recommendation of the Subordinate Selection Board, Haryana.
3. In case of posts, which do not fall under (1) and (2) above mentioned, recruitment should be made through the concerned employment exchange.
4. All promotions, exceeding a period of six months shall be made subject to the approval of the government or the Public Service Commission or Subordinate Selection Board as the case may be.

While making recruitment, the policy of government regarding the reservation of posts for the members of Scheduled Castes (SC) and Backward Classes (BC) and for any other category in relation to the services under it, shall be followed.[24] However, if suitable candidates are not available by direct recruitment for promotion then appointment could be made by transfer/ deputation.

Methods of Recruitment: Table 3.6 and Table 3.7 indicate the methods adopted to make recruitment to various posts at both the State and the District level services:

Table 3.6
Method of Recruitment for Municipal State Level Service

Name of the Post	*Method of Recruitment*
Engineer	Only by direct recruitment
Superintendent (Office)	Only by promotion on seniority cummerit
Superintendent (Tax and Octroi)	basis
Accountant	
Chief Sanitary Inspector	
Executive Officer	50 per cent direct recruitment and 50 per cent
Secretary	by promotion
Fire Station Officer	

Sources: Establishment Branch of Municipal Council, Panchkula.

Table 3.6 depicts that the method of recruitment for engineers is only by direct recruitment. The posts of Superintendent (Office), Superintendent (Tax and Octroi), Accountants, Chief Sanitary Inspector are recruited only by promotion on seniority-cum-merit basis and the posts of Executive officer, Secretary and Fire Station Officer are recruited by 50 per cent direct recruitment and 50 per cent by promotion.

Table 3.7
Methods of Recruitment for Municipal District Level Service

Name of the Post	*Method of Recruitment*
Work Inspector (Technical)	Only by direct Recruitment
Fire Men	
Peon cum Chowkidar	
Bhawan Nirman Nirikshak	
Superintendent	
Patwari	
Clerk	
Sub Fire Officer	50 per cent direct recruitment and 50 per cent by
Office Assistant	promotion

Leading Fire Men	
Sanitary Inspector Driver Fire Brigade Driver	80 per cent direct recruitment and 20 per cent by promotion

Source: Establishment Branch of Municipal Council, Panchkula

Table 3.7 depicts that Work Inspector (Technical), Fire Men, Peon cum Chowkidar, Bhawan Nirman Nirikshak, Superintendent, Patwari and Clerk are recruited by direct recruitment. The posts of Sub Fire Officer, Office Assistant and Leading Fire Men are recruited by 50 per cent direct recruitment and 50 per cent by promotion. The posts of Sanitary Inspector, Driver and Fire Brigade Driver are recruited by 80 per cent direct recruitment and 20 per cent by promotion.

Thus, according to HMSIRCS, Rules of 1982, recruitment to Municipal Council, Panchkula, are made mainly by three methods:

1. Direct Recruitment
2. Promotion
3. Deputation

1. Direct Recruitment

Direct recruitment is made either through interview or through written examination. The minimum qualification for various categories of posts has been specified in column four of the rules. The general conditions relating to recruitment to municipal services like nationality, domicile etc., are more or less similar to the conditions applicable in the State Public Services in Haryana. The age limit for direct recruitment to these services has been defined between 17-35 years. In case, the candidate belongs to Scheduled Caste and Backward Class category, the upper age limit shall be such as may be fixed by government, from time to time, for their appointment to a government service. Direct recruitment is made either by Haryana Public Service Commission or Subordinate Selection Board, Haryana, or through the concerned employment exchange.

A. Qualification and Experience for Direct Recruitment

The details of qualifications and experience for direct recruitment have been given in Table 3.8 and 3.9.

Table 3.8
Details of Qualifications and Experience for Direct Recruitment and Promotion of Employees of Municipal Council, Panchkula

Sr. No.	*Name of Post*	*Class of Municipal Committee*	*Qualifications and Experience for Direct Recruitment*	*Qualifications and Experience for Promotion*
1.	Executive Officer	A	Post-Graduate in any subject or Graduate in Law. Preference shall be given to those, with Diploma in Higher Officers' Course in the Local Government.	Should be a Graduate and have worked as Secretary in A Class Committee for at least five years or as Executive Officer in B Class committee for at least five years.
		B	Same as for A Class Committee: provided that candidates next in order of merit after providing for vacancies in A Class Committees would be considered.	Should be a Graduate and should have worked as Secretary in B Class and C Class Committees for at least three years.
2	Secretary	A	Graduate with second division. Preference shall be given to those with Diploma in Higher Officers' Course in the Local Government.	Should have worked as Secretary in B or C Class Committee or as Superintendent on the Office, Tax or Octroi side in A Class Committee for at least five years.
3	Superintendent (Tax)	B & C	Same as for A Class Committees: provided that candidates next in order of merit after providing for vacancies in A Class Committee would be considered.	Should have worked as Superintendent on the Office, Tax or Octroi side in B and C Class Committee or as Accountant who has passed the departmental examination of Accountant in A, B and C Class Committee for at least three years.
4	Engineer	A	Such qualifications as may be prescribed by the State Government from time to time	Such qualifications as may be prescribed by the State

			for direct recruitment of Sub-divisional Engineer/ Assistant Executive Engineer in the State Public Works Departments.	Government from time to time for promotion to the posts of Sub-divisional Engineer/ Assistant Executive Engineer in the State Public Works Departments.
5.	Superintendent (Office)	A	...	At least three years service as Superintendent (Office) in a B Class Committee.
		B	...	Should be a Matriculate with at least three years service as Assistant Head Clerk in A, B and C Class committee.
6.	Superintendent Tax and Octroi	A	...	At least three years service as Superintendent (Tax Octroi) in B or C Class Committees.
		B & C	...	Should be a Matriculate with at least three years as Asstt. Octroi Superintendent or five years service as Tax Inspector/ Octroi Inspector/ Licence Inspector in A, B or C Class Committees.
7.	Accountant	A, B & C	Matric with diploma from I.T.I.	Should be a Graduate with three years service or Matriculate with C Class Committees and have passed the departmental examination prescribed for Municipal Accountants A Grade five years service as Assistant Accountant/ Senior Accounts, Clerk/ Head Cashier in A, B, or 3. or B Grade.

8.	Chief Sanitary Inspectors	A, B & C	...	Should be Matriculate with at least eight years service as Sanitary Inspector in A, B or C Class Committees and possess a Certificate for Sanitary Inspectors' Course.
9.	Fire Station Officers	A & B	(i) Graduate (ii) Should have passed the Station Officer Instructor Course from National Fire Service College, Nagpur,or Divisional Officer Course in Fire Engineering from National Fire Service College, Nagpur.	

Source: Municipal Act of Haryana.

Table 3.9
Details of Qualification and Experience for Direct Recruitment and Promotion District Level Services of Haryana Municipal

Sr. No.	*Name of Post*	*Class of Municipal Committee*	*Qualifications and Experience for Direct Recruitment*	*Qualifications and Experience for Promotion*
1.	Sanitary Superintendent	A	...	Should be a Matriculate and qualified Sanitary Inspector with five years' service in A, B or C Class Committees.
2.	Sub-fire Officer	A & B	...	Should be a Matriculate and possess a certificate of Sub-Officer's Course from National Fire Service College, Nagpur, with five years service as Leading Fireman in A or B Class Committees.
3.	Assistant (including Asstt. Octroi Superintendent, Assistant, Asstt. Accountant, Senior Account Clerk, Head Cashier, Water Rate Assistant and Public Health Assistant)	A & B	...	Should be a Matriculate with at least five year service in the clerical cadre of A, B or C Class Committees.
4.	Light Inspector		Matriculate with course	...
5.	Leading Fireman	A & B	...	Should be Matriculate and efficient in the theory and practice of fire fighting and rescue having qualified the

				departmental examination for promotion to Leading Fireman, with at least five years' service as Fireman A or B Class Committees.
6.	Fire Brigade Driver	A & B	Matriculate with driving licence of Heavy Vehicles with knowledge of automobile engine and pumps and very efficient in driving.	Should be very efficient in driving with knowledge of automobile engine and pumps and possess a licence of driving heavy vehicles and at least three years' experience as a whole time firemen in operational fire service in A or B Class Committees.
7.	Firemen	A & B	(1) Knows swimming and diving in deep water;(2) Is capable to run a distance of 100 metres with a load of 50 kilogram, on both shoulders per minute;(3) Is capable of climbing a rope or a vertical pipe to a height of three metres from the ground;(4) Is capable of lifting a hook ladder to vertical position by 3rd to 6th round or capable of pitching an extension ladder properly against the wall; and (5) Passed matric with science from a recognized University/ Board.	...

Source: Municipal Act of Haryana, 1973.

3.9 Employees Satisfaction About Recruitment System

(I) Responses of Permanent Employees

In case of recruitment system, out of the sample respondents, 48 per cent employees were either dissatisfied or highly dissatisfied, 30 per cent were satisfied, highly satisfied and the remaining 22 per cent were indifferent. The level of satisfaction further has been examined on the basis of gender, education, age and grade. The employees were asked about their satisfaction regarding the recruitment system. The responses of the respondents have been given in Table 3.10.

Table 3.10
Satisfaction with Recruitment Policy of MCP
(Figures in Parenthesis Represent Percentages)

		Highly Satisfied	*Satisfied*	*Indifferent*	*Dissatisfied*	*Highly Dissatisfied*
Gender	Male	0	0	19(35.2%)	31(57.4%)	4(7.4%)
Gender	Male	1(1.9%)	15(27.7%)	12(22.2%)	24(44.4%)	2(3.7%)
	Female	0	0	1(25.0%)	3(75.0%)	0
Education	Illiterate	0	3(33.3%)	3(33.3%)	3(33.3%)	0
	Below matric	0	1(14.3%)	2(28.6%)	3(42.9%)	1(14.3%)
	Matric and above	1(2.4%)	11(26.2%)	8(19.0%)	21(50.0%)	1(2.4%)
Age	Below30	1(14.3%)	4(57.1%)	1(14.3%)	1(14.3%)	0
	30 to 40	0	5(21.7%)	6(26.1%)	12(52.2%)	0
	40 to 50	0	5(21.7%)	6(26.1%)	10(43.5%)	2(8.7%)
	50 and above	0	1(20.0%)	0	4(80.0%)	0
Grade	A	0	2(50.0%)	0	2(50.0%)	0
	B	0	1(20.0%)	1(20.0%)	2(40.0%)	1(20.0%)
	C	0	4(25.0%)	2(12.5%)	10(62.5%)	0
	D	1(3.0%)	8(24.2%)	10(30.3%)	13(39.4%)	1(3.4%)

Source: Field Survey.

Out of the total male respondents, 1.9 per cent were highly satisfied, 27.7 per cent satisfied, 22.2 per cent indifferent, 44.4 per cent opined dissatisfaction and the remaining 3.7 per cent were highly dissatisfied. In the case of females, 25.0 per cent were indifferent while 75.0 per cent were dissatisfied about the recruitment policy.

The analysis on the basis of education reveals that among the illiterates, 33.3 per cent were satisfied, 33.3 per cent indifferent and remaining 33.3 per cent were highly dissatisfied. In the case of below matric, 14.3 per cent expressed satisfaction, 28.6 per cent indifferent and 14.3 per cent were dissatisfied. Around 2.4 per cent above matric, were highly satisfied, 26.2 per cent satisfied, 19.0 per cent indifferent, 50 per cent dissatisfied and remaining 2.4 per cent reported being highly dissatisfied.

On the basis of age, out of the total employees having an age below 30 years, 14.3 per cent were highly satisfied, 57.1 per cent reported satisfied, 14.3 per cent were indifferent and 14.3 per cent were dissatisfied. Out of total employees between the age group of 30 to 40 years, 21.7 per cent were satisfied, 26.1 per cent were indifferent and the remaining 52.2 per cent expressed dissatisfaction. In the case of employees between the age group of 40 to 50 years, 21.7 per cent reported satisfied, 26.1 per cent were indifferent, 43.5 per cent expressed dissatisfaction and remaining 8.7 per cent were highly dissatisfied. Out of the total employees having an age above 50 years, 20.0 per cent were satisfied and the remaining 80 per cent expressed dissatisfaction.

On the basis of grade, in the Grade A category, 50 per cent were satisfied and 50 per cent were dissatisfied. In the case of B grade, 20 per cent were satisfied, 20.0 per cent indifferent, 40.0 per cent expressed dissatisfaction and the remaining 20.0 were expressed highly dissatisfaction. In the Grade C category, 25.0 reported satisfied, 12.5 per cent were indifferent and the remaining 62.5 per cent expressed dissatisfaction. In the case of Grade D employees, 3.0 per cent answered highly satisfied, 24.2 per cent expressed satisfaction, 30.3 per cent were indifferent, 39.4 per cent reported dissatisfied and the remaining 3.0 per cent were highly dissatisfied with the recruitment policy.

(II) Responses of Contractual Employees

In case of recruitment system, out of 21 respondents, 90 per cent employees were either dissatisfied or highly dissatisfied and the remaining 10 per cent were indifferent. The level of satisfaction further has been examined on the basis of gender, education and age. The employees were asked about their satisfaction regarding the recruitment system. The responses of respondents have been given in Table 3.11.

Table 3.11
Satisfaction with Recruitment Policy of MCP
(Figures in Parenthesis Represent Percentages)

		Highly Satisfied	*Satisfied*	*Indifferent*	*Dissatisfied*	*Highly Dissatisfied*
Gender	Male	0	0	1(5.3%)	8(42.1%)	10(52.6%)
	Female	0	0	1(50.0%)	1(50.0%)	0
Education	Illiterate	0	0	0	0	0
	Below matric	0	0	0	1(20.0%)	4(80.0%)
	Matric and above	0	0	2(12.5%)	8(50.0%)	6(37.5%)
Age	Below30	0	0	1(7.7%)	7(53.8%)	5(38.5%)
	30 to 40	0	0	1(12.5%)	2(25.0%)	5(62.5%)

Source: Field Survey.

Out of the total male respondents, 5.3 per cent were indifferent, 42.1 per cent reported dissatisfaction and the remaining 52.6 per cent were highly dissatisfied. In the case of female, 50 per cent were indifferent while 50 per cent expressed dissatisfaction with the recruitment system.

The analysis on the basis of education shows that among below matric, 20.0 per cent were dissatisfied while 80 per cent reported being highly dissatisfied. Around 12.5 per cent, matric and above contractual employees were indifferent, 50 per cent were dissatisfied and remaining 37.5 per cent reported high dissatisfaction.

On the basis of age, out of total employees between the age groups of 20 to 30 years, 7.7 per cent were indifferent, 53.8 per cent expressed dissatisfaction and the remaining 38.5 per cent were highly dissatisfied. Out of total employees between age groups of 30 to 40 years, 12.5 per cent were indifferent, 25.0 per cent dissatisfied and the remaining 62.5 per cent were highly dissatisfied with the recruitment system.

It can be inferred that a large numbers of employees of MCP were either dissatisfied or highly dissatisfied with the recruitment system.

2. Promotion

Promotion is very significant in personnel administration. Competent and promising employees must have avenues for advancement in the service to ensure not only effective and better utilisation of available human resources but also to retain those who have demonstrated professional competence and administrative ability.[25]

Promotion, as defined by L. D. White is "an appointment from a given position to a position of higher grade, involving a change of duties to a more difficult type of work and greater responsibility, accompanied by change of title and usually an increase in pay." [26]

Promotion is advancement in rank, status, and salary/pay. It also involves a change in duties and responsibilities. Promotion should be based on sound principles of merit and seniority. Seniority or length of service of an employee is an important factor in promotion. According to this principle, an employee whose length of service is more than that of other candidates should be promoted i.e., the senior most should get the advantages of promotion.[27]

Under the principle of merit, promotions are based upon performance, expertise and technical qualifications of each employee, measured objectively. The various methods of testing candidates ability are promotional examinations, service record and judgment of the head of department.[28]

Promotion in Municipal Council, Panchkula

For the purpose of promotion, employees of the Municipal Council, Panchkula are governed by the rules/acts applicable to Haryana Government employees.[29] Generally, there are two basic principles of promotion viz., seniority and merit or promotional examinations. The qualifications and experiences for promotion to different categories of post have been specified in Column five of Table 3.8 and 3.9.

All promotions exceeding a period of six months shall be made subject to the approval of Government or Haryana Public Service Commission or Subordinate Service Selection Board, Haryana (SSC), as the case may be.[30]

In MCP two employees were promoted from clerk to superintendant and Sanitary Inspector to Chief Sanitary Inspector. However, some aspects of promotional methods were ignored where it took place.

3.10 Employees' Satisfaction About Promotion System

Responses of Permanent Employees

In case of promotion system, out of the sample respondents, 62 per cent employees are either dissatisfied or highly dissatisfied and the remaining seven per cent were satisfied, highly satisfied and 33 per cent were indifferent. The level of satisfaction further has been examined on the basis of gender, education, age and grade. The employees were asked about their satisfaction regarding the promotion policy. The responses of the respondents have been given in Table 3.12.

Table 3.12
Satisfaction with Promotion Policy
(Figures in Parenthesis Represent Percentages)

		Highly Satisfied	*Satisfied*	*Indifferent*	*Dissatisfied*	*Highly Dissatisfied*
Gender	Male	0	4(7.4%)	18(33.3%)	14(25.9%)	18(33.3%)
	Female	0	0	0	3(75.0%)	1(25.0%)
Education	Illiterate	0	0	0	2(22.2%)	7(77.8%)
	Below matric	0	1(14.3%)	0	2(28.6%)	4(57.2%)
	Matric and above	0	3(7.2%)	18(43.2%)	13(31.2%)	8(19.2%)
Age	Below30	0	0	5(71.4%)	1(14.3%)	1(14.3%)
	30 to 40	0	1(4.3%)	10(43.5%)	7(30.4%)	5(21.7%)
	40 to 50	0	2(8.7%)	3(13.0%)	6(26.1%)	12(52.2%)
	50 and above	0	1(20%)	0	3(60.0%)	1(20.0%)
Grade	A	0	1(25%)	2(50%)	0	1(25%)
	B	0	1(20.0%)	2(40%)	1(20%)	1(20%)
	C	0	2(12.5%)	2(12.5%)	6(37.5%)	6(37.5%)
	D	0	0	12(36.4)	10(30.3%)	11(33.3%)

Source: Field Survey.

Out of the total male respondents, 7.4 per cent were satisfied, 33.3 per cent indifferent, 25.9 per cent dissatisfied and the remaining 33.3 per cent opined high dissatisfaction. In the case of female, 75.0 per cent were dissatisfied and 25.0 per cent highly dissatisfied about the promotion policy.

The analysis on the basis of education reveals that among the illiterates, 22.2 per cent were dissatisfied and 77.8 per cent opined dissatisfaction. In the case of below matric, 14.3 per cent expressed satisfaction, 28.6 per cent were dissatisfied and the remaining 57.2 per cent reported being dissatisfied. Around 7.2 per cent above matric were satisfied, 43.2 per cent indifferent and 31.2 per cent dissatisfied and the remaining 19.8 per cent expressed highly dissatisfied with the promotion policy.

On the basis of age, out of the total employees having an age below 30 years, 71.4 per cent were indifferent, 14.3 per cent ewere dissatisfied and the remaining 14.3 per cent were highly dissatisfied. Out of the total employees between the age group of 30 to 40 years, 4.3 per cent answered being satisfied, 43.5 per cent being indifferent, 30.4 per cent expressed dissatisfaction and the remaining 21.7 per cent were highly dissatisfied. In the case of employees between the age group of 40 to 50 years, 8.7 per cent reported being satisfied, 13.0 per cent were indifferent, 26.1 per cent expressed dissatisfaction and the remaining 52.2 per cent reported being highly dissatisfied. Out of the total employees having an age above 50 years, 20.0 per cent were satisfied, 60.0 per cent expressed dissatisfied and the remaining 20.0 per cent were highly dissatisfied.

On the basis of grade, out of the total employees and 25 per cent of those in Grade A were satisfied, 50 per cent were indifferent and the remaining 25.0 per cent were highly dissatisfied. In the case of Grade B, 20.0 per cent expressed satisfaction, 40.0 per cent were indifferent, 20.0 per cent expressed dissatisfaction and the remaining 20.0 were highly dissatisfied. In the Grade C category, 12.5 were satisfied, 12.5 per cent were indifferent, 37.5 expressed dissatisfaction and the remaining 37.5 per cent reported being highly dissatisfied. In the case of Grade D employees, 36.4 per cent were indifferent, 30.3 per cent reported dissatisfaction and the remaining 33.3 per cent were highly dissatisfied with the promotion policy.

On the basis of the study, it is concluded that a large number of employees of MCP were either dissatisfied or highly dissatisfied with the promotion policy.

3. Deputation

Rule 10 (2) of Haryana Municipal Service (Integration Recruitment and Condition of Service), Rules 1982 provides that if no suitable candidate is available for appointment by direct recruitment or by promotion, the vacancies may be filled up by transfer or by deputation of suitable persons. The Officials of executive and technical sides are drawn from different departments of Haryana Government for deputation. The time period for deputation posting varies from six months to two years in Municipal Council, Panchkula.

Deputation in Municipal Council, Panchkula

In MCP, one clerk came on deputation from Municipal Council, Hisar in 2007 and one Junior Engineer also came on deputation from the Panchayat Department in 2007 for one year.

3.11 Training

Training is the "process of developing skills, habits, knowledge and attitudes in employees for the purpose of increasing the effectiveness of employees in their present positions as well as preparing employees for future government positions".[31]

It is a well articulated effort directed towards inculcating occupational skills and knowledge in the employees and making them familiar with the objectives of the department to which they belong and their potential contribution in the furtherance of the departmental goals. Training, however, cannot confine itself to mere inculcation of occupational skills and knowledge. It must set a wider goal and be set against a wider background. The function of training is to help employees grow not only from the standpoint of mechanical efficiency but also in terms of broad outlook and perspective which public servants need. Training must aim at broadening the mental horizons/sphere of the employees and help them build integrity and morale by instilling the right mental attitude on the question of personal and public conduct. Training would thus help employees, become people oriented and can set the tone and quality of the organisation. Training is accordingly, vital to a career service which provides for the recruitment of persons of young age and their subsequent promotions.[32]

Objectives of Training

The objective of training is to impart an individual with the knowledge of environment in which he is to function. The knowledge of administrative management is to achieve optimum performance and the cultivation of necessary attitudes. The specific objectives of training are as following:

1. ***Understanding of Environment:*** An employee must know the legal framework under which he/she has to work. He must be provided with the basic knowledge of social sciences in order to understand the intricacies of social environment. With the knowledge of social sciences, he can react with the environment favourably. Tyagi has justified it, from three different perspectives:

    i. Administration is the human process largely depending upon first hand experience drawn from the actual administrative situation in all its facets and on weighing each problem from every angle.
    ii. The role of public servant in a welfare state is that of a social scientist in action. In order to be able to act properly and effectively, he/she must have scientific acumen which

he can develop only by a systematic and sustained education in the theory and practice of social science.

iii. The need for a basic training in the fundamentals of Social Science becomes all the more necessary in the context of our public recruitment being based on lower age limit, which limits the entry of advanced research student to the public service. [33]

2. ***Improving Administrative Capability:*** There is a great need to enhance the administrative capability of public services so that they can achieve the objectives of the government in the shortest possible time. Administrative capability is an important means of converting or processing programme inputs into outputs such as goods and services, as Kantz says, "Administrative Capability for development involves the ability to mobilise, allocate and combine the action that are technically needed to achieve development objective." [34]
3. ***Cultivating Genuine Attitude:*** Training must also aim to cultivate a new attitude and behaviour in employees in the public services. This is all the more important. Marshal suggests the development of the following ingredients to promote the right rationale and attitude:
   a. Development of rational thinking;
   b. Development of objective thinking;
   c. Development of social understanding;
   d. Development of aesthetic responsiveness;
   e. Development of practical abilities; and
   f. Development and placement of memories in action.[35]

Training of Municipal Personnel

The need and importance of training is yet to receive adequate recognition in case of municipal personnel administration. The employees of local bodies also need to be exposed to outside development and major national problems, so that their vision widens and they adapt to comprehensive approach to the problems confronting them.[36]

While in countries like U.K., U.S.A., Canada, Netherlands, Germany and Sweden, education and training in municipal government has made significant progress, the Government of India has shown little interest in this regard.

Before independence, some universities, like Nagpur, Allahabad and Lucknow started courses in Municipal Administration and the

Institute of Local Self Government, Bombay (1927) made pioneer progress training municipal officials.[37]

The Centre for Training and Research now known as the Centre for Urban Studies, an organ of the Indian Institute of Public Administration, has done a commendable work in this regard. It was only in 1963 that the Government of India appointed a Committee known as Nuruddin Committee on the Training of Municipal Employees. The Committee emphasised the need for imparting training to the municipal personnel in different types of municipal bodies. Professionalisation in municipal administration was considered necessary in view of the increasing complexities of the urban administration. The committee recommended the setting up of a training institute at the central level which would organise high level imaginative training programmes and co-ordinate the training activities throughout the country and promote necessary uniformity in the programmes of different state level institutes. The Committee observed, "It would be one of the central institute's major responsibility to prescribe the standard of training and research and it should serve as a model in this respect". The Committee did not rule out the need for setting up a state institute but it was felt that lack of adequate resources, equipment and faculty might stand in the way of simultaneous development of a number of state institutes in different parts of the country.[38]

The Rural Urban Relationship Committee (1963-66), also stressed the urgency of setting up a training and research institute in the field of municipal administration. As a sequel to these recommendations, Central Institute was attached to Indian Institute of Public Administration, New Delhi and Regional Centers were set up at Lucknow, Hyderabad, Bombay and Calcutta.[39]

In the Northwestern region of the country including Punjab and Haryana, there is no institute as such to impart training to the municipal employees. The Punjab Local Government (Urban Inquiry Committee 1957) had among other things, recommended for the establishment of a training institute for municipal personnel. And though the government had accepted the recommendations, yet the government did not take any steps to implement them.

Training in Municipal Council, Panchkula

There is no specialised or separate training institute for the personnel of local bodies in Haryana.The training to municipal personnel is being imparted at the Haryana Institute of Public Administration (HIPA), Gurgaon. It was established in 1983 with the objective of providing training, research and consultancy to improve efficiency in the administration. HIPA is an autonomous society registered under the Societies Registration Act, 1860. The Chief Minister of Haryana is also the President of general body. The executive council is the apex policy-making body, which guides the institute in all its major policies, strategies and setting up its long-term agenda. The Chief Secretary of the State is the Executive Council's Chairperson.

Training activities of HIPA are broadly grouped into the following categories:

1. Institutional Training Course;
2. Fundamental Training Course;
3. In service training for Haryana Civil Services (HCS);
4. Subject specified short-term in service training course;
5. Need Based Training Course For various corporations/board and other autonomous bodies of the state government and Central Government;
6. Training courses for ministerial staff;
7. Department of personnel and training;
8. Seminars and Workshop: In view of growing multi-disciplinary approaches, the institute conducts seminars and workshops for administrators, academics and professionals, on various subjects of topical interest; and
9. Researches and Consultancy.

The various training programmes conducted from time to time by Haryana Institute of Public Administration (HIPA) for urban local bodies officials are mentioned in Table 3.13.

Table 3.13
Training Programmes Conducted by Haryana Institute of Public Administration for Urban Local Bodies

Sr. No.	*Name of the Programme*	*Period*	*Participants*
1.	Municipal Finance and Accounts Reform	Data not available	Data not available
2.	New Concept in Management of Municipal Services.	do	do
3.	Integrated infrastructure project formulations, and appraisal and implementation with special reference to IDSMT	do	do
4.	A course on Girl Child in India:	4/8/2005 to	do

	Challenges and Responses	8/8/2005	
5.	Sustainable Solid Waste Management.	25/5/2005 to 27/5/2005	do
6.	Disaster Management and Urban Planning.	30/5/2005 to 3/6/2005	5 Executive Officers
7.	Municipal Accounts Reform	6/6/2005 to 9/6/2005	5 Accountant
8.	Urban Transport System and Management	13/6/2005 to 17/6/2005	5 Executive Officers
9.	Tackling Urban Slum (Sponsored by Department of Urban Planning and Transport)	20/6/2005 to 24/6/2005	5 Executive Officers
10.	Public Private Partnership in Urban Development	27/6/2005 to 1/7/2005	5 Secretaries
11.	Training on "Sustainable Solid Waste Management"		
12.	A one week training course on Environment Management	13/6/2005 to 17/6/2005	5 Secretaries
13.	Earthquake Management	16/5/2005 to 20/502005	
14.	Ground Water Management	30/5/2005 to 3/6/2005	
15.	Training Course on Legal Aspects of Personnel Management (Sponsored by Construction Industry Development		Not attended
16.	Disaster Management: Role of Nagar Palika	28/6/2005 to 30/6/2005	5 Executive Officers
17.	Prevention of HIV/AIDS among Risk Individuals	23/1/2006 to 27/1/2006	6 Secretaries

Source: Directorate of Urban Local Bodies, Haryana.

Information of relevant training programmes is sent by HIPA to the Directorate of Urban Local Bodies. The Directorate is requested to depute their officers for undergoing training at the institute. In case an officer so deputed fails to attend the training programme workshop/course, the Directorate is required to seek an explanation from the concerned officer.

In Municipal Council, Panchkula only one accountant has received training between 6.6.2005 to 9.6.2005 on the topic of Municipal Accounts Reform.

3.12 Employees' Satisfaction About Training System

Responses of Permanent Employees

In case of training system, out of 58 respondents, 71 per cent employees expressed either dissatisfaction or high dissatisfaction and the remaining 29 per cent were indifferent. The level of satisfaction further has been examined on the basis of gender, education, age and grade. The employees were asked about their satisfaction regarding the training system. The responses of the respondents have been given in Table 3.14.

Table 3.14
Satisfaction with Training Policy
(Figures in Parenthesis Represent Percentages)

		Highly Satisfied	*Satisfied*	*Indifferent*	*Dissatisfied*	*Highly Dissatisfied*
Gender	Male	0	0	15(27.8%)	15(27.8%)	24(44.4%)
	Female	0	0	2(50.0%)	0	2(50%)
Education	Illiterate	0	0	3(33.3%)	1(11.1%)	5(55.6%)
	Below Matric	0	0	2(28.6%)	2(28.6%)	3(42.9%)
	Matric and above	0	0	12(28.6%)	12(28.6%)	18(42.9%)
Age	Below30	0	0	2(28.6%)	1(14.3%)	4(57.1%)
	30 to 40	0	0	7(30.4%)	9(39.1%)	7(30.4%)
	40 to 50	0	0	7(30.4%)	3(13.0%)	13(56.5%)
	50 and above	0	0	1(20.0%)	2(40.0%)	2(40.0%)
Grade	A	0	0	3(75.0%)	1(25%)	0
	B	0	0	1(20.0%)	2(40.0%)	2(40%)
	C	0	0	5(31.2%)	3(18.7%)	8(50%)
	D	0	0	8(24.2%)	9(22.9%)	16(48.5%)

Source: Field Survey.

Out of total male respondents, 27.8 per cent were dissatisfied and 44.4 per cent were highly dissatisfied. In the case of females, 50.0 per cent were highly satisfied and 50.0 per cent opined indifferent response about the training system.

The analysis on the basis of education reveals that among the illiterate 55.6 per cent were highly dissatisfied, 33.3 per cent indifferent and the remaining 11.1 per cent were dissatisfied. In the case of below matric, 42.9 per cent were highly dissatisfied, 28.6 per cent indifferent and the remaining 28.6 per cent were dissatisfied. Around 28.6 per cent above matric reported being dissatisfied, 42.9 per cent highly dissatisfied and remaining satisfied, and 28.6 per cent indifferent with the training system.

On the basis of the age out of the total employees having an age below 30 years, 14.3 per cent reported being dissatisfied, 57.1 per cent were highly satisfied and remaining 28.6 per cent were indifferent. Out of total employees between the age group of 30 to 40 years, 30.4 per cent were being highly satisfied, 39.4 per cent dissatisfied and the remaining 30.4 per cent were indifferent. In the case of employees between the age group of 40 to 50 years, 56.5 per cent were highly dissatisfied, 30.4 per cent indifferent and the remaining 13.0 per cent were dissatisfied. Out of the total employees having an age above 50 years, 40.0 per cent were highly satisfied, 40.0 per cent expressed dissatisfaction and remaining 20.0 per cent were indifferent on account of the training system.

On the basis of grade, in the case of Grade A category, 25 per cent were satisfied and the 75 per cent were indifferent. In the case of Grade B, 40 per cent were highly satisfied, 20 per cent expressed indifference and the remaining 40 per cent were dissatisfied. In the Grade C category, 50.0 per cent reported being highly satisfied 18.7 per cent dissatisfied and the remaining 31.2 per cent were indifferent. In the case of Grade D employees, 48.5 per cent answered highly satisfied, 22.9 per cent being dissatisfied and remaining 24.2 per cent were indifferent with the training system.

Thus, on the basis of fieldwork, it is concluded that most of the employees of MCP were either satisfied or highly satisfied with training system.

A perusal of the training facilities for Municipal Employees at Haryana in general and Municipal Council, Panchkula in particular reveal that the training facilities have not been provided to the entire staff of the Municipal Council. Only selected categories level of municipal personnel attend such training programmes. Majority, mainly the lower category of staff, adopt "Learning by Doing" method for enhancing their job skills. Municipal authorities, however, do not encourage and facilitate the training of employees by grant of study leave, payment of fees, etc. for undergoing training regarding municipal administration in the various state/private institutes.

3.13 Determination of Pay

It is needless to mention that pay and compensation are very important for an employee. The standard of living and the social prestige of an employee depend to great extent on the pay he draws. A man chooses a career on the basis of the pay, which he expects to receive. The health and vitality of services depend on the levels of remuneration. Therefore, the salary system must be so designed as to attract, motivate and retain the staff.

An analysis of the conditions of services and pay scales of the municipal personnel reveals that these compare very unfavourably with equivalent post under the government. It is difficult to attract suitable candidates to the municipal services and still more difficult to retain them. Even the Rural Urban Relationship Committee had recommended that the pay scale and emoluments of municipal employees of various classes should be comparable to those of the corresponding state government employees.[40] The scale of pay, should be both fair and adequate with regard to duties, responsibilities, qualification and length of service. Inadequate salaries have been responsible for keeping the competent people away from the services of local body.

Determination of Pay in Municipal Council, Panchkula

The pay and other conditions of the service are statutory determined by Government of Haryana under Section 38 (3) (c) of Haryana Municipal Act, 1973. It provides that the State Government shall have the power to make rules and regulations regarding pay and other conditions of service of persons appointed to municipal services of Haryana. In the exercise of this power, the Government of Haryana has made Haryana Municipal Services Integration, Recruitment and Condition of Service (H.M.S.I.R.C.S) Rules, 1982. Rule 11 (2) of these rules provides that the scales of pay of the post in various services shall be as given in Appendix A of the rules, as revised from time to time. It also provides that the government may review the scale of posts in a service, as it may deem proper from time to time. Rule 11 (3) of the rules provide that appointing authority may, for special reason to be recorded in writing, sanction start of higher pay than the minimum of the scale of the first appointment to any person.

In municipalities of Haryana as well as Municipal Council, Panchkula, there are mostly uniform systems of pay and allowances as compared to other government departments. In Haryana, the pay scale of the municipal employees are treated at par with the employees of the State Government.

Table 3.15 shows the pay scales of different categories of staff in the Municipal Council, Panchkula:

Table 3.15
Pay Scales of Different Categories of Employees in Municipal Council, Panchkula as Per 6th Pay Commission, Report 2008

Sr. No.	*Name of the Post*	*Pay-scale as Revised upto 2008*	*Grade Pay*
1.	SDE (Sub Divisional Engineer)	15600-39100	5400
2.	ME (Municipal Engineer)	15600-39100	5400
3.	JE (Junior Engineer)	9300-34800	3600
4.	Work Inspector	5200-20200	1900
5.	House Tax Superintendent	9300-34800	3600
6.	Clerk	5200-20200	1900

7.	Sanitation Supervisor	5200-20200	1900
8.	Staff Worker	4440-7440	1300
9.	Chief Sanitation Supervisor	9300-34800	3600
10.	Accountant	9300-34800	3600
11.	JE (Electrical)	9300-34800	3600
12.	Assistant Town Planner	15600-39100	5400
13.	Bhawan Nirman Nirikshak	5200-20200	2400
14.	Patwari	5200-20200	1900
15.	Fire Sub Officer	9300-34800	3600
16.	Assistant Fire Sub-Officer	9300-34800	3200
17.	Leading Fire Men	5200-20200	2400
18.	Fire Men	5200-20200	1900
19.	Driver	5200-20200	2400
20.	Peon	4440-7440	1300
21.	Executive Officer	15600-39100	5400
22.	Secretary	9300-34800	4600
23.	Officer Superintendent	9300-34800	3600
24.	Office Assistant	9300-34800	3200

Source: Establishment Branch of Municipal Council, Panchkula.

A. Increment

In the light of Sixth Pay Commission recommendations, the Government of Haryana has fixed three per cent increment in basic pay and grade pay on every pay band of the State Government employees or the municipal employee annually. So, employees of Municipal Council, Panchkula get an increment in their pay at the rate of 3 per cent increase on their basic pay.

B. Allowances

Besides basic salary, the employees of Municipal Council, Panchkula also receive certain allowances.

The allowances given to employees of Municipal Council, Panchkula have been given in Table 3.16.

Table 3.16
Allowances Given to the Employees at Municipal Council, Panchkula

Sr. No.	*Name of the Allowance*	*Amount*
1.	**D. A.** :Dearness Allowance	Per cent of the Basic Pay. Government announces increase of D.A. twice in a year on 1st January and 1st July.
2.	**H.R.A.**: House Rent Allowance	20 per cent of the basic-pay as per pay scales implemented in A class cities. 10 per cent for other cities than A class. 30 per cent for metro cities.
3.	**C.C.A.**: City Compensatory Allowance	This allowance is being given in urban areas such as Chandigarh and Panchkula etc.
4.	**T.A.**: Travelling Allowance	As per the government norm

Source: Establishment Branch of Municipal Council, Panchkula.

C. Provident Fund

The employees are entitled to subscribe to the provident fund of the Municipal Council where they are employed for the time being, provided that a transfer of an employee from one Municipal council to another, the balance of provident fund at his credit along with interest accrued there on up-to-date shall be transferred to the Municipal Council to which an employee has been transferred, within a period of 15 days from the date of his transfer.[41] All the employees of MCP are required to deduct 10 per cent of their salary as a deduction of Provident Fund from their basic pay and grade pay in every pay band.

Gratuity

The municipal Employees are also entitled to gratuity at such rates as notified by the government from time to time. Presently, employees of Municipal Council, Panchkula get gratuity equal to 16½ months salary on the basis of the last drawn salary.

D. Pension

According to Haryana Municipal Employee Pension and General Provident Fund Rules, 1993, the Municipal employees are entitled to pension at such rates as may vary from time to time notified by the Government.

For the purpose of the payment of pension, there shall be established a Pension Fund by the Director of Urban Local Bodies, Haryana.

The share of money along with the interest standing in the contributory provident fund account to the credit of an employee of municipality who opts or who is governed by these rules, shall stand transferred to the pension fund to the extent it was contributed by the concerned municipality during the period of service of an employee along with any loss caused to the contribution of the concerned municipality through withdrawal during the service which shall be made good by the employee paying the amount along with interest due for that period to the pension fund.

A municipality shall make monthly contribution towards the fund at the rate of 10 per cent of the basic pay of all municipal employees who opt for pension under these rules.

The money of the pension fund shall be kept in the Nationalised banks of Haryana or Haryana Co-operative bank or a post office and would be suitably invested in government securities so as to earn the maximum interest. The Employees of MCP can also receive their pension and make their contribution in accordance with said procedure.

3.14 Employees' Satisfaction With Pay Scale System

(I) Responses of Permanent Employees

In case of a pay scale system, out of the 58 respondents, 79 per cent employees expressed either dissatisfaction or high dissatisfaction and the remaining five per cent opined satisfaction, and 16 per cent were indifferent. The level of satisfaction further has been examined on the basis of gender, education, age and grade. The employees were asked about their satisfaction regarding the pay scale system. The responses of the respondents have been given in Table 3.17.

Table 3.17
Satisfaction with Pay Scale Policy
(Figures in Parenthesis Represent Percentages)

		Highly Satisfied	*Satisfied*	*Indifferent*	*Dissatisfied*	*Highly Dissatisfied*
Gender	Male	0	0	15(27.8%)	15(27.8%)	24(44.4%)
Gender	Male	0	3(5.6%)	9(16.7%)	36(66.7%)	6(11.1%)
	Female	0	0	0	3(75.0%)	1(25.0%)
Education	Illiterate	0	0	1(11.1%)	6(66.7%)	2(22.2%)
	Below matric	0	0	0	5(71.4%)	2(28.6%)
	Matric and above	0	3(7.1%)	8(19.0%)	28(66.7%)	3(7.1%)
Age	Below 30	0	1(14.3%)	3(42.9%)	3(42.9%)	0
	30 to 40	0	1(4.3%)	4(17.4%)	17(73.9%)	1(4.3%)
	40 to 50	0	1(4.3%)	2(8.7%)	14(60.9%)	6(26.1%)
	50 and above	0	0	0	5(100.0%)	0
Grade	A	0	0	2(50.0%)	2(50.0%)	0
	B	0	2(40.0%)	0	3(60.0%)	0
	C	0	0	0	15(93.8%)	1(6.2%)
	D	0	1(3.0%)	7(21.2%)	19(57.6%)	6(18.2%)

Source: Field Survey.

Out of the total male respondents, 5.6 per cent were satisfied, 16.7 per cent indifferent, 66.7 per cent dissatisfied and remaining 11.1 per cent expressed high dissatisfaction. In the case of females, 75 per cent were dissatisfied while 25 per cent opined high dissatisfaction with pay scale policy.

The analysis on the basis of education reveals that among the illiterates, 11.1 per cent were indifferent, 66.7 per cent were dissatisfied and the remaining 22.2 per cent reported being highly dissatisfied. In the case of below matric, 71.4 per cent were dissatisfied while 28.4 per cent reported high satisfaction. Around seven per cent above matric were dissatisfied, 19.0 per cent indifferent, 66.7 per cent dissatisfied and the remaining 7.1 per cent expressed high dissatisfaction with their pay scale.

On the basis of age, out of total employees having an age below 30 years, 14.3 per cent were satisfied, 42.9 per cent indifferent and remaining 42.9 per cent were dissatisfied. Out of the total employees between the age groups of 30 to 40 years, 4.3 per cent were satisfied, 17.4 per cent were indifferent, 73.9 per cent were dissatisfied and the remaining 4.3 per cent reported being highly dissatisfied. In the case of employees between the age groups of 40 to 50 years, 4.3 per cent reported satisfied, 8.7 per cent were indifferent, 60.9 per cent expressed dissatisfied and the remaining 26.1 per cent opined highly dissatisfaction. Out of the total employees having an age above 50 years, cent per cent expressed dissatisfaction with the pay scale system.

On the basis of grade, in the Grade A category, 50 per cent were indifferent while 50 per cent reported dissatisfaction. In the Grade B, 40 per cent expressed satisfaction and 60 per cent expressed dissatisfaction. In the Grade C category, 93.3 per cent expressed dissatisfaction while 6.2 per cent reported being highly dissatisfied. In the case of Grade D employees, 3.0 per cent answered satisfaction, 21.2 per cent were indifferent, and 57.6 per cent reported dissatisfaction and the remaining 18.2 per cent opined high dissatisfaction with the pay scale policy.

The above findings suggest that a huge number of employees of MCP were either dissatisfied or highly dissatisfied with the pay scale system.

(II) Responses of Contractual Employees

In case of the pay scale system, out of 21 respondents, 100 per cent employees were either dissatisfied or highly dissatisfied. The level of satisfaction further has been examined on the basis of gender, education and age. The employees were asked about their satisfaction regarding the pay scale policy. The responses of the respondents have been given in Table 3.18.

Table 3.18
Satisfaction with Pay Scales of Contractual Employees
(Figures in Parenthesis Represent Percentages)

		Highly Satisfied	*Satisfied*	*Indifferent*	*Dissatisfied*	*Highly Dissatisfied*
Gender	Male	0	0	15(27.8%)	15(27.8%)	24(44.4%)
Gender	Male	0	0	0	3(15.8%)	16(84.2%)
	Female	0	0	0	1(50.0%)	1(50.0%)
Education	Illiterate	0	0	0	0	0
	Below matric	0	0	0	0	5(100.0%)
	Matric and above	0	0	0	4(25.0%)	12(75.0%)
Age	Below 30	0	0	0	3(23.1%)	10(76.9%)
	30 to 40	0	0	0	1(12.5%)	7(87.5%)

Source: Field Survey.

Out of the total male respondents, 15.8 per cent were found to be dissatisfied while 84.2 per cent were found to be highly dissatisfied. In the case of female, 50 per cent were indifferent while 50 per cent were dissatisfied.

The analysis on the basis of education shows that among below matric, cent per cent were highly dissatisfied. Around 25 per cent matric and above were dissatisfied and the remaining 75 per cent were highly dissatisfied.

On the basis of age, out of total employees between the age groups of 20 to 30 years, 23.1 per cent were dissatisfied and 76.9 per cent were highly dissatisfied. Out of the total employees between the age groups of 30 to 40 years, 12.5 per cent were dissatisfied while 87.5 per cent expressed highly dissatisfaction.

On the basis of study it is concluded that most of the employees of MCP were either dissatisfied or highly dissatisfied with the pay scale system.

3.15 Employees' Satisfaction With Fringe Benefit System

Fringe Benefits

Fringe benefits are compensations made to an employee beyond the regular benefit of being paid for their work. Compensation in addition to direct wages or salaries, such as company car, house allowance, medical insurance, paid holidays, pension schemes, subsidised meals are the examples of it. Some fringe benefits are regarded part of a taxable income.[42]

Responses of Permanent Employees

In case of the fringe benefit system, out of 58 respondents, 76 per cent employees expressed either dissatisfaction or high dissatisfaction and 59 per cent opined satisfaction, while the remaining 20 per cent were indifferent. The level of satisfaction has further been examined on the basis of gender, education, age and grade. The employees were asked about their satisfaction regarding the fringe benefit system. The responses of the respondents have been given in Table 3.19.

Table 3.19
Satisfaction with Fringe Benefits System
(Figures in Parenthesis Represent Percentages)

		Highly Satisfied	*Satisfied*	*Indifferent*	*Dissatisfied*	*Highly Dissatisfied*
Gender	Male	0	0	15(27.8%)	15(27.8%)	24(44.4%)
Gender	Male	0	2(3.7%)	11(20.4%)	31(57.4%)	10(18.5%)
	Female	0	0	0	1(25.0%)	3(75.0%)
Education	Illiterate	0	0	0	5(55.6%)	4(44.4%)
	Below matric	0	0	1(14.3%)	3(42.9%)	3(42.9%)
	Matric and above	0	2(4.8%)	10(23.8%)	24(57.1%)	6(14.3%)
Age	Below30	0	0	2(28.6%)	4(57.1%)	1(14%)
	30 to 40	0	1(4.3%)	5(21.7%)	14(60.9%)	3(13.0%)
	40 to 50	0	0	2(8.7%)	12(52.2%)	9(39.1%)
	50 and above	0	1(20.0%)	2(40.0%)	2(40.0%)	0
Grade	A	0	1(25.0%)	2(50.0%)	1(25.0%)	0
	B	0	0	1(20.0%)	3(60.0%)	1(20.0%)
	C	0	0	5(31.2%)	8(50.0%)	3(18.8%)
	D	0	1(3.0%)	3(9.1%)	20(60.6%)	9(27.3%)

Source: Field Survey.

Out of the total male respondents, 3.7 per cent were satisfied, 20.4 per cent indifferent, 57.4 per cent dissatisfied and the remaining 18.5 per cent reported being highly dissatisfied. In the case of females, 25 per cent were dissatisfied while 75 per cent reported being highly dissatisfied about the fringe benefits system.

The analysis on the basis of education reveals that among the illiterates 55.6 per cent were dissatisfied and 44.4 per cent were highly dissatisfied. In the case of below matric, 14.3 per cent were indifferent, 42.9 per cent were dissatisfied and the remaining 42.9 per cent were highly dissatisfied. Around 4.8 per cent above matric were highly satisfied, 26.2 per cent satisfied, 23.8 per cent indifferent, 57.1 per cent dissatisfied and the remaining 14.3 per cent expressed high dissatisfaction with the fringe benefits system.

On the basis of age, out of the total employees having an age below 30 years, 28.6 per cent were indifferent, 57.1 per cent were dissatisfied and remaining 14.3 per cent were highly dissatisfied. Out of total employees between the age groups of 30 to 40 years, 4.3 per cent answered satisfied, 21.7 per cent were indifferent, 60.9 per cent expressed dissatisfaction and the remaining 13 per cent reported being highly dissatisfied. In the case of employees between the age groups of 40 to 50 years, 8.7 per cent were indifferent, 52.2 per cent expressed dissatisfaction and the remaining 39.1 per cent were highly dissatisfied. Out of the total employees having an age above 50 years, 20 per cent were satisfied, 40 per cent indifferent and the remaining 40 per cent expressed dissatisfaction.

On the basis of grade out of total employees 25 per cent of Grade A employees were satisfied, 50 per cent indifferent and 25 per cent were dissatisfied. In the case of Grade B employees, 20 per cent were indifferent, 60 per cent expressed dissatisfaction and remaining 20 per cent reported being highly dissatisfied. In the Grade C category, 31.2 per cent were indifferent, 50 per cent expressed dissatisfaction and remaining 18.8 per cent were highly dissatisfied. In the case of Grade D employees, 3.0 per cent were satisfied, 9.1 per cent were indifferent, 60.6 per cent reported dissatisfied and the remaining 27.3 per cent reported being highly dissatisfied about fringe benefits system.

Thus, on the basis of fieldwork, it is concluded that a large number of employees of MCP were either dissatisfied or highly dissatisfied with the fringe benefits system.

G. Other Benefits

Leave

The employees of Municipal Council, Panchkula are entitled to various kinds of leave. Some of these are: Casual Leave, Medical Leave, Earned Leave, etc.

(1) ***Casual Leave:*** The employees of Municipal Council, Panchkula are entitled to casual leave. Those who have put in service from 1 to 10 years get casual leave of 10 days in a year and between 10 –15 years of service get 15 days in a year and 20 years and above get 20 days in a year. Women are entitled to casual leave of 30 days in a year.

An unavailed casual leave gets converted into an earned leave. But it can not be more than 300 days for any employee throughout one's whole service.

(2) Employees can get medical leave for 10 days with full pay on the submission of medical certificate and 20 days with half pay, in a year.

3.16 Employees' Satisfaction With Leave System

In case of the leave system, out of 58 respondents, 82 per cent employees expressed either dissatisfaction or high dissatisfaction and nine per cent opined satisfaction, and the remaining nine per cent were indifferent. The level of satisfaction has further been examined on the basis of gender, education, age and grade. The employees were asked about their satisfaction regarding the leave system. The responses of respondents have been given in Table 3.20.

Table 3.20
Satisfaction with Leave System
(Figures in Parenthesis Represent Percentages)

		Highly Satisfied	*Satisfied*	*Indifferent*	*Dissatisfied*	*Highly Dissatisfied*
Gender	Male	0	0	15(27.8%)	15(27.8%)	24(44.4%)
Gender	Male	0	4(7.4%)	5(9.3%)	20(37.0%)	25(46.3)
	Female	0	1(25.0%)	1(25%)	1(25%)	1(25%)
Education	Illiterate	0	0	2(22.2%)	2(22.2%)	5(55.6%)
	Below Matric	0	1(14.3%)	0	4(57.1%)	2(28.6%)
	Matric and above	0	4(9.5%)	4(9.5%)	15(35.7)	19(45.2%)
Age	Below 30	0	0	2(28.6%)	3(42.9)	2(28.6%)
	30 to 40	0	2(8.7%)	2(8.7%)	7(30.4%)	12(52.2%)
	40 to 50	0	2(8.7%)	1(4.3%)	9(39.1%)	11(47.8%)
	50 and above	0	1(20%)	1(20%)	2(40%)	1(20%)
Grade	A	0	1(25%)	1(25%)	2(50%)	0
	B	0	0	1(20%)	3(60%)	1(20%)
	C	0	2(12.5%)	1(6.2%)	7(43.8%)	6(37.5%)
	D	0	2(6.1%)	3(9.1%)	9(27.3%)	19(57.6%)

Source: Field Survey

Out of the total male respondents, 7.4 per cent were satisfied, 9.3 per cent indifferent, 37 per cent dissatisfied and the remaining 46.3 per cent reported being highly dissatisfied. In the case of females, 25 per cent were satisfied, 25 per cent were indifferent, 25 per cent were dissatisfied and the remaining 25 per cent reported being highly dissatisfied with leave system.

The analysis on the basis of education reveals that among the illiterates, 22.2 per cent were indifferent, 22.2 per cent dissatisfied and remaining 55.6 per cent expressed high dissatisfaction. In the case of below matric, 14.3 per cent expressed satisfaction, 57.1 per cent were dissatisfied and the remaining 28.6 per cent reported being highly dissatisfied. Around 9.5 per cent above matric were satisfied, 9.5 per cent indifferent, 35.7 per cent dissatisfied and the remaining 45.2 per cent opined high dissatisfaction with the leave system.

On the basis of age, out of total employees having an age below 30 years, 28.6 per cent were indifferent, 42.9 per cent expressed dissatisfaction and the remaining 28.6 per cent reported being highly dissatisfied. Out of total employees between the age groups of 30 to 40 years, 8.7 per cent answered satisfied, 8.7 per cent were indifferent, 30.4 per cent expressed dissatisfaction and the remaining 52.2 per cent reported high dissatisfaction. In the case of employees between the age groups of 40 to 50 years, 8.7 per cent reported satisfied, 4.3 per cent were indifferent, 39.1 per cent expressed dissatisfaction and the remaining 47.8 per cent reported high dissatisfaction. Out of total employees having an age above 50 years, 20 per cent were satisfied, 20 per cent indifferent, 40 per cent expressed dissatisfaction and remaining 20 per cent reported being highly dissatisfied.

On the basis of grade, out of total employees 25 per cent Grade A employees were satisfied, 25.0 per cent indifferent and the remaining 50 per cent reported dissatisfied. In the case of Grade B, 20 per cent were indifferent, 60 per cent expressed dissatisfaction and the remaining 20 per cent were highly dissatisfied. In the Grade C category, 12.5 per cent reported satisfied, 6.2 per cent were indifferent, 43.2 per cent expressed dissatisfaction and remaining 37.5 per cent opined being highly dissatisfied. In the case of Grade D employees, 6.1 per cent expressed satisfaction, 9.1 were indifferent, 27.3 per cent reported dissatisfied and the remaining 57.6 per cent were highly dissatisfied with the leave system.

Based on the earlier examination of findings, it can be concluded that most of the employees of MCP were either dissatisfied or highly dissatisfied with the leave system.

3.17 Conduct and Discipline

The need of inculcating in the municipal employees a spirit of single-minded devotion to the services of local bodies and loyalty to them can hardly be over emphasised. The people expect from municipal employees high standards of honesty, good conduct and municipal personnel should always make an effort to live upto the expectations of the people to achieve this objective. Generally, municipalities formulate and enforce a code of rules to regulate the conduct of their employees. According to rule 15 (4) of Haryana Municipal Services (IRCS) Rules, 1982, the Government Employees (Conduct) Rules, 1966 as amended from time to time and applicable to the state of Haryana shall apply to the members of the municipal services. The Conduct Rules regulate, inter alias, proper behaviour towards superiors, code of ethics in official's private life, political activities, honesty and integrity by prohibiting acceptance of gifts, engaging in private trade or business, capacity of debts, acquisition and disposals of properties, etc. According to Haryana Municipal Act, 1973, the employees of MCP are bound to follow the said rule.

Punishment

The violation of conduct rules by municipal employees should result in disciplinary action because, if misconduct and fault go unpunished, it will encourage other employees to commit the same norm and this may corrupt the whole system. The Haryana government has, therefore, provided that the Haryana Civil Services (Punishment and Appeal) Rules, 1987 as amended from time to time, shall apply to the members of the municipal services so far as they are not inconsistent with the provisions of the Haryana Municipal Act, 1973.[43] The authority empowered to impose penalties (minor and major) and Appellate authority in respect of a category of posts in services shall be as specified in the Haryana Civil Services (Punishment and Appeal) Rules, 1987.

The details of Punishing Authority and Appellate Authority for the Employee of Municipal Council, Panchkula are given in Table 3.21:

Table 3.21
Details of Punishing Authority and Appellate Authority of Employees for Municipal Council, Panchkula
Haryana Municipal State Level Services

Sl. No.	*Designation of Post*	*Appointing Authority*	*Nature of Penalty*	*Punishing Authority*	*Appellate Authority*
1.	Executive Officer	Government	Minor	Municipal	Government
2.	Medical Officer of Health		Penalties	Committee/ Administrator	
3.	Engineers		Major Penalties	Government	
4	Secretaries	Government	Minor	Municipal	Government
5.	Superintendent (Office)		Minor penalties	Municipal Committee/ Administrator	Director, Local Bodies
6.	Superintendent (Tax/Octroi)	Director, Local Bodies	Major penalties	Director, Local Bodies	Government
7.	Accountants				
8.	Fire Station Officers				
9.	Sectional	Director,	Minor	Municipal	Director

	Officers	Local Bodies	Penalties	Engineer and where this post does not exist or is vacant, Municipal Committee/ Administrator	Local Bodies
			Major penalties	Director, Local Bodies	Government
10.	Chief Sanitary Inspector	Director, Local Bodies	Minor penalties	Medical Officer of Health and where this post does not exist or is vacant Municipal Committee/ Administrator	Director Local Bodies
			Major penalties	Director, Local Bodies	Government
	Haryana Municipal District Level Services				
11.	Light Inspectors	Not Mentioned	Not Mentioned	Not Mentioned	Not Mentioned
12.	Foreman				
13.	Asstts. (Including Asstt. Octroi Supdts., Asstts., Asstt./ Accountants, Senior Accounts Clerks, Head Cashiers, Water Rate Assistants and Public Health Assistants	....	...		
14.	Inspectors (Non-Technical), Grade II (including Traffic Inspectors, Vehicle Inspectors, Wheel Tax Inspectors, Pound Inspectors, Water Rate Inspectors, Street Light Inspectors, Assistant Sanitary Inspectors				

	and Assistant Octroi Inspectors)	....	
15.	Clerks (including Accounts Clerks, Assistant Cashiers, Water Meter Readers Tax/ House Tax Clerks, Rent Collectors, Fee Collectors, Octroi Rent Clerk-cum-Sub-Inspectors, Tax Collectors, General Clerks, Record Keeper, Typists, Store-keepers, Audit Clerks, Assistant Record-keepers, Tax Clerks, Clerks, Compost Keepers, Octroi Moharris /Clerks, Tehbazari Moharrirs, Cattle Pound Moharrirs/ Clerks, Library Moharrirs, Perokars)	....	....
16.	Sub-Fire Officers		
17.	Leading Firemen		
18.	Fire Brigade Drivers		
19.	Firemen		
20.	Head Clerks		
21.	Steno-Typists		
22.	Drivers (including Cars/ Jeeps, Ambulance Drivers and Head Drivers)	....	....

Source: Municipal Act of Haryana, 1973.

Further, Haryana Municipal Act, 1973 makes provision for action against misconduct and is as discussed below:

Action against Misconduct

Every municipal employee is liable to have his increments or promotions. In case of misconduct, this provision may be denied to the employees. In addition to this they could face censure, reduction in rank, compulsory retirement, removal or dismissal for breach of any departmental regulation or indiscipline or for carelessness, unfitness, neglect of duty or other misconduct after being given a reasonable opportunity for explanation. However, a show cause notice could not be issued where an officer or an employee is removed or dismissed on the ground of conduct which has led to his conviction on criminal charge or where the authority empowered to remove or dismiss such an officer/ employee is satisfied that for some reason to be recorded by that authority, it is not reasonably practicable to give that person an opportunity of showing cause. Further, an employee \ officer could not be compulsory retired, removed or dismissed by an authority subordinate to that by which he was appointed.[44]

Misconduct in MCP

In MCP, there is less usage of disciplinary action and even in those cases especially at District level services employees, where it was attempted, political interference and favoritism resulted in shielding the guilty. This is more so in case of District Level Municipal employees, where penal as well as appellate authorities have not even been mentioned.

3.18 Employees' Satisfaction With Disciplinary Action System

(I) Responses of Permanent Employees

In case of disciplinary action system, out of 58 respondents, 62 per cent employees expressed either dissatisfaction or high dissatisfaction, 10 per cent opined satisfaction, high satisfaction and the remaining 28 per cent were indifferent. The level of satisfaction further has been examined on the basis of gender, education, age and designation. The employees were asked about their satisfaction regarding the disciplinary action system. The responses of respondents have been given in Table 3.22.

Table 3.22
Satisfaction with Disciplinary Action Policy
(Figures in Parenthesis Represent Percentages)

		Highly Satisfied	*Satisfied*	*Indifferent*	*Dissatisfied*	*Highly Dissatisfied*
Gender	Male	1(1.9%)	5(9.3%)	15(27.8%)	19(35.2%)	14(25.9%)
	Female	0	0(0 %)	1(25.0%)	2(50.0%)	1(25.0%)
Education	Illiterate	0	1(11.1%)	2(22.2%)	3(33.3%)	3(33.3%)
	Below matric	0	2(28.6%)	0	4(57.1%)	1(14.3%)
	Matric and above	1(2.4%)	2(4.8%)	14(33.3%)	14(33.3%)	11(26.2%)

Age	Below30	0	1(14.3%)	4(57.1%)	0	2(28.6 %)
	30 to 40	1(4.3%)	0	7(30.4%)	12(52.2%)	3(13.0%)
	40 to 50	0	3(13.0%)	4(17.4%)	7(30.7%)	9(39.1%)
	50 and above	0	1 (20.0%)	1(20.0%)	2(40.0%)	1(20.0%)
Grade	A	0	1(25.0%)	1(25.0%)	1(25.0%)	1(25.0%)
	B	0	1(20.0%)	1(20.0%)	2(40.0%)	1(20.0%)
	C	0	1(6.2%)	1(6.2%)	9(56.2%)	5(31.2%)
	D	1(3.0%)	2(6.1%)	13(39.4%)	9(27.3%)	8(24.2%)

Source: Field Survey.

Out of the total male respondents, 1.9 per cent were highly satisfied, 9.3 per cent satisfied, 27.8 per cent indifferent, 35.2 per cent dissatisfied and remaining 25.9 per cent reported highly dissatisfied. In the case of females, 25 per cent were indifferent and 50 per cent were dissatisfied and the remaining 25 per cent reported highly dissatisfied with disciplinary action system.

The analysis on the basis of education reveals that among illiterates, 11.1 per cent were satisfied, 22.2 per cent indifferent, 33.3 per cent dissatisfied and again 33.3 per cent were highly dissatisfied. In the case of below matric, 28.6 per cent expressed satisfaction, 57.1 per cent were dissatisfied and the remaining 4.3 per cent were highly dissatisfied. Around 2.4 per cent above matric were highly satisfied, 4.8 per cent satisfied 33.3 per cent indifferent, again 33.3 per cent dissatisfied and the remaining 26.2 per cent reported highly dissatisfied.

On the basis of age, out of total employees having an age below 30 years, 14.3 per cent reported satisfied, 57.1 per cent were indifferent, 28.6 per cent expressed high dissatisfaction. Out of total employees between the age groups of 30 to 40 years, 4.3 per cent answered highly satisfied, 30.4 per cent were indifferent, 52.2 per cent expressed dissatisfaction and the remaining 13.0 per cent were highly dissatisfied. In the case of employees between the age groups of 40 to 50 years, 13.0 per cent reported satisfied, 17.4 per cent were indifferent, 30.4 per cent expressed dissatisfaction and the remaining 39.1 per cent were highly dissatisfied. Out of total employees aged above the 50 years, 20 per cent were satisfied, 20 per cent indifferent, 40 per cent expressed dissatisfaction and the remaining 20 per cent were highly dissatisfied.

On the basis of grade, out of total employees 25 per cent Grade A employees were satisfied, 25 per cent indifferent, 25 per cent were dissatisfied and the remaining 25 per cent were highly dissatisfied. In the case of Grade B, 20 per cent answered satisfied, 20 per cent were indifferent, 40 per cent expressed dissatisfaction and remaining 20 per cent were highly dissatisfied. In the Grade C category, 6.2 per cent reported satisfied, 6.2 per cent were indifferent, 56.2 per cent expressed dissatisfaction and the remaining 31.2 per cent opined highly dissatisfied. In the case of Grade D employees, 3.0 per cent answered highly satisfied, 39.4 per cent were indifferent, and 27.3 per cent reported dissatisfied and the remaining 24.2 per cent were highly dissatisfied with disciplinary action system.

The study thus, concluded that a large number employee of MCP were either dissatisfied or highly dissatisfied with the disciplinary action system.

(II) Responses of Contractual Employees

In case of disciplinary action system, out of 21 contractual employees, 68 per cent employees were either dissatisfied or highly dissatisfied while 32 per cent reported indifferent. The level of satisfaction has further been examined on the basis of gender, education and age. The responses of respondents have been given in Table 3.23.

Table 3.23
Satisfaction with Disciplinary Action System
(Figures in parenthesis represent per centages)

		Highly Satisfied	*Satisfied*	*Indifferent*	*Dissatisfied*	*Highly Dissatisfied*
Gender	Male	0	0	6(31.6%)	4(21.1%)	9(47.4%)
	Female	0	0	0	0	2(100.0 %)
Education	Illiterate	0	0	0	0	0
	Below matric	0	0	1(20.0%)	2(40.0%)	2(40.0%)
	Matric and above	0	0	5(31.2%)	2(12.5%)	9(56.2%)
Age	Below30	0	0	4(30.0%)	3(23.1%)	6(46.2%)
	30 to 40	0	0	2(25.0%)	1(12.5%)	5(62.5%)

Source: Field Survey.

Out of the total male respondents, 31.6 per cent were indifferent, 21.1 per cent reported dissatisfaction and remaining 47.4 per cent were highly dissatisfied. In the case of females, cent per cent expressed high dissatisfaction.

The analysis on the basis of education shows that among below matric, 20 per cent were indifferent, 40 per cent dissatisfied and remaining 60 per cent were highly dissatisfied. Around 31.2 per cent matric and above were indifferent, 12.5 per cent dissatisfied and remaining 56.2 per cent were highly dissatisfied.

On the basis of age, out of total employees between the age groups of 20 to 30 years, 30.8 per cent were indifferent, 23.1 per cent dissatisfied and the remaining 46.2 per cent were highly dissatisfied. Out of total employees between the age groups of 30 to 40 years, 25.0 per cent were indifferent, 12.5 per cent dissatisfied and the remaining 62.5 per cent were highly dissatisfied.

Thus, it can be concluded that a large number employees of MCP were either dissatisfied or highly dissatisfied with the disciplinary action system.

3.19 Employees' Satisfaction With Service Conditions Policy

(I) Responses of Permanent Employees

In case of service conditions, out of 58 respondents, 84 per cent employees expressed either dissatisfaction or high dissatisfaction and nine per cent opined satisfaction, high satisfaction and the remaining seven per cent were indifferent. The level of satisfaction further has been examined on the basis of gender, education, age and designation. The responses of the respondents have been given in Table 3.24.

Table 3.24
Satisfaction with Service Conditions
(Figures in Parenthesis Represent Percentages)

		Highly Satisfied	*Satisfied*	*Indifferent*	*Dissatisfied*	*Highly Dissatisfied*
Gender	Male	0	0	6(31.6%)	4(21.1%)	9(47.4%)
Gender	Male	0	5(9.3%)	4(7.4%)	16(29.6%)	29(53.7%)
	Female	0	0	0	3(75.0%)	1(25.0%)
Education	Illiterate	0	0	1(11.1%)	3(33.3%)	5(55.6%)
	Below matric	0	0	1(14.3%)	4(57.1%)	2(28.6%)
	Matric and above	0	5(11.9%)	2(4.8%)	12(28.6%)	23(54.8%)
Age	Below30	0	1(14.3%)	1(14.3%)	2(28.6%)	3(42.9%)
	30 to 40	0	3(13.0%)	0	5(21.7%)	15(65.2%)
	40 to 50	0	1(4.3%)	3(13.0%)	7(30.4%)	12(52.2%)
	50 and above	0	0	0	5(100.0%)	0
Grade	A	0	2(50.0%)	1(25.0%)	1(25.0%)	0
	B	0	0	1(20.0%)	3(60.0%)	1(20.0%)
	C	0	2(12.5%)	0	9(56.2%)	5(31.2%)
	D	0	1(3.0%)	2(6.1%)	6(18.2%)	24(72.7%)

Source: Field Survey.

Out of the total male respondents, 9.3 per cent were satisfied, 29.6 per cent indifferent, 29.6 per cent dissatisfied and the remaining 53.7 per cent were highly dissatisfied. In the case of females, 75.0 per cent were dissatisfied while 25 per cent highly dissatisfied about service conditions.

The analysis on the basis of education reveals that among the illiterates, 11.1 per cent were indifferent, 33.3 per cent dissatisfied and the remaining 55.6 per cent were highly dissatisfied. In the case of below matric, 14.3 per cent were indifferent and 57.1 per cent were dissatisfied and the remaining 28.6 per cent reported highly dissatisfied. Around 11.2 per cent above matric were satisfied, 4.8 per cent indifferent, 28.6 per cent dissatisfied and the remaining 54.8 per cent were highly dissatisfied.

On the basis of age, out of total employees having an age below 30 years, 14.3 per cent reported satisfied, 14.3 per cent were indifferent, 28.6 per cent expressed dissatisfaction and the remaining 42.9 reported highly dissatisfied. Out of total employees between the age groups of 30 to 40 years, 13 per cent answered satisfied, 21.7 per cent expressed dissatisfaction and remaining 65.2 per cent reported highly dissatisfied. In the case of employees between the age groups of 40 to 50 years, 4.3 per cent reported satisfied, 13 per cent were indifferent, 30.4 per cent expressed dissatisfaction and remaining 52.2 per cent were highly dissatisfied. Out of total employees having an age above the 50 years, cent per cent expressed dissatisfaction.

On the basis of grade out of total employees 50 per cent of the Grade A employees 50.0 per cent were satisfied, 25 per cent indifferent and the remaining 25 per cent were dissatisfied. In the case of B grade, 20 per cent were indifferent, 60 per cent expressed dissatisfaction and the remaining 20 per cent were highly dissatisfied. In the Grade C category, 12.5 reported satisfied, 56.2 expressed dissatisfaction and remaining 31.2 per cent reported highly dissatisfied. In the case of Grade D employees very few answered satisfied, 6.1 per cent were indifferent, 18.2 per cent reported dissatisfied and the remaining 72.7 per cent expressed high dissatisfaction about service conditions.

It can be thus, inferred that a large number of employees of MCP were either dissatisfied or highly dissatisfied with the service conditions system.

(II) Responses of Contractual Employees

In case of service conditions out of 21 respondent contractual employees, cent per cent employees expressed highly dissatisfaction. The level of satisfaction further has been examined on the basis of gender, education and age. The responses of the respondents have been given in Table 3.25.

Table 3.25
Satisfaction with Service Conditions of Contractual Employees (Figures in Parenthesis Represent Percentages)

		Highly Satisfied	*Satisfied*	*Indifferent*	*Dissatisfied*	*Highly Dissatisfied*
Gender	Male	0	0	0	0	19(100.0%)
	Female	0	0	0	0	2(100.0%)
Education	Illiterate	0	0	0	0	0
	Below matric	0	0	0	0	5(100.0%)
	Matric and above	0	0	0	0	16(100.0%)
Age	Below30	0	0	0	0	13(100.0%)
	30 to 40	0	0	0	0	8(100.0%)

Source: Field Survey.

Out of the total male respondents, cent per cent expressed high dissatisfaction. In the case of females, again cent per cent expressed high dissatisfaction.

The analysis on the basis of education shows that among below matric, cent per cent expressed high dissatisfaction. In the case of matric and above, cent per cent reported high dissatisfaction.

On the basis of age, out of total employees between the age groups of 20 to 30 years, cent per cent expressed high dissatisfaction. Out of total employees between the age groups of 30 to 40 years, again cent per cent expressed highly dissatisfaction.

The above results clearly exhibit that a large number of employees of MCP were either dissatisfied or highly dissatisfied with their service conditions.

3.20 Employees' Satisfaction With Management Employee Relations

(I) Responses of Permanent Employees

In case of management employee relations, out of 58 respondents, 69 per cent employees expressed either dissatisfaction or high dissatisfaction and four per cent opined satisfaction, high satisfaction and the remaining 27 per cent were indifferent. The level of satisfaction further has been examined on the basis of gender, education, age and designation. The responses of the respondents have been given in Table 3.26.

Table 3.26
Satisfaction with Management-Employee Relations
(Figures in Parenthesis Represent Percentages)

		Highly Satisfied	*Satisfied*	*Indifferent*	*Dissatisfied*	*Highly Dissatisfied*
Gender	Male	0	0	0	0	19(100.0%)
Gender	Male	1(1.9%)	1(1.9%)	15(27.8%)	21(38.9%)	16(29.6%)
	Female	0	0	0	3(75.0%)	1(25.0%)
Education	Illiterate	0	0	1(11.1%)	4(44.4%)	4(44.4%)
	Below matric	1(14.3%)	0	1(14.3%)	3(42.9%)	2(28.6%)
	Matric and above	0	1(2.4%)	13(31.0%)	17(40.5%)	11(26.2%)
Age	Below30	0	0	5(71.4%)	2(28.6%)	0
	30 to 40	1(4.3%)	1(4.3%)	8(34.8%)	8(34.8%)	5(21.7%)
	40 to 50	0	0	2(8.7%)	9(39.1%)	12(52.2%)
	50 and above	0	0	0	5(100.0%)	0
Grade	A	0	0	2(50.0%)	1(25.0%)	1(25.0%)
	B	0	0	0	5(100.0%)	0
	C	2(12.5%)	0	2(12.5%)	9(55.8%)	3(18.6%)
	D	0	1(3.0%)	11(33.3%)	9(27.3%)	12(36.4%)

Source: Field Survey.

Out of the total male respondents, 1.9 per cent were highly satisfied, 1.9 per cent satisfied, 27.8 per cent indifferent, 38.9 per cent dissatisfied and the remaining 29.6 per cent reported highly dissatisfied. In the case of female respondents, 75 per cent were dissatisfied while 25 per cent highly dissatisfied with management-employee relations.

The analysis on the basis of education reveals that among the illiterates, 11.1 per cent were indifferent, 44.4 per cent dissatisfied and again 44.4 per cent were highly dissatisfied. In the case of below matric, 14.3 per cent expressed high satisfaction, 14.3 per cent indifferent and 42.9 per cent were dissatisfied and the remaining 28.6 per cent reported high dissatisfaction. Around 2.4 per cent of above matric were satisfied, 31 per cent indifferent, 40.5 per cent dissatisfied and remaining 26.2 per cent were highly dissatisfied.

On the basis of age, out of total employees the age group of below 30 years, 71.4 per cent were indifferent and 28.6 per cent expressed dissatisfaction. Out of total employees between the age groups of 30 to 40 years, 4.3 per cent answered satisfied, 34.8 per cent were indifferent, 34.8 per cent dissatisfied and the remaining 21.7 per cent expressed high dissatisfaction. In the case of employees between the age groups of 40 to 50 years, 8.7 per cent were indifferent, 39.1 per cent expressed dissatisfaction and the remaining 52.2 per cent were highly dissatisfied. Out of total employees in the above the 50 years age group, cent per cent expressed dissatisfaction.

On the basis of grade out of total employees 50 per cent of the Grade A employees were indifferent, 25 per cent dissatisfied and the remaining 25 per cent were highly dissatisfied. In the case of Grade B, cent per cent expressed dissatisfaction. In the Grade C category, 12.5 per cent reported highly satisfied, 12.5 per cent were indifferent, 55.8 per cent expressed dissatisfaction and the remaining 18.6 were highly dissatisfied. In the case of Grade D employees, very few expressed satisfaction, 33.3 were indifferent, 27.3 per cent reported dissatisfied and the remaining 36.4 per cent reported highly dissatisfied about management employee relations.

On the basis of study, it is concluded that large number employees of MCP were either dissatisfied or highly dissatisfied with management employee relations system.

(II) Responses of Contractual Employees

In case of management employer relations, out of 21 respondent contractual employees, 57 per cent employees expressed high dissatisfaction, while 43 per cent reported indifferent. The level of satisfaction further has been examined on the basis of gender, education and age. The responses of the respondents have been given in Table 3.27.

Table 3.27
Satisfaction with Management Employee Relations of Contractual Employees (Figures in Parenthesis Represent Percentages)

		Highly Satisfied	*Satisfied*	*Indifferent*	*Dissatisfied*	*Highly Dissatisfied*
Gender	Male	0	0	0	0	19(100.0%)
Gender	Male	0	0	9(47.4%)	0	10(52.6%)
	Female	0	0	0	0	2(100.0%)
Education	Illiterate	0	0	0	0	0
	Below matric	0	0	3(60.0%)	0	2(40.0%)
	Matric and above	0	0	6(37.5%)	0	10(62.5%)
Age	Below 30	0	0	6(46.2%)	0	7(53.8%)
	30 to 40	0	0	3(37.5%)	0	5(62.5%)

Source: Field Survey.

Out of the total male respondents, 47.4 per cent were indifferent and 52.6 per cent expressed high dissatisfaction. In the case of females, 100 per cent expressed high dissatisfaction.

The analysis on the basis of education shows that among below matric, 60.0 per cent were indifferent and 40 per cent highly dissatisfied. Around 37.5 per cent, matric and above were indifferent and 62.5 per cent were highly dissatisfied.

On the basis of age, out of total employees having an age between 20 to 30 years, 46.2 per cent were indifferent and 53.8 per cent were highly dissatisfied. Out of total employees having an age between the age of 30 to 40 years, 37.5 per cent were indifferent and 62.5 per cent were highly dissatisfied.

Based on above analysis, it can be concluded that large numbers of employees of MCP were either dissatisfied or highly dissatisfied with management-employee relations system.

3.21 Transfer Policy

According to Rule 13 (HMSIRCS), Rule, 1982 a member of state level service shall be liable to serve at any place in the state of Haryana. A member of the district level service may be transferred out side the district, if it is considered expedient in the public interest. A member of municipal service may be transferred to another municipal committee of the same class.

Transfers in MCP

In MCP frequent transfers have been seen for the post of secretaries as during the study period, secretaries were transferred four times. However no transfers took place for the post of Executive Officer and District Level employees. This poses a serious question mark on the authencity of the transfer system.

3.22 Employees' Satisfaction With Transfer

In case of transfer system, out of 58 respondents, 70 per cent employees expressed either dissatisfaction or highly dissatisfaction and four per cent opined satisfaction, highly satisfaction and remaining 26 per cent indifferent response. The level of satisfaction further has been examined on the basis of gender, education, age and designation. The responses of the respondents have been given in Table 3.28.

Table 3.28
Satisfaction with Transfer Policy
(Figures in Parenthesis Represent Percentages)

		Highly Satisfied	*Satisfied*	*Indifferent*	*Dissatisfied*	*Highly Dissatisfied*
Gender	Male	0	2(3.7%)	14(25.9%)	19(35.2%)	19(35.2%)
	Female	0	0	0	2(50.0%)	2(50.0%)
Education	Illiterate	0	0	1(11.1%)	3(33.3%)	5(55.6%)
	Below matric	0	0	0	2(28.6%)	5(55.6%)
	Matric and above	0	2(4.8%)	13(31.0%)	16(38.1%)	11(26.2%0

Age	Below30	0	1(14.3%)	4(57.1%)	1(14.3%)	1(14.3%)
	30 to 40	0	0	6(26.1%)	11(47.8%)	6(26.1%)
	40 to 50	0	0	3(13.0%)	7(30.4%)	13(56.5%)
	50 and above	0	1(20.0%)	1(20.0%0	2(40.0%)	1(20.0%)
Grade	A	0	1(25.0%)	1(25.0%)	1(25.0%)	1(25.0%)
	B	0	1(20.0%)	0	2(40.0%)	2(40.0%)
	C	0	0	2(12.5)	7(43.8%)	7(43.8%)
	D	0	0	11(33.3%)	11(33.3%)	11(33.3%)

Source: Field Survey.

Out of the total male respondents, 3.7 per cent were satisfied, 25.9 per cent indifferent, 35.2 per cent dissatisfied and the remaining 35.2 per cent reported highly dissatisfied. In the case of females, about 50.0 per cent were dissatisfied and remaining 50.0 per cent expressed high dissatisfaction about transfer policy.

The analysis on the basis of education reveals that among the illiterates, 11.1 per cent were indifferent, 33.3 per cent dissatisfied and the remaining 55.6 per cent were highly dissatisfied. In the case of below matric, 28.6 per cent were dissatisfied and 71.4 per cent highly dissatisfied. Around 4.8 per cent above matric were satisfied, 31 per cent indifferent, 38.1 per cent dissatisfied and the remaining 26.2 per cent were highly dissatisfied.

On the basis of age out of total employees having an age below 30 years, 14.3 per cent reported satisfied, 57.1 per cent were indifferent, 14.3 per cent expressed dissatisfaction and remaining, 14.3 per cent were highly dissatisfied. Out of total employees between the age groups of 30 to 40 years, 26.1 per cent were indifferent, 26.1 per cent highly dissatisfied and the remaining 47.8 per cent expressed dissatisfaction. In the case of employees between the age groups of 40 to 50 years, 13 per cent were indifferent, 30.4 per cent expressed dissatisfaction and the remaining 56.5 per cent were highly dissatisfied. Out of total employees having an age above the 50 years, 20 per cent were satisfied, 20 per cent indifferent, 20 per cent highly dissatisfied and the remaining 40 per cent expressed dissatisfaction.

On the basis of grade, out of total employees 25 per cent of the Grade A employees were satisfied, 25 per cent indifferent, 25 per cent were dissatisfied and remaining 25 per cent highly dissatisfied. In the case of Grade B employees, 20 per cent answered satisfied, 40 per cent expressed dissatisfaction and the remaining 40 per cent were highly dissatisfied. In the Grade C category, 12.5 per cent were indifferent, 43.8 per cent expressed dissatisfaction and remaining 43.8 per cent reported highly dissatisfied. In the case of Grade D employees, 33.3 per cent were indifferent, 33.3 per cent reported dissatisfied and remaining 33.3 per cent were highly dissatisfied.

Thus, it can be concluded that large number of MCP were either dissatisfied or highly dissatisfied with transfer policy.

3.23 Working Hours

The opinion of contractual employees about working hours system of Municipal Council Panchkula has been analysed on the basis of Gender, Education, and Age. Out of 21 respondents cent per cent were dissatisfied and highly dissatisfied with working hours. The responses have been reported in Table 3.29.

Table 3.29
Satisfaction with Working Hours of Contractual Employees
(Figures in Parenthesis Represent Percentages)

		Highly Satisfied	*Satisfied*	*Indifferent*	*Dissatisfied*	*Highly Dissatisfied*
Gender	Male	0	2(3.7%)	14(25.9%)	19(35.2%)	19(35.2%)
Gender	Male	0	0	0	2(10.5%)	17(89.5%)
	Female	0	0	0	1(50.0%)	1(50.0%)
Education	Illiterate	0	0	0	0	0
	Below matric	0	0	0	0	5(100.0%)
	Matric and above	0	0	0	3(18.8%)	13(81.2%)
Age	Below30	0	0	0	2(15.4%)	11(84.6%)
	30 to 40	0	0	0	1(12.5%)	7(87.5%)

Source: Field Survey.

Out of the total male respondents, 10.5 per cent reported dissatisfaction and 89.5 per cent were highly dissatisfied. In the case of females division across level of dissatisfaction and highly dissatisfaction is even.

The analysis on the basis of education shows that among below matric, 100 per cent were highly dissatisfied while around 18.8 per cent matric and above were dissatisfied and 81.2 per cent were highly dissatisfied.

On the basis of age, out of total employees the age group of between 20 to 30 years, 15.4 per cent reported dissatisfied and 84.6 per cent were highly dissatisfied. Out of total employees the age group of between the age group of 30 to 40 years, 12.5 per cent expressed dissatisfaction and 87.5 per cent were highly dissatisfied.

On the basis of the study, it is concluded that most of the employees of MCP were either dissatisfied or highly dissatisfied with the working hours.

The analysis of the responses of permanent employees of MCP reveals that as far as the classification system, pay scales policy, training policy, transfer policy, promotion policy, leave system, fringe benefits, disciplinary action system, service conditions and management employees' relations are concerned, most of the employees were dissatisfied. However, in case of recruitment policy is concerned no conclusion can be drawn.

The analysis of the responses of the contractual employees of MCP reveals that as far as recruitment policy, pay scales policy, promotion policy, leave system, disciplinary action system, service conditions, working hours and management employees relations is concerned, most of the employees were dissatisfied.

3.24 Analysis of Personnel Policy of Mcp on the Basis of Secondary Data

An analysis of the personnel policy of MCP, on the basis of present study reveals certain factors which affects its performance. These factors have been discussed as under:

I. Shortage of Staff

The study of personnel administration of Municipal Council, Panchkula (MCP) reveals that there is a huge shortage of staff at all levels. Against the sanctioned strength of 104 employees, the MCP is managing its affairs with only 50 employees. This causes a lot of strain on the human resources of the Council. At the time of its establishment in the year 2001, Haryana Urban Development Authority (HUDA) had given an assurance to transfer personnel to MCP. However, this transfer could not take place despite repeated reminders sent to it by MCP. Some of the employees were brought on deputation from the concerned department of Haryana government to overcome this shortage.

1. Lack of Proper Method Adopted in Contracting Out

There has hardly been any recruitment campaign undertaken by the government to fulfill the human resources requirement of MCP. Therefore, in order to meet its day-to-day activities and provide effective delivery of services, MCP has been left with no other option but to contract out some of its services. The contracted-out services are mentioned below:

I. Sanitation
II. Street Light
III. Park

IV. Fire Services
V. Road

The contracting out of the above-mentioned services has delivered mixed results. On one hand, this arrangement has helped MCP to carry out its functions while on the other, several questions have been raised about the quality of service delivery. Ineffective monitoring and collusion between MCP officials and contractors are mainly responsible for the poor service delivery.

2. **Exploitation of Employees**

In addition, the study has also found large-scale exploitation of the personnel employed by the contractor. This takes place in an open violation of contract agreement. Many times employees are paid less wages, the contractor seldom contributes the matching contribution for the employee provident fund and holidays are rarely given. In certain cases, even the medical grounds are not considered for allowing the worker to go on leave. The trade unions have also been largely ineffective in working for the cause of the contractual workers. The study reveals that the workers who express their grievances are not given employment opportunities again.

3. **Ineffective Monitoring**

Lack of monitoring and corruption has resulted in supply of substandard materials for most of the services, which have been contracted out by MCP. [45]

4. **Ineffective Training**

Though training is a very important aspect of Human Resource Development, the study found that except few senior officials, the training has largely been neglected by most of the employees at Municipal Council Panchkula.

In Municipal Council, Panchkula only one employee accountant has received training between 6/6/2005 to 9/6/2005, on the topic of Municipal Accounts Reform. No improvement in his work has been seen after attaining training programme.

5. **Inadequate Promotional Avenues**

The promotional avenues play an important role in career development and the effective performance of an organisation. It was observed that in Municipal Council, Panchkula, the opportunities for promotion especially at the lower level are negligible.

6. **Less Usage of Disciplinary Action**

For the smooth running of an organisation, discipline assumes a vital importance. The study found less usage of displinary action and even in those cases where it was attempted, political interference and favoritism resulted in shielding the guilty.

7. **Tenure System**
One of the important aspects of personnel administration is the tenure system wherein officials are regularly transferred from one place to another. This is done with an objective to ensure, check on corruption, bringing fresh ideas etc. However, it was seen that in case of MCP very few transfers have taken place. This could be due to nexus between official and political masters and corrupt practices adopted.

8. **No Effective Procedure for Deputation**
During the study it was found that MCP had neither made an effective policy for availing employees for deputation nor is it even a will bit interested in this regard.

3.25 Status of Hypothesis

The analysis of both primary and secondary data is used to check the status of Hypothesis 2: "The employees of Municipal Council, Panchkula are dissatisfied with the personnel policy of the Council". Further this hypothesis has been split into sub-hypotheses covering areas such as recruitment policy; classification system; pay scale policy; training system; promotion system; leave system; fringe benefit system, disciplinary action; service conditions; management-employee relations; and working hours.

More than half of the total permanent employees reported that they were not satisfied with the personnel policy of the MCP. In the case of Contractual employees, 100 per cent reported dissatisfaction about the recruitment policy, working hours, pay scale policy, leave system and service conditions. The major findings have been summarized in the Matrix 1.

Matrix 1
Summing up the Testing of Hypothesis 2

Sr. No.	*Sub Hypothesis*	*Sources of Data*	*Analysis*	*Status of Sub Hypothesis Y Valid N Invali*
1.	Employees of MCP are not satisfied with recruitment Policy	Primary	**1. Permanent employees:** About 48% employees are dissatisfied with the recruitment policy and 22 per cent were indifferent	No conclusion can be drawn
			2. Contractual employees: About 90% employees are	Y

			dissatisfied and very few are indifferent towards the recruitment policy	
2.	Employees of MCP are not satisfied with the classification system	Primary	**Permanent employees:** About 66% employees are dissatisfied with the classification system	Y
3.	Employees of MCP are not satisfied with the pay scale policy	Primary	**1.Permanent employees:** Around 80 per cent employees are dissatisfied with the pay scale policy **2. Contractual employees:** All the contractual employees are dissatisfied with the pay scale policy	Y Y
4.	Employees of MCP are not satisfied with the training policy	Primary	**Permanent employees:** Around 71 per cent employees are dissatisfied with the training policy	N
5.	Employees of MCP are not satisfied with the transfer Policy	Primary	**Permanent employees:** About 73 per cent employees are dissatisfied with the transfer policy	Y Y
6.	Employees of MCP are not satisfied with the promotion policy	Primary	**Permanent employees:** About 62% employees are dissatisfied with the promotion policy	Y
7.	Employees of MCP are not satisfied with the leave system	Primary	**1. Permanent employees:** About 81% employees are dissatisfied with the leave system **2. Contractual employees:** All the contractual employees are dissatisfied with the leave system	Y Y
8.	Employees of MCP are not satisfied with the fringe benefits system	Primary	**1. Permanent employees:** About 78% employees are dissatisfied with the fringe benefits system	Y
9.	Employees of MCP are not satisfied with the disciplinary action	Primary	**1.Permanent employees:** About 63% employees are dissatisfied with the disciplinary action system **2. Contractual employees:** About 71% employees are dissatisfied and only 29% are indifferent with the disciplinary action system	Y Y

10. Employees of MCP are not satisfied with the service conditions	Primary	**1. Permanent employees:** About 84% employees are dissatisfied with the service conditions	Y
		2. Contractual employees: All the contractual employees are dissatisfied with service conditions	Y
11. Employees of MCP are not satisfied with the management employees relation	Primary	**1. Permanent employees:** About 71% employees are dissatisfied with the management employer relations	Y
		2. Contractual employees: About 53% employees are dissatisfied with the management – employer relations	Y
12. Employees of MCP are not satisfied with the Working hours	Primary	**Contractual employees:** All the contractual employees are dissatisfied with the working hours	Y

Source:

Thus, on the basis of the above analysis of sub hypotheses, the Hypothesis 2: "The employees of Municipal Council Panchkula are dissatisfied with the personnel policy of the Council" is accepted.

Concluding Observation

The analysis of the Personnel Administration of MCP in terms of satisfaction, reveals mixed out come. The study shows that as far as recruitment is concerned, no definite conclusion can be drawn as in addition to around half of the respondent employees of MCP being dissatisfied, a substantial per centage was found to be indifferent. In case of all other facets of personnel administration, the study found that the employees of MCP were dissatisfied. The dissatisfaction was particularly more pronounced in terms of classification, training, pay scale policy, transfer policy, promotion policy, leave system, fringe benefits system, disciplinary action, service conditions, management employee relations, working hours. The secondary data also brought forth the acute problem of shortage of manpower, lack of promotional avenues and exploitation of employees, as the significant factors for the poor personnel administration in MCP. Thus, study lays bare the fact that situation of personnel Administration in MCP far from good. It has some road blocks w\c if not faster seriously, can further dampln its reputation in the coming times.

REFERENCE

1. C. B. Mamoria and S.V Gankar, *Personnel Management*, Himalya Publishing House, Mumbai, 2007, p.5.
2. S. L. Goel, *Personnel Administration and Management*, Sterling Publishers Private Ltd, New Delhi, 1993, p.7.
3. Thomes G. Spates quoted in Mamoria and Gankar, *op.cit.*, p. 7.
4. Jucious quoted in *Ibid.*, p. 8.
5. Raymond W. Cox III, Susan J. Buck, Betty N. Morgan, Public Administration in Theory and Practice, Pearson Education (Singapore) Pvt. Ltd., Delhi, 2005, p. 53.
6. Sahib Singh and Swinder Singh, Local Government in India, New Academic Publishing Co., Jalandhar, 2000, p. 121.
7. Maheshwari, *op. cit.* p. 324.
8. *Ibid.*, p. 327.
9. *Ibid.*, p. 331.
10. *Ibid.*, p. 333.
11. Khem Singh, *Organisation And Working of Municipal Corporation Shimla*, Unpublished Thesis, Department of Public Administration, Panjab University, Chandigarh, 1990, p. 185.
12. *Ibid.*, p. 186.
13 Rural Urban Relationship Committee, *op.cit.*
14. *Ibid.*, p. 188.
15. W.F. Willoughby, *Principle of Public Administration*, New York, 1964, p. 220.
16. F.M. Marx, *Element of Public Administration*, Harper and Row Publishers, New York, 1966, p. 10.
17. Herman Finer, *Theory and Practice of Modern Government*, Hereditary Holt and Company, New York, 1949, p. 856.
18. *Haryana Municipal Act*, 1973, p.65.
19. *Haryana Municipal Safai Majdoor Service Rules*, 1976.
20. Glen, O. Stahl, *Public Personnel Administration*, New York, Harper and Row Publishers, 1966, p. 59.
21. E. N. Gladden, *The Civil Services, Its Problems and Future*, Staples Press, London, 1945, p. 64.
22. Stahl, *op. cit.,* p. 60.
23. Singh, *op. cit.*, p. 208.
24. *Haryana Municipal Act*, *op. cit.*, p. 706.

25. Pigours Paul and Charles A Myers, *Personnel Administration – A Point of View and Method*, McGraw Hill, New York, 1965, p. 49.
26. L. D. White, *Introduction to the Study of Public Administration*, Eurasia Publishing House (P) Ltd, New Delhi, 1968, p. 400.
27. Amreshwar Avasthi & A. Avasthi, Administrative Theory, Lakshmi Narain Agarwal, Agra, 1996, p. 297.
28. *Ibid.*, pp.301-304.
29. *Rule 18, H.M.S.I.R.C.S Rules*, 1982.
30. *Rule 9 (1) (IV), H.M.S.I.R.C.S, Rules*, 1982.
31. William G. Torpey, *Personnel Management*, D. Van Nostrand, New York, 1953, p. 154.
32. Maheswari, *op. cit.*, pp. 318-322.
33. A.R. Tyagi, "Administrative Training: A Theoretical Postulate", *International Review of Administrative Science*, Vol. XI, No. 2, 1974, p.157.
34. Singh, *op. cit.*, p. 217.
35. Marsheil. *Development Teaching*, New York, 1949, p.190.
36. Maheshwari, *op.cit.,* p. 338.
37. Henary Maddic, *Democracy, Decentralization and Development*, Asia Publishing House, Bombay, 1963, pp. 184-185.
38. Government of India, *Report of the Committee on the Training of Municipal Employees*, 1963, Part-II, Para 20.
39. Pradeep Sachdeva, *Urban Local Government and Administration in India*, Kitab Mahal, Allahabad, 1993, p. 172.
40. Government of India, *Rural Urban Relationship Committee Report*, Volume 1, 1978.
41. *H. M. S. I.R.C.S, Rule*, 1982.
42. http://www.businessdictionary.com/definition/fringe-benefit.html#ixzz2CvL1AVzm access on 21\11\2012
43. *H.M.S I. R.C.S Rule,* 1982 .
44. *Haryana Municipal Act, 1973,* p.708.
45. B.S Ghuman and A. Mehta, "Privatisation of Public Services by Urban Local Governments in India: A Case Study of Municipal Council, Panchkula", *Nagarlok,* Vol. XLII, No. 1, Jan- March, 2010, p.54.

4

FINANCIAL ADMINISTRATION OF THE MUNICIPAL COUNCIL PANCHKULA

Finance is the quite essential fuel which churns the wheels of the administrative machinery at all levels of the government i.e. national, state and local Level. White has rightly observed, "Finance and administration are in fact inseparable. Every administrative act has its financial implications, either creating a charge on treasury or making a contribution to it. Nothing can be done without the expenditure of money, at the very minimum for the payment of the salary or wage of the official or employee who acts. Available financial resources set a maximum limit for administrative activity as a whole and on each of its separate parts. The management of finance is therefore one of the first and one of the inescapable responsibilities of the administrators".[1]

The goal of the modern welfare state is to provide quantitative and qualitative public services to its citizens. This requires the availability of sufficient finances along with their prudent utilization.

4.1 Administration of Finance

"Financial administration occupies a pivotal importance today because of the tremendous increase in the amount of money being expended towards the provision of government services. It is already a well established fact that everything government does require money. It is therefore utterly essential that sound principles and techniques of financial administration be employed in the administrative set up."[2]

Financial administration is one of the most important facets of public administration as it is concerned with all the aspects of financial management of the state. In a broad sense, it includes all the processes involved in collecting, budgeting, expending public money, accounting for the financial transaction of the government and auditing income and expenditure[3].

According to White, "Fiscal management includes those operations designed to make funds available to officials and to ensure their lawful and efficient use. It also includes the control of the accounting and reporting system; treasury management and revenue collection; and audit".[4]

The need for finance has always been felt indispensable at all levels of administration for a smooth delivering of goods and services. But local government finance assumes great importance as it is nearer to people. In order to enable municipal bodies to discharge their obligation in respect of development and improvement of their respective areas, provision of civic amenities and welfare services, they require adequate financial resources commensurate with tasks assigned to them. But unfortunately, the municipal bodies in our country generally suffer from scarcity of financial resources. As far back as 1925, the Indian Taxation Enquiry Committee had noted that the finances of local bodies were inadequate for the services they were required to perform.[5]

4.2 Municipal Finance in India

The Municipal Acts of various states set out an elaborate list of obligatory and discretionary functions entrusted to the local bodies. However, besides these legally allocated functions, their responsibilities have been growing far and wide in the wake of rapid urbanization exerting a colossal pressure on the civic facilities and amenities. But, it is regrettable that the importance of these obligations with adequate resources has never been sufficiently recognized.

Table 4.1 shows the major sources of income for Municipal Bodies in India.

Table 4.1
Major Sources of Income for Municipal Bodies in India

	Source	*Component*
I	Internal Taxes	Property taxes, taxes on vehicle, animals, trade and professions: theatre/ show tax, taxes on advertisements, boats, etc.
II	Non-Tax Revenue	Rent from municipal assets, income from municipal undertakings, user charges, fees and fines, income from municipal investments.
III	External Sources grants-in-aid, shared taxes, compensation given on the lieu of abolished tax.	General purpose, specific purpose entertainment tax, motor vehicle tax, land revenue, stamp duties, exercise duties, etc.
IV	Borrowing	Municipal bodies to borrow from state government and municipals bonds.

Source: Directorate of Urban Local Bodies, Haryana.

Table 4.1 shows that the major sources of income of municipal bodies are internal taxes; non-tax revenues; external sources including grants-in-aid, shared taxes, compensation given in lieu of abolished taxes; and borrowings.

4.3 Statutory Taxation Powers of Municipalities in Haryana

According to Section 69 of The Municipal Act, Haryana 1973 (here after refer as the Act)[6], the taxation powers of the municipalities in Haryana have been divided into two parts: A. Obligatory taxes and B. Discretionary taxes.

A. Obligatory Taxes

Obligatory taxes are compulsory change the language in municipality. These taxes are as follows:

(a) A tax payable by the owner on buildings and land which should not be less than two and a half percent and more than fifteen percent , of the rate that is determined by the state government on the basis of annual value of buildings and lands;

(b) A duty on the transfer of immovable properties situated within the limits of the municipality in addition to the duty imposed under the Indian Stamp Act, 1899, on every instrument of the description specified below. The rate of such a tax should not be less than one percent and more than three percent on the amount specified below, against instrument.[7]

Description of Instruments on which Duty shall be levied

1. Sale of immovable property:- The amount or value of the consideration for the sale as set forth in the instrument.
2. Gift of immovable property: - The value of the property as set forth in the instrument.
3. Mortgage with possession of immovable property:- The amount secured by the mortgage as set forth in the instrument.
4. Lease in perpetuity of immovable property:- The amount equal to one –sixth of the whole amount or value of the rent which would be paid or delivered in respect of the first fifty years of the lease.

The above mentioned duties are collected by the Registrar or the Sub Registrar in the shape of non judicial stamp paper at the time of registration of the document. The amount of the duty so collected is paid to the Committee concerned.

B. Discretionary Taxes

According to Section 70 of the Act, the State Government can authorize the committee by general or special order from time to time, to impose any of the following taxes, tolls and fees in the whole or any part of the municipality such as : -

1. A tax on professions, trades, callings and employments;
2. A tax on vehicles, plying for hire or kept or registered under the Motor Vehicle Act, 1988,within the municipality;
3. A tax on animals used for riding, draught or burden, kept for, within or outside the municipality;
4. A tax on dogs kept within the municipality;
5. A Show Tax;
6. A toll on vehicles entering the municipality;
7. A tax on boats moved within the municipality;
8. A tax on consumption of electricity at the rate of five paise for every unit of electricity consumed ,by any person within the municipality;
9. A fire tax;
10. A sanitation tax;
11. A tax on driving licences issued under the Motor Vehicle Act, 1988, within the municipality;
12. A development tax on the increase in urban land value caused by the execution of any development or improvement work;
13. A general tax not more than 15 percent of the annual value of buildings and lands within the municipal area;

14. A fee with regard to pilgrimages;
15. A fee with regard to drainage;
16. Lighting;
17. Scavenging;
18. A fee for cleansing of latrines and privies;
19. A fee in the nature of costs for providing internal services under the scheme framed under Section 203; and
20. With the previous sanction of the state government, any other tax, toll or fee which the State Legislature has the power to impose in the state under the Constitution of India.

The rates of any tax, toll or fee mentioned above except electricity duty, is determined by the Committee concerned at such rates which are determined by the state government from time to time.[8]

4.4 Power of State Government in Respect of Taxation

According to Section 75 of the Act, the State Government can authorize the Committee to impose any tax mentioned in Section 70. However, the rate and time period of such a tax shall be determined by the State Government. The state government can direct the Committee to modify the rate of any taxes already imposed. The Committee is bound to modify such taxes within a certain period.[9]

Thus, the state government plays a pivotal role in the levy of taxes and modification of the Committee in general and Municipal Council, Panchkula, in special.

4.5 Financial Administration of Municipal Council, Panchkula

Financial administration in brief, comprises a raising of resources and their utilization by incurring expenditure with efficiency and economy. It also implies a proper co-ordination of resources and expenditure through a well considered and carefully formulated budget plan.

The financial administration of MCP has been discussed under the heads of :

A. Budgetary Process of Municipal Council, Panchkula.

In this head, the budgetary process of MCP has been discussed especially as to the entire process how is the budget passed in MCP and what are the stages involved in the intire process.

B. Income of Municipal Council Panchkula.

The income of MCP has been analysed on the following accounts: (A) the sources of income i.e. Taxes and Non Taxes Revenues (like own generated revenues) of MCP has been discussed under: (i) Major Heads of income, (ii) Income from Share Tax, and (iii) Income from Minor Heads; and (B) Grants-in-aid (financial resources transferred from state and central government).

C. Expenditure of Municipal Council, Panchkula

The expenditure pattern of MCP has been discussed in terms of the 1) Total expenditure of MCP; 2) established expenditure; 3)contingency expenditure;4) development work expenditure; and5) miscellaneous expenditure.

D. Audit and Accounts Process in Municipal Council, Panchkula

The audit and accounts process in the local bodies Haryana, and MCP has been explained, and the shortcomings of the existing audit and accounting process of MCP have also been discussed at length.

E. Analysis of the Financial Administration of Municipal Council, Panchkula

The analysis of the financial administration of MCP has been carried out on the basis of (A) Income; (B) Expenditure; and (C) Management of finances.

4.6. Budgetary Process of Municipal Council, Panchkula

As is already known, a budget is tool of financial administration. It is an important financial document. Which consists estimates of income and expenditure for the coming financial year. The Haryana Municipal Act, 1973, deals with the preparation and enactment of the budget of the municipal body in Haryana.

In MCP, the preparation of the budget is initiated by the Accounts Branch, which is headed by the Accountant. Accounts Branch issues a circular to the different departments/ wings of the Municipal Council, for submitting figures of estimated/ proposed income and expenditure during the coming financial year, in the month of September. The Departments/wings are required to submit their estimated income and expenditure by the first week of October. These estimates are then compiled by the Accounts Branch. The compilation of budget is almost over by the month of January. After the compilation of budget by the Accounts Branch, the budget is placed before the Secretary. The Secretary along with the Executive Officer and the accountant goes into the details of the budget. A thorough scrutiny of the budgetary estimates is made and necessary changes in these estimates are made after discussion. Thereafter, the budget is presented before the General House of the Council for its consideration. After the General House of the Council has passed the budget, it is sent to the District Collector for his approval.

The interactions with officials of MCP reveal that there has been delay in the approval of the budget by the State Government.

4.7 Income of Municipal Council, Panchkula

Statement of total income of MCP between 2001-2010 has been given in Table 4.2 and Figure 4.1.

Table 4.2
Statement of Total Income of the Municipal Council, Panchkula
(Figures in Rs)

Year	*Total income*
2001-02	35,597,210
2002-03	76,541,848
2003-04	75,623,413
2004-05	101,853,755
2005-06	140,808,496
2006-07	150,448,993
2007-08	224,780,000
2008-09	204,619,960
2009-10	343,255,735

Source: Accounts Department of Municipal Council, Panchkula.

Figure 4.1 Statement of Total Income of the Municipal Council, Panchkula

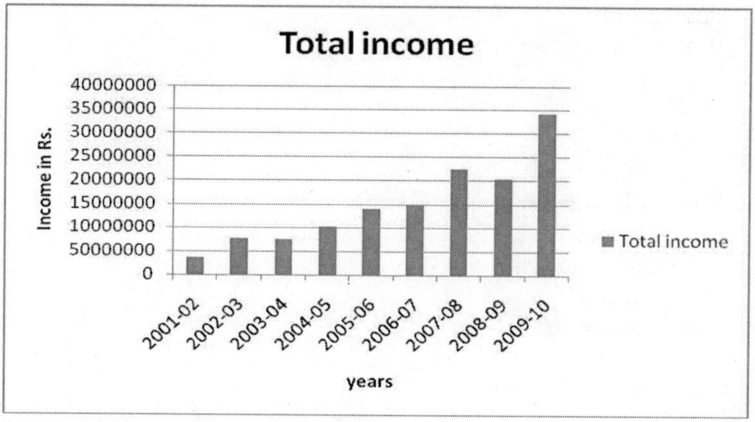

Table 4.2 and Figure 4.1 show that the total income of the Municipal Council, Panchkula increased from Rs 3.5 crore in 2001-02 to Rs 22.47 crore in the year 2007-08. This continuous increase in income over the years however was not witnessed during the year 2006-07, when it was Rs 15.04 crore as compared to Rs 14.08 crore in 2005-06. It decreased to Rs 20.46 crore in 2008-09 but again increased to Rs 3 4.32 crore in year 2009-10. An analysis of total income of MCP between 2001 to 2010 reveals that there is about 12 times increase in the total income. However, the total income of MCP has been fluctuating year wise as is evident that it was Rs 15 crore in 2006-07 but increased to Rs 22.47 crore in the year 2007-08, while in the year 2008-09 it came down to Rs 20.48 crore and then again increased to Rs 34.79 crore in the year 2009-10.

4.7.1 Sources of the Income of Municipal Council, Panchkula

The sources of income of the Municipal Council, Panchkula can be divided into the following categories:

A. Heads of Income

(i) Major Heads of Income

a. Income from Interest on Investment
b. Electricity Duty
c. House Tax
d. Show Tax
e. License U/S 12 B
f. License Vehicles
g. Fire Tax.

(ii) Income from Minor Heads

h. Copying Fee
i. Tehbazari / *Malba*
j. Fire Tax
k. Roadside Trees
l. Rent of Shops
m. Sale of Night Soil
n. Fire Call Charges
o. Dead Animals
p. Road Cut Charges
q. Composition Fees
r. Advertisement/Park Booking
s. Stray Cattle
t. Advance and Deposit

u. Buildings Application Fees
v. Miscellaneous.

(iii) Share Tax

w. Stamp Duty
x. Excise share
y. Development Charges.
z. Token Tax Driving License (Issued by the Registration Authority)

iv) Other Receipts

Za. LADT (Local Area Development Tax)
Zb. Professional Tax
Zc. Advance and deposits.

B. Grants-in-aid: Another source of income for MCP are the grants-in aid, which are received by the MCP from the centre as well as State Government from time to time .The details of this have been discussed subsequently in the chapter.

Let us now look into these sources of income in detail. Various sources have been shown in Table 4.3 and Figures 4.2.

A. Heads of Income

(i) Major Source of Income of Municipal Council, Panchkula
(a) Interest on Investment.

The income of the Municipal Council, Panchkula from interest on investment was 0.30 per cent of the total income from major heads in 2001-02. It increased to 29.19 per cent of the total income from major heads in 2004-05. However, it decreased to Rs 50 lakhs in 2007-08 during which it was 5.87 per cent of the total income from major heads. It then increased to Rs 1.7 crore in the year 2008-09, i.e., 8.2 percent of the total income from major heads. It again increased to Rs 2 crore in the year 2009-10, when it was 15.99 per cent of the total income from major heads as shown in Table 4.3 and Figure 4.2.

The income of the Municipal Council, Panchkula from electricity duty increased from Rs 32.19 lakhs in 2001-2002, i.e., 10.12 per cent of the total income to 1.05 crores in 2003-2004 which was 19.85 per cent of the total income from major heads. But, it was 25 lakhs in 2004-05, which was 5.17 per cent of the total income from major heads. It increased to one crore in 2007-08, which was 11.74 per cent of the total income from major heads. It then increased to Rs.,1.02 crore in 2008-09, which was 17.05 per cent of the total income from major heads. It further increased to Rs 2 crore in the year 2009-10, which was 15.99 per cent of the total income from major heads as shown in Table 4.3 and Figure 4.2.

Table 4.3 Sources of Income of Municipal Council Panchkula From Major Heads (Figures are in Rs)

Year	*Interest on investment*	*Electricity duty*	*House tax*	*Show tax*	*License*	*Licence vehicles U/S 12 B*	*Development charges*	*Total Income from major head*
2001-02	94,940	3,219,040	4,529,511	18,208	20,020	127,875	23,797,018	31,806,612
Percentage	0.30	10.12	14.24	0.06	0.06	0.40	74.82	100.00
2002-03	278,895	5,000,000	26,047,123	12,416	15,160	10,002	57,527	31,421,123
Percentage	0.89	15.91	82.90	0.04	0.05	0.03	0.18	100.00
2003-04	909,851	10,500,000	41,453,275	13,728	7,635	904	—	52,885,393
Percentage	1.72	19.85	78.38	0.03	0.01	0.00	-	100.00
2004-05	14,108,567	2,500,000	31,652,063	2,912	64,071	10,684	—	48,338,297
Percentage	29.19	5.17	65.48	0.01	0.13	0.02	-	100.00
2005-06	7,029,040	13,423,684	33,394,183	660	79,272	56,996	—	53,983,835
Percentage	13.02	24.87	61.86	0.00	0.15	0.11	-	100.00
2006-07	10,594,469	12,818,513	35,314,411	0	94,563	37,290	289,028	59,148,264
Percentage	17.91	21.67	59.70	0.00	0.16	0.06	0.49	100.00
2007-08	5,000,000	10,000,000	40,000,000	10,000	100,000	50,000	30,000,000	85,160,000
Percentage	5.87	11.74	46.97	0.01	0.12	0.06	35.23	100.00
2008-09	17,071,224	10,253,366	32,747,237	0	65,300	7,786	0	60,144,913
Percentage	28.38	17.05	54.45	0.00	0.11	0.01	0.00	100.00
2009-2010	20,000,000	20,000,000	45,000,000	1,000	100,000	15,000	40,000,000	125,116,000
Percentage	15.99	15.99	35.97	0.00	0.08	0.01	31.97	100.00

Source: Accounts Branch of MCP.

Figure 4.2 Sources of Income of Municipal Council Panchkula From Major Heads

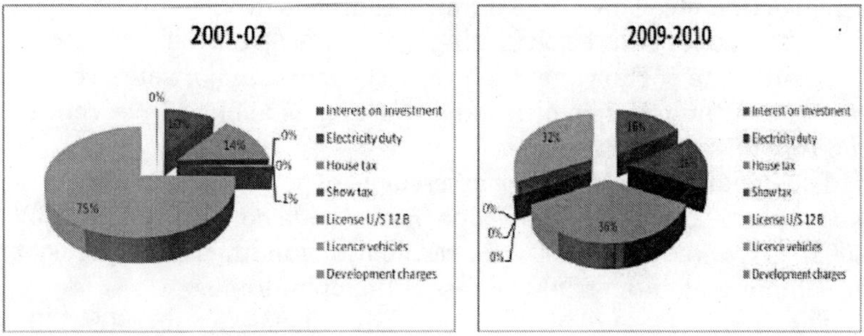

(b) Electricity Duty

Under the provisions of the Haryana Municipal Act, a tax on the consumption of electricity at the rate of one paisa per unit of electricity consumed within the limits of the municipality, can be levied subject to general or special order of the state government. The state government vide its notification dated 28-12-1990 decided that each Municipal Committee shall impose this tax within a period of one year from the date of issue of the notification, on the basis of resolution to be passed by the individual municipality. But factually, this levy came in operation from 1.7.1992 in all municipalities uniformly, at the rate of one paisa per unit. This levy was to be collected by the power utilities and paid to the concerned municipalities in the same manner as electricity duty is paid by the power utilities to the State Government. Subsequently, the State Government vide order dated 16th May, 2000 revised the rates of tax on electricity from one paisa to five paisa per unit of electricity consumed within the municipal limit.

(c) House Tax (Property Tax)

Property Tax is one of the major sources of revenue for municipalities all over the country. It has been estimated that nearly 30 per cent to 40 per cent of the municipal revenue is generated by this tax alone. Normally, this tax levied in terms of the annual rental value, is highly subjective, giving rise to malpractices at every level. However, in view of the difficulties faced in knowing the actual rent charged from different categories of buildings and the prevailing malpractices, many states have delinked property tax from the rental value concept and have switched over to the area linked scheme based on standardised plinth area costs. The "unit area" value is to be determined based on the location, structural characteristics, age of the building, use to which the building is being put, the quality of construction etc. The entire municipal area is divided into various zones/sub zones before calculating the unit area annual value.[10]

In the state of Haryana, the property tax is a major source of tax revenue of the municipalities and constitutes about 46 per cent of their own revenues.

The Rental Value Method of assessment of property tax in Haryana was replaced by the Capital Value System vide notification No.9/32/2001-5C1, dated 13-12-2001, for residential buildings and 5 per cent on commercial, industrial and institutional buildings [11].

The House Tax is levied on an annual basis. From 2006-2007 onwards there was a provision for 10 per cent rebate (discount) on the payment of house tax within 30 days of the receipt of the House Tax Bill. Now, this rebate has been increased to 15 per cent of the total dues. In case the due amount is not paid within 30 days, there is a provision for penalty being charged at the rate of 10 per cent of the total amount.

From the year 2004-2005, the Haryana Government has initiated certain new policy measures with respect to House Tax. Some of the important measures are as follows:

- i The House Tax on construction over an area less than 100 yards would be exempted.
- ii There would be no House Tax levied to the tune of Rs 8,000/ per year in case of widows.
- iii Now in addition to the ex-servicemen, who were earlier exempted from the House Tax, even the property in the name of their family members will be exempted.
- iv All government offices/buildings have been exempted from the payment of House Tax.
- v Special relaxation was given to those who had for some reason, failed to deposit this House Tax. All of them were given an opportunity to deposit the same within the time period from July 2007 to September 2008 with a provision that no penalty/additional charges will be levied on them[12].

The income of the Municipal Council, Panchkula, from house tax increased from Rs 45.23 Lakhs to Rs 4.14 crores from 2001-02 to 2003-04. It was 11.69 per cent of the total income from major heads in 2001-02. It then increased to a 78.38 per cent of the total income from major heads in 2003-04 but then decreased to Rs four crore in 2007-08 which was 46.97 per cent of the total income from major heads. The reason for this decline was the time to time exemption given to the citizens by the State Government. It is relevant to note here that the percentage recovery of House Tax and Rent was far below than 90 per cent of the norms fixed by the Government[13]. It again decreased to Rs 3.2 crore in the year 2008-09 which was 54.45 percent of the total income from major heads. It increased to Rs 4.5 crore in the year 2009-10, which was 35.97 per cent of the total income from major heads as shown in Table 4.3 and Figure 4.2.

(d) Entertainment Duty and Show Tax

The entertainment tax is levied by all the states primarily on all cinema halls/video parlours etc. located in an urban area. Many states also impose a surcharge as well as a Show Tax Commercial Taxation Department is the agency which administers this Act. The entertainment Tax/Show Tax is basically levied in lieu of all the municipal services being availed by the owners of the cinema halls/ video parlours. Since entertainment tax is essentially local in character, it is paid by the local residents and therefore, there is a strong case for passing on wholly or partly the income from this source to the local bodies.

The Zakaria Committee (1963) was set up to recommend measures for the augmentation of financial resources of the urban bodies. It recommended that 25 per cent of the proceeds of the entertainment tax should be earmarked for the urban local bodies.[14]

The First State Finance Commission of Haryana had also recommended a transfer of 50 per cent of net income from entertainment tax and the entire net income from Show Tax to the urban local bodies.[15]

As regards to the Show Tax, presently, it stands abolished. Even if levied, it would be paid by the proprietors. The Second State Finance Commission is of the view that the Show Tax should be re-imposed on the entertainment duty at the rate of 10 per cent and the entire amount should be passed on to the concerned municipality within whose area the collection is made.[16]

The income of the Municipal Council, Panchkula from Show tax was Rs 18.20 thousands in 2001-02 but it started decreasing in the subsequent years, and in 2006-07, it was nil. It was 10 thousand in 2007-08 ,while in the year 2008-09,the collection under this head was again nil. It was five thousand rupees in 2009-10 as shown in Table 4.3 and Figure 4.2.

The Show Tax is collected from cinema halls on the basis of their seating capacity of the cinema hall.[17]

The entertainment duty and show tax are collected by the Excise and Taxation Department in Haryana under the provisions of "The Punjab Entertainment Duty Act, 1955" and "The Punjab Entertainments Tax (Cinematograph Shows) Act, 1954", respectively.[18]

The entertainment duty was levied at the rate of 12.5 per cent over the past many years in the State. A show tax at the rate of 9 per cent was charged on the total collection of entertainment duty before 1-7-2001, which was paid solely by the proprietors of the cinema halls. The State Government reduced the rate of entertainment tax from 50 per cent to 12.5 per cent on the basic admission rates on cinema halls/video parlors, and to 25 per cent on all other entertainments w.e.f. 1.7.2001 with a view to encourage cinema industry in the State.[19]

(e) Licences Under Section 12 B

Under the Haryana Municipal Act, 1973, Section 12 B, Municipal Council, Panchkula collects tax on the licenses issued for items such as *Karyana*, Coal, Broom, Kerosene Oil and Factory, etc. under the jurisdiction of Municipal Council, Panchkula etc.[20]

The total income of Municipal Council, Panchkula from major head licence under Section 12 B increased from Rs 20 thousand in year 2001-2002 to Rs one lakh in the year 2009-2010 as shown in Table 4.3 and Figure 4.2.

(f) Licensed Vehicles

Motor vehicles of different descriptions are registered under the provisions of the Indian Motor Vehicles Act, 1988 and rules made there under. Taxes/fees are levied under the provision of Punjab Motor Vehicles Taxation Act/Rules as applicable to the State of Haryana. The Vehicle Tax has been a good source of income for the states but the local bodies have been demanding their share of revenue since the infrastructure of the cities, especially roads are used by the transporters and vehicles of different categories that put a lot of pressure on other urban infrastructure.[21]

Recommendations were made by the Rural Urban Relationship Committee (1966), Central Council of Local Government and Urban Development and the All India Council of Mayors (1970-1980), that a part of the Vehicle Tax should be transferred to the urban local bodies.

First State Finance Commission also recommended that 20 per cent of the net proceeds of vehicle tax be transferred to urban local bodies.[22]

The State Government issued a notification w.e.f. 16.5.2000 to impose a tax on vehicles at the time of new registration/payment of token tax @ of lump sum of Rs 50 for moped, Rs 100 for scooter/ motor cycle, Rs 500 for car and at the rate of five per cent of the token tax payable on other heavy vehicles. This amount so collected shall be paid to the municipality by the registering authority.[23]

A tax on driving license @ Rs 100 per driving licence issued under the Motor Vehicles Act of 1988 has been levied w.e.f. 16.5.2000. The amount so collected by the Licensing Authority is to be remitted to the concerned municipal body.

In Municipal Council, Panchkula, the licenses are given to the vehicles such as rehri, rickshaw, pony, etc. The licence fee levied on rehries was Rs 35 per rehries. However, this tax on rehries has been reduced to Rs one per *rehri*.[24]

Income from license vehicles in Municipal Council, Panchkula decreased from Rs 1.27 lakhs in 2001-02 to Rs 37.2 thousands in 2006-07. It then increased to Rs 57 thousand in 2008-09 and it then decreased to Rs 15,000 in the year 2009-10 as shown in Table 4.3 and Figure 4.2.

(g) Development Charges

This tax is collected by Haryana Urban Development Authority (HUDA) on an agreement with the Municipal Council, Panchkula that 75 per cent of the charges thus collected, would be given to Municipal Council, Panchkula. The Development Charges are imposed on new sectors being developed, for example, Sector – 31, Panchkula. These charges are to the tune of Rs 120 per square meter. In case of new development activity taking place in old sectors, the charges imposed are to the tune of Rs 55 per square meter. However, unfortunately, HUDA has failed to honour the agreement and has not paid even a single rupee for the years 2003-04 to 2005-06.

The income of Municipal Council, Panchkula from the development charges decreased from Rs 2.37 crores in 2001-02 to Rs 2.8 lakhs in 2006-07. It then increased to Rs three crores in 2007-08 which was 35.23 percent of the total income from major heads. However, the income from this head was nil in 2008-09. It increased to Rs four crore in the year 2009-10 which was 31.97 per cent of the total income from major heads as shown in Table 4.3 and Figure 4.2.

It is noteworthy to mention here that thoughts the income from this source is not much, still the Municipal Council Panchkula should have taken effective steps to get the agreement between HUDA

(Haryana Urban Development Authority) and Municipal Council, Panchkula implemented in letter and spirit.

(ii) Minor Sources of Income of Municipal Council Panchkula

Income from minor sources of MCP has been shown in Table 4.4.

(h) Copying Duty

A copying fee to the tune of Rs.10 per page, is being charged. The sources of copying fee include copy of the building maps, copy of the land record, information sought under RTI, etc. Earlier during the time periods 2001-02 and 2002-03, Haryana Urban Development Authority used to levy this tax.[25]

The income of Municipal Council Panchkula from copying fee increased from Rs 375 in the year 2003-2004 to Rs 10,000 in year the 2007-08. It decreased to Rs 4,000 in the year 2008-09 and increased to Rs 5,000 in the year 2009-10, which was 0.04 percent of the total income as shown in Table 4.4.

(i) Tehbazari / Malba

It is collected by the Municipal Council, Panchkula for picking *Malba* from houses in the jurisdiction of Municipal Council, Panchkula.

The income of Municipal Council, Panchkula from *Tehbazari-Malba* increased from Rs 72 thousands in 2002-03 to Rs 1.5 lakhs in 2007-08. It then decreased to 50 thousand in 2008-09 but again increased to Rs 1.5 lakhs in the year 2009-10 as shown in Table 4.4.

(j) Road Side Trees

This income comes through selling of roadside trees falling within the Municipal Council, Panchkula jurisdiction. The income of Municipal Council, Panchkula from road side trees was Rs 1.4 lakhs in the year 2001-02. It was Rs 10 thousand in the year 2007-08. It then decreased to nil in 2008-09. But it again increased to Rs 10 thousand in the year 2009-10 as shown in Table 4.4.

(k) Rent of Shops

This rent is collected and levied by Municipal Council, Panchkula. For example, there are thirteen shops in the Majri village, which are owned by Municipal Council, Panchkula. The shops are charged a rent of Rs 800 to Rs 1000 per month.[26]

Table 4.4 Income of MCP from Minor Heads (Figures are in Rs)

Year	*Copying duty*	*Tehbazari / Malba*	*Road side trees*	*Rent of shops*	*Fire call charges*	*Dead animals*	*Road cut charges*
2001-02	—	1,057,903	140,483				7,285
Percentage	-	83.51	11.09	0.00	0.00	0.00	0.58
2002-03	0	72,000	0	163,360	3,500	10,462	250
Percentage	0.00	0.78	0.00	1.76	0.04	0.11	0.00
2003-04	375	94,010		168,645	2,973	110,500	57,612
Percentage	0.00	0.85	0.00	1.52	0.03	1.00	0.52
2004-05	3,485	85,500		138,280	3,390	70,000	260,112
Percentage	0.09	2.09	0.00	3.39	0.08	1.71	6.37
2005-06	1,030	61,200		88,881	10,760	190,000	3,743,972
Percentage	0.01	0.67	0.00	0.98	0.12	2.10	41.29
2006-07	2,900	95,000		91,554	6,800	165,000	975,850
Percentage	0.03	1.02	0.00	0.99	0.07	1.78	10.50
2007-08	10,000	150,000	10,000	150,000	60,000	190,000	2,800,000
Percentage	0.10	1.51	0.10	1.51	0.60	1.92	28.23
2008-09	4,000	50,400	0	61,873	55,242	126,000	906,120
Percentage	0.13	1.61	0.00	1.97	1.76	4.01	28.86
2009-10	5,000	150,000	10,000	100,000	60,000	150,000	1,500,000
Percentage	0.04	1.10	0.07	0.73	0.44	1.10	10.98

Source: Accounts Branch of MCP.

Composition fees	Advertisement/ Park booking	Stray cattle	Building Application fees	Miscellaneous	Fire tax	Fire call charges	Total Income from Minor Head
			40,845	20,225			1,266,741
0.00	0.00	0.00	3.22	1.60	0.00	0.00	100.00
32430	0	872,454	0	2,000,000	6,103,585	3,500	9,261,541
0.35	0.00	9.42	0.00	21.59	65.90	0.04	100.00
55232	331,325		10,980		10,224,855	2,973	11,059,480
0.50	3.00	0.00	0.10	0.00	92.45	0.03	100.00
40345	1,167,987		8,713		2,302,883	3,390	4,084,085
0.99	28.60	0.00	0.21	0.00	56.39	0.08	100.00
51980	454,963		7,331	377,275	4,069,167	10,760	9,067,319
0.57	5.02	0.00	0.08	4.16	44.88	0.12	100.00
112769	230,302	12,900	17,426	299,000	3,640,737	3640,737	9,290,975
1.21	2.48	0.14	0.19	3.22	39.19	39.19	100.00
100000	550,000	100,000	40,000	700,000	5,000,000	60,000	9,920,000
1.01	5.54	1.01	0.40	7.06	50.40	0.60	100.00
70150	83,581	47,300	27,354	190,694	1,461,779	55,242	3,139,735
2.23	2.66	1.51	0.87	6.07	46.56	1.76	100.00
50000	1,000,000	100,000	30,000	500,000	4,000,000	6,000,000	3,139,735
0.37	7.32	0.73	0.22	3.66	29.29	43.94	100.00

The income of Municipal Council, Panchkula from rent of shops was Rs 1.63 lakh during the year 2002-03 and it decreased to Rs 1.5 lakhs in 2007-08. It again decreased to Rs.61 thousand in the year 2008-09. However, it again increased to Rs one lakh in the year 2009-10 ,as shown in Table 4.4.

(l) Fire Call Charges

Municipal Council Panchkula collects this charge on the fire calling. The fire call charges are as follows:

No fire call charges are levied if a call is received for a fire incident within the jurisdiction of Municipal Council, Panchkula. This charge is collected for the fire incident outside the jurisdiction of Municipal Council, Panchkula at the rate of Rs 300 per hour.

The income of Municipal Council, Panchkula from fire call charges increased from Rs 3,500 in 2002-03 to Rs 55 thousands in 2008-09 and again increased to Rs 60 thousand in the year 2009-10, as shown in Table 4.4.

(m) Sale of Dead Animals

It comes through the contract awarded, whereby a fixed amount is collected from the contractor. The contractor, in turn derives his income by selling the skin, bones etc of the dead animal.

The income of Municipal Council, Panchkula from dead animals increased from Rs 10.4 thousands in 2002-03 to Rs 1.9 lakhs in 2007-08. It increased to Rs 1.26 lakhs in 2008-09 and again increased to Rs 1.5 lakhs in the year 2009-10, which was 1.10 per cent of the total income from minor heads, as shown in Table 4.4.

(n) Road Cut Charges

The Road Cut Tax charge is collected on account of cuts /damages made and the digging of roads for the purpose of laying cable, sewerage/drainage pipe, water pipes, etc.

The Income of Municipal Council, Panchkula from roads cut charges increased from Rs 7285 in the year 2001-02 to Rs 28 lakhs during 2007-08.But it then decreased to Rs nine lakhs during 2008-09. However, it again increased to Rs 15 lakhs which was 10.98 per \cent of total income from minor heads in the year 2009-10, as shown in Table 4.4. It is pertinent to note here that the residents of various localities rue that roads cut by different agencies are hardly ever repaired by Municipal Council, Panchkula.

(o) Composition Fee

It is collected by Municipal Council, Panchkula, by imposing fine on those violating the license condition. The composition fee starts from Rs 250 and can be charged up to Rs5,000. For example, those selling polythene are liable to pay a fine of Rs 1,000.

The income from Composition Fee of Municipal Council, Panchkula increased from Rs 32.4 thousands in 2002-2003, to Rs one lakh which was 1.01 per cent of the total income from minor heads in 2007-08. But it decreased to Rs 70 thousand in 2008-09 and further decreased to Rs 50 thousand in the year 2009-10, as shown in Table 4.4.

(p) Park Booking

Park booking charges are collected by Municipal Council, Panchkula for the purposes such as bookings for marriages, other functions/ parties/ ceremonies, etc. These charges are Rs 5,000 in case of underdeveloped parks.

The income of Municipal Council, Panchkula from park booking was Rs 3.31 lakhs in 2003-04 and Rs 5.5 lakhs in 2007-08 which was 3.31 per cent and 5.54 per cent of the total income from minor heads, respectively. It decreased to Rs 83 thousand in 2008-09, but increased to Rs 10 lakhs in the year 2009-10, as shown in Table 4.4.

(q) Stray Cattle

It comes through the catching of stray animal at the time of their subsequent release. An owner of stray cattle has to pay a penalty of Rs 500 in case of young cattle and Rs 1,000- in case of fully-grown cattle. The income of Municipal Council, Panchkula from stray cattle was Rs 8.7 lakhs in 2002-03 which was 9.42 per cent of the total income from minor heads and it decreased to Rs 12.9 thousands in 2006-07. It increased to Rs one lakh in 2007-08 which was 1.01 per cent of the total income from minor heads. It decreased to 47 thousands in 2008-09, but increased to Rs one lakh in the year 2009-10, as shown in Table 4.4.

(r) Building Application Fee

This fees is collected by Municipal Council, Panchkula from two types of applicants, namely, domestic users and commercial users. Domestic users are charged a building application fees at the rate of Rs one per square feet. Commercial users are charged a building application fees of Rs five per square feet. However, since the year 2004, the building application fee rates have been revised. The new rates are as follows:

I Domestic users: 20 paisa per square feet.
II Commercial users: Re one per square feet.

The income of Municipal Council, Panchkula from Building Application Fee decreased from Rs 40 thousand in 2001-02 to Rs 27 thousand in the year 2008-09, as shown in Table 4.4.

(s) Fire Tax

Municipal Council Panchkula collects Fire Tax at the rate of 2.5 per cent from domestic users and five per cent from commercial users. In the year 2002-03, it was 65.90 per cent of the total income from minor heads and increased to 92.45 per cent of the total income in 2003-04. The onus of depositing this tax lies with the house owners and owners of commercial properties. A perusal of the Table 4.4 shows that there has been a huge decrease in income from this source. This can be attributed to the fact that neither the property owners have been serious in depositing this tax, nor the municipal officers have made any serious attempt to realize this tax from the property owners. This has resulted in substantial loss of revenue to the Municipal Council, Panchkula. Further, it increased to Rs 50 lakhs in 2007-08 which was 50.40 per cent of total income from minor heads, but decreased to Rs 14 lakhs during 2008-09. It again increased to Rs 40 lakhs in the year 2009-10 which was 29.29 per cent of the total income from minor heads, as shown in Table 4.4.

(iii) Income from Share Tax of Municipal Council, Panchkula

The share tax is the tax which is transferred by the State Government to MCP. The income of MCP from share tax has been shown in Table 4.5 and Figure 4.3.

(t) Stamp Duty

Stamp Duty is an important source of revenue for the State Government. It is imposed on transfer of immoveable property both in rural and urban area, in the State. This is an elastic source of revenue.

In the case of municipal areas, the local bodies are empowered to impose an additional duty on the transfer of immoveable property within the limit of municipalities in addition to the duty imposed under the Indian Stamp Act.[27]

Table 4.5 Income of MCP from Share Tax (Figures are in Rs)

Year	*Stamp Duty*	*Token Tax Driving License*	*Excise Share*	*Total Income from Share Tax*
2001-02	0	21,07,154	0	2,107,154
	0.00	100.00	0.00	100.00
2002-03	33049902	2,053,592	0	35,103,494
	94.15	5.85	0.00	100.00
2003-04	5475819	2,259,453	0	7,735,272
	70.79	29.21	0.00	100.00
2004-05	44894345	2,349,404	323,000	47,566,749
	94.38	4.94	0.68	100.00
2005-06	56676739	2,105,622	0	58,782,361
	96.42	3.58	0.00	100.00
2006-07	46189828	3,083,714	2,919,528	52,193,070
	88.50	5.91	5.59	100.00
2007-08	100000000	3,000,000	5,000,000	108,000,000
	92.59	2.78	4.63	100.00
2008-09	135302379	2,260,579	0	137,562,958
	98.36	1.64	0.00	100.00
2009-10	200000000	3,000,000	10,000,000	213,000,000
	93.90	1.41	4.69	100.00

Source: Accounts Branch of MCP.

Figure 4.3 Income of MCP from Share Tax

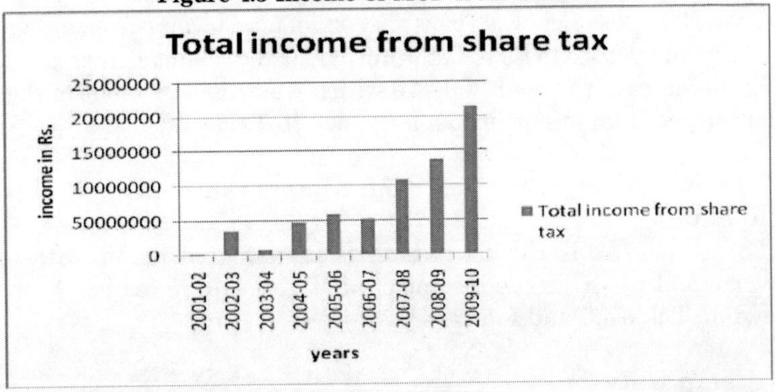

The stamp duty was being charged at the rate of 15½ per cent in municipal areas, up to February, 2004. The state government reduced the stamp duty rates w.e.f. 1.3.2004 to 8 per cent in urban areas.[28]

Municipal Council, Panchkula, collected stamp duty on the registry of land/ property. Earlier Haryana Government used to collect 15 per cent stamp duty out of which 3 per cent was the share of Municipal Council, Panchkula. However, from the year 2004, this stamp duty levied by Haryana Government and its share distributed to Municipal Council, Panchkula has been worked out on the basis of the following categories:

I In case where properties are owned by a male, eight per cent stamp duty has been imposed, out of which 2 per cent is given to Municipal Council, Panchkula.

II In case where properties are owned by both male and female, seven per cent stamp duty has been imposed, out of which two per cent is given to Municipal Council, Panchkula.

III In case where property is owned by a female, four per cent of stamp duty has been imposed, out of which two per cent is given to Municipal Council, Panchkula.

The income of Municipal Council, Panchkula from stamp duty increased from Rs 3.3 crores in 2002-03 to Rs 4.6 crore during the year 2006-07, which was 94.15 and 88.50 per cent of the total income from share tax respectively. It increased to Rs 10.0 crores in 2007-08, which was 44.49 per cent of the total income. It again increased to Rs 13 crore in 2008-09, which was 65.7 per cent of the total income from share tax. It further increased to Rs 20 crore in the year 2009-10, which was 54.3 per cent of the total income from share tax, as shown in Table 4.5 and Figure 4.3.

(u) Tax on Driving Licences

Tax on driving @ Rs 100 per driving license issued under the Motor Vehicles Act of 1988, has been levied w.e.f. 16.5.2000. The amount collected by the licensing authority is to be remitted to the concerned municipal body.

The income of Municipal Council, Panchkula from token tax on driving license increased from Rs 21.0 lakhs in 2001-02 to Rs 30.83 lakhs in 2006-07 and it decreased to Rs 30 lakhs in 2007-08, which was 2.78 per cent of the total income from share tax. It decreased to Rs 22 lakhs in 2008-09, which was 1.64 per cent of total income from share tax. It further, increased to Rs 30 lakhs in the year 2009-10, which was 1.41 per cent of the total income as shown in Table 4.5 and Figure 4.3.

(v) Excise Share

Excise duty falls in the category of shared taxes. An excise duty at the rate of Re one per bottle of liquor sold in jurisdiction of the local bodies is passed on to the concerned Municipal Council as per their entitlement and Rs five per bottle of wine. But in Municipal Council, Panchkula, no excise share was transferred to the Council during the years 2001-02, 2002-03, 2003-04 and 2005-06. It shows that no specific sharing criterion for excise duty was observed by Municipal Council, Panchkula. Recently, a request was made to the government to transfer the excise duty to Municipal Council, Panchkula.

The income of Municipal Council, Panchkula from excise share increased from Rs 3.2 lakhs in 2004-05 to Rs 29.1 lakhs in 2006-07. It furtherto Rs 50 lakhs in 2007-08, which was Rs 4.63 per cent of total income from share tax. In 2008-09 the collection under this head was nil. It increased to Rs one crore in the year 2009-10, which was 4.69 per cent of the total income from share tax as shown in Table 4.5 and Figure 4.3.

(iv) Other Money Receipts by MCP

The income of MCP between 2001 to 2010 from other sources has been shown in Table 4.6 and Figure 4.4.

(w) Advance and Deposit

It is a type of earnest money, that comes from the contractor. This is a type of security which is deposited by a contractor at the time of sanctioning of a contract. But, it has to be returned to the contractor .Therefore, it cannot be counted as income.

The income of Municipal Council, Panchkula from advance and deposit increased from Rs 3.2 lakhs in 2001-02 to Rs 51 lakhs in 2006-07, which was 17.29 per cent of the total income from other sources. It decreased to Rs 37 lakhs in 2008-09 and further decreased to Rs 20 lakhs in the year 2009-10, which was cent per cent of the total income from other sources as shown in Table 4.6 and Figure 4.4.

Table 4.6 Income of MCP from Other Sources (Figures are in Rs)

Year	*Advance and Deposit*	*Professional Tax*	*Local Area Development Tax*	*Total Income from Other Sources*
2001-02	325,643	91,060	0	416,703
	78.15	21.85	0.00	100.00
2002-03	0	755,690		755,690
	0.00	100.00	0.00	100.00
2003-04	3,800,768	142,500	0	3,943,268
	96.39	3.61	0.00	100.00
2004-05	1,864,624	0	0	1,864,624
	100.00	0.00	0.00	100.00
2005-06	1,974,981	0	17,000,000	18,974,981
	10.41	0.00	89.59	100.00
2006-07	5,156,684	0	24,660,000	29,816,684
	17.29	0.00	82.71	100.00
2007-08	1,700,000	0	20,000,000	21,700,000
	7.83	0.00	92.17	100.00
2008-09	3,772,354	0	0	3,772,354
	100.00	0.00	0.00	100
2009-10	2,000,000	0	0	2,000,000
	100.00	0.00	0.00	100

Source: Accounts Branch of MCP.

Figure 4.4 Income of MCP from Other Sources

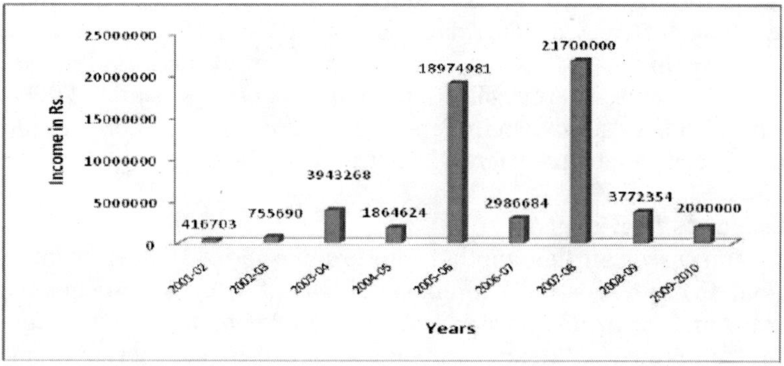

(x) Professional Tax

Professional tax was initially levied on professionals such as engineers, doctors, and managers of coaching centers, which was abolished later. Municipal Council, Panchkula prior to the year 2004, used to collect Professional Tax.

The income of Municipal Council, Panchkula from professional tax increased from Rs 91.06 thousand in 2001-2002 to Rs 1.42. Lakhs, which was 3.61 per cent of the total income from other sources in 2003-2004. The professional tax remained much below the sanctioned budget estimate for the year 2003-2004, i.e., the target was Rs 7,00,000 and the actual collection was Rs 1,42,500. [29]

In terms of proportion of the percentage in total receipts, the professional tax increased from 0.23 per cent in 2001-02 to 0.98 per cent in 2003-04 of the total expenditure. And in terms of proportion in total receipts, the professional tax came down to 0.18 per cent in 2003-04 of the total expenditure as shown in Table 4.6 and Figure 4.4.

(y) Local Area Development Tax

The State Government abolished octroi in the State from 1.11.1999. This measure pre-empted the municipalities of their major source of tax revenue. Since the decision to abolish octroi was taken in the interest of free flow of trade and industry, it became a moral duty of the State Government either to compensate the municipalities of the consequential loss or to provide alternate sources of revenue.

Accordingly, the Haryana Local Area Development Tax Act, 2000 (LADT Act) was enacted to provide for levy and collection of tax on the entry. The LADT Act, 2000 came into force w.e.f. 5th May, 2000. The authority for the tax administration is the Excise and Taxation Department of the local areas.

The income of Municipal Council, Panchkula from Local Area Development Tax was Rs 1.7 crore in 2005-06 and it increased to Rs 2.46 crore in 2006-07, which was 82.1 per cent of the total income from other sources. And collection under this head was nil in 2008-09 and 2009-10, as shown in Table 4.6 and Figure 4.4. There are no specific criteria for transfer of LADT to Local Bodies.

B. Grants-in-Aid

As discussed earlier, another source of income of MCP is Grants-in-aid. In any discussion of municipal finance, the role of government grants and contributions assume considerable importance. 'Grants' may be defined as a sum of money assigned by a superior to an inferior governmental authority to aid it in the discharge of its function. There are four types of grants.

1. **General Purpose Grants:** These grants are primarily intended to substantially bridge the gap between the needs and resources of the local bodies. The only condition laid down in the rules for their eligibility is that the municipal council should have imposed taxes prescribed by the municipal laws and taken all necessary steps for their realization.
2. **Specific Purpose Grants**: These grants are tied to the provision of certain services for the performance of certain tasks. Such services rendered by the municipal bodies may fall under the obligation of the state government also or they may be national in character. These grants cover the provision of services such as water supply and drainage; housing, public works, roads, drains etc; maintenance of dispensaries, schools, fire-fighting services and so on. It is also called conditional grant.
3. **Statutory and Compensatory Grants**: These grants are given under various enactments of local bodies and compensations on account of loss of any revenue on taking over a tax by the state government from the local government. It is a compulsory transfer. Statutory grants are compulsory transfers which may also be in lieu of abolition or withdrawal of certain taxes such as octroi.
4. **Grants from Central Government**: Inadequate financial resources and financial crisis bounds the local bodies to seek grants-in-aid from the Central Government. grants-in-aid given by the State government are ad-hoc and discretionary in nature, depending largely on the availability of funds with the State.[30]

There is often a confusion between grants-in-aid of revenue and grants-in-lieu of some tax abolished or withdrawn from the local domain. The latter is a kind of compensation for loss of revenue because of dis-empowering of a local body by a legislative action. This should therefore, be treated as a local body share in general pool of net proceeds. The grants in aid are given to urban local bodies by the state government in accordance with certain mandatory principles.

4.7.2 Sources of Grants in Aid to Local Bodies in Haryana

The Grants Transferred to Urban Local Bodies in Haryana by Central Finance Commissions

Consequent to the 73rd Constitutional Amendment Act, 1992, the new sub-clauses (b and c) were inserted in clause (3) of the Art 280 of the Constitution relating to the function of Finance Commission requiring Central Finance Commission to suggest:

"The measures needed to augment the Consolidated Fund of a State to supplement the resources of the rural and urban local bodies in the state on the basis of the recommendations made by the Finance Commission of the state".[31]

On the basis of this, various Central Finance Commissions have made recommendations for the local self governments as discussed below:

(A) Tenth Finance Commission:

Though the above stated Amendment (73rd) came after setting up of the tenth Finance Commission yet keeping in view the spirit of these amendments and likely changes in the status of local bodies, the 10th Finance Commission recommended an ad-hoc provision of grants of Rs 1,000 crore for urban local bodies for the period 1995-2000. This amount was to be distributed among the states on the basis of the inter-state ratio of slum population. The share of State of Haryana in the total allocation was Rs 16.58 crore.[32]

However, Rs 12.44 crore against the allocation of Rs 16.58 crore grant was received from the Government of India which was transferred to the urban local bodies and distributed as per the laid down criteria. The balance grant of Rs 4.14 crore was not released to the State Government as election of (ULB) urban local bodies were not held as per the schedule.[33]

(B) Eleventh Finance Commission (EFC)

The term of reference of the EFC required it to make recommendations on the measures needed to augment the Consolidated Fund of the State to supplement the resources of the panchayats and municipalities on the basis of the recommendations of the State Finance Commissions (SFCs). However, where SFCs were not constituted or did not submit the recommendations, the EFC was required to make its own assessment on the matter.

The EFC recommended grants amounting to Rs. 2000 crore for the municipalities for the period between 2000-2005. The EFC desired that the local bodies grant should be utilised for maintenance of civic services in urban areas which include provision of primary education, primary healthcare, safe drinking water, street lighting, sanitation, maintenance of cremation and burial grounds, public conveniences and other common property resources. The EFC allocated Rs 36.64 crore to Haryana State Government for the development of urban local bodies. Henceforth, Rs 7.33 crore are being transferred to ULB annually.[33] However, MCP received Rs 45 lakhs, 27 lakhs and 51 lakhs grant in the year 2005-06, 2006-07 and 2007-08 respectively (See Table 4.7).

(C) Twelfth Finance Commission (TFC)

The Twelfth Finance Commission (TFC) felt that at least 50 per cent of the grants-in-aid provided to each state for the urban local bodies should be earmarked for the scheme of solid waste management, through public private partnership. According to TFC, the municipalities should concentrate on the collection, segregation and transportation of solid waste. The cost of these activities whether carried out in house or sourced could be met from the grants.

The TFC has urged that the states may require municipalities of towns of over 1,00,000 population as per 2001 census, to prepare acomprehensive scheme including composting and waste to energy programs to be undertaken in the private sector for appropriate funding from the grants recommended by the TFC.

The TFC attempted to adopt the equalisation principle and provided only a grant of Rs 20,000 crore for PRI and Rs 5,000 crore for Urban Local Bodies. The share of the State of Haryana was Rs 91 crore. However, MCP received Rs 18 lakhs and 27 lakhs grant in the year 2007-08 and 2008-09 respectively (See Table 4.7).

(D) Thirteenth Finance Commission

The report of the Thirteenth Finance Commission (FC) is a mark departure from the earlier reports and has for the first time, recommended a share transfer from the divisible pool being a general basic grant amounting to 1.5 per cent and performance grant amounting to one per cent of the divisible pool. This method has increased the volume of transfers to the tune of Rs 231,110 million which is four and a half (4½) times higher than 50,000 million of TFC. The Thirteenth Finance Commission also introduced a reform agenda to be linked with the performance grants.

4.7.3 The State Finance Commission (SFC) (Article 243Y)

The State Finance Commission constituted under Article 243(Y) reviews the financial position of the municipalities and make recommendations to the Governor:

(a) The principles, which should govern

i. the distribution between the state and the municipalities of the net proceeds of the taxes, duties, tolls and fees leviable by the state, which may be divided between them under this part and the allocation between the municipalities at all levels of their respective shares of such proceeds.
ii. the determination of the taxes, duties, tolls and fees which may be assigned to or appropriated by, the municipalities;
iii. the measures needed to improve the financial position of the municipalities;
iv. The grants-in-aid to the Local Self Body;
v. Other matter referred to the Finance Commission by the Governor in the interest of sound finance of the municipalities.

The Governor shall cause to lay every recommendation made by the Commission under this article together with an explanatory note before the Legislature of the State.[34]

Grants to local bodies from the Consolidated Fund of the State are supposed to meet the gap between the resources required for meeting the cost, providing certain minimum standards of certain basic services to the citizens in a given municipality irrespective of the domicile within the state and the resources the municipality in question should be able to generate on objective grounds rather than actual resources they are generating on both the sides, revenue and cost. There is thus, an insistence for the use of normative standards while the citizens should get the same level of local public goods/local public utility services and perhaps, publicly provided services such as public health and primary education (not listed in the domain of municipalities) in all urban habitations. There is a suggestion that they must contribute as much as they can.[35]

4.7.4 Grants Given by State Government on the Recommendation of the State Finance Commission of Haryana

After the enactment of the 73rd and 74th Constitutional Amendments, every State is required to constitute, at regular intervals of five years, a Finance Commission, under Article 243 (I) and 243 (Y). Each State is further required to assign to the State Finance Commission, the task of reviewing the financial position of the local bodies and making recommendation on the sharing and assignment of various taxes, duty, tolls, fees, etc. and giving recommendations with respect to the grants-in-aid to be given to the local body from the Consolidated Fund of the State.[36]

The scope of enquiry of the State Finance Commission is much wider as compared to the Central Finance Commission, which besides recommending the sharing of State resources suggests measures to improve the financial position of these bodies so as to enable them to become viable units of the local government.

As a logical sequel to these Constitutional Amendments, the Haryana Municipal Amendment Act, 1994 and the Haryana Municipal Corporation Act, 1994 were enacted and the Haryana Finance Commission Rules, 1994 were formulated.

In pursuance of the constitutional provisions, the Article 243 I and 243 Y and Section 213 of the Haryana Panchayati Raj Act, 1994 and 68A of Haryana Municipal Act, 1973 and Rules 1994 the Government of Haryana has so for appointed three State Finance Commissions.

The terms of reference of these State Finance Commissions are as follows:

These Commissions are required to make recommendations related to the following matters:

The principles which should govern

(i) The distribution of the net proceeds of the taxes, duties, tolls and fees leviable by the State which may be divided between them under Part IX -A of the Constitution of India and the allocation between the Municipalities at all levels of their respective shares of such proceeds;
(ii) The determination of the taxes, duties, tolls and fees which may be assigned to or appropriated by the Municipalities;
(iii) The grants-in-aid to the Municipalities from the Consolidated Fund of the State; and
(iv) The measures needed to improve the financial position of the Municipalities.

In making these recommendations, the Commission shall have regard among other considerations to:

(i) The objective of balancing the receipt and expenditure of the State and for generation of surplus for capital investment;
(ii) The resources of the State Government and demands therein particularly in respect of the expenditure on civil administration, maintenance and up-keep of capital assets, maintenance expenditure on plan schemes and other committed expenditures or liabilities of the State; and

(iii) The requirement of the Panchayati Raj Institutions and the Municipalities, their potential for raising resources and reducing expenditure.[37]

The following State Finance Commission were set-up by the State Government to make recommendations of the local bodies:

(A) First State Finance Commission

To comply with the provisions made under Article 243 (Y) of the Constitution of India, the Governor of Haryana constituted the First State Finance Commission of Haryana on May 31, 1994 and it submitted its report in March, 1997. The report was examined by the State Finance Department and placed before the State Legislature in September 2001. The Commission made the following recommendations:

In case of grants to Urban Local Bodies, 50 per cent capital (1991 Census) to all Municipal Council/Committees for total population of Rs 32.19 lakhs with 10 per cent step up each year due to loss of excise duty. The funds transferred ass per the first State Finance Commission recommendations were Rs 21.5 crores and for the period 2001-02 and Rs 74.92 crores to the Urban Local Bodies (ULB) for the total period of 1997-2001.

(B) Second State Finance Commission

The Governor of Haryana constituted the Second State Finance Commission on 6th of September 2000 under the chairmanship of Sh. Suraj Bhan along with three members and a Member Secretary. The Commission submitted its report in September 2004, for a period of 5 years from 2001-05. A Cabinet Sub-committee was constituted on May 09, 2005 under the Chairmanship of the Finance Minister to examine the recommendations of the Second Finance Commission and submit its report to the State Government. This Sub-Committee finalized its report on sharing the state taxes, duties, fees and grants-in-aid to the local bodies, on October 18, 2005.

After analyzing the financial position of the Municipal bodies, the Commission recommended a per capita grant of Rs25/- (2001 Census) for all Municipal Councils/Committees per annum. The annual amount of grant works out at Rs 11.87 crore based on Rs 47.48 lakh population; and 10 per cent step up has been given for further years.[38] However, MCP received Rs 78 lakhs and Rs 49 lakhs grant in the year 2006-07 and 2008-09, respectively (See Table 4.7).

(C) Third State Finance Commission

The Governor of Haryana constituted the 3rd State Finance Commission, Haryana on December 22, 2005. Sh. N. Mathur (IAS

Retd.) was appointed as the Chairman of the Commission. Along with him,three members and a member Secretary was also appointed. The Commission was expected to submit its report by December 31, 2006. But the tenure of Commission was extended up to December 31, 2007. It submitted its report in the year 2008.

Report of 3rd State Finance Commission Haryana (2008)[39]

In pursuance section 213 of the Haryana Panchyati Raj Act 1994 (Act-II of 1994) and rule 3 of Haryana Finance Commission Rules, 1994, the Governor of Haryana constituted the 3rd State Finance Commission in four stages vide notification Nos. 18/1//2005-Pol(2P) dated December 22, 2005, (ii) 1/11/2006-1511 dated January 16, 2006, (iii) 18/1/2005-Pol(2) dated December 4, 2006 and (iv) 18/1/2005-POL (2P) dated 28.5.2007 in the Chairmanship of Sh.A.N. Mathur alongwith 5 members on the request of State Government. The Commission submitted its interim report on February 29, 2008 covering the period 2006-07, 2007-08 and 2008-09 falling under its revenue period. And finally recommended total devolution of fund 4192.40 to local bodies for the period 2006-2011. And advocated devolution of fund to the PRI's and ULB on the basis of following criteria should be considered for population (40%), BPL Population (25 %), area (25%) and Literacy Gap (10%) while deciding the share .

Apart from this, the Commission has vouches for devolution of funds for various special purposes amounting to Rs.45.00 crore to enhance capacity building, creating data base and proper maintenance of accounts and audit, strengthening of engineering wings, upgradation of fire services and pension liabilities of Local Bodies.

Commission also emphasized and put up social audit for effecting transparency in the functioning of institutions, facilitates public activities, works or programmes being undertaken by Local Bodies for their timely completion, costs, achievements and quality of works and for maintaining of roads correctly. With warranty the quality of works, plugging leakages in the system and reduces manipulation.

Capacity building and empowerment of the various stakeholders of local bodies i.e. elected representatives, functionaries and civil societies and empowerment of citizens and secure e-community participation were others remarkable enjoinder of the commission.

The commission has observed that the data base of local bodies is very precious. There is no reliable mechanism for collection of data at any level i.e. local body, departmental and government level. So, it suggested that there should be creation of effective and appropriate database.

Due to prior financial state of urban local bodies are unable to provide quality civic services on the requisite scale. So, commission suggested adoption of privatisation of municipal services as alternative and efforts should also be made for enhancing Public Private Partnership (PPP).

The commission also recommended for increasing the functions of District Planning Committees besides preparation of draft development plan, they not only may be engaged in co-ordination and monitoring of the implementation of District Development Plan and but also involved in allocation of resources to local bodies for planning and implementation of local level projects contained in District Development Plan.

And calls for various improvement in local bodies such as; transfer of water supply functions to urban local bodies, a separate list of local taxation and identified new horizon of Taxes i.e. Mobile Cess, Cable Tax and Vacant Land Tax and measure optimum recovery on services of the basis of cost incurred; application of effective E-Governance at relevant level. Steps to rationale the municipal personnel system and promote an effective management system for development of man power. Launching of Effective collection drive e-collection, method alongwith collection at door-steps; mutual resolution of disputes through lok adalats, display of defaulters name in the locality itself, attractive incentives and penalties; like including attachment of bank account and levy of penal interest. And creation of institution Centre for Civic Governance.

4.7.5 Other Grants

In addition, some other grants have been made under the following schemes:

(A) Environmental Improvement of Urban Slum (E.I.U.S.)

This scheme was started in the financial year 1986-87. The scheme which is an integrated part of the 20-Point Programme and also tied with the scheme of 'Special Component Plan' for Scheduled Castes is being implemented in the sector, which seeks to improve the living condition of inhabitants residing in slum areas/*basties* through providing low cost drinking water supply, storm water drains, However, MCP received Rs 4.5 lakhs and Rs 11 lakhs in grants in the years 2004-05 and 2005-06, respectively (See Table 4.7).

Table No. 4.7 Grant Statement of Municipal Council, Panchkula (Figures are in Rs.)

Year	*Environment Improvement of Urban Slum (EIUS)*	*Urban Infrastructure*	*Central 11th Finance Commission*	*Central 12th Finance Commission*	*2nd State Finance Commission*	*House Tax Compensation*	*C.M Announcement*	*Total Grant*	*Toal Income*
2004-05	4,12,000	4,55,000	—		—			867000 (0.85)	101853755
2005-06	4,23,000	11,79,000	45,99,000	—				6201000 (4.4)	140808496
2006-07	—	—	27,04,000	—	78,09,800			10513800 (6.9)	150448993
2007-08	—	—	51,61,000	18,44,000	—			7005000 (3.1)	224780000
2008-09	—	—-	——-	27,00,000	49,37,000	43,74,450	10,500,000	22511450 (11.0)	204619960
2009-10	—	—	—	—	—	—	—	—	—

Source: Accounts Branch of Municipal Council, Panchkula.

(B) Adhoc Revenue Earning Scheme (ARES)

This scheme was started in the financial year 1996-97. Its purpose was to increase the income of Municipal Bodies. Under this scheme the Municipal Bodies are expected to prepare revenue generating projects. For example, construction of shops, auto- rickshaw stands, parking areas, etc. The projects so prepared are sent to the state government through the Directorate of Urban Local Bodies Haryana. According to this scheme, the financing is undertaken in such a way that 20 per cent of the resources are contributed by the municipalities by themselves and 60 per cent is borrowed from the financial institutions by the municipality concerned. Later on, the Government made the provision that municipalities could borrow up to 75 per cent from the financial institution instead of 60 per cent. The grant component is distributed on the basis of the class of municipalities, population and economic conditions.

(C) Centrally Sponsored Project- Integrated Development of Small and Medium Town (IDSMT)

This scheme was started in the financial year 1996-97. It is a Central Government sponsored scheme for Integrated Development of Small and Medium Towns. Under this scheme, the Central Government contributes/ is to contribute 60 per cent of the total budgetary estimate and the rest 40 per cent is to be contributed by the state government. The central assistance shall be provided within one month to the state government. If this grant is not spent for the specified purposes or any money remains unspent, that has to be returned back to the Centrel Government. The Local Government Department of Haryana is expected to prepare and send a component wise physical and financial progress report of the scheme to the Ministry of Urban Development, Government of India.

(D) Urban Infrastructure (UI)

This scheme was started in the financial year 2002-03. This scheme is related to strengthening of the urban infrastructure like filling of concrete pavings and drains, construction of drains, roads and street repairs as per the demand of welfare association asides the development of parks. This scheme is not applicable to slum areas.

(E) House Tax Compensation

MCP received Rs 43 lakhs special grant as a House Tax Compensation in the year 2008-09 (See Table 4.7).

(F) Chief Minister (C.M.) Announcement

MCP received a special grant of Rs one crore as a result of an announcement made by the Chief Minister in the year 2008-09 (See Table 4.7).

4.7.6 Grants Received by Municipal Council, Panchkula

The various grants released by the State Government to MCP between year 2001 to 2010 have been given in Table 4.7.

Table 4.7 reveals that in the year 2004-05, MCP received a grant of Rs 8.6 lakhs. In the year 2005-06, it received Rs 62 lakhs grant which was 4.4 percent of the total income. In the year 2006-07, it received a grant of Rs 1crore which was 8.6 percent of the total income. In the year 2007-08, it received a grant of Rs 70 lakhs grant, which was 3.1 percent of the total income. In the year 2008-09, it also received a grant of Rs two crore which was 10.9 per cent of the total income.

The study reveals that the total income of MCP is fluctuating year wise and the contributions of grants-in aid in total income are less and there is no effective tax compliance.

4.8 Expenditure of Municipal Council, Panchkula

The total expenditure of MCP from 2001 to 2010 has been shown in Table 4.8 and Figure 4.5.

Table 4.8 Statement of Total Expenditure of the Municipal Council, Panchkula (Figures are in Rs)

Year	*Total Expenditure*
2001-2002	4,322,361
2002-2003	29,010,228
2003-2004	70,758,292
2004-2005	155,197,234
2005-2006	91,408,811
2006-2007	274,058,233
2007-2008	342,555,000
2008-2009	246,007,889
2009-2010	446,915,000

Source: Accounts Branch, Municipal Council, Panchkula.

Figure 4.5 Statement of Total Expenditure of the Municipal Council, Panchkula

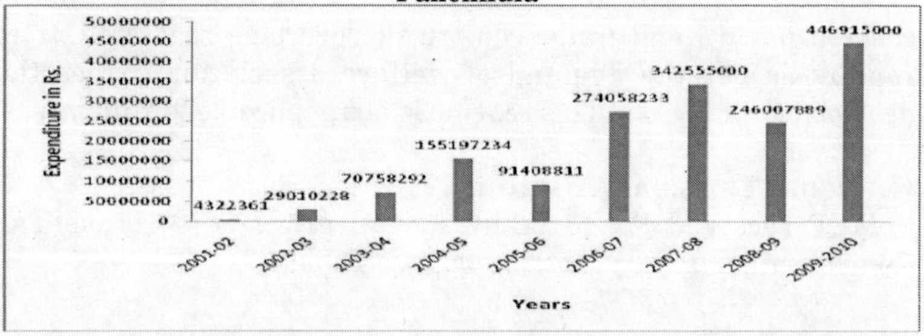

Table 4.8 clearly shows that the total expenditure of the Municipal Council increased from Rs 43.2 lakhs in 2001-02 to Rs 34.2 crore in 2007-08. But in the year 2008-09 it decreased to Rs 24.6 crore. But again it increased to Rs 44 crore in the year 2009-10 as shown in Table 4.8 Figure 4.5. It is relevant to mention here that the expenditure of MCP between 2001-2010 kept fluctuating year wise and the annual compound growth rate of expenditure was 68.80 percent during the period between 2001-02 to 2009-10.

The Municipal Council, Panchkula has made the following classification of expenditure made under various heads:

1. Establishment
2. Contingency
3. Development Work
4. Miscellaneous

Table 4.9 Heads-wise Distribution of Expenditure (Figures are in Rs)

Years	*Establishment*	*Contingency*	*Development*	*Miscellaneous*	*Expenditure*
2001-2002	781,645	875,258	701,396	10,000	2,368,299
Percentage	33.00	36.96	29.62	0.42	100.00
2002-2003	1,967,994	6,675,402	9,129,667	1,674,280	19,447,343
Percentage	10.12	34.33	46.95	8.61	100.00
2003-2004	3,889,840	21,347,645	20,993,100	354,899	46,585,484
Percentage	8.35	45.82	45.06	0.76	100.00
2004-2005	4,967,056	32,883,406	55,488,463	6,184,988	99,523,913
Percentage	4.99	33.04	55.75	6.21	100.00
2005-2006	4,887,510	27,399,173	27,192,571	4,233,880	63,713,134
Percentage	7.67	43.00	42.68	6.65	100.00
2006-2007	5,741,529	35,773,381	111,575,838	9,205,931	162,296,679
Percentage	3.54	22.04	68.75	5.67	100.00
2007-2008	14,600,000	53,824,006	261,300,000	15,940,000	345,664,006
Percentage	4.22	15.57	75.59	4.61	100.00
2008-2009	8,138,092	47,077,436	186,007,691	5,127,918	246,351,137
Percentage	3.30	19.11	75.51	2.08	100.00
2009-10	31,600,000	61,765,000	158,100,000	12,150,000	263,615,000
Percentage	11.99	23.43	59.97	4.61	100.00

Source: Municipal Council, Panchkula.

Figure 4.6 Head wise Distribution of Expenditure

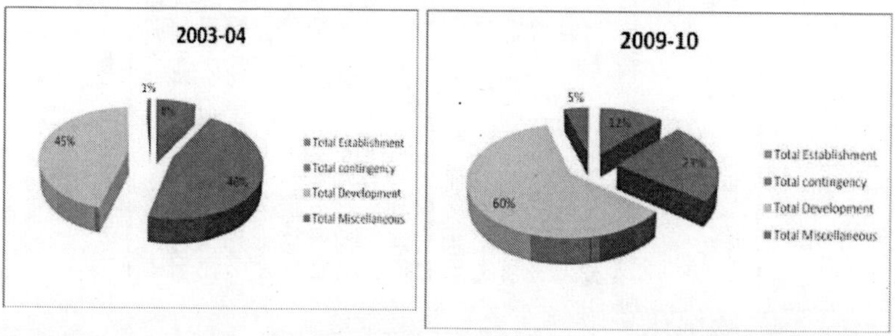

Table 4.10 Establishment Expenditure of MCP

Years	*General Administration*	*Taxes*	*Fire*	*Engineering branch / building branch*	*Street light*	*Public health direction*	*Sanitation removal*	*Public health*	*Total*
2001-2002	645,799	0	0	135,846	0	0	0	0	781,645
Percentage	82.62	0.00	0.00	17.38	0.00	0.00	0.00	0.00	100.00
2002-2003	773,022	373,090	307,750	139,995	77,716	29,250	267,171	0	1,967,994
Percentage	39.28	18.96	15.64	7.11	3.95	1.49	13.58	0.00	100.00
2003-2004	884,558	334,565	1,279,549	384,665	156,624	117,119	732,760	0	3,889,840
Percentage	22.74	8.60	32.89	9.89	4.03	3.01	18.84	0.00	100.00
2004-2005	902,574	420,247	1,701,091	606,594	190,179	100,608	761,665	284,098	4,967,056
Percentage	18.17	8.46	34.25	12.21	3.83	2.03	15.33	5.72	100.00
2005-2006	984,393	373,234	1,677,258	429,636	207,567	152,167	828,263	234,992	4,887,510
Percentage	20.14	7.64	34.32	8.79	4.25	3.11	16.95	4.81	100.00
2006-2007	1,525,223	505,877	1,630,070	371,765	290,682	231,108	926,426	260,378	5,741,529
Percentage	26.56	8.81	28.39	6.48	5.06	4.03	16.14	4.53	100.00
2007-2008	3,500,000	600,000	5,500,000	1,500,000	450,000	400,000	1,400,000	1,250,000	14,600,000
Percentage	23.97	4.11	37.67	10.27	3.08	2.74	9.59	8.56	100.00
2008-09	2,251,551	594,610	2,521,386	978,158	361,231	348,524	1,031,083	51549	8,138,092
Percentage	27.67	7.31	30.98	12.02	4.44	4.28	12.67	0.63	100.00
2009-10	7,100,000	1,200,000	12,300,000	5,200,000	800,000	700,000	2,300,000	2,000,000	31,600,000
Percentage	22.47	3.80	38.92	16.46	2.53	2.22	7.28	6.33	100.00

Source: Accounts Branch of MCP.

1. Establishment Expenditure

The details of the establishment expenditure has been reported in Table 4.10.

The expenditure on establishment includes salary of employees, pension share[41] (It is 10 per cent of the basic pay and dearness allowance paid to the employees. Under the Pension Scheme, the share is paid by Municipal Council, Panchkula to Local Bodies, Haryana).

The expenditure of Municipal Council, Panchkula, on establishment was Rs 7.81 lakhs in 2001-02, which increased to Rs 57.41 lakhs in 2006-07. It further increased to Rs 1.46 crore in 2007-08, which was 4.2 per cent of the total expenditure on establishment. It decreased to Rs 81 lakhs in the year 2008-09, which was 3.3 per cent of the total expenditure on establishment. It again increased to Rs 3.16 crore in the year 2009-10, which was 11.9 per cent of the total expenditure on establishment as shown in Table 4.10 and Figure 4.7.

Figure 4.7 Establishment expenditure of MCP

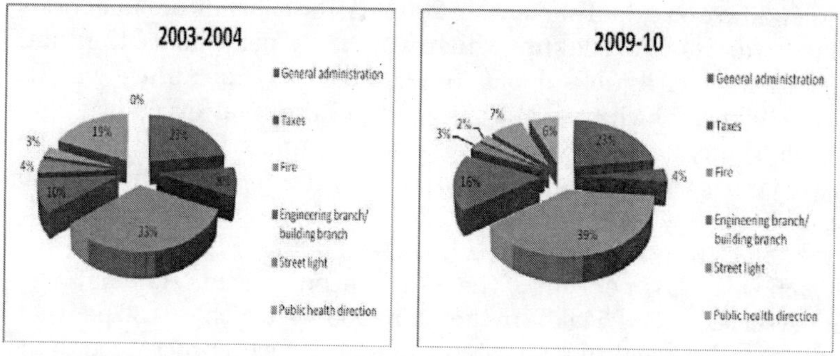

The expenditure on establishment is made under following heads:

(A) General Administration

In the year 2001-02, the expenditure of establishment under the head General Administration was Rs 6.45 lakhs, which was 82.62 per cent of the total expenditure on establishment. It increased to Rs 9.02 lakhs during the year 2004-05 but in terms of percentage, it came down to 18.17 per cent of the total expenditure on establishment. In the year 2006-07, the expenditure under this head increased to Rs 15.25 lakhs, which was Rs 26.56 per cent of the total expenditure on establishment. It increased to Rs 35 lakhs in 2007-08, which was 23.97 per cent of the total expenditure on establishment. It again increased to Rs 22 lakhs in 2008-09, which was 27.6 per cent of the total expenditure on establishment. It further increased to Rs 71 lakhs in 2008-09, which was 22.4 per cent of the total expenditure on establishment as shown in Table 4.10 and Figure 4.7.

(B) Taxes

In the year 2002-03, the expenditure on establishment under the head of taxes was Rs 3.73 lakhs which was 18.95 per cent of the total expenditure on establishment. In the year 2005-06, it was Rs 3.73 lakhs, which was 7.63 per cent of the total expenditure on establishment. In the year 2006-07, it was Rs 5.05 lakhs, which was 8.81 per cent of the total expenditure. In the year 2007-08, it increased to Rs six lakhs, which was 4.10 per cent of the establishment expenditure. It decreased to Rs five lakhs in the year 2008-09, which was 7.3 per cent of the establishment expenditure.It again increased to Rs 12 lakhs in 2009-10, which was 3.79 per cent of the total expenditure on establishment as shown in Table 4.10 and Figure 4.7.

C) Fire Brigade

In 2002-03, Municipal Council, Panchkula made an expenditure of Rs 3.07 lakhs under this head, which was 15.63 per cent of the total expenditure on establishment. In 2004-05, the expenditure under this head was Rs 17.01 lakhs, which was 32.24 per cent of the total expenditure of establishment. In 2005-06, the expenditure was Rs 16.77 lakhs, which was 34.31 per cent of the total expenditure on establishment. In 2006-07 the expenditure under this head was Rs 16.3 lakhs, which was 28.39 per cent of the total expenditure on establishment. There was a small decrease in expenditure under this head since the year 2005-06. It increased to Rs 55 lakhs in 2007-08, which was 37.67 per cent of the total expenditure on establishment. It decreased to Rs 25 lakhs in the year 2008-09, which was 30 per cent of the total expenditure on establishment. It further increased to Rs 1.2 crore in 2009-10, which was 38.9 per cent of the total expenditure on establishment as shown in Table 4.10 and Figure 4.7.

(D) Engineering Building Branch

The establishment expenditure under the head of Engineering / Building Branch was Rs 1.35 lakhs in the year 2001-02 and it was 17.37 per cent of the total expenditure of establishment. In the year 2006-07, the expenditure under this head was Rs 3.71 lakhs, which was 6.47 per cent of the total establishment expenditure and it increased to Rs 15 lakhs in 2007-08, which was 10.27 per cent of the total expenditure on establishment. It further increased to Rs 52 lakhs in 2009-10, which was 16.45 per cent of the total expenditure on establishment as shown in Table 4.10 and Figure 4.7.

(E) Street Light

In the year 2001-02, the expenditure on establishment under the head of street light by the MCP was nil. This was because the function of streetlighting was under the jurisdiction of Haryana Urban Development Authority (HUDA).[42] This function was transferred to the MCP in the financial year 2002-03 and the Municipal Council incurred an expenditure of Rs 77 thousand under this head, which was 3.94 per cent of the total expenditure of establishment. This expenditure increased to Rs 2.90 lakhs in the year 2006-07, which was 5.06 per cent of the total expenditure of establishment in the year 2007-08. It increased to Rs 4.5 lakhs, which was 3.08 per cent of the total establishment expenditure. But it declined to Rs three lakhs in the year 2008-09, which was 4.4 percent of the total establishment expenditure.Further, it again increased to Rs eight lakhs in 2009-10, which was 2.5 per cent of the total expenditure on establishment as shown in Table 4.10 and Figure 4.7.

(F) Public Health Direction

No expenditure was incurred by the Council on Public Health Direction during 2001-02.

In 2002-03, Municipal Council made an expenditure of Rs 19,000 which was 1.48 per cent of the total expenditure on establishment. In 2006-07, the establishment expenditure under this head was Rs 2.31 lakhs, which was 4.02 per cent of the total expenditure on establishment. It decreased to Rs four lakhs in 2007-08, which was 2.73 per cent of the total expenditure on establishment. Further, it declined to Rs three lakhs in 2008-09, which was 4.2 per cent of the total expenditure on establishment. Again it increased to Rs seven lakhs in 2009-10, which was 2.21 per cent of the total expenditure on establishment as shown in Table No. 4.10 and Figure 4.7.

(G) Sanitation / Removal

The establishment expenditure under the head of sanitation/ removal was nil in the year 2001-02. In the year 2002-03, the expenditure under this head was Rs 2.67 lakhs, which was 13.57 per cent of the total expenditure of establishment. In the year 2006-07, the expenditure under this head increased to Rs 9.26 lakhs which was 16.13 per cent of the establishment expenditure. Again it increased to Rs. 14 lakhs in the year 2007-08, which was 9.58 percent of the total expenditure on establishment. But it decreased to Rs 10 lakhs in 2008-09, which was 12.6 per cent of the total expenditure on establishment. It again increased to Rs 23 lakhs in the year 2009-10, which was 7.2 per cent of the total expenditure on establishment as shown in Table 4.10 and Figure 4.7.

(H) Public Health

There was no establishment expenditure under this head from the year 2001-02 to 2003-04. In the year 2004-05, the expenditure under this head was Rs 2.84 lakhs which was 5.72 per cent of the total establishment expenditure. In the year 2006-07, the expenditure under this head was Rs 2.60 lakhs, which was 4.5 per cent of the total expenditure of establishment. It increased to Rs 12.5 lakhs in 2007-08, which was 8.56 per cent of the total expenditure of establishment. But it decreased to Rs nine lakhs, which was 12.0 per cent of the total expenditure on establishment. It further increased to Rs 20 lakhs in the year 2009-10, which was 6.3 per cent of the total expenditure on establishment as shown in Table 4.10 and Figure 4.7.

2. Contingency Expenditure

The second category of expenditure is that of contingency. The nature of contingency expenditure varies under different heads. A description of contingency expenditure under various heads is as follows:

The details of Contingency expenditure has been given in Table 4.11 and Figure 4.8.

(A) General Administration

Under the General Administration head, the contingency expenditure is made on the Travel Allowance (TA) which is given to the President and officials of the Municipal Council for travelling outside the jurisdiction of Municipal Council, Panchkula. The allowance bear the cost of petrol, oil, lubricants and repair of office vehicles, traveling allowances, telephone bills, etc.

The contingency expenditure under this head in the year 2001-02 it was Rs 2.42 lakhs which was 27.70 per cent of the total contingency expenditure under this head. By 2004-05, it rose to Rs 7.95 lakhs, which was 2.42 per cent of the total contingency expenditure. But in 2005-06, it came down to Rs 4.64 lakhs, which was 1.70 per cent of the total contingency expenditure. In 2006-07, it increased to Rs 7.11 lakhs, which was 1.93 per cent of total contingency expenditure.[43] Again it increased to Rs 8 lakhs in 2007-08, which was 1.49 per cent of the total expenditure on contingency. But it decreased to Rs five lakhs in the year 2008-09, which was 1.08 per cent of the total expenditure on contingency. It Further, increased to Rs. 10 lakhs in 2009-10, which was 1.6 per cent of the total expenditure on contingency as shown in Table 4.11 and Figure 4.8.

Table 4.11 Contingency Expenditure of MCP (Figures are in Rs.)

Years	*General Administration*	*Fire Brigade*	*Sanitation Removal*	*Licenses*	*Parks*	*Street Light Bill*	*Taxes*	*Engineering branch/ building branch*	*Rent & Tehbazari*	*Library*	*Epidemic*	*Stray cattle*	*Total contigency*
2001-2002	242,430	239,686	32,270	358,099	0	2,773	0	0	0	0	0	0	875,258
	27.70	27.38	3.69	40.91	0.00	0.32	0.00	0.00	0.00	0.00	0.00	0.00	100.00
2002-2003	368,391	329,691	2,730,546	36,650	0	2,977,177	213,069	19,878	0	0	0	0	6,675,402
	5.52	4.94	40.90	0.55	0.00	44.60	3.19	0.30	0.00	0.00	0.00	0.00	100.00
2003-2004	567,539	464,451	9,295,735	10,379	0	9,572,717	130,901	101,817	0	0	0	1,204,106	21,347,645
	2.66	2.18	43.54	0.05	0.00	44.84	0.61	0.48	0.00	0.00	0.00	5.64	100.00
2004-2005	795,311	683,319	16,196,516	27,259	4,154,947	9,749,197	429,409	191,370	7,400	6,081	19,521	623,076	32,883,406
	2.42	2.08	49.25	0.08	12.64	29.65	1.31	0.58	0.02	0.02	0.06	1.89	100.00
2005-2006	464,957	330,561	12,576,442	35,625	880,609	11,913,546	209,933	185,518	0	5,440	7,764	788,778	27,399,173
	1.70	1.21	45.90	0.13	3.21	43.48	0.77	0.68	0.00	0.02	0.03	2.88	100.00
2006-2007	711,802	498,913	16,860,469	51,420	2,927,571	13,041,107	77,353	490,364	0	1,950	53,039	1,059,393	35,773,381
	1.99	1.39	47.13	0.14	8.18	36.45	0.22	1.37	0.00	0.01	0.15	2.96	100.00
2007-2008	800,000	700,000	20,000,000	100,000	10,000,000	15,000,000	600,000	5,000,000	0	15,000	109,006	1,500,000	53,824,006
	1.49	1.30	37.16	0.19	18.58	27.87	1.11	9.29	0.00	0.03	0.20	2.79	100.00
2008-09	507,436	549,201	28,039,741	39,500	4,425,829	10,813,533	257,054	308,720	0	3,245	100,906	2,032,271	47,077,436
	1.08	1.17	59.56	0.08	9.40	22.97	0.55	0.66	0.00	0.01	0.21	4.32	100.00
2009-10	1,000,000	500,000	35,000,000	100,000	7,500,000	15,000,000	1,500,000	500,000	0	15,000	150,000	500,000	61,765,000
	1.62	0.81	56.67	0.16	12.14	24.29	2.43	0.81	0.00	0.02	0.24	0.81	100.00

Source: Accounts Branch of MCP.

Figure 4.8 Contingency Expenditure of MCP

Year 2001-2002 **Year 2009-2010**

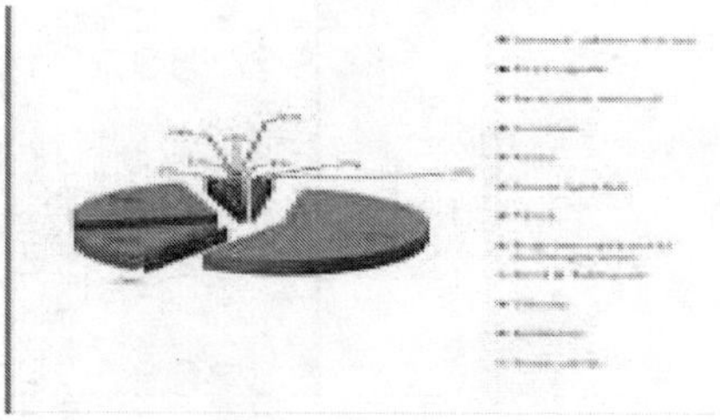

(B) Fire Brigade

The contingency expenditure under this head includes contingency, petrol, oil, lubricants, repair of office vehicles, traveling allowances, telephone bills etc. In the year 2001-02, the expenditure under this head was Rs 2.39 lakhs, which was 27.38 per cent of the total contingency expenditure. In the year 2006-07, the expenditure under this head was Rs 4.98 lakhs, which was 1.39 per cent of the total contingency expenditure. It increased to Rs 7 lakhs in 2007-08, which was 1.30 per cent of the total contingency expenditure .But it decreased to Rs 5.4 lakhs in the year 2008-09, which was 1.17 per cent of the total expenditure of contingency. Thereafter, It decreased to Rs five lakhs in the year 2009-10 which was 0.8 per cent of the total expenditure on contingency as shown in Table 4.11 and Figure 4.8.

(C) Sanitation / Removal

The expenditure under this head is made with respect to the payment of the contractor for providing sanitation services. In 2001-02, the contingency expenditure under this head was Rs 32,270, which was 3.69 per cent of the total contingency expenditure. By 2006-07, the expenditure under this head increased to Rs 1.68 crore, which was 47.13 per cent of the total contingency expenditure and it further increased to Rs two crores in the year 2007-08, which was 37.16 per cent of the total of contingency expenditure. Agaian it increased to Rs 2.8 crore in the year 2008-09, which was 59.56 per cent of the total expenditure of contingency. Again it increased to Rs. 3.5 crore in the year 2009-10 which was 56.6 per cent of the total expenditure on contingency as shown in Table 4.11 and Figure 4.8.

(D) Licenses

The expenditure under this head is made with respect to issue of licence number plates and receipts to rehri, rickshaws, ponies, etc.

The expenditure under this head in the year 2001-02 was Rs 3.58 lakhs, which was 40.91 per cent of the total contingency expenditure. In the year 2006-07, this expenditure got reduced significantly to Rs 51 thousand, which was 0.14 per cent of the total contingency expenditure. In the year 2007-08, it again increased to Rs one lakh, which was 0.13 per cent of the total contingency expenditure. It remained at Rs. 1 lakh in 2009-10, which was 0.16 per cent of the total expenditure on contingency as shown in Table 4.11 and Figure 4.8.

(E) Parks

The contingency expenditure under this head is made on the maintenance of parks, payment to Parks Development Societies, etc.

No contingency expenditure under this head was made by the Municipal Council, Panchkula during the year 2001-02, 2002-03 and 2003-04, as this function was looked after by the Haryana Urban Development Authority (HUDA). In the year 2004-05, the contingency expenditure made under this head was Rs 41.4 lakhs, which was 12.64 per cent of the total contingency expenditure. In the year 2005-06, this expenditure came down to Rs 8.8 lakhs, which was 3.21 per cent of the total contingency expenditure. In the year 2006-07, the expenditure under this head increased to Rs 29.27 lakhs, which was 8.18 per cent of the total contingency expenditure and it increased to Rs one crore in 2007-08, which was 18.58 per cent of the total of contingency expenditure. It then decreased to Rs 44 lakhs in 2008-09, which was 9.40 per cent of the total expenditure of contingency. However, it increased to Rs 75 lakhs in 2009-10, which was 12.14 per cent of the total expenditure on contingency as shown in Table 4.11 and Figure 4.8.

(F) Street Light Bill

The contingency expenditure under this head is made on the payment of street lighting bills to the Uttar Haryana Viduyat Vitran Nigam (UHVUM). In the year 2001-02, the expenditure under this head was Rs 2,773,[44] which was 0.3 per cent of the total contingency expenditure. In 2006-07, the expenditure made under this head was Rs 1.3 crores, which was 36.45 per cent of the total contingency expenditure. It then increased to Rs 1.5 crores in 2007-08, which was 27.87 per cent of the total expenditure of contingency expenditure. It declined to Rs.1 crore in 2008-09, which was 22.97 per cent of the total expenditure of contingency.

It again increased to Rs 1.5 crore in 2009-10, which was 24.29 per cent of the total expenditure on contingency as shown in Table 4.11 and Figure 4.8.

(G) Taxes

The expenditure under this head is made regarding the House Tax Bill printing and distribution. The contingency expenditure under the head taxes in the year 2001-02 was Nil. In the year 2002-03, the expenditure under this head was Rs 2.13 lakhs, which was 3.19 per cent of the total contingency expenditure. In the year 2006-07, the expenditure under this head came down to Rs 77 thousand, which was 0.22 per cent of the total contingency expenditure. It then increased to Rs six lakhs in 2007-08, which was 1.11 per cent of the total expenditure of contingency expenditure. And it further decreased to Rs 2.5 lakhs in the year 2008-09, which was 0.55 per cent of the total expenditure of contingency. But it further increased to Rs 15 lakhs in the year 2009-10, which was 2.43 per cent of the total expenditure on contingency as shown in Table 4.11 and Figure 4.8.

(H) Engineering Branch

The expenditure under this head includes sundry expenditure like purchase of small items of building materials (lock, replacement of broken window pane), patchwork on broken roads. There was no expenditure under this head in the year 2001-02. In the year 2002-03, a sum of Rs 19,000 was spent under this head, which was 0.30 per cent of the total contingency expenditure. In 2006-07, sum of Rs 4.9 lakhs was spent under this head, which was 1.37 per cent of the total contingency expenditure and it increased to Rs 50 lakhs in 2007-08, which was 9.29 per cent of the total expenditure of contingency expenditure. Again it decreased significantly to Rs three lakhs in 2008-09, which was 0.66 per cent of the total expenditure of contingency. And it decreased to Rs 50 lakhs in 2009-10, which was 0.8 per cent of the total expenditure on contingency as shown in Table 4.11 and Figure 4.8.

(I) Library

The contingency expenditure under this head includes cost of newspapers and magazines subscribed for the office and old age home. There was no expenditure under this head during the year 2001-02, 2002-03, and 2003-04. In the year 2004-05, contingency expenditure under this head was Rs 6,081 which was 0.02 per cent of the total expenditure. In the year 2006-07, the expenditure under this head was Rs 1,950. In the year 2007-08, it increased to Rs 15 thousand, which was 0.03 percent of the total contingency expenditure. Thereafter, it decreased to Rs three thousand in the year 2008-09, which was 0.01 percent of the total expenditure on contingency. It increased to Rs 15 thousand in 2009-10 as shown in Table 4.11 and Figure 4.8.

(J) Epidemic

The contingency expenditure under this head is made on petrol and diesel, given to Civil Hospitals and District Health Authorities for the purpose of fogging/spraying of insecticides/mosquito repellents, etc. This spraying is done for the prevention of epidemic. No expenditure was made under this head during 2001-02, 2002-03 and 2003-04. In the year 2004-05, the expenditure under this head was Rs 19.5 thousand, which was 0.06 per cent of the total contingency expenditure. In the year 2006-07, the expenditure under this head was Rs 53,000, which was 0.15 per cent of the total contingency expenditure and it increased to Rs one lakh in the year 2007-08, which was 0.20 per cent of the total of contingency expenditure. It remained almost same at Rs one lakhs in the year 2008-09, which was 0.21 per cent of the total expenditure on contingency. But it increased to Rs 1.5 lakhs in 2009-10, which was 0.81 per cent of the total expenditure on contingency as shown in Table 4.11 and Figure 4.8.

(K) Stray Cattle

The expenditure under this head is made the regarding contract amount paid to the contractor for catching stray cattle and taking those cattle to the cattle ponds, maintained by Municipal Council, Panchkula. No expenditure was made under this head during 2001-02 and 2002-03. In 2003-04, a sum of Rs 12.04 lakhs was spent under this head, which was 5.64 per cent of the total contingency expenditure. In the year 2006-07, a sum of Rs 10.59 lakhs was spent under this head, which was 2.96 per cent of the total contingency expenditure while increased to Rs 15 lakhs in the year 2007-08, which was 2.75 per cent of the total of contingency expenditure. It increased to Rs 20 lakhs in the year 2008-09, which was 4.32 per cent of the total expenditure of contingency. It was Rs. five lakhs in the year 2009-10 which was 0.8 per cent of the total expenditure on contingency as shown in Table 4.11 and Figure 4.8.

3. Development Work Expenditure

The third category of expenditure of the Municipal Council, Panchkula as per the statement of expenditure is on development works. The expenditure under this category is made on the construction of shops, development of parks, construction of drains, constructions of roads, concrete paving, office land and building, etc. The head-wise description of the expenditure is made under this headgiven below:

The details of development expenditure of MCP has been given in Table 4.12.

(A) Construction of Roads

The expenditure under this head includes construction of mettled roads in urban areas under the jurisdiction of Municipal Council, Panchkula. Roads in Panchkula have been categorized into three categories: A, B and C.

Category A: Main Roads,
Category B: Sector Dividing Roads,
Category C: Roads within the sector.

The construction of roads of all the categories has been the responsibility of Municipal Council, Panchkula.

In the year 2001-02, Municipal Council, Panchkula had spent Rs. 6.96 lakhs under this head, which was 99.37 per cent of the total expenditure on development works. No expenditure was made under this head during the year 2002-03. In the year 2003-04, a sum of Rs 1.56 crores was spent under this head, which was 74.71 per cent the total expenditure on development works.

In the year 2006-07, a sum of Rs 6.50 crores was spent under this head, which was 58.27 per cent of the total expenditure on development works. It increased to Rs 10 crore in the year 2007-08, which was 74.05 per cent of the total expenditure on development works. It decreased significantly to Rs 1.7 crore in the year 2008-09, which was 93.26 per cent of the total expenditure on development works while again it increased to Rs 15 crore, which was 94.8 per cent of the total expenditure on development works, as shown in Table 4.12.

(B) Construction and Development of Parks

The expenditure under this head includes the expenditure made on the construction and development of new parks and repair of parks. The work related to maintenance of parks is done through

Table 4.12 Development Works Expenditure of MCP (Figures are in Rs.)

Year	*Construction of Roads*	*Development of Parks*	*Concrete Paving*	*Construction of Drains*	*Office Land and Building*	*Fire Brigade*	*Repair of cattle pond / catcher*	*Repair construction of Shops*	*Total*
2001-2002	696,973	4,423	0	0	0	0	0	0	701,396
	99.37	0.63	0.00	0.00	0.00	0.00	0.00	0.00	100.00
2002-2003	0	0	9,129,667	0	0	0	0	0	9,129,667
	0.00	0.00	100.00	0.00	0.00	0.00	0.00	0.00	100.00
2003-2004	15,683,976	596,843	4,712,281	0	0	0	0	0	20,993,100
	74.71	2.84	22.45	0.00	0.00	0.00	0.00	0.00	100.00
2004-2005	25,631,762	15,050,842	10,254,365	674,321	3,778,794	98,379	0	0	55,488,463
	46.19	27.12	18.48	1.22	6.81	0.18	0.00	0.00	100.00
2005-2006	21,748,294	3,444,663	1,763,958	0	235,656	0	0	0	27,192,571
	79.98	12.67	6.49	0.00	0.87	0.00	0.00	0.00	100.00
2006-2007	65,012,664	19,965,859	24,483,871	957,414	839,383	316,647	0	0	111,575,838
	58.27	17.89	21.94	0.86	0.75	0.28	0.00	0.00	100.00
2007-2008	193,500,000	25,000,000	20,000,000	15,000,000	2,500,000	3,000,000	2,000,000	300,000	261,300,000
	74.05	9.57	7.65	5.74	0.96	1.15	0.77	0.11	100.00
2008-2009	173,475,321	6,046,610	5,463,428	559,561	462,771	0	0	0	186,007,691
	93.26	3.25	2.94	0.30	0.25	0.00	0.00	0.00	100.00
2009-10	150,000,000	5,000,000	1,500,000	1,000,000	500,000	0	100,000	0	158,100,000
	94.88	3.16	0.95	0.63	0.32	0.00	0.06	0.00	100.00

Source: Accounts Branch of MCP.

the Sector Welfare Associations of the Municipal Council, Panchkula. For this purpose, Municipal Council, Panchkula pays Re one per square meter to the Resident Welfare Associations (RWAs).

In the year 2001-02, the expenditure under this head was Rs. 4,423 which was 0.63 per cent of the total expenditure incurred on the development work.

No expenditure was made under this head in the year 2002-03. In 2003-04, it was Rs 5.9 lakhs, which was 2.84 per cent of the total expenditure on development work. In 2006-07, a sum of Rs 1.9 crore was spent under this head, which was 17.89 per cent of the total expenditure on development works. It increased to Rs 2.5 crore in the year 2007-08, which was 9.51 per cent of the total expenditure of development works. It then decreased to Rs 60 lakhs, which was 3.25 per cent of the total expenditure on development works. It again decreased significantly to Rs 50 lakhs in the year 2009-10, which was 3.16 per cent of the total expenditure on development works,as shown in Table 4.12.

(C) Concrete Paving

The expenditure under this head is made on cement concrete roads, in areas where proper drainage facilities are not available. Many such roads have been constructed in villages falling under the jurisdiction of Municipal Council, Panchkula.

In the year 2001-02, no expenditure was made under this head. In 2002-03, a sum of Rs 91.29 lakhs was spent under this head, which was 100 per cent of the total expenditure on development works. In the year 2006-07, a sum of Rs 2.44 crores was spent under this head which was 21.94 per cent of the total expenditure on development works and in the year 2007-08, the expenditure under this head was Rs two crore, which was 7.65 per cent of the total expenditure on development works. It then decreased to Rs 54 lakhs in the year 2008-09,which was 2.94 per cent of the total expenditure on development works. It again decreased to Rs 15 lakhs, which was 0.9 per cent of the total expenditure on development works, as shown in Table 4.12.

(D) Construction of Drains

The expenditure under this head includes construction of drains and kerb channel along the roads and construction of drains in villages under the jurisdiction of Municipal Council, Panchkula.

Under this head, no expenditure was made in the years 2001-02, 2002-03 and 2003-04. In 2004-05, a sum of Rs 6.74 lakhs was spent under this head, which was 1.22 per cent of the total expenditure on development works. Again in 2005-06, there was no expenditure under this head. In 2006-07, a sum of Rs 9.57 lakhs was spent under this head, which was 0.86 per cent of the total expenditure on development works. It then increased to Rs 1.5 crores in 2007-08, which was 5.74 percent of the total expenditure. It then decreased significantly to Rs 5.5 lakhs, which was 0.30 per cent of the total expenditure uncured on development works. It then increased to Rs 10 lakhs which was 0.6 percent of the total expenditure on development works as shown in Table 4.12.

(E) Office Land and Building

The expenditure made under this head includes the amount spent on the purchase of land for office buildings (though no construction might have taken place as yet), maintenance of Municipal Council Office (being run from Community Hall, Sector-4, Panchkula), and maintenance of public toilets.

During the year 2001-02 to 2003-04, the Municipal Council, Panchkula made no expenditure under this head . In the year 2004-05, a sum of Rs 37.78 lakhs was spent under this head which was 6.81 per cent of the total expenditure. In the year 2006-07, a sum of Rs 8.39 lakhs was spent under this head, which was 0.75 per cent of the total expenditure.It then increased to Rs 30 lakhs in the year 2007-08, which was 1.34 per cent of the total expenditure on development works. It further decreased to Rs 4.6 lakhs in the year 2008-09, which was 0.25 per cent of the total expenditure on development works. It increased to Rs five lakhs, which was 0.3 per cent of the total expenditure on development works ,as shown in Table 4.12.

(F) Fire Brigade

The expenditure under this head is made on the repair and construction of building. No expenditure was made under this head during the years 2001-02, 2002-03 and 2003-04. In the year 2004-05, a sum of Rs 98 thousands was spent under this head, which was 0.18 per cent of the total expenditure on development works. In the year 2006-07, a sum of Rs 3.16 lakhs was spent under this head, which was 0.28 per cent of the total expenditure on development works while expenditure under this head was nil in the year 2008-09 and 2009-10, as shown in Table 4.12.

(G) Repair of Cattle Pond Catcher

In the year 2007-08, the MCP expended some money for the repair of cattle ponds. The amount spent was Rs 20 lakhs which was 0.77 per cent of the total expenditure incurred on the development works. The expenditure under this head was nil in 2008-09. It then increased to Rs 1 lakh in the year 2009-2010, as shown in Table 4.12.

(H) Construction of Shops

No expenditure was made by the Municipal Council, Panchkula under this head till 2007, since its inception. Though a provision for this had been made in the budgets of Municipal Council, Panchkula. However, in 2007-08, Rs three lakhs were spent under this head which was 0.11 per cent of the total expenditure incurred on the development works. Moreover, the expenditure under this head was nil in the year 2008-09 and 2009-10, as shown in Table No. 4.12.

4. Miscellaneous Expenditure

The expenditure incurred under this head is in the nature of general expenses, street lightings, fires, etc.

The details of this miscellaneous expenditure have been shown in Table 4.13.

Table 4.13 Miscellaneous Expenditure of MCP (Figures are in Rs)

Year	*D.U.D. share*	*Street Light*	*Fire*	*Law Charges*	*Election Charges*	*Audit Fee*	*Loan For General Purpose*	*Total*
2001-2002	0	0	0	10,000	0	0	0	10,000
	0.00	0.00	0.00	100.00	0.00	0.00	0.00	100.00
2002-2003	1,961	974,675	0	93,100	4,064	600,480	0	1,674,280
	0.12	58.21	0.00	5.56	0.24	35.86	0.00	100.00
2003-2004	0	293,446	0	42,278	0	19,175	0	354,899
	0.00	82.68	0.00	11.91	0.00	5.40	0.00	100.00
2004-2005	500,000	3,915,216	1180869	97,583	0	491,320	0	6,184,988
	8.08	63.30	19.09	1.58	0.00	7.94	0.00	100.00
2005-2006	1,000,000	2,43,866	0	20,3803	0	597,211	0	4,233,880
	23.62	57.46	0.00	4.81	0.00	14.11	0.00	100.00
2006-2007	1,133,577	7,247,172	0	17,1850	0	586,332	67,000	9,205,931
	12.31	78.72	0.00	1.87	0.00	6.37	0.73	100.00
2007-2008	1,500,000	10,000,000	2500000	300,000	10,0000	640,000	900,000	1,594,000
	9.41	62.74	15.68	1.88	0.63	4.02	5.65	100.00
2008-2009	1,000.000	2,020,471	1207500	138,830	61,117	700,000	0	5,127,918
	19.50	39.40	23.55	2.71	1.19	13.65	0.00	100.00
2009-10	500,000	10,000,000	100000	400,000	50,000	1,000,000	100,000	1,215,000
	4.12	82.30	0.82	3.29	0.41	8.23	0.82	100.00

Source: Accounts Branch of MCP.

(A) Directorate of Urban Development (DUD) SHARE

The expenditure under this head is incurred on account of the supervision charges paid to the Directorate of Urban Development of Haryana as Share. In 2006-07, Rs 11.33 lakhs was paid as D.U.D. Share, which was 12.31 per cent of total miscellaneous expenses. It increased to Rs 15 lakhs in 2007-08, which was 9.41 per cent of total expenditure on miscellaneous expenses. It then decreased to Rs 10 lakhs in 2008-09, which was 19.50 per cent of the total expenditure uncured on miscellaneous tasks. It further decreased to Rs 5 lakhs in 2009-10, which was 4.12 per cent of the total miscellaneous expenditure, as shown in Table 4.13.

(B) Street Light

The expenditure under this head includes fixing of streetlights including chowks, parks, cables and conductors, payment to street light contractors for maintenance etc. In the year 2002-03, a sum of Rs 9.74 lakhs was spent under this head, which was 58.21 per cent of the total miscellaneous expenditure. In the year 2006-07, a sum of Rs 72.47 lakhs was spent under this head which was 78.72 percent of the total miscellaneous expenditure. It increased to Rs one crore in the year 2007-08, which was 62.74 per cent of the total expenditure incurred on miscellaneous expenditure. It decreased to Rs 20 lakhs in 2008-09, which was 39.40 per cent of the total expenditure incurred under the miscellaneous category. It again increased to Rs one crore in 2009-10, which was 5.12 per cent of the total miscellaneous expenditure as shown in Table 4.13.

(C) Fire

The expenditure under this head includes expenditure on acquisition / purchase of new fire tenders, etc. In the year 2004-05, a sum of Rs 11.8 lakhs was spent under this head, which was 19.09 per cent of the total miscellaneous expenditure. In the year 2007-08, MCP spent Rs 25 lakhs which was 15.68 per cent of the total miscellaneous expenditure. The expenditure then decreased to Rs 12 lakhs in 2008-09, which was 23.55 per cent of the total miscellaneous expenditure. It again decreased to Rs1 lakh in 2009-10, which was 0.82 per cent of the total expenditure of miscellaneous as shown in Table 4.13.

(D) Law Charges

The expenditure under this head includes payment made to lawyer for legal advices. In 2001-02, a sum of Rs 10,000 was spent under this head. In 2006-07, a sum of Rs 1.71 lakhs was spent under this head and it increased to Rs three lakhs in 2007-08, which was 1.88 per cent of the total expenditure on miscellaneous. It then decreased to Rs 1.3 lakhs, which was 2.7 per cent of the total expenditure on miscellaneous in 2008-09. It again increased to Rs four lakhs in 2009-10, which was 3.29 per cent of the total expenditure on miscellaneous, as shown in Table 4.13.

(E) Election Charges

The expenditure under this head was made in the year 2002-03 and a sum of only Rs 4,000 was spent during this year for the official work relating to Municipal Council, Panchkula elections. In 2007-08, elections were conducted for MCP and it spent Rs one lakh for this purpose. It decreased to Rs 61 thousand in year 2008-09, which was 1.19 per cent of the total miscellaneous expenditure. It further decreased to Rs 50 thousands in 2009-10, which was 0.41 per cent of the total expenditure on miscellaneous as shown in Table 4.13.

(F) Audit Fee

The expenditure under this head includes the Audit Fee paid to the Director of Local Audit, Haryana for auditing the accounts of Municipal Council, Panchkula. The Directorate of Local Audit, Haryana is responsible for the audit of Accounts of local bodies. The audit fee is paid on an annual basis. In the year 2002-03, a sum of Rs 6 lakhs was paid as audit fee, which was 35.86 per cent of the total miscellaneous expenditure. In the year 2006-07, a sum of Rs 5.86 lakhs was paid as audit fee, which was 6.37 per cent of the total miscellaneous expenditure. In the year 2007-08, it further increased to Rs. 6.4 lakhs, which was 4.02 per cent of total miscellaneous expenditure. It then , increased to Rs seven lakhs in the year 2008-09, which was 13.65 per cent of the total miscellaneous expenditure. It then increased to Rs 10 lakhs in 2009-10, which was 8.23 per cent of the total miscellaneous expenditure, as shown in Table 4.13.

(G) Loan for General Purpose

Under this head the outflow is on account of loans given to employees for general purposes. In the year 2007-08, the outflow under this head was Rs 67,000, which was 0.73 per cent of the total miscellaneous expenditure. In 2008-09, the outflow under this head was Rs nine lakhs, which was 5.65 per cent of the total miscellaneous expenses. While the expenditure under this head was nil in the year 2008-09. It then increased to Rs one lakh in the year 2009-10, which was 0.82 per cent of the total miscellaneous expenditure as shown in Table 4.13.

The study of the expenditure pattern of MCP reveals that it has been fluctuating year wise. Though a proper classification of the expenditure is not there and the non-developmental expenditure seems to have consumed more revenue than the development one.

4.9 Audit and Accounts Process in Municipal Council Panchkula

A proper system of accounting and audit is an indispensable feature for the smooth and effective functioning of any administration it not only prevents misappropriation and wastage of funds of local bodies but also to ensure proper control over the expenditure and provide necessary information for policy making along with the increase in resource available to the local bodies through additional resources mobilization and transfers from the State and Central Governments.

A. Accounting

The accounting system is the major quantitative information system in almost every organisation. It is concerned with accumulation, classification and interpretation of information that assists individual executives to fulfill organisational objectives as defined by the top management. An effective accounting system provides information for three broad purposes:

(1) Internal reporting to managers for use in planning and controlling current operation;
(2) Internal reporting to managers for use in strategic planning, i.e., in special decision makings and in the formulating of overall policies and long range plans; and
(3) External reporting to stock holders, government and other outside parties.[45]

Municipal bodies are required to maintain accounts in the form and manner as prescribed by the state government and to follow the accounts code which inter alia describes the officials connected with the financial transactions and lays down procedure for the disbursement of money.

Article 243Z of the Constitution of India, provides that the Legislature of a State, may, by law, make provisions, with respect to the maintenance of accounts by the Municipalities and the audit of such accounts.[46]

In Haryana, Municipal accounts are maintained in accordance with the provision of the Municipal Account Code 1930 and the

Haryana Municipal Act 1973. The Accounts Branch of the concerned municipal body is entrusted with the preparation and maintenance of the accounts.

For withdrawal of money for various purposes, the bills are submitted to the Accounts Branch which gets these bills passed by the Resident Audit Officer (RAO).

B. Audit System

Audit is an examination of the accounts in order to discover and report to the legislature the unauthorised, illegal or irregular expenditure and unsound financial practices on the part of the administration.

The objective of the audit is to see that the expenditure incurred with the sanctions of the competent authority, and made for the purpose for which it was sanctioned by legislature.

Types of audit system

(i) **Pre-audit**:- If the audit occurs before the money is spent or during the process of spending, it is called pre audit system.

(ii) **Post-audit**:- If the audit occurs after the money is spent, it is called post audit system.

The audit and account process in Municipal Council, Panchkula has been discussed as under:-

(A) Audit and Accounts of Local Bodies in Haryana

There is a pre-audit system also called the Resident Audit Scheme under which pre-audit is currently being conducted in respect of 20 Municipal Councils and seven Municipal Committees in the State. Municipal Corporation Faridabad is also covered under the pre-audit scheme as provided under Section 168(3) of Haryana Municipal Corporation Act, 1994. Under the pre-audit system, a day-to-day audit of accounts is conducted.

The remaining Municipal Committees in the State are covered under the post audit system by which accounts of Municipal Committees with annual income more than Rs five lakhs are audited biannually and, Municipal Committees with annual income below Rs five lakhs are conducted annually, as per the provisions of the Municipal Accounts Code.

(B) Audit System in Municipal Council Panchkula

The Municipal Account Code, 1930 and Haryana Municipal Act 1973, provides for the Audit of Accounts of the Municipal Council,

Panchkula. The responsibility for auditing lies with Director, Local Audit who is under the administrative control of the Finance Department. There is a pre-audit system also called the Resident Audit Scheme under which pre-audit is currently being conducted in the Municipal Council, Panchkula, under the pre-audit system, a day to day audit of account is conducted. The Resident Audit Officer as well as other auditors is appointed by the Government. After the close of every financial year, Municipal Council is required to pay an audit fee as per rules to Director Local Audit, Haryana.

The Comptroller and Auditor General of India conducts audit of the accounts as far as the utilisation of governments grant and loan is concerned.[47]

(C) Audit Reports

The auditor prepares reports on Annual Audit, which consist of audit notes dealing with serious irregularities, requiring particular attention of the local and higher authorities, objection statement relating to technical irregularities, mistake and defects. The council is required to consider both the audit notes and the objection statement and to express its opinion on them to examiner.

(D) Shortcomings of the Existing System of Audit and Accounts

In the pre-audit system, a raising of objections is a continuous process and every payment/claim is approved by audit before the actual payment is made. As and when objection is made, it is intimated to the head of the concerned local body by the Resident Auditor. At the close of the year, a draft audit report on the accounts of the local body for the preceding year is submitted to the approving authority. In the case of the Corporation, the approving authority is the Director, Local Audit and in the case of Councils and Committees, it is the concerned Zonal Deputy Director. Copies of audit reports are sent to various authorities for information and compliance.

It has been seen that very little interest is taken by the bodies to settle objections which keep on piling year after year, and there is no system for monitoring the compliance of Council with the audit reports, where as provisions have been made in the Accounts Code wherein specific time limits have been given for compliance at various levels.

As per the notification dated 14th January, 1982, two Committees, one at the divisional level and the other at the district level, were constituted to examine and discuss the annual accounts and reports of the municipalities and to suggest remedial measures. These committees have mostly remained non-functional because of the pre-occupation of various government functionaries in their day-to-day affairs.

It has also been noticed that the audit reports are seldom placed before the general house of the ULBs and generally the audit objections are settled only at the time of the next audit and the audit objections, which remain unsettled, are included in the new audit report. The First Haryana State Finance Commission, in para 24.5 of its Report, recommended that a State level Public Accounts Committee for municipal finances should be constituted to be headed by the Secretary, Urban Development. It should have non-officials as well as officials of the concerned departments as members and Director Local Audit as the Member Secretary. The Committee shall have powers to call for and scrutinise the accounts of any municipality, examine the audit report and make suitable recommendations including dropping of objections, etc. The Report of this Committee shall be submitted to the State Government for final disposal. These recommendations have, however, not been implemented. At present, there are no local, regional or state level bodies to monitor the disposal of the audit objections.

4.10 Factors Affecting Financial Administration of MCP

A couple of factors play a crucial role in the Financial Administration of MCP. These factors are:

1. Delay in Budgetary Process

The above mentioned analysis reveals that the surplus of MCP was not merely because of increased resources mobilisation but also because of less money being spent by MCP due to procedural delay like delays in State Government to grant permission for spending money. For example, MCP had passed the budget in month of February in the year 2004 as well as in 2007 and 2009, but the State Government had delayed it upto the month of June.

2. Grant –in-aid

The analysis on the basis of grants–in-aid shows that the MCP was neither aware about its balance of grants nor showed much interest to make any efforts in this regard to receive the grants with in the stipulated time.

3. No proper Classification of expenditure

Classification of expenditure are made on the basis of requirements and the need of services[48]. In the study,it was found that MCP has not adopted any appropriate classification of its expenditure on the priority basis for select services,i.e.,sanitation, street light, parks and fire brigade services.

4. None of the objections of audit were removed in the stipulated period

The study of audit and accounts reveals that many objections were made by Audit Authority regarding its audit. It was seen during the study that MCP has neither removed the objection year-wise nor has shown any interest in this regard.

4.11Analysis of Financial Administration of Municipal Council Panchkula in The Context of Status of Hypotheses

The financial Administration of the local government can be called efficient if it takes necessary steps in raising resources, ensures effective tax compliance, distributes resources to different services in balanced manner and maintains a ratio of adequate development expenditure with respect to non-developmental expenditure[49].

Briefly the financial administration of MCP has been examined with reference to two hypotheses namely: Hypothesis 3 "The MCP does not manage its financial resources properly", and split into three sub-hypothesis,namely: (i) "The MCP does not prepare budget estimates properly especially in case of taxes"; (ii) "Non-developmental expenditure consumes maximum revenue of MCP and in the process, the development of the city suffered"; (iii) " There is an imbalance in the expenditure on select services by MCP", and Hypothesis 4: "The sources of Income of MCP are inadequate resulting in its over dependence upon grants-in aid."

Hypothesis 3, Sub Hypothesis (i): The MCP does not prepare budget estimates properly especially in case of taxes.

For testing the effectiveness of the budget estimates for tax collection of MCP over the years, a comparison between the budgeted income and the actual income from major head and minor head was made as shown in Tables 4.14, 4.14A & 4.14B.

Table 4.14 Estimated and Actual Income on Major heads of MCP (2001-02 to 2004-05) (Figures are in Rs.)

Years	*2001-02*			*2002-03*			*2003-04*			*2004-05*		
Services	*Budge-ted (Rs.)*	*Actual (Rs.)*	*Actual as a per centage of budgeted*	*Budge-ted (Rs.)*	*Actual (Rs.)*	*Actual as a as a per centage of budgeted*	*Budge-ted (Rs.)*	*Actual (Rs.)*	*Actual as a per centage of budgeted*	*Budge-ted (Rs.)*	*Actual (Rs.)*	*Actual per centage of budgeted*
Electricity Duty	6,000,000	3,219,040	53.6	6,000,000	5,000,000	83.3	6,000,000	10,500,000	175	8,000,000	2,500,000	31.2
House Tax	5,500,000	4,529,511	8.2	30,000,000	26,047,123	86.8	27,500,000	41,453,275	150.7	30,000,000	31,652,063	105.5
Fire Tax	5,500,000	0	0	2,000,000	6,103,585	305.1	5,000,000	10,224,855	204.4	7,000,000	2,302,883	32.89
S Duty	15,000,000	0	0	20,000,000	33,049,902	165.25	27,500,000	5,475,819	19.9	30,000,000	44,894,345	149.64
E-Share	0	0	0	0	0	0	0	0	0	0	323,000	0
Rent Shops	0	0	0	150,000	163,360	108.9	150,000	168,645	112.4	150,000	138,280	92.1
Interest On Investment	0	94,940	0	200,000	278,895	139.4	300,000	909,851	303.28	1,500,000	14,108,567	940
Development work	30,000,000	23,797,018	79.3	30,000,000	57,527	0.1	30,000,000	0	0	30,000,000	0	0

Source: Accounts Branch of MCP.

Table 4.14A Estimated and Actual Income on Major heads of MCP (2005-06 to 2008-09) (Figures are in Rs.)

Years	*2005-06*			*2006-07*			*2007-08*			*2008-09*		
Services	*Budge-ted (Rs.)*	*Actual (Rs.)*	*Actual as a per centage of budgeted*	*Budge-ted (Rs.)*	*Actual (Rs.)*	*Actual as a per centage of budgeted*	*Budge-ted (Rs.)*	*Actual (Rs.)*	*Actual as a per centage of budgeted*	*Budge-ted (Rs.)*	*Actual (Rs.)*	*Actual as a per centage of budgeted*
Electricity Duty	6,000,000	3,219,040	53.6	6,000,000	5,000,000	83.3	6,000,000	10,500,000	175	8,000,000	2,500,000	31.
Electricity Duty	8,000,000	13,423,684	167.7	8,000,000	12,818,513	160.3	10,000,000	10,000,000	100	75,000,000	10,253,366	68.35
House Tax	30,000,000	33,394,183	111.31	30,000,000	35,314,411	117.7	40,000,000	40,000,000	100	27,500,000	32,747,239	119.8
Fire Tax	15,000	4,069,167	27,127.70	15,000	6,800	45.33	5,000,000	5,000,000	100	4,000,000	1,461,779	36.5
S Duty	30,000,000	56,676,739	59.2	30,000,000	46,129,828	61.0	50,000,000	100,000,000	100	160,000,000	135,302,379	170.7
Rent of Shops	150,000	88,881		15,000	91,554		150,000	150,000		100,000	61,873	61.87
Interest on Investment	3,000,000	7,029,040	234.3	3,000,000	10,594,469	353.1	5,000,000	5,000,000	100	10,000,000	17,071,224	170.7
Development work	30,000,000	0	0	30,000,000	289,028	0.9	30,000,000	30,000,000	100	30,000,000	0	0
Excise share	500,000	0	0	500,000	2,919,528	583.1	5,000,000	5,000,000	100	7,500,000	0	0

Source: *Ibid.*

Table 4.14B Estimated and Actual Income on Major heads of MCP (2009-2010) (Figures are in Rs)

Year	2009-10		
Services	*Budge-ted (Rs)*	*Actual (Rs)*	*Actual as a per centage of budgeted*
Electricity Duty	20,000,000	20,000,000	100
H Tax	45,000,000	45,000,000	100
Fire Tax	4,000,000	4,000,000	100
S Duty	200,000,000	200,000,000	100
Rent of Shops	100,000	100,000	100
Interest on Investment	20,000,000	20,000,000	100
Development work	40,000,000	40,000,000	100
Excise share	10,000,000	10,000,000	100

Source : *Ibid.*

(i) Major heads of Income

Tables 4.14, 4.14A and 4.14B reveal that on the whole, Municipal Council Panchkula has failed to ensure effective tax compliance in its jurisdiction .The data about major heads of income shows that there was huge variation between the budgeted estimates of tax revenues and actual tax revenues, thereby, reflecting ineffective tax compliance. This trend is particularly visible in the case of Development Work wherein on an average, only 22.53 per cent of the proposed taxes have been collected between 2001 to 2009.

In case of some taxes, the comparison between budgeted income as well as actual income shows that MCP has failed to prepare proper budget estimates by following the principles of public finance and administration. Tables 4.14, 4.14A and 4.14B clearly show that Fire tax, Interest on investment, Rent of Shops and Electricity duty have always been much higher than the budgeted estimates. During the years 2001-09, the income from the fire tax, interest on investment, rent of shops and electricity duty as percentage of budgeted estimates was 3481 per cent, 280 per cent, 135 per cent and 104.9 per cent of the budgeted estimate respectively, as shown in Tables 4.14, 4.14A and 4.14B.

(ii) Minor heads of Income

In case of income from minor heads of MCP, the comparison between the budgeted income and the actual income shows that MCP has failed to prepare the budget estimate by following a rigorous exercise of budget preparation. Tables 4.15, 4.15A and 4.15B clearly show that for Road cut charges, Tehbazari Malba and Composition Fees, the actual income from these taxes have always been much higher than their budgeted estimates during the years 2001 to 2009. The actual income was 1,513 per cent of the estimate in case of road

Table 4.15 Estimated and Actual Income from Minor Heads of MCP (2001-02 to 2004-05) (Figures are in Rs)

Years / *Minor Head*	*2001-02* *Budge-ted (Rs)*	*Actual (Rs)*	*Actual as a per centage of budgeted*	*2002-03* *Budge-ted (Rs)*	*Actual (Rs)*	*Actual as a per centage of budgeted*	*2003-04* *Budge-ted (Rs)*	*Actual (Rs)*	*Actual as a per centage of budgeted*	*2004-05* *Budge-ted (Rs)*	*Actual (Rs)*	*Actual as a per centage of budgeted*
Composition Fees	0	0	0	50,000	32,430	0.6	20,000	55,232	276	20,000	40,345	201.7
Tehbazari Malba	0	1,057,903	-	25,000	72,000	288	20,000	94,010	470	20,000	85,500	427.5
Licence Us 12	1,200,000	20,020	1.6	500,000	15,160	3.03	100,000	7,635	7.6	100,000	64,071	64.0
Road Cut Charges	0	7,285	0	75,000	250	0.3	25,000	57,612	230	25,000	260,112	

Source: *Ibid.*

Table 4.15A Estimated and Actual Income from Minor Heads of MCP (2005 -06 to 2008-09) (Figures are in Rs)

Years / *Minor Head*	*2005-06* *Budge-ted (Rs)*	*Actual (Rs)*	*Actual as a per centage of budgeted*	*2006-07* *Budge-ted (Rs)*	*Actual (Rs)*	*Actual as a per centage of budgeted*	*2007-08* *Budge-ted (Rs)*	*Actual (Rs)*	*Actual as a per centage of budgeted*	*2008-09* *Budge-ted (Rs)*	*Actual (Rs)*	*Actual as a per centage of budgeted*
Composition Fees	25,000	51,980	207.9	25,000	112,769	451.0	100,000	100,000	100	50,000	70,150	140
Tehbazari Malba	50,000	61,200	122.4	50,000	95,000	190	50,000	150,000	300	150,000	50,400	33.6
Licence Us 12	100,000	79,272	79.27	100,000	94,563	94.5	100,000		100	100,000	65,300	64.07
Road Cut Charges	50,000	3,743,972	7487	50,000	975,850	1951	200,000	2,800,000	1400	1,500,000	906,120	0.60

Source: *Ibid.*

cut charges, 228 per cent in case of Tehbazari Malba and 122 per cent for composition fees of the Budgeted estimate, respectively, as shown in Tables 4.15, 4.15A and 4.15B.

Table 4.15B Estimated and Actual Income from Minor Heads of MCP (2009 -10) (Figures are in Rs)

Year / *Minor Head*	*2009-10* *Budge-ted (Rs)*	*Actual (Rs)*	*Actual as a per centage of budgeted*
Composition Fees	50,000	50,000	100
Tehbazari Malba	150,000	150,000	100
Licence Us 12	100,000	100,000	100
Road Cut Charges	150,000	150,000	100

Source: *Ibid.*

Hypothesis 3, Sub Hypothesis (ii): Non developmental expenditure consumes maximum revenue and in the process, the development of the city suffered.

For testing of sub–hypothesis (ii), a comparison of developmental expenditure vis-à-vis non developmental expenditure for the period 2001-2010 was undertaken as shown in Table 4.16.

Tables 4.16, 4.16A and 4.16B reveal that the ratio of development expenditure to the non development expenditure has been low. The average of development expenditure as a percentage of non-development for the years 2001 to 2010 was 8.2 per cent, 25.5 per cent, 36.5 per cent, 26.2 per cent, 24.7 per cent, 21.8 per cent, 20.2 per cent, 18.3 per cent and 17.0 per cent respectively. This shows that the non development expenditure was more than the development expenditure and thus, adversely affected the development works of MCP.

Hypothesis 3, sub hypothesis (iii): There is an imbalance in the expenditure on select services by MCP

For testing of this sub-hypothesis, a comparative analysis of expenditure was undertaken on select services.

There is imbalance in expenditure on select services provided by MCP. For example, over the years the expenditure on roads has been higher than other services like sanitation, parks, street lights and fire services. The Tables 4.16, 4.16A and 4.16B have shown that the expenditure on roads, parks, sanitation, street light and fire brigade as a percentage of development expenditure was 60.5 per cent, 13.40 per cent, 15.09 per cent, 4.87 per cent, 1.79 per cent, respectively. Thus, it can be concluded that if Rs 100 was spent between 2001 to 2010 for select services than, Rs 57.53, Rs 12.88, Rs

Table 4.16 Ratio of Total Expenditure Given for Development Expenditure of MCP (2001-02 to 2004-05)

Year\Total Expenditure Services	*2001-02\2368299*		*2002-03\19447345*		*2003-04\46585484*		*2004-05\99523913*	
	Total Expenditure	*Ratio Of Total Expenditure*	*Expenditure*	*Ratio Of Total Expenditure*	*Expenditure*	*Ratio Of Total Expenditure*	*Expenditure*	*Ratio Total Expenditure*
Road+ Cc Paving	696,993	29.4	9,129,668	46.9	62,806,786	134.0	35,886,127	36.0
Sanitation	32,270	1.3	2,730,546	14.04	9,295,735	19.9	22,939,726	23.0
Parks	4,423	0.1	0	0	596,843	1.2	56,610,212	56.8
Street Light	2,773	0.1	12,723,927	65.4	12,507,181	26.04	13,664,413	13.7
Fire Brigade	239,686	10.1	329,691	1.6	464,451	0.9	1,962,567	1.97
	AVG	**8.2**		**25.5**		**36.5**		**26.28**

Source: *Ibid.*

Table 4.16A Ratio of Total Expenditure Given for Development Expenditure of MCP (2005-06 to 2008-09) (Figures are in Rs.)

Year\Total Expenditure Services	*2005-06\63713134*		*2006-07\162296679*		*2007-08\345664006*		*2008-09\246351137*	
	Total Expenditure	*Ratio Of Total Expenditure*	*Expenditure*	*Ratio Of Total Expenditure*	*Expenditure*	*Ratio Of Total Expenditure*	*Expenditure*	*Ratio Total Expenditure*
Road+ Cc Paving	39,387,874	61.8	89,496,535	55.1	213,500,000	61.9	178,938,749	72.6
Sanitation	12,576,442	1927	17,817,883	10.9	70,000,000	20.2	28,599,302	11.6
Parks	12,250,753	19.0	49,241,569	30.3	35,000,000	10	4,425,829	1.79
Street Light	14,350,412	22.5	20,288,279	12.5	25,000,000	7.2	12,834,004	5.2
Fire Brigade	330,561	0.5	815,560	0.5	7,700,000	2.2	1,756,701	0.7
	AVG	**24.74**		**21.86**		**28**	**AVG**	**18.36**

Source: *Ibid.*

13.65, Rs 4.95 and Rs 1.60 were spent on roads, sanitation, parks, street light and fire brigade, respectively. The biasness of expenditure in favour of roads adversely effects the provision and quality of other services like sanitation, parks, street light and fire brigade.

Table 4.16B Ratio of Total Expenditure Given for Development Expenditure of MCP (2009-10) (Figures are in Rs)

Year\Total Expenditure Services	*2009-10\263615000* Total Expenditure	Ratio Of Total Expenditure
Road+ Cc Paving	151,500,000	57.4
Sanitation	36,000,000	13.6
Parks	12,500,000	4.7
Street Light	25,000,000	9.4
Fire Brigade	510,000	0.1
	AVG	**17.04**

Source: *Ibid.*

Hypothesis 4: The sources of income of MCP are inadequate resulting in its over dependence upon grants-in aid.

For testing of Hypothesis 4 related to grants-in–aid, an analysis of the total grants received by the MCP from Centrel as well as State governments and the ratio of this as a percentage of total income was undertaken as shown in Table 4.17.

Table 4.17 Grants-in aid of MCP (Year-Wise) (Figures are in Rs)

Year	*Grant*	*Total Income After Including Grant*	*Percentage of Grants-in-aid in Total Income*
2001-02	0	35,597,210	0
2002-03	0	76,541,848	0
2003-04	0	75,623,413	0
2004-05	867,000	102,720,755	0.0
2005-06	6,201,000	147,009,496	4.40
2006-07	10,513,800	160,962,793	8.6
2007-08	7,005,000	231,785,000	3.11
2008-09	22,511,450	365,767,185	10.9
2009-10	0	0	0
Average	**2.29**		

Source: *Ibid.*

Table 4.17 reveals that the contribution of grants-in-aid received by the MCP is only 2.29 per cent (average of the period 2001-2010) of the total income. This shows that MCP is not depending much upon grant-in-aid. It manages to raise resources for its working from its own sources. Also during the period 2001-2003, MCP received no grants-in-aid, suggesting its non-dependence on grants.

4.12 Status of Hypotheses

The analysis of both primary and secondary data was used to check the status of Hypothesis 3: "The Municipal Council, Panchkula

Matrix 2 Summing up the Testing of Hypotheses 3 and 4

Hypothesis	*Sub-hypothesis*	*Sources of data*	*Analysis*	*Status of Sub Hypothesis* Valid Y Invalid N
Hypothesis 3: The Municipal Council, Panchkula does not manage its financial resources properly.	I. The MCP does not prepare its budget estimates properly especially, in case of taxes.	Secondary data	The data about major and minor heads of income from taxes shows huge variation between the budgeted estimates and the actual income, thereby reflecting a lack of undertaking scientific exercise to estimate the revenue from taxes and also indicating poor tax compliance. This trend is particularly visible in case of development work s where in, on an average, only 22.53 per cent of the estimated taxes were actually realised between 2001 and 2009. In case of minor heads, the actual income from fire tax, interest on investment, rent of shops and electricity duty has always been much higher than the budgeted estimates. For example, between year 2001-09, the income from the fire tax, interest on investment, rent of shops and electricity duty as percentage of budgeted estimates was 3481 per cent, 280 percent, 135 per cent and 104.9 per cent, respectively. In case of road cut charges, tehbazari malba and composition fees, it was 1513 per cent, 228 per cent and 172 percent of the budgeted estimates respectively.	Y

	II. Non developmental expenditure consumes maximum revenue and in the process, the development of the city suffers.	Secondary data	The ratio of development expenditure to the non-development expenditure has been low. The average of development expenditure as a percentage of non-development for the years 2001 to 2010 was only 8.2 per cent, 25.5 per cent, 36.5 per cent, 26.2 per cent, 24.7 per cent, 21.80 per cent, 20.82 per cent, 18.30 per cent and17.08 per cent, respectively.	Y
	III. There is an imbalance in the expenditure on select services by MCP.	Secondary data	There is an imbalance in the expenditure on select services delivered by MCP. For example, over the years the expenditure on roads has been larger than that on other services like sanitation, parks, street lights and fire services. The expenditure on road as a percentage of development expenditure for the years from 2001 to 2010 was 60.5 per cent, 13.40 per cent, 15.09 per cent, 4.87 per cent, 1.79 per cent, respectively. If Rs 100 were spent between 2001 to 2010 for select services, Rs 57.53 were allocated for road, Rs 12.88 for sanitation, Rs 13.65 for Parks, Rs 4.95 for street light and Rs 1.60 for fire brigade.	Y
Hypothesis 4: The sources of income of MCP are inadequate resulting in its overdependence upon grants-in-aid.		Secondary data	The contribution of grant-in-aid received by the MCP as a percentage of total income is only 2.9 per cent (average of the period 2001-2009). During the period 2001-2004, MCP did not receive grant-in-aid.	N

does not manage its financial resources properly" and Hypothesis 4 "The sources of income of MCP are inadequate resulting in its over dependence upon grants in aid".

Thus, on the basis of the above analysis of sub hypothesis, the Hypothesis 3: "The Municipal Council, Panchkula does not manage its financial resources properly" stands validated and Hypothesis 4: "The sources of income of MCP are less resulting in its over dependence upon grants-in-aid" get rejected.

Concluding Observations

The study revealed that MCP has failed to prepare proper budget estimates for tax collection in its jurisdiction over the years. MCP has also failed to ensure proper tax compliance. Huge variations between the budgeted estimates and actual tax revenue have been found in the study. As far as the expenditure is concerned, non-development expenditure consumes maximum revenue of MCP and in the process, the development of the city suffers. Further, more the study also reports an imbalance in the expenditure on select services by MCP. Roads take the lion's share of total expenditure and subsequently other services suffer. The study identified crucial factors affecting the financial administration of MCP. These are the delays in approval of budget by the district administration, improper classification of expenditure, non-adherence to the reports of audit and accounts for improving its financial health. On the whole, the study found that the MCP does not follow the cannons of efficient financial administration.

REFERENCES

1. L.D. White, Introduction to the Study of Public Administration, McMillan, New York, 1955, p. 215.
2. Felix Nigro, Public Administration Readings and Documents, Rinehart and Co-Inc., New York, 1951, p. 312.
3. S.L. Goel, Public Financial Administration, Deep & Deep Publication, 2002, p. 11.
4. White, op.cit. p. 220.
5. Government of India, Report of the Committee on Budgetary Reform in Municipal Administration, Ministry of Works and Housing, New Delhi, 1974.
6. *Haryana Municipal Act, op*.cit.
7. *Ibid.*, Section, 70.

8. *Ibid*., Sec. 70.
9. *Ibid*., Sec. 75.
10. Government of Haryana, Second State Finance Commission Report, 2005.
11. *Directorate of Urban Local Bodies, Finance Department,* Haryana
12. *Ibid*.
13. *Municipal Council, Panchkula*, Audit's Inspection Note, 2005-06.
14. *Ibid*.
15. *Ibid*.
16. *Ibid*.
17. Officials of Account Department of Municipal Council, Panchkula.
18. Second Finance Commission Report, op. cit.
19. *Ibid*.
20. Haryana Municipal Act, 1973, op. cit.
21. Second Finance Commission Report, op. cit.
22. Government of Haryana, 1st State Finance Commission Report, 1997.
23. *Directorate* of Urban Local Bodies, op.cit.
24. *Ibid*.
25. *Accounts* Branch, Municipal Council, Panchkula
26. *Ibid*.

27 Haryana Municipal Act, 1973.

28. *Account*s Branch, op.cit.
29. *Ibid*.
30. Maheshwari, op. cit., p. 342.
31. Bakshi, op. cit., Art. 280.
32. Finance Branch, Directorate of Urban Local Bodies of Haryana.
33. *Ibid*.
33. Second State Finance Commission Report, op.cit.
34. Bakshi, op.cit., Art 243Y.
35. P.K. Dubey, "Strengthening Urban Local Bodies in Chattisgarh", Nagarlok, Vol. XXXVIII, No.2, April-June, 2006.
36. Bakshi, op.cit., Art. 243I.
37. Bakshi., op.cit.
38. Second State Finance Commission Report, op.cit.
39. Report of 3rd state Commission Haryana, 2008.
40. *Directorate of Urban Local Bodies Haryana, op.cit*.
41. Finance Department, Directorate of Urban Local Bodies, Haryana
42. Accounts Branch of Municipal Council, Panchkula.
43. Accounts Branch of Municipal Council, Panchkula.

44. *Ibid*.
46. Charles-T Horn, Accounting for Management Control: An Introduction, Prentice-Hall of India Pvt. Ltd., New Delhi, 1976, p.4.
46. Bakshi, op.cit., Art 243Z.
47. Second State Finance Commission Report, op.cit.
48. D.H.L. Bhatia, Public Finance, Vikas Publishing House Pvt. Ltd., Alahabad, 2008, pp. 193-198.
49. Olu Ojo, "Efficient Financial Management for Local Governments: The Nigerian Experience", Blutinul Universitatic Petrol-Gazedin Ploiosts, Vol. LXI, No. 2, 2009, pp. 36-44.

5

The Physical Performance of Municipal Council Panchkula With Special Reference to Select Services

Performance measurement happens to be an way by which the services provided by the organisation can be judged *efficiently* in the terms of their output, efficiency, effectiveness and quality with respect to input. A performance measurement therefore is essential in order to ensure better decision making, performance appraisal, accountability, better service delivery and effective public participation.

Urban Local bodies all over the world are the primary agencies for meeting social, cultural and physical needs of the citizens. They provide a variety of public utility services for the convenience of healthy living and welfare of individuals and community. The growth of trade and industry in the city in general also depends upon an efficient performance of the Municipal Services[1].

People generally tend to judge an urban government's performance by the standard of services its agencies provide. It is therefore, essential that the Municipal Services should be adequately and efficiently provided not only for the convenience and healthy living of citizens, but also for the promotion of the social and economic development of the local community as well as the overall national development.

In this chapter, the physical performance of MCP with special reference to select services has been examined. The performance of MCP from citizens' perspective has been analysed in the subsequent chapter.

5.1 The Physical Performance of Municipal Council, Panchkula (MCP) with Special Reference to Select Services

The physical performance of Municipal Council, Panchkula (MCP) has been analysed on the basis of activities undertaken with regard to the following basic services:

1. Sanitation
2. Roads
3. Street Lights
4. Fire
5. Parks.

5.2 Physical Performance of MCP Regarding Sanitation Services

The Sanitation services in the Municipal Area Panchkula are provided by MCP mainly by adopting contracting out mode. An analysis of the physical performance of MCP with regard to the sanitation services has been undertaken on the basis of comparison with select benchmarks, assessment of government agencies, pictorial depictions of conditions of sanitation services and content analysis of news reports. Efforts have also been made to visit different areas under the municipal jurisdiction and use observation as a method of data collection about the activities undertaken and their impact on the sanitation conditions in the area.

5.2.1 Sanitation Services Provided by Municipal Council, Panchkula

The following sanitation services are provided by the MCP to the citizens in its jurisdiction.

(i) Street Cleaning
(ii) Collection of Waste
(iii) Transportation of Waste
(iv) Disposal of Waste

(i) Street Cleaning

Municipal Council, Panchkula has been entrusted with the

responsibility of cleaning the streets. In an area falling under the jurisdiction of MCP, the process of street cleaning is carried out manually by sweepers working in groups, who are assigned specific areas within their respective zones.

(ii) Collection of Waste

The second service includes the collection of waste from roadsides and from within the sectors, villages and colonies, and transferring it to near-by community bins through hand cart. These community bins are installed on the roadsides and are owned by the MCP.

Community bins have been installed on roadsides all over the city under Council area with the a vision that the waste collected by the sweepers on roadsides is transferred to such bins through handcarts. However, most of the citizens hire private garbage collectors for door to door collection of their daily household waste on a monthly payment.

(iii) Transportation of Waste

This is normally done by the garbage collecting staff, which transfers garbage from bins to the vehicles. After bins are emptied, the vehicle along with the workers moves to the next bin till it is fully loaded. Municipal vehicles such as trucks and trolleys are used for transportation of waste to a dumping site which is located near Sector 23 , Panchkula.

(iv) Disposal of Waste

The final function i.e. disposal of collected waste is performed by M.C.P. This disposal of waste refers to dumping of waste into a landfill.

5.2.2 Analysis of Physical Performance of MCP regarding Sanitation Services

An analysis of the physical performance of MCP regarding sanitation services has been undertaken on the basis of: I. Select Benchmarks; II. Assessment of Government Agencies; III. Pictorial depictions; and IV. Content Analysis of News Reports.

I. Select Benchmarks of Sanitation Services

There are some parameters for the delivery of sanitation services by the municipalities to the citizens. These have been taken from select studies / research works published in the journals. An analysis of the sanitation services provided by the Municipal Council Panchkula has been undertaken on the basis of these select benchmarks and is presented in Table 5.1.

Table 5.1

Benchmarks for Sanitation Services

Sr. No.	*Benchmark*	*Performance of MCP*	*Comment*
1.	100% household level coverage of solid waste	About 70% of the households are covered.	Around 30%, villages and colonies are not covered on account of solid waste (Primary data, pictorial depiction and content analysis).
2.	100% collection of Municipal waste	About 50%	Half of the waste in the MCP jurisdiction is not collected.
3.	100% scientific disposal of Municipal waste	0%	MCP has not made an arrangement for Scientific disposal of municipal waste (Primary data, pictorial depiction and content analysis).
4.	100% segregation of solid waste*	0%	There is no provision for segregation of solid waste in the MCP jurisdiction.
5.	Hazardous wastes such as hospital wastes must be incinerated in all cases whereas mechanized composing and incineration for large urban areas. Sanitary landfill method of disposal used in small and medium towns.	0%	No provision.
6.	Number of Bins should be 1 for 75 persons	1 for 1373 persons	The number of Bins per person in MCP jurisdiction are significantly lower than the prescribed norm.
7.	Number of sanitary workers should be 2.8 per thousand population***.	1.54 per thousand population/1,000	The number of contractual sanitary workers in MCP

		jurisdiction are significantly lower than the prescribed parameter.

Source* Government of India, *Handbook on Service Level Benchmarking*, Ministry of Urban Development, 2009.

** M.P. Mathur, "Norms and Standards of Municipal Basic Services in India", *National Institute of Urban Affairs*, 2007.

*** Simanty Bundyopadhya, "Decentralization in Jharkhand: Some Implication for Urban Service Delivery", *International Study Programme Working Paper* 11-14, 2011.

Table 5.1 reveals that in case of solid waste the coverage of household is 70 per cent against a norm of 100 per cent. The benchmark for collection of municipal waste is 100%.Therefore, it seems that MCP is rint half way to this parameter. The performance of MCP with regard to scientific disposal of municipal waste, segregation of solid waste and management of hazardous waste is hitting rock bottom. In case of number of bins and sanitary workers, the performance of MCP is again below norms.

Hence, the performance of sanitation services provided by MCP undertaken on the basis of select benchmarks reveals that the sanitation services in the jurisdiction of MCP are deficient as compared to the select benchmarks.

II. Assessment of Government Agencies

The service delivery system of MCP is audited by Government agencies. According to the report of Urban Estate Department of Haryana, the quality of sanitation services is sub standard (The *Tribune*, January 14, 2005). The District administration report is also very critical about the sanitation services being provided in the city (*The Tribune*, April 23, 2005). It clearly states that the sanitation services in the jurisdiction of MCP is not up to the mark.

III. Pictorial Depiction of Sanitation Services in MCP jurisdiction

In order to analyse the physical performance of MCP regarding sanitation services, a pictorial analysis has been used. The status of sanitation conditions has been captured from the four broad areas falling within the jurisdiction of MCP. These include the posh sectors, the other sectors, villages and colonies. A snapshot of the sanitation services in these four broad areas have been presented in photographs 1 to 18.

Photographs 1-18
Pictorial Depiction of Sanitation Services in Different Areas of MCP

Posh Sectors	**Other Sectors**

Photograph 1

Clean Garbage Bin (Sector 2)

Photograph 2

Garbage Lying Scattered in the Park (Sector 11)

Photograph 3

Clean Road (Sector 7)

Photograph 4

Scattered Garbage Behind Park (Sector 12)

Posh Sectors
Photograph 5

Clean Road
(Sector 8)

Other Sectors
Photograph 6

Heap of Garbage in Front of Park(Sector 12)

Photograph 7

Clean Road
(Sector 6)

Photograph 8

Scattered Garbage
(Sector 16)

Posh Sectors
Photograph 9

Clean Sanitation
(Sector 8)

Other Sectors
Photograph 10

Overflowing Garbage Bin
(Sector 16)

Photograph 11

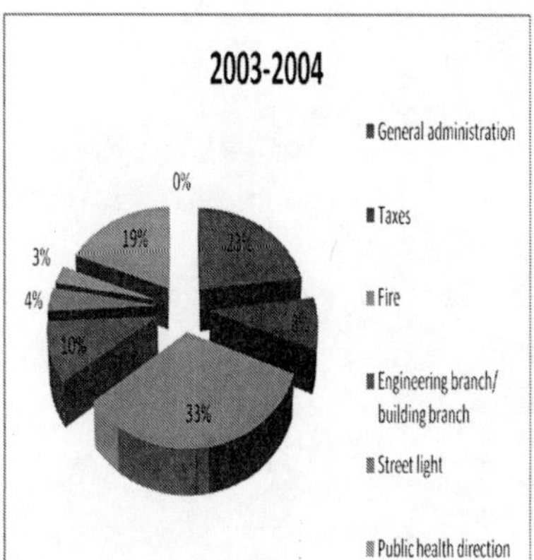

Clean Sanitation
(Sector 7)

Photograph 12

Burning of Garbage in Sector 19
(The Tribune, Feb 28, 2010).

Photograph 13

Stray Cattle Menace in Sector 17 (*The Tribune* Feb 03,2004)

Photograph 14

Burning of Garbage in Sector 17 (*The Tribune*, November 6, 2005)

Villages

Photograph 15

Scattered Garbage (Village Bhainsa Tibba)

Colony

Photograph 16

Depolarable Sanitary conditions in Rajiv Colony (*The Tribune*, 16 July, 2008)

Photograph 17

Garbage on Road
(Village Haripur)

Photograph 18

Pathetic Sanitary Conditions
in Rajiv Colony
(*The Tribune*, 22 July, 2008)

A pictorial analysis of the sanitation services being provided by the MCP reveals that there is a huge variation in the quality of services being delivered across locations. In case of posh areas, the quality of sanitation services is better which deteriorates as we move from posh sectors to other sectors to colonies and then villages.

IV. Content Analysis of News Reports

For collecting information about the performance of MCP regarding the sanitation services, a content analysis of news reports was also undertaken. The major findings in this regard are reported in Table 5.2.

Table 5.2 Content Analysis of News Reports

Sr. No.	*Theme*	*News Reports*	*Analysis of News Reports*
1.	Sweepers are irregular their duties	Dainik Bhaskar, September 5,2007;	Sanitary conditions in MCP jurisdiction are in a deprived state because sweepers employed by MCP are irregular in their duties. The problem is more acute in Sectors 19, 20 and in some villages.
2.	Burning of leaves	The Tribune, November 06, 2005;	Burning of leaves and other wastes especially in Sector 19,

		February 28, 2006. Dainik Bhaskar, July, 16, 2008.	3, 7 and Mansa Devi Complex and generally in the jurisdiction of MCP is continuing, despite a strict ban imposed by the Apex court. The terms of contract signed with the sanitation contractors clearly specify that they can't burn waste. According to the Municipal Corporation Solid Waste Management Rule, 2000, the Municipal Council is also required to frame by- laws to check this hazardous practice
3.	Overflowing garbage bins and scattered garbage	The Tribune, February 03, 2004; December 08, 2004; September 15, 2005; February 28, 2010. Dainik Bhaskar, August 29, 2007; October 5, 2007; October 20, 2007; October 30, 2007; July 16, 2008.	The news paper reports reveal that there is overflowing of garbage bins and heaps of garbage are scattered in most of areas of MCP jurisdiction especially in Sectors 17, 19, 10 21,23 and the area around Mansa Devi Complex.
4.	Foul smell	Dainik Bhaskar, September 24, 2007; November 16, 2007. The Tribune, November 16, 2007; February 28, 2010.	An adverse affect on the general health of public around sectors 23, 24, 25 of Panchkula has been observed due to bad order arising as a result of burning practices in the dumping grounds.
5.	Problems of stray cattle	The Tribune, February 03, December 8, 2004; September 15, 2005. Dainik Bhaskar, August 29, 2007; October 30, 2007.	Stray cattle are the major menace, especially in Sectors 17, 19, 21 and Rajeev colony and occasionally, result in serious accidents also. It is relevant to mention here that major efforts have not been made for catching the stray cattle in MCP jurisdiction.
6.	No systematic disposal and treatment of solid waste	The Tribune, November 06, 2005; August 7, 2005; March 04, 2009; February 28, 2010. Dainik Bhasker, September 24, 2007;	In MCP jurisdiction, there is no systematic disposal or treatment of solid waste. It is simply dumped in vacant plots and on *Nullah* that passes through the various sectors. It leads to insanitary conditions in the city, specially in Sectors, 19, 3, 7, and Mansa Devi Complex.
7.	Water logging	The Tribune, September 13, 2007; October 30, 2007; July 27, 2008.	The rain water logged for days together in the absence of proper drainage system resulted into muddy road conditions, especially in Sector 10.

8.	Mosquito Menace	Dainik Bhasker, November 16, 2007 **The Tribune,** July 27, 2008.	Some areas of MCP jurisdiction have been turned into breeding grounds for mosquitoes and lies, due to insanitary conditions prevalent in the city.
9.	Outbreak of Cholera and Dengue	The Tribune, July 18, 2008 July 20, 2008 Dainik Bhasker, October 30, 2007.	Due to bad conditions of the sanitation services in the city, there was an outbreak of cholera which resulted in few deaths in Rajeev colony.
10.	Problem of Congress grass	The Tribune, August 7, 2005; August 28, 2007.	In the MCP jurisdiction, the congress grass pervaded the entire city and leads to pitiable conditions of sanitation system in the city, especially in Sector 6 Hospital.

Analysis of news paper reports reveal very bad conditions of sanitary system in MCP jurisdiction.

Factors responsible for the Poor Performance of Sanitation Services

Factors responsible for the poor performance of MCP in case of sanitation services have been listed as follows:

(a) Inadequate Manpower

The ideal number of employees in the sanitation department should be 532 for the satisfactory delivery of services. The number of sanitation employees is awfully low, it is only 310. This glaring difference is emerging as a major stumbling block in the satisfaction of citizens with regard to the sanitation services in MCP jurisdiction. Within the department, a majority of workers are contractual and hired by the contractors. As mentioned in the chapter on personnel administration, they are paid very low wages and suffer from unfavorable service conditions. MCP provides sanitation services to the citizens of Panchkula mainly by the method of contracting out since 2002 due to a shortage of permanent staff. The Executive Officer (E.O) of the Council has been authorized to invite tenders from private parties for giving each zone on contract on an annual basis. He is responsible for fixing the terms and conditions of the tender in accordance with the Haryana Municipal Act, 1973 and guidelines of the Government of Haryana from time to time. After awarding the tender, an agreement is signed between the private contractor and the EO and the President of MCP. The main provisions of such an agreement have been mentioned in Annexure I. MCP provides the sanitation services through contracting out .The status of contractual sanitation workers has been given in Table 5.3.

Table 5.3 Number of Contractual Sanitation Workers for Sanitation Service at MCP (year wise)

Year	*Number of workers*
2001-02	Not available
2002-03	-do-
2003-04	395
2004-05	417
2005-06	297
2006-07	297
2007-08	297
2008-09	297
2009-10	310

Sources: Sanitation Branch of Municipal Council, Panchkula, 2010.

Table 5.3 reveals that the strength of contractual employees over the past five years has decreased from 417 in 2004-05 to 310 in 2009-10. The decline in the number of workers adversely affects the performance of sanitation services.

(b) Lack of Capacity Building of Existing Manpower

The employees of the sanitation department including the sanitary workers have not been provided training and this has lead to ineffective service delivery. In MCP, there is just only one employee i.e. an accountant who had been trained between 2001 to 2010 in the Haryana Institute of Public Administration (HIPA). Neither MCP nor the state government has made any efforts for capacity building of employees of the sanitation department.

(c) Ill-equipped Infrastructure

The MCP does not have sufficient physical equipment to provide sanitation services

The physical equipment for providing sanitation services by MCP have been reported in Table 5.4.

Table 5.4 Physical Equipments for Providing Sanitation Services for the Years 2001-02 and 2009-2010

Tools & Equipments	*No. of Equipments 2001-02*	*No. of Equipments 2009-10*
Tricycle	60	60
Community Bins	140	140
Dumper Placer Type Containers	84	84
Dumper Placer Machines	2	2
Skip Lifter	1	4
Tractors	1	2

Sources: Sanitation Branch of Municipal Council, Panchkula, 2010.

Table 5.4 reveals that the Municipal Council, Panchkula had 60 Tricycles, 140 Community Bins, 84 Dumper Placer Type Containers, two Dumper Placer Machines, one Skip Lifter and one Tractor in 2001-02. A look at the records of the Sanitation Branch over a period of 9 years (2001-02 to 2009-10) shows that the physical equipment have remained same except in the case of skip lifter and tractor which increased from one to four and one to two, respectively in the year 2009-10 in comparison to the year 2001-02. The officials of the Sanitation Branch also revealed that the branch at present does not have containers that tackle hazardous waste and Bull Dozers, etc, which are important for sanitation service delivery. It is relevant to mention here that the ideal number of collection bins in sanitation branch should be approximately 2,533 against 140 available with the MCP.

Physical equipment are the most important vehicles for catering of services and the sanitation services are no exception. In case of MCP, the study reveals that there has been a marginal increase in the physical equipment between the year 2001 to 2010. For example, there were only 290 equipment during 2001, which increased to only 292 in the year 2010. The availability of equipment per 1,00,000 population was 193 in 2001, which further declined to 153 in 2010. Thus, this mismatch between increase in the equipment and increase in population clearly suggests that MCP has not succeeded in providing adequate equipment for the delivery of sanitation services.

(d) Absence of Modern Solid Waste Management Practices

There is a strict need of modern Solid Waste Management practices in MCP jurisdiction because of the huge solid waste generation. The total solid waste generated in MCP jurisdiction has been shown in Table 5.5.

Table 5.5 Solid Waste Generated in Municipal Council, Panchkula

Sr. No	*Solid Waste Generated in Tonnes/Day*	*No. of Collection Bins*	*Placement Area*
1.	1.12 MT	2	Bana Madenpar
2.	2.80 MT	5	Fakh pur Kundi
3.	1.68 MT	4	Rajiv Colony
4.	1.68 MT	4	Sector 8
5.	1.68 MT	4	Khadak Mangoli
6.	1.68 MT	4	Devi Nagar
7.	1.68 MT	4	Azad Colony
8.	1.12 MT	3	Maheshpur
9.	1.68 MT	3	Sector. 16
10.	2.72 MT	4	Sector. 17

11.	1.68 MT	3	MDC Sec. 5
12.	5.60 MT	12	MDC Sec. 4
13.	5.04 Mt	9	Sector 12 A
14.	5.60 MT	10	Sec. 14
15.	5.04 MT	9	Sec. 15
16.	4.48 MT	8	Sec. 7
17.	2.80 MT	5	Sec. 9
18.	0.56 MT	3	Sec 10
19.	3.36 MT	6	Sec. 11
20.	3.38 MT	6	Sec. 12
21.	3.92 MT	7	Sec. 19
22.	4.48 MT	8	Sec. 2
23.	3.80 MT	5	Sec. 4
24.	5.04 MT	9	Sec. 6
25.	2.80 MT	5	Ind. Ph-I
26.	4.48 MT	5	Ind. Ph-II
Total	**78.40 MT**	**140**	

Sources: Sanitation Branch of Municipal Council, Panchkula, 2010.

Table 5.5 depicts that in Municipal Council, Panchkula jurisdiction, the solid waste generated daily is about 78.40 metric tonnes while the number of bins allocated for their collection are 140 in number. This solid waste is brought for disposal to the disposal ground which is located in Sector 23 and known as the Dumping Ground.

The dumping ground is a common dumping place of MCP and Haryana Urban Development Authority (HUDA). Recently this place has been in controversy. Because of the expansion of Panchkula and the development of new sectors beyond river Ghaggar, the dumping ground has now occupies a central place. The people living in the new sectors are thus, demanding that this dumping ground be shifted as foul smell emanating from the waste makes living conditions difficult particularly, during the rainy season.

The study reveals that Municipal Council, Panchkula despite having sufficient funds at its disposal, has failed to adopt the modern waste management methods like (i) Segregation; (ii) Composting/ Recycling; and (iii) Incineration. These methods have tremendous utility as discussed below and therefore, by not adopting them the MCP depriving its population of their benefits:

(i) Segregation of Waste

Certain waste components such as paper, plastics, glass and metals can be recovered from the collected waste and be reused or remanufactured into new products. The process of sorting the usable materials such as paper, plastics, glass and metals from the commingled waste is known as segregation[2].

In Panchkula, the waste at the dumping site is segregated by the rag- pickers. Generally, rag pickers come early in the morning or in the afternoon before the arrival and departure of the council staff at the dumping site. They collect the recyclable materials such as bottles, paper, metal and plastic from the waste and sell it to scrap dealers. The scrap dealer contact the private firms, who after buying the waste from rag pickers sell it to such firms for recycling. The M.C.P is not directly involved in the performance of any of the above mentioned activities.

(ii) Composting/Recycling

Composting is considered to be a form of recycling. It is also a form of bio-treatment as in the process, the microorganisms degrade the biodegradable waste to yield manure. The biodegradable waste arises from a variety of human, agricultural and horticultural sources and can be considered to form three general groups: waste of direct animal origin (faeces/ manures), plant materials (grass clippings, vegetable pilings) and processed materials (food wastes). In Panchkula, unfortunately MCP has not been able to do this .

(iii) Incineration of Waste

Incineration represents a treatment option for the destruction and safe transformation or reduction of waste. It is a process of destroying or inactivating the hazardous waste metals, iron containing material gaseous, liquids etc. produced by industrial processing units and hazardous waste (human anatomical waste, tissues, organs, body parts, hypodermic needles, syringes etc.) produced by medical institutions. However, a good incineration system not only makes good use of waste but also generates electric power[3].

However, MCP has failed to adopt the above mentioned modern waste management techniques. In the absence of solid waste management system, M.C.P is failing in its basic duty of providing clean and hygienic environment to the residents of the city.

5.3 Physical Performance of MCPRegarding Road Services

The road services in the Municipal Area, Panchkula are provided by MCP. Mainly contracting out mode is adopted for the delivery of these services. The analysis of physical performance of MCP with regard to road services has been undertaken on the basis of comparison with select benchmarks; assessment of government agencies; pictorial depiction of condition of road services; and content analysis of news reports. Efforts have also been made to visit different areas under the municipal jurisdiction and use observation as a method of data collection about the activities being undertaken and their impact on the road conditions in the area.

5.3.1 MCP and Road Services

For providing road services, MCP performs the following two functions :

(1) Construction of Roads, and
(2) Maintenance of Roads

The construction and maintenance of roads comes under the purview of the Engineering Wing of MCP which covers all types of settlement i.e. sectors, colonies and villages. A municipal engineer has been charged with the responsibility of construction and maintenance of roads, footpaths, round-about, parking lots, road berms and back lanes in the city.

MCP performs both the above mentioned functions i.e. construction and maintenance of roads through the process of contracting out.

For this, MCP invites tenders and gives work on contract basis to some private agencies. The contract mentions the terms and conditions, which the contractor has to follow during a given period of time for the completion of work, maintenance of roads, cleaning of road berms and back lanes. Under the agreement signed between the contractor on the one side and the Executive Officer and the Municipal Engineer on the behalf of MCP on the other, the provisions relating to construction as well as maintenance of roads have been mentioned in Annexure II.

5.3.2 Analysis of Physical Performance of MCP Regarding Road Services

The analysis of the physical performance of MCP regarding sanitation services has been undertaken on the basis of: I. Select depiction; and IV. Content Analysis of News Reports.

I. Select Benchmarks for Road Services

There are some benchmarks for the Road Services being provided by municipalities to the citizens. These have been taken from select studies /research work published in various journals. The analysis of the Road Services being provided by Municipal Council, Panchkula has been undertaken on the basis of these select parameters and is presented in Table 5.6.

Table 5.6 Analysis of MCP on the Basis of Benchmarks for Quality and Availability of Road Services

Sr. No.	*Indicators*	*Benchmarks*	*Performance of MCP*	*Comments*
1.	Quality of Road	(i) Proper layering with Standard Base Course and Surface Course. (ii) Proper thickness of layer. (iii) Proper Density	Not satisfactory	According to the Third Party Inspection Report i.e. by National Institute of Technical Teacher Training and Research (NITTTR) and District Administration the quality of roads in MCP jurisdiction was sub standard.
2.	Mix Design Ratio for different ingredients	(i) Stone aggregate of different size (ii) Stone of dust (iii) Bitumen	Not satisfactory	According to the Third Party Inspection Report i.e. by NITTTR and District Administration, the quality of roads in terms of Mix Design Ratio for different ingredients of MCP jurisdiction was sub standard.
3.	Preparation	(i) Proper Surface Preparation (ii) Proper Rolling	Not satisfactory	The Third Party Inspection Report i.e. by District Administration reveals that the quality of roads in MCP jurisdiction in area of preparation was sub standard.
4.	Density	Proper density	Not satisfactory	The Third Party Inspection Report i.e. by District Administration reveals that the quality of roads in MCP jurisdiction was sub standard because proper density was not maintained.
5.	Comprehensive strengths*	Proper	Not satisfactory	The Third Party Inspection Report i.e. By NITTTR and District Administration shows that the quality of roads in MCP jurisdiction was sub standard, because it had improper comprehensive strength.

6.	Requirement of roads per thousand population road length [per km square] **	Class I [1 lakh and above population] = 11.09 km/1000	2.11Km/1000 population	The performance of MCP in this regard is immensely poor as its performance is less than even 20 percent of the parameters.

****Sources***: Parameters of quality of Road adopted by NITTTR, Sector 26, Chandigarh.

** Simanty Bundyopadhya, "Decentralization in Jharkhand: Some Implication for Urban Service Delivery", *International Study Programme Working Paper*, 11-14, 2011.

II. Assessment of Government Agencies

According to the District Administration Report: (1) Many cement \ concrete works were found sub standard; (2) Less cement has been used while filling kerbs channel; (3) All the works in general for cement concrete kerbs were substandard and the contractors had carried out pilferage of cement on a large scale due to the fact that the comprehensive strength of the concrete kerbs had not attained even 50% strength, as per requirement and in work under head; (4) The comprehensive strength of kerbs was approximately 20% of the required strength resulting in pilferage of cement more than 60% to 70%. Thus, almost all the works of cement concrete kerbs were found to be substandard and waited that a large scale pilferage/saving of cement had been carried out by the contractors; (5) No cement was found beneath the lane concrete; (6) Wrong and excessive entries had been made in the logs e.g. in Sector 8, the length of Kerbs Channel was 4230 running ft, but it had been written as 5598 feet in the Measurement Book. So it resulted in a loss of about Rs. 34 thousands MCP funds (Dainik Bhaskar, 4 September, 2007).The Municipal Council samples failed all quality tests. Out of the 250 development works carried out in the district, 30 works were selected at random of which 12 samples were sent to the Shri Ram Laboratory of Research Institute, Delhi for testing the ratio of ingredients and their comprehensive strength. According to the test report, "The test results showed that the sample failed badly in quality. Besides, substandard works have been carried out for road footpaths, repair of roads and bogus payments had been detected in one such case. The estimates of various developmental works had been split up intentionally to keep the maximum number of works within the financial powers of the president of MCP, thereby enhancing the scope of financial manipulation". It was also mentioned in the report that excess payments to contractors, wrong entries in the register and poor supervision were the major reasons amongst various others for substandard quality of work (*The Tribune*, August 30, 2007). When Head of NITTR, Civil Department Professor A K Duggal was interviewed by the researcher, he said that he was not satisfied with the raw materials used by Municipal Council, Panchkula and many a times,the guidelines were violated.The District Administration Report about physical performance of MCP was also critical.

III. Pictorial Depiction of Road Services in MCP Jurisdiction

In order to analyze the physical performance of MCP regarding Road Services, a pictorial analysis has been used. The status of roads condition had been captured from the four broad areas falling within the jurisdiction of MCP. These are posh sectors, other sectors, villages and colonies. A snapshot of the roads in these four broad areas has been presented in Photographs 19 to 36.

Photographs 19 - 36
Pictorial Depiction of Road Services

Posh Areas
Photograph 19

Good Condition of Road
(Sector 6)

Other Sectors
Photograph 20

No Proper Maintenance of Road
(Sector 31)

Photograph 21

Good Quality of Road
(sector 7)

Photograph 22

Worse Condition of Road
(Sector 7)

Posh Areas
Photograph 23

Well-maintained Road
(sector 7)

Other Sectors
Photograph 24

Potholed Road
(Sector 7)

Photograph 25

Good Condition of Road
(sector 7)

Photograph 26

Deplorable Condition of Road
(Sector 4)

Photograph 27

Good Condition of Road
(sector 8)

Photograph 28

Worse Condition of Road
(Sector 4)

Photograph 29

Well Maintained Road
(sector 5)

Photograph 30

Path holed Road
(Sector 7)

Village
Photograph 31

Worse Condition of
Budhanpur Road
(sector 5)

Colony
Photograph 32

Ill Maintained Road
Indira Colony
(sector 5)

Photograph 33

Worse Condition of Road (Tribune New Service January 3, 2006)

Photograph 34

Worse Condition of Road

Photograph 35

Worse Condition Village Marji

Photograph 36

Pathetic Condition of India Colony Road

The pictorial analysis of the roads services provided by the MCP reveals that there is a huge variation in the quality of roads across locations. In case of Posh areas, the quality of roads is high which decreases at the level of other sectors. Whereas, the quality of roads is worse in the case of colonies and relatively better in the case of villages.

IV. Content Analysis of News Reports

For collecting information about the performance of MCP regarding roads, a content analysis by news reports was undertaken. The major findings in this regard are reported in Table 5.7.

Table 5.7 Content Analysis of News Reports

Sr. No.	*Theme*	*News Reports*	*Analysis of News Reports*
1.	Deplorable conditions of roads and they are full of pot holes	*Dainik Bhaskar,* September 3, 19, 21, 26, 2007; October 5, 2007 *The Times of India,* March 2, 2009.	Bad conditions of roads are prevalent throughout the MCP area especially in Sectors 15, 19, 20, and 7 (near school).
2.	Substandard road works	*Dainik Bhaskar* September 6, 19, 21, 2007; October 5, 2007 *The Tribune,* September 30, 2007. The Times of India, March 02, 2009.	The quality of roads in MCP jurisdiction is substandard especially in Sectors 15, 9, and 2-A.
3.	Shortage of Technical staff	*Dainik Bhaskar,* September 26, 2007; October 5, 2007.	In MCP, there is a shortage of technical staff for catering to road works. As a result, the quality of roads in its jurisdiction is below the expectations of the residents.
4.	Lack of supervision in road work	*Dainik Bhaskar,* December 18, 2007	In MCP jurisdiction, the road work has not been done properly due to lack of supervision.
5.	Neither repaired nor patch work done	*Dainik Bhaskar,* September 3, 2007. *The Tribune,* January 7, 2005; October 5, 2007	The roads are broken at most of the places in MCP jurisdiction. No repair work has not been done from a long time specially in Sector 15 and Industrial area, Phase-1.

Factors responsible for the Poor Performance of Road Services

The factors responsible for the poor performance of MCP in case of Road Services are as follows:

(a) Inadequate Manpower

The Roads Department of MCP is being looked after by the Engineering Branch and the details of its personnel had been discussed in the Third Chapter of Personnel Administration of MCP. It has been found that five employees are required for the Engineering Branch for provision of road services. In contrast, only three employees are present in the branch. The gap of two employees emerges as a factor in the provision of road services by MCP.

(b) Lack of Capacity Building of Existing Manpower

The employees of the Engineering Branch have not been provided training and it has lead to ineffective service delivery. Neither MCP nor state government has made efforts for the capacity building of employees of the Roads Department.

(c) Lack of Physical Infrastructure and Dependence on Contractors

The Roads Department of MCP not only lacks appropriate physical equipments but is also depend upon contractors for providing road services. If MCP receives any complaint about road services it has to look towards other agencies/ contractors to redress the complaints for even the work related to filling the pot holes of the roads and all of this effects the performance of MCP.

(d) Inadequate Roads Constructed and Maintained by MCP between 2001-2010

Table 5.8 Road Maintained, Repaired and Constructed between 2001-2010

Nature of Work	*Area in Kilometers*
Strengthening	27.2
Patchwork	13.0
Construction	3.4
C C Pavement	6.9
Repair of Road	93.4
Development of Road	2.5
PFs Interling	0.3
Premixing	35.9
PF Kerb Channel	3.2
P F Road Making	0.02
Widening Road	0.2
Total	196.2

Source: Engineering Branch of Municipal Council,Panchkula,2010.

The total length of roads in MCP is 406.43 km including 67.08 km of Concrete Road which is 15.41 per cent of the total length and

339.35 km of the Tarred Road which constitute 84.59 per cent of the total length. Further, an analysis of the area wise distribution of the roads reveals that 346.76 km, i.e., 85.22 percentage of the total road length in MCP is in sectors and the remaining 67.08 km, i.e., 14.78 percentage is in villages and colonies. A look at the maintenance, repair and construction work regarding roads undertaken by MCP between 2001-2010 shows that the MCP had done road strengthening of about 27.20 km, patch work of 13 km and constructed road of about 3.50 km. It had also done CC Pavement work of seven km, repair of roads about 93 km and premixing of road of 35.93 km.

MCP had also done Pot Filling (P.F.) on roads for 0.36 km, P.F. kerb channel for 3.21 km and PF road making for 20 km. As far as the development and widening of roads is concerned the MCP had developed 2.59 km road and it had also done widening of roads for only 0.22 km. Total of Road maintained and repaired by MCP between 2001 to 2010 were approximately 196.2 km and it was mostly in urban areas and little in rural areas, where only seven km road was maintained and repaired and colonies were totally neglected in this period. In conclusion, we can say that MCP had undertaken little work regarding road services between 2001-2010 (See Table 5.8).

The analysis of Table 5.8, content analysis of news reports, pictorial depiction and observation clearly shows that MCP had paid less attention to maintain, repair and construction work regarding roads between 2001-2010.

5.4 Physical Performance of MCP Regarding Street Light Services

The Street Light Services in the Municipal area Panchkula are provided by MCP through the contracting mode.

Two types of activities are performed by MCP while providing street light services to its citizens:-

1. Development of new Street Light Points and Poles.
2. Maintenance of Street Lights (including change and repair of points).

MCP performs both of the above mentioned functions through contracting out mode. Tenders are invited every year and contractors are liable to do both of the functions as per a pre-determined agreement. The contract agreement is signed between the Executive Officer and the Municipal Engineers on one side and contractors on the other side. The main provisions of the contract agreement are provided in Annexure III.

5.4.1 Analysis of Physical Performance of MCP Regarding Street Light Services

The analysis of physical performance of MCP regarding street light services has been undertaken on the basis of: I. Select Benchmarks; II. Assessment of Government Agencies; III. Pictorial depiction; IV. Content Analysis of News Reports.

I. Select Benchmarks for Street Light Services

There are some parameters for the delivery of Street Light Services by municipalities to the citizens. These have been taken from select studies /research works published in the journals. The analysis of Street light services provided by Municipal Council Panchkula has been undertaken on the basis of these select parameters and is presented in Table 5.9 and 5.10.

(i) Benchmarks for quality of Street Light services: Benchmarks for quality of Street Light services has been presented in Table 5.9.

Table 5.9 Benchmarks for Quality Of Street Light Services

	Indicators	*Units*	*Performance of MCP*	*Observations*
1.	Personnel -Supervisor – Technical Qualified.	2 x 31 = 62	In MCP there were 2 supervisors for 31 Wards.	An analysis of the performance reveals a huge deficit in the number in the supervisors for street light services. Instead of 62 supervisors, there are merely 2 in M CP.
2.	On/Off in particular time*	Particular time	According to citizens of MCP the Street lights do not operate in particular time.	The primary data as well as observation shows irregularities on the part of employees of the Electricity Department in switching on and switching off the lights, on particular time, resulting in a wastage of energy.

* Street Light Contract Agreement of Municipal Council, Panchkula.

Table 5.9 reveals that in MCP personnel for providing street light services were not as per the minimum standards.

(ii) Benchmarks for Availability of Street Light Services: The Parameter, for availability of Street Light Services have been given in Table 5.10.

Table 5.10 Benchmarks for Availability of Street Light Services

Sr. No	*Street light indicators*	*Physical norms*	*Performance of MCP*	*Comments*
1	Number of street lights per 1000 population*	25	44.75/1000	On this account, the performance of MCP is better than the bench marks.
2	Distance between two Poles**	28 meters	35 Meter in sectors and 60 to 150 Meter in Villages	The distance between two poles in MCP is slightly less than the benchmarks. In few sectors, villages and colonies, as there is no provision of Street Lights, the comparison with benchmarks is not possible.

* R. Ramanathan and S. Das Gupta, *Estimates of Urban Infrastructure & Financing* (2006-2007), 2009.

** Simanty Bundhoupdhayay , " Decentralization in Jharkhand: Some Implications for Urban Service Delivery", *International Study Programme Working Paper 11-14.*, 2011.

Table 5.9 and 5.10 reveals that in MCP, Street Lights equipment and personnel were not as per the minimum standards.

II. Assessment by Government Agencies

The performance of MCP regarding street light services is audited by government agencies. The District Administration Report regarding the maintenance of street lights is very critical (The Tribune, December 20, 2004). According to the report of Urban Estate Department Haryana, dysfunctional street lights are not repaired on time (The Tribune, January 14, 2005). The committee formed by the district administration was dissatisfied with the street light services provided by MCP (The Tribune, January 14, 2006)

I. Pictorial Depiction of Street Light Services in MCP jurisdiction

In order to analyse the physical performance of MCP regarding Street Lights Services, a pictorial analysis has been used. The status of street light services has been captured from the four broad areas falling within the jurisdiction of MCP. These are the posh sectors, other sectors, villages and colonies. A snapshot of the street lightsw services in these four broad areas have been presented in Photographs 37 to 47.

Photographs 37 - 47
Pictorial Depiction of Street Light Services

Posh Areas
Photograph 37

Well-maintained Street Light (Sector 4)

Other Sectors
Photograph 38

Ill Maintained Street Light (Sector 2)

Photograph 39

Working Street Light Point Properly (Sector 6)

Photograph 40

Street Light Not Working (Sector 16)

Posh Areas

Photograph 41

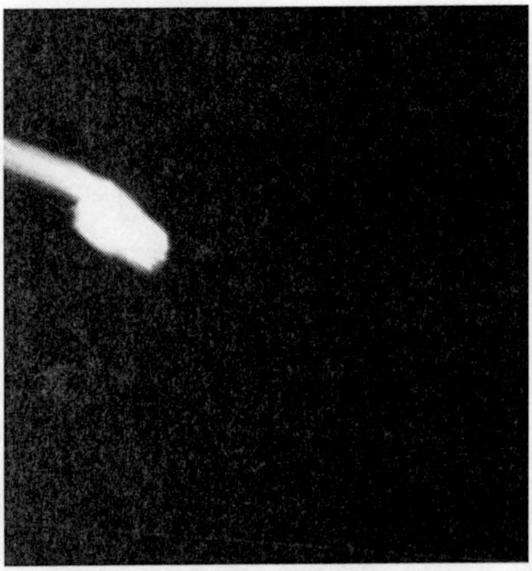

Maintained Street Light
(Sector 7)

Other Sectors

Photograph 42

No Street Light Point
(Sector 10)

Photograph 43

No Electrical Meter
(Sector 1)

Photograph 44

No Street Light Point
(Sector 10)

Posh Areas
Photograph 45

Working Street Light Point

Other Sectors
Photograph 46

No Street Light poles

IN

(Sector 14)

(Sector 10)

Village
Photograph 47

Village Bhainsa Tibba

Colony
No provision

The pictorial analysis of the Street Light services provided by MCP reveals that there is a huge variation in the quality of services delivered across locations. In case of posh areas, the quality of Street light services is high which decreases at the level of other sectors. Whereas, there is no provision of Street light services in case of colonies and some villages.

II. Content Analysis of News Reports

For collecting information about the performance of the MCP regarding street lights services, a content analysis of news reports was undertaken. The major findings in this regard are reported in Table 5.11.

Table 5.11 Content Analysis of News Reports

Sr. No.	*Theme*	*News Reports*	*Analysis of News Reports*
1.	Street Lights are reveal	*Dainik Bhaskar,* *The Tribune,* December 20, 2004; August 9, 2008.	The news paper reports reveal September 6, 2007 April 21, 2007; that the street lights in MCP properly jurisdiction are not working properly.
2.	Missing electric reveal poles	*Dainik Bhaskar,* September 6, 2007.	The newspaper reports reveals that there some electric poles are missing in some areas of MCP jurisdiction.
3.	Redressal of reveal grievances	*Dainik Bhaskar,* September 6, 2007. The Times of India December 18, 2008.	The newspaper reports that there is no action taken by MCP to the redressal of citizen grievances.
4.	Inadequate street lights maintenance	*Dainik Bhaskar,* April 21, 2007; *The Tribune,* December 20, 2004; January 14, 2005; January 14, 2006; and November 16, 2007. The Times of India, December 18, 2008.	In MCP jurisdiction, there is no proper maintenance of street lights.
5.	Dysfunctional reveal street light	*The Tribune,* January 14, 2005; *The Tribune,* December 8, 2004; January 14, 2006: and August 9, 2008.	The newspaper reports reveals that there are a large number of dysfunctional street lights in MCP jurisdiction.

6.	No street light points and absence of meter	*The Tribune,* October 7, 2005; and August 9, 2008.	In MCP jurisdiction, there is absence of street light points in some areas. No electric meters are installed at poles and this leads to financial loss to council.
7.	Contract agreement is not implemented	*The Tribune,* January 14, 2006.	Contracting out of street lights is not free from corruption. At times, the provisions of agreement are not followed.
8.	External audit of street light services is critical	*The Tribune,* January 14, 2005; and January 14, 2006.	According to Urban Estate Department Report of Haryana, the dysfunctional street lights were not repaired in time. According to District Administration Report, the defunct streetlights were not being repaired.

An analysis of news paper reports reveals worse condition of street lights system in MCP jurisdiction.

Factors responsible for Poor Performance of Street Light Services

The factors responsible for poor performance of MCP in case of Street lights services are as follow:

(a) Inadequate Manpower

The personnel of electrical branch are awfully low. The personnel of Electrical Branch, zone wise has been reported in Table 5.12.

Table 5.12 Personnel of Electrical Branch

Years	*Zone 1*	*Zone 2*	*Total*
2001-02	6	7	13
2002-03	6	8	14
2003-04	5	7	12
2004-05	8	6	14
2005-06	9	7	16
2006-07	8	9	17
2007-08	8	8	16
2008-09	10	11	21
2009-2010	11	10	21

Source: Electrical Branch of Municipal Council, Panchkula, 2010.

Table 5.12 reveals that Street light contractual workers are less than the required against the demand of employees. The number of employees was 13 in 2001-02 and increased to only 21 in 2009-10.

(b) Lack of capacity building of existing man power

The employees of the Electrical Branch have not been provided training and it has lead to ineffective service delivery. Neither MCP nor state government has made efforts for capacity building, for employees of street lights.

(c) Ill-equipped infrastructure

The MCP lacks sufficient physical equipment to provide street light services. The Physical equipment of the Electrical Branch has been shown in Table 5.13.

Table 5.13 Physical Equipment

Equipment	*2001-02*	*2009-10*
Ladder	2	2
Van	1	1
Total	3	3

Sources: Electrical Branch of Municipal Council, Panchkula.

Table 5.13 reveals that this branch has inadequate physical equipment. No new infrastructural facilities have been added over time.

(d) Only limited Street Lights Points Repaired and Maintained by MCP between year 2001 to 2010

MCP has total 8607 Street light points in its jurisdiction. It has 2959 Tube Points and 831 Sodium Points in Sectors 12 A, 14,15,16,17,18 and Sector 19, Village Rallay, Budan Pur, Fateh Pur, Kundi, Maheshpur, Devinagar, Abhaypur, RajivNagar and divide Road in Zone -1.

It has 4236 Tubelights and 581 Sodiums in Sector 2,4,6,7,8,9,11,12 and MDC 4 and 5 Village Majri, Raila Haripur and Bhainsa Tibha in Zone -2.

The above discussion reveals that the existing street lights points are not fulfilling the expectations of citizens which come to installation of 1,500, for the covering of area especially in village and colony. Limited Street Lights Points were repaired and maintained by MCP between year 2001 to 2010 (See Table No. 5.14).

Table 5.14 Repaired and Developed Street Lights

Year	*2001 – 2010*
Street Light Developed	Repaired and
Mini High mast light in Park	35
Mini High mast light in Sector	56
Solar Light	65
Total	156

Sources: Electrical Branch of Municipal Council, Panchkula,2010

Table 5.14 reveals that MCP had repaired 35 Mini High Mast Light in Parks and 56 Mini High Mast Light in Sectors and 65 Solar Lights in Sectors. It may be concluded that total only 156 Street lights had been repaired by MCP between 2001 to 2010.

5.5 Physical Performance of MCP Regarding Fire Services

Two types of functions are performed by MCP while providing the Fire services:-

1) Fire prevention :
   Providing guidance to citizens for adopting safety measures in their residential and commercial buildings.
2) Fire fighting

5.5.1 Analysis of Physical performance of MCP regarding Fire services

The analysis of physical performance of MCP regarding Fire Services has been undertaken on the following basis:

I. Select Benchmarks; II. Assessment by Government Agencies; and III. Content Analysis of News Reports

I. Benchmarks for Fire services

There are some parameters for the delivery of Fire services by municipalities to the citizens. The analysis of Fire services provided by Municipal Council, Panchkula has been undertaken on the basis of these select parameters and is presented in Table 5.15, 5.16, 5.17 and 5.18.

(i) Benchmarks for Physical Infrastructure of Fire Services:

The benchmarks for Fire Services identified by National Disaster Management Authority, Government of India have been given in Table 5.15.

Table 5.15 Benchmarks for Fire Services

Physical Equipments	*Norms*	*Performance of MCP upto 31 March 2010*	*Requirement*
Fire station (10 square km)	1	1 for 39.5 square Kilometer area	4
Rescue Tender with required equipment	1	1	4
Ambulance	1	x	4
Mini water Tender	1	x	4
Motor Cycle based Water Mist Technology equipped Fire Party	1	x	4
Water browser detachable [10,000-20,000 meters]	2 tanks	x	2

Break down van	1	x	3
Response Time Urban Rural	5 min. 20 min.	Average 30 minutes in Urban and 40 minutes in Rural	—

Source: National Disaster Management Guidelines, *National Disaster Management Authority*, Government of India, 2010.

Table 5.15 reveals that in MCP, there is only one fire station an areas of 39.5 square kilometer against the norm of four laid down in the National Disaster Management Guidelines and there is only one Rescue Tender against the norms of three. Apart from this, there is no provision for several other physical equipments such as Break Down Van and Ambulance as prescribed in the norms.

(ii) Benchmarks for Water Tender:

The benchmarks for Water Tender stipulated by National Disaster Management Authority (N.D.M.A) have been shown in Table 5.16.

Table 5.16 Benchmarks for Water Tender

Population	*Tenders (Norms)*	*Position in MCP upto 31 March 2010*	*Required*
50,000	1	——	——
1,00,000	2	——-	——
3,00,000	6	2	4
Additional 1 lakh	1	——	——

Source: National Disaster Management Guidelines National Disaster Management Authority, Government of India, 2010.

Table 5.16 reveals that MCP has only 2 Water Tenders against the norms of 6 and clearly show deficiency in the equipment.

(iii) Benchmarks for Fire Safety Equipment:

The parameters for Fire Safety Equipment as per the National Disaster Management guidelines have been shown in Table 5.17.

Table 5.17 Benchmarks for Fire Safety Equipment

Fire Safety Equipments	*Norms*	*Condition in MCP upto 31 March 2010*	*Requirements*
Helmet	According to requirement	15	60
Water bottle with sling	,,	X	4
Eye protection	,,	4	16
Ear protection	,,	1	10
Safety steel-toe boots	,,	X	10
Safety Whistle	,,	X	10
Knee pads	,,	X	20

Work gloves	,,	4	20
Overalls	,,	X	20
Personal safety line Sashcord) 15"length	,,	X	20
Gum boot	,,	1	20
Fire Entry Suits	,,	X	20
Fire Proximity Suits	,,	X	20
Fire Approach Suits	,,	X	20

Source: National Disaster Management Guidelines, *National Disaster Management Authority*, Government of India, 2010.

Table 5.17 reveals that MCP is far behind in the Fire Safety Equipment as laid down by National Disaster Management Authority (N.D.M.A) guidelines.

(iv) Norms for Physical Equipment:

The norms for Physical Equipments laid down by National Disaster Management Authority have been shown in Table 5.18.

Table 5.18 Norms for Physical Equipment

Physical Equipments	*Norms*	*Condition in MCP upto March 2010*	*Requirements*
Turn Table Ladder	1	1	3
Hydraulic Platform	1	Not available	2
Hazmat	1	Not available	1
Advance Rescue/ Emergency Tender	2	Not available	2
Hose Laying Tender	2	Not available	2
Lighting Van	1	Not available	1
Central Post Van	1	Not available	1
Canteen Van	1	Not available	1
Mobile Work shop for repair of Fire Appliances	1	Not available	1
Mobile Work shop for Telecommunication equipment	1	Not available	1
Disaster Management equipment Van	1	Not available	1
High Capacity Pumps	2	Not available	1
Special Personal Protective equipment for NBC Disasters	1	Not available	1

Source: National Disaster Management Guidelines, *National Disaster Management Authority*, Government of India, 2010.

Table 5.18 reveals that norms for physical equipment with the fire department of MCP in comparison with the norms of National Disaster Management Authority present a very poor picture except for the Turn Ladder.

II. Assessment of Government Agencies

According to District Administration Report, the quality of fire services in MCP jurisdiction is substandard(*The Tribune*, August 30, 2007).

III. Content Analysis of News reports

For collecting information about the performance of MCP regarding fire services, a content analysis of news reports was undertaken. The major findings in this regard are reported in Table 5.19.

Table 5.19 Content Analysis of News Reports

Sr. No.	*Theme*	*Source*	*Analysis of News Reports*
1.	Bad condition of fire services	*Dainik Bhaskar,* September 5, 2007; *The Tribune,* July 16, 2008.	The news paper reports reveal that the fire brigade services in MCP jurisdiction are far below the residents expectations.
2.	Lack of Physical Infrastructure, modern technique and lack of adequate staff	*Dainik Bhaskar,* September 5,2007; August 2,2008; April 8,2008; and August 2, 2008. *The Tribune,* July 16, 2008.	The news paper reports reveal that there is a lack of physical infrastructure and modern techniques to provide fire services in the fire brigade department of MCP. Moreover, lack of staff in fire services contributes to poor performance of fire services by MCP.
3.	Delay reaction in case of fire break out	*The Times of India,* March 2, 2007.	In MCP jurisdiction, the fire brigade Van is not able to reach in time to the fire fighting site.

Source: News paper reports.

An analysis of news paper reports reveals a worse condition of fire services in MCP jurisdiction.

Factors responsible for Poor Performance of Fire Services

The factors responsible for poor performance of MCP in case of Fire services are as follows:

(a) Inadequate manpower

MCP has inadequate manpower to provide fire brigade services. The details of the personnel of Fire Departments of MCP have been reported in Table 5.20.

Table 5.20 Contractual Personnel of Fire Branch of MCP

Contractual Personnel	*Number as on 12-06-2010*	*Salary (according to Commissioner Rate Wage)*
Fire man	12	4500
Fire Station Driver	5	4500

Source : Fire Branch of Municipal Council, Panchkula, 2010.

Table 5.20 reveals that there were 17 contractual fire personnel in the Fire Branch of MCP in 2010 against the requirement of 40.

(b) Lack of capacity building of existing man power

The employees of Fire Branch including the Sub Fire Officers have not been provided training by MCP.

(c) Ill-equipped infrastructure

The MCP lacks sufficient physical equipment to provide fire brigade services. The existing status of Physical equipment of Fire Branch has been given in Table 5.21.

Table 5.21 Physical Equipment of Fire Branch for the Years 2001-02 and 2009-10

Equipment	*2001-02*	*2009-10*
Van Including Ladder	2	2
Breezing Operator	2	2+2 = 4
Firing Entry Suit	1	1
Pipe	600Mtr-20*30 Pipe Meter.	1800 Meter.
Foam Compound	100Litre	100 Litre.

Source: Fire Branch of Municipal Council, Panchkula, 2010.

Table 5.21 depicts that there is a lack of proper physical equipment with the Fire Branch of Municipal Council, Panchkula. The physical equipment remained constant except the Breezing Operator suggesting deterioration in fire brigade services in the light of manifold increase in the population of Panchkula.

(d) Poor handling of complaints by Fire Branch

The fire Branch of MCP is not handling fire complaints properly. The handling of complaints with respect to Fire Services has been given in Table 5.22.

Table 5.22 Handling of Complaints by Fire Branch

Years	*Number of Complaints*	*Handling of Complaints*	*Not handled Properly*	*False Complaints*
2003-04	154	140	14	4
2004-05	131	131	06	5
2005-06	178	178	12	4
2006-07	192	192	08	6
2007-08	200	192	08	4
2008-09	198	197	10	8
2009-2010	220	220	12	10

Source : Fire Branch of Municipal Council, Panchkula, 2010.

Table 5.22 depicts that over the year, number of complaints increased from 154 in the year 2003-04 to 192 in the year 2010.

5.6 Physical Performance of MCP Regarding for Park Services

The Park Srvices in the Municipal Area, Panchkula are being provided by MCP. Mainly contracting out mode has been adopted for providing Park Services. Two types of activities are performed by MCP as far as the Parks Services are concerned, namely;

(1) Development of new parks; and
(2) Maintenance of existing parks

MCP performs both the above mentioned functions through Park Development Societies and, agreements have been signed between both i.e. MCP on the one hand and Park Development Society on the other. For main provisions of the agreement, see Annexure IV.

5.6.1 Analysis of Physical Performance of MCP regarding Park Services

The analysis of physical performance of MCP regarding park services has been undertaken on the following basis:

I. Select Benchmarks laid down by HUDA; II. Assessment by Government Agencies; III. Pictorial depiction; and IV. Content Analysis of News Reports.

I. Select Benchmarks for Park Services

There are some parameters that guide the delivery of Park Services by municipalities to the citizens. An analysis of Park Services provided by Municipal Council Panchkula has been undertaken on the basis of these select parameters and is presented in Table 5.23.

Table 5.23 Benchmarks for Park Services

Sr. No.	*Items*	*Norms*	*Condition in MCP*
1.	Provision of park	For 250 Acres area two parks	Instead of 2 parks for 250 acres area in MCP, there is provision of only one park.
2.	Toe wall	1½Feet.	Partially fulfilled in Sectors.
3.	Angle Iron	2½Feet.	Partially fulfilled in Sectors.
4.	Fencing	Four horizontal and two across wires of 12 x 12 gauge.	Partially fulfilled in Sectors.

Source: HUDA Horticulture Division, Norms for Horticulture Works, 1997.

Table 5.23 reveals that sectors considered as posh areas fulfilled partially all the norms. However, some of the sectors not being part of the posh areas, hardly fulfilled the above norms.

II. Assessment of Government Agencies

The Services Delivery System of MCP is usually audited by the Government agencies. According to the report of Urban Estate Department of Haryana, there are irregularities in the Park Services provided by MCP. The wings and benches fixed in the parks and other development works under taken in over 200 parks are of inferior quality (The Tribune, January 14, 2005). According to the report of District Administration of Panchkula, the park services in MCP jurisdiction are not as per the expectations of its citizens (The Tribune, January 14, 2006).

III. Pictorial Depiction of Park Services in MCP Jurisdiction

In order to analyze the physical performance of MCP regarding park services, a pictorial analysis has been used. The status of conditions of Parks has been captured from the three broad areas falling within the jurisdiction of MCP. These are posh sectors, other sectors and villages. A snapshot of the Quality of Parks in these three broad areas have been presented in Photographs 48 to 62.

Photographs 48 - 62
Pictorial Depiction of Park Services

Posh Areas
Photograph 48

Well-maintained Parks
(Sector 6)

Other Sectors
Photograph 49

Bad Condition of Park
(Sector 12)

Photograph 50

Good Quality of Park
(Sector 6)

Photograph 51

No Wall and Fencing in Parks
(*The Tribune* July 27, 2008)
(Sector 9)

Posh Areas
Photograph 52

Good Condition of Parks
(Sector 7)

Other Sectors
Photograph 53

Worse Condition of Parks
(Sector 14)

Photograph 54

Well-maintained Park
(Sector 8)

Photograph 55

Deporable Condition Park
(Sector 15)

Posh Areas
Photograph 56

Parks with Good Infrasturcture
(Sector 8)

Other Sectors
Photograph 57

Pathetic Condition Park
(Sector 12)

Photograph 58

Well-maintained Park
(Sector 5)

Photograph 59

Park with no Wall and Fencing
(Sector 14)

Posh Areas
Photograph 60

Good Quality of Park
(Sector 7)

Other Sectors
Photograph 61

Worse Condition of Park
(Sector 14) An analysis of An

Village	**Colony**
Photograph 62	No provision

Village Haripur

The pictorial analysis of the Park Services provided by MCP reveals that there is a huge variation in the quality of Parks across locations. In case of posh areas, the quality of Parks is better which deteriorates gradually as one moves from the posh sectors to villages via other sectors.

IV. Content Analysis of News Reports

For collecting information about the performance of MCP regarding Park Services, a content analysis of news reports was undertaken. The major findings in this regard are reported in Table 5.24.

Table 5.24 Content Analysis of News Reports

Sr. No.	*Themes*	*News Reports*	*Analysis of News Reports*
1.	Poor development and maintenance of parks	*The Tribune,* August 7, 2005; January 19, 2006; and October 5, 2007.	MCP are far from the expectations of residents of Panchkula.
2.	Worse condition of parks worsened	*The Tribune,* July 27, 2008. *The Times of India,* February 12, 2007.	The conditions of parks with in MCP jurisdiction have overtime.
3.	Corrupt practices in park development and maintenance	*The Tribune,* May 10,2005; and January 19,2006 *The Times of India,* March 27, 2007.	The corrupt practices have been rampant in parks devlopment and maintenance.

4.	No proper implementation of contract.	*The Times of India,* February, 2008.	The contract agreement with private service provides are adhered to.

Source: News Paper Reports.

An Analsis of newspaper reports reveals that the parks services provided by MCP are not as per the norms laid down.

Factors responsible for Poor Performance of Park Services

Factors responsible for poor performance of MCP in case of park services are as follow:

(a) Inadequate Manpower

The parks services of MCP are looked after by the Engineering Branch, as there is no separate machinery for catering to Parks Services. There are only three personnel in the Engineering branch . The Park Development Society (PDS) is constituted by MCP in different areas providing Park Services. But the societies do not have adequate number of employees. There are 70 PDS in MCP jurisdiction and only few societies have their personnel, i.e., Malis (gardeners).

(b) Few Parks Developed and Maintained by MCP between Years 2001 to 2010

Around 204 open spaces were provided by HUDA to MCP. However, only 78 parks were developed and maintained by MCP between the Years 2001 to 2010.The details of this are reported in Table 5.25.

Table 5.25 Parks Developed and Maintained between 2001-2010

	Urban	*Rural*	*Total*
Development of Parks	73	5	78
Repair of Park Grill, Fencing, etc.	2	1	3
Construction work	1 km	0	1 km

Source: Engineering Branch of Municipal Council, Panchkula, 2010.

Table 5.25 reveals that MCP had developed 73 parks in urban areas and five parks in rural areas between the years 2001 to 2010. Further MCP repaired two parks in sectors and one in rural areas between the period 2001-2010.

5.7 Status of Hypothesis

For evaluating the status of the Hypothesis 5: "The physical performance of Municipal Council Panchkula in not satisfactory", the results have been summarised in the Matrix 3.

Matrix 3 Summing up the Status of Hypothesis 5

Sub hypothesis	*Source of data*	*Analysis*	*Status of Sub Hypothesisþ Y Valid N valid*
(i) The Physical performance of MCP with regard to sanitation services is not satisfactory due to drastic decline over time in physical equipment per thousand population, inadequate manpower, lack of modern waste management methods and deviation of provision of sanitation services from the prescribed benchmarks	Primary and Secondary data	• In 2001 MCP had 290 equipment which increased marginally to 292 in 2010. • Equipment per 1000 population suggest that the same declined drastically from 193 to153 between 2001 and 2010. • Further it was found that no practice of segregation of waste, recycling and incineration of waste was adopted by the MCP. • Pictorial depictions indicate worse conditions of sanitation services specifically, in villages and colonies. • Sanitation services were not extended up to 30 percent of the population. • Collection of waste was 50 per cent of the total. • Disposal of waste 70per cent against the standards of 100 per cent. • The number of Disposal Bins 1/1373 population against the norm of 1/75. • The number of sanitary workers was 1.54 per thousand population against the benchmark of 2.8.	Y
(ii) The Physical performance of MCP with regard to road services is not satisfactory on account of lack of inadequate manpower, physical equipment, poor maintenance of roads, improper monitoring of the contractual work and provision of road services not according to the benchmarks	Primary and secondary data	• The Engineering Branch has only three employees against the requirement of 20 employees. • Further the existing staff of Engineering Branch is mainly non-technical and cannot ensure compliance of terms and conditions of the contracts. • Between 2001 to 2010 only 186 km roads were repaired and maintained. • MCP has no equipment of its own for road services. It mainly depends upon equipment of contractors which are many	N

		time made available slowly. • District Administration Reports and Urban Estate Department Reports of Haryana were very critical of road services. • Pictorial depictions indicate very bad conditions of roads in MCP jurisdiction. • In MCP, there are only 2.11 km roads per thousand population against the prescribed benchmark of 11.09 km roads. Roads cover only 70 per cent of the population.	
(iii) The physical performance of MCP in terms of Street light satisfactory owing to inadequate physical equipment, shortage of employees, negligence by MCP, the provision of services not in consonance with increase in population, poor monitoring and standard of street light services not being as per the prescribed standards	Primary and secondary	• The Electrical Branch has only 2 employees against the requirement of 58 employees. Engineering Branch is mainly non technical and cannot ensure compliance of terms and conditions of the contracts. • The number of street lights was 8607 in 2001 which increased only to 8,763 in 2010 thus adding only 156 street lights. • Street lights per thousand of population clearly suggests that MCP has failed to provide street lights in tune with growing population. • Street lights per thousand were only 44.75 in 2001 which declined drastically to 21.68 in 2010. • Between 2001 to 2010 physical equipment with Electrical Branch remained three only. • Pictorial depiction indicates very bad conditions of Street light in MCP jurisdiction. • Distance between two poles was not as per the benchmarks. The distance between two poles should be 28 meters, whereas, in case of MCP, the distance is of 35 meters. • The number of contractual workers was 13 in 2001, which increased only to 21 in 2010. During this period population of Panchkula increased manifold. • Performance of MCP on account of street lights is not satisfactory	Y

		as per the report of District administration and Urban Estate Department of Haryana.	
(iv) The physical performance of MCP in regard to fire services is not satisfactory due to insufficient physical equipment, absence of up gradation and modernization, inadequate manpower and provision of fire services not being in consonance with the benchmarks prescribed by National Disaster Management Authority	Primary and secondary data	• The number of contractual employee was 20 in 2001, which decreased to 17 in 2010. During this period population of Panchkula increased manifold. • Between 2001 to 2010 physical equipment with Fire Branch increased from five to seven only. MCP could not upgrade and modernize its physical equipment according to demand of present fire situation. • The prescribed norms are four fire tenders, two water tenders. Against these MCP has only two fire tenders and two water tenders.	Y
(v) The physical performance of MCP in terms of park services is not satisfactory owing to inadequate provision of parks viz-a-viz population, absence of physical equipment, non monitoring of the works of Parks Development Society, deprivation of parks services for the resident of colonies and slums, and absence of services in relation to prescribed standard.	Primary and secondary data	• MCP has no separate personnel for catering is to parks services. This function is looked after by Engineering Branch. • Further the existing staff of Engineering Branch mainly consists of non technical staff and cannot ensure compliance of terms and conditions of the contracts. • Only 78 parks were developed and maintained against the requirement of 204 parks. • MCP has no physical equipments for providing park services adequately to residents. • Pictorial depictions indicate worse conditions of parks in MCP jurisdiction. • In case of villages and colonies there are no parks. MCP has only one park for 250 meters areas against the prescribed benchmarks two for same area. • No proper physical infrastructure in parks as per the prescribed benchmarks. • Urban Estate Department of Haryana finds irregularities in development of park and inferior quality of park in MCP jurisdiction.	N

An analysis of sub hypotheses reveals that the Hypothesis 5: "The physical performance of Municipal Council Panchkula is not satisfactory" **stands validated**.

Concluding Observations

MCP has been providing several services to the citizens of Panchkula. An assessment of the physical performance in terms of select basic services namely Sanitation, Parks, Street Lights, Fire and Roads paints a poor picture of MCP. According to the present study, Sanitation Services are poor on account of parameters such as the number of bins per thousand population, number of sanitary workers per thousand population, non-segregation of solid waste, and less collection of households waste. The study also found that the provisions of road services are at variance with prescribed norms. Further, the performance in terms of Street lights and Fire services is no way better than Sanitation and Roads. It was also seen that the park services in MCP suffer the most. Inadequate staff; lack of capacity building programmes for employees; lack of equipment; lack of upgradation and modernisation of equipment; contracting out of service and the poor monitoring of contracts; and corrupt practices are some of the factors constraining the physical performance of Civic Services in MCP.

6

Performance of the Municipal Council Panchkula from Citizens' Perspective

An evaluation of the performance of an organisation from the users perspective has assumed an added importance in the backdrop of the new paradigm, articulating citizen-centric or citizen-friendly administration. A user of any services is a King in the alternative paradigm of administration. Keeping this in view, the focus of the present chapter is on the performance assessment of MCP from the citizens' perspective. The level of satisfaction has been selected as an indicator of the citizens' assessment of the MCP's performance.

6.1 Salient Features of Sample Population's Profile

As mentioned in the section dealing with research methodology, a sample of 305 citizens was taken for evaluating the performance of MCP. The sample was drawn from posh areas, other sectors, colonies and villages. Prior to showcausing analysis the level of satisfaction of the sample population, it is desirable to describe some salient features of the sample population on the following accounts:

(1) ***Area:*** Out of 305 respondents, 80 were from rural area, 200 from urban and 25 from colonies.

(2) ***Gender:*** On the basis of gender 293 were male and 12 were female respondents.

(3) ***Employment:*** On the basis of employment, 261 were employed and 44 unemployed.

(4) ***Education:*** On account of education, 74 were below matric and 231 matric and above.

(5) ***Income:*** As per the level of income, 16 respondents were in the category of income above Rs.20,000, 243 having earned between Rs 5000-20000 and 46 with no income.

(6) ***Age:*** On the basis of age, 107 respondents were below 30 years, 182 between 30 to 60 years of age and 16 respondents were 60 years and above in age.

The profile of the respondents has been described below on the basis of their area, gender, employment, education, income and age in Table 6.1.

Table 6.1
Category-wise Number of Respondents

Category	*Sub category*	*Number of Respondents*
Area	Rural	80
	Urban	200
	Colony	25
Gender	Male	293
	Female	12
Employment	Employed	261
	Unemployed	44
Education	Below Matric	74
	Matric and above	231
	No income	46
Income monthly	Between Rs. 5000 to 20,000	243
	Above Rs. 20,000	16
	Below 30	107
Age	30 to 60	182
	60 and above	16

Source: Field survey.

6.2 Major Findings

As stated earlier, the study has been confined to select the basic services being provided by Municipal Council, Panchkula. The citizens satisfaction level on account of these services has been described as under:

6.2.1 Sanitation

Sanitation is the business of keeping places clean and healthy. It directly affects the health of the people. Poor sanitary conditions and lack of adequate sewerage disposal methods can result into water borne diseases, heaps of garbage lying in bad odour; attracting stray cattle or animals which may also result in accidents.

The respondents' opinion about the status of sanitation services being provided by Municipal Council, Panchkula has been discussed on the basis of (i) Garbage collection, (ii) Cleanliness, (iii) Spraying activities, and (iv) Privatisation.

(i) Garbage Collection

In case of garbage collection, out of the 305 sample population only 63 (20 per cent) were found to be satisfied, while the remaining 242 (80 per cent) expressed their clear dissatisfaction.

The level of satisfaction has further been examined on the basis of area, gender, employment, education, income and age of the respondents. The level of significance across these attributes of sample population has been examined by using chi-square (÷2).

Area:-

The area wise responses of the citizens with regard to their satisfaction with the garbage collection have been depicted in Table 6.2.

Table 6.2
Satisfaction with Garbage Collection (Area wise)

		Satisfied	*Dissatisfied*
Area	Rural	0	80(100.00%)
	Urban	63(31.50%)	137(68.50%)
	Colony	0	25(100.00%)

(Figures in parentheses represent percentages).

Out of all rural respondents, none was found to be satisfied with the garbage collection. Out of the total urban respondents, 31.5 per cent were found to be satisfied while 68.5 per cent were found to be dissatisfied. From the colonies, again none of the respondent was found to be satisfied with the services being provided (See Table 6.2).

The analysis of the responses sought from the rural areas and colonies put together clearly suggests that Municipal Council, Panchkula has failed to provide sanitation services to the satisfaction of residents of the area and in the process, has made these areas vulnerable to many deadly diseases.

Gender

The gender wise responses of citizens with regard to their satisfaction with the garbage collection have been given in Table 6.3.

Table 6.3
Satisfaction with garbage collection (Gender wise)

		Satisfied	*Dissatisfied*
Gender	Male	57(19.50%)	236(80.50%)
	Female	6(50.00%)	6(50.00%)

X2 = 6.5, d.f = 1,P > 0.05
(Figures in parentheses represent percentages).

The analysis on the basis of gender reveals that, 19.5 per cent male expressed their satisfaction while the majority 80.5 per cent were not satisfied. In case of female respondents the division across level of satisfaction was even.

The chi square test value works out to be 6.5, which is significant at five per cent level and d.f=1.This suggests that the level of satisfaction is influenced by gender.

Employment

Employment wise responses of the citizens with regard to satisfaction with the garbage collection have been given in Table 6.4.

Table 6.4
Satisfaction with Garbage Collection (Employment wise)

		Satisfied	*Dissatisfied*
Employment	Employed	51(19.5%)	210(80.5%)
	Unemployed	12(27.30%)	32(72.70%)

X2 =1.3, df = 1, P > 0.05
(Figures in parentheses represent percentages).

Employment wise, around 19.5 per cent of the employed people were satisfied while 80.5 per cent expressed their dissatisfaction. In case of unemployed, 27.3 per cent opined satisfaction while 72.7 per cent were not satisfied.

The chi square test value works out to be 1.3, which is insignificant at five per cent level and d.f.=1.This suggests that the level of satisfaction is not influenced by employment.

Education

The education-wise responses of the citizens with regard to satisfaction with the garbage collection have been given in Table 6.5.

Table 6.5
Satisfaction with Garbage Collection (Education wise)

		Satisfied	*Dissatisfied*
Employment	Below matric	5(6.76%)	69(93.24%)
	Matric and above	58(25.10%)	137(74.90%)

X2 =11.5, df = 1, P > 0.05
(Figures in parentheses represent percentages).

The analysis on the basis of education shows that amongst the below matric, 6.76 per cent expressed satisfaction while majority 93.24 per cent were not satisfied. Furthermore, around 25 per cent above matric were satisfied while the remaining 75 per cent were not satisfied.

The chi square test value works out to be 11.5, which is significant at five per cent level and d.f=1. This indicates that the level of satisfaction depends on education.

Income

The income wise responses of the citizens with regard to satisfaction with the garbage collection have been given in Table 6.6.

Table 6.6

Satisfaction with Garbage Collection (Income wise)

		Satisfied	*Dissatisfied*
Income	No income	12(26.10%)	34(73.90%)
	between Rs. 5000 to 20000	46(18.90%)	197(81.10%)
	Rs. 20000 and above	5(31.20%)	11(68.80%)

X2 =2.3, df = 2, P > 0.05

(Figures in parentheses represent percentages).

On the basis of income, out of the total respondents having no income, 26.1 per cent were satisfied where as 73.9 per cent were found to be dis satisfied. Furthermore, about 19 per cent of the respondents having income between Rs 5,000 to Rs 20,000 were found to be satisfied while majority 81.1 per cent reported as not satisfied. Out of the total respondents having income Rs 20,000 and above, 31.2 per cent reported being satisfied and 68.8 per cent reported being dissatisfied.

The chi square test value works out to be 2.3, which is insignificant at five per cent level and d.f.=2. This indicates that the level of satisfaction is not influenced by the income of respondents.

Age

The age wise responses of the citizens with regard to satisfaction with the garbage collection have been given in Table 6.7.

Table 6.7

Satisfaction with Garbage Collection (Age wise)

		Satisfied	***Dissatisfied***
Age	Below30	18(16.80%)	89(83.20%)
	30 to 60	36(19.80%)	146(80.20%)
	60 and above	9(56.20%)	7(43.80%)

X2 =13.4, df = 2, P > 0.05

(Figures in parentheses represent percentages).

On the basis of age, out of the total respondents having an age below 30 years, 16.80 per cent were satisfied while 83.2 per cent were not satisfied. Out of total respondents having an age between 30 to 60 years, 19.8 per cent were satisfied and 80.20 per cent reported not satisfied. Out of the total respondents having an age 60 and above years, 56.2 per cent were satisfied while 43.8 per cent were not satisfied.

The chi square test value works out to be 13.4, which is significant at 5 per cent level and d.f.=2. This indicates that the age of the respondents influences the level of satisfaction.

(ii) Cleanliness

In case of cleanliness, out of 305 sample population, 25 per cent were satisfied, whereas the remaining 75 per cent expressed dissatisfaction.

The level of satisfaction further has been examined on the basis of area, gender, employment, education, income and age of the respondents. The level of significance across these attributes of sample population has been examined by using ÷2.

Area

The area wise responses of the citizens with regard to satisfaction with cleanliness have been reported in Table 6.8.

Table 6.8
Satisfaction with Cleanliness (Area Wise)

		Satisfied	*Dissatisfied*
Area	Rural	1(1.20%)	7998.80%)
	Urban	7638.00%)	12462.00%)
	Colony	0	25(100.00%)

(Figures in parentheses represent percentages).

The respondents were asked about their satisfaction level regarding the cleanliness of their locality. Out of rural respondents, 1.20 per cent were satisfied while 98.80 per cent were dissatisfied. Out of the total urban respondents, 38 per cent were satisfied whereas 62 per cent were not satisfied. From the colonies none was satisfied with the cleanliness.

An analysis of the responses from the colonies clearly suggests that Municipal Council, Panchkula has failed to provide sanitation services to the marginalised areas.

Gender

The gender-wise responses of the citizens with regard to satisfaction with cleanliness have been given in Table 6.9.

Table 6.9
Satisfaction with Cleanliness (Gender Wise)

		Satisfied	*Dissatisfied*
Gender	Male	71(24.30%)	222(75.70%)
	Female	6(50.00%)	6(50.00%)

÷2 =4.0, df = 1, P > 0.05

(Figures in parentheses represent percentages).

The analysis, on the basis of gender reveals that 24.3 per cent males expressed their satisfaction while 75.70 per cent in contrast expressed clear dissatisfaction. In case of female respondents, the division across the level of satisfaction was even.

The chi square test value works out to be 4.0, which is significant at five per cent level and d.f=1. This indicates that the level of satisfaction is influenced by gender.

Employment

The employment-wise responses of the citizens with regard to satisfaction with cleanliness have been given in Table 6.10.

Table 6.10
Satisfaction with Cleanliness (Employment Wise)

		Satisfied	*Dissatisfied*
Employment	Employed	63(24.13%)	198(75.87%)
	Unemployed	14(31.80%)	30(68.20%)

÷2 =1.8, df = 1, P > 0.05

(Figures in parentheses represent percentages).

Out of the total respondents, around 24.3 per cent expressed satisfaction while 75.8 per cent expressed dissatisfaction. In case of unemployed, 31.8 per cent opined satisfaction while 68.2 per cent were found to be dissatisfied.

The chi square test value works out to be 1.8, which is insignificant at five per cent level and d.f.=1. This indicates that the level of satisfaction is not influenced by the employment of respondents.

Education

The education wise responses of the citizens with regard to satisfaction with cleanliness have been given in Table 6.11.

Table 6.11
Satisfaction with Cleanliness (Education Wise)

		Satisfied	*Dissatisfied*
Education	Below matric	7(12.50%)	67 (87.50%)
	Matric and above	70(30.30%)	161(69.70%)

÷2 =12.9, df = 1, P > 0.05
(Figures in parentheses represent percentages).

The analysis on the basis of education shows that among below matric, 12.5 per cent expressed satisfaction while 87.5 per cent expressed dissatisfaction. About 30.3 per cent of above matric were satisfied while the remaining 69.7 per cent were not satisfied.

The chi square test value works out to be 12.9, which is significant at five per cent level and d.f=1. This indicates that the level of satisfaction varies across the educational background of respondents.

Income

The income-wise responses of the citizens with regard to satisfaction with cleanliness have been given in Table 6.12.

Table 6.12
Satisfaction with Cleanliness (Income Wise)

		Satisfied	*Dissatisfied*
Income	No income	14(30.40%)	32(69.60%)
	Between Rs. 5000 to 20000	58(23.90%)	185(76.10%)
	Rs. 20000 and above	5(31.20%)	11(68.80%)

÷2 =1.2, df = 2, P > 0.05
(Figures in parentheses represent percentages).

On the basis of income, 30.4 per cent respondents having no income were satisfied while 69.6 per cent were not satisfied. Out of the total respondents having income between Rs. 5000 to Rs. 20,000, 23.9 per cent reported satisfaction and majority 76.1 per cent reported clear dissatisfaction. Out of total respondents having income above Rs. 20,000, 31.2 per cent were satisfied while 68.8 per cent were not satisfied.

The chi square test value works out to be 1.2, which is insignificant at five per cent level and d.f.=2. This indicates that the level of satisfaction does not vary with the income of the respondents.

Age

The age wise responses of the citizens with regard to satisfaction with cleanliness have been given in Table 6.13.

Table 6.13
Satisfaction with Cleanliness (Age Wise)

		Satisfied	*Dissatisfied*
Age	Below30	22(20.60%)	85(79.40%)
	30 to 60	47(25.80%)	135(74.20%)
	60 and above	8(50.00%)	8(50.00%)

÷2 =6.4, df = 2, P > 0.05
(Figures in parentheses represent percentages).

On the basis of age, out of the total respondents having an age below 30 years, 20.6 per cent were satisfied where as 79.4 per cent were not satisfied. Out of the total respondents having an age between 30 to 60 years, 25.8 per cent were satisfied, while 74.2 per cent reported clear dissatisfaction . Out of the total respondents having an age of 60 years and above, the division across level of satisfaction was even.

The chi square test value works out to be 6.4, which is insignificant at five per cent level and d.f=2. This indicates that the level of satisfaction is not influenced by the age.

Thus, it can be concluded that a large number of citizens in MCP jurisdiction are not satisfied with the cleanliness services being accorded to them.

(iii) Spraying Activities

The respondents opinions, about the status of sanitation services provided by Municipal Council, Panchkula, on the basis of spraying activities have been analysed on the basis of area, gender, employment, education, income and age.

Out of rural respondents, 85.0 per cent said that MCP undertook spraying activities once in a year, 5.0 per cent said more than once in a year, while 10 per cent said MCP did not initiate spraying activitiesat all. Out of the total urban respondents, 2.0 per cent reported it to be that the frequency was once in a month, .5 per cent said once in three months, 23.5 per cent as once in six months, 30.5 per cent as once in a year, while 43.5 per cent reported that MCP did not initiate it at all. Municipal Council, Panchkula has not taken any initiative to spray in colonies.

The respondents were asked whether Municipal Council, Panchkula had been spraying in their area and how often. The responses have been given in Table 6.14.

Table 6.14
Time of Spraying in Municipal Council, Panchkula

		Once in a Months	*Once in Three Months*	*Once in Six Months*	*Once in Year*	*In More than a Year*	*Not Taken any Initiative*
Area	Rural	0(0.00%)	0(0.00%)	0(0.00%)	68(85.00%)	4(5.00%)	8(10.00%)
	Urban	4(2.00%)	1(0.50%)	47(23.50%)	61(30.50%)	0(0.00%)	87(43.5%)
	Colony	0(0.00%)	0(0.00%)	0(0.00%)	0(0.00%)	0(0.00%)	25(100%)
Gender	Male	4(1.40%)	1(0.30%)	47(16.10%)	122(41.80%)	4(1.40%)	115(39.25%)
	Female	0(0.00%)	0(0.00%)	0(0.00%)	7(58.30%)	0(0.00%)	5(41.70%)
Employment	Employed	3(1.14%)	0(0.00%)	38(14.55%)	126(48.27%)	4(1.53%)	100(38.31%)
	Unemployed	1(2.30%)	1(2.30%)	9(20.50%)	13(29.50%)	0(0.00%)	20(45.40%)
Education	Below matric	0(0.00%)	0(0.00%)	1 (1.35%)	35(47.29%)	1(1.35 %)	37(50.00%)
	Matric and above	4(1.70%)	1(0.40%)	46(19.90%)	94(40.70%)	31.30%)	8335.60%)
Income	No income	1(2.20%)	1(2.20%)	11(23.90%)	14(30.40%)	00.00%)	1941.30%)
	Between Rs 5,000 to 20,000	3(1.20%)	0(0.00%)	36(14.80%)	110(45.30%)	41.60%)	9037.10%)
	Rs. 20,000 and above	0(0.00%)	0(0.00%)	0(0.00%)	5(31.20%)	00.00%)	1169.8 %)
Age	Below30	1(0.90%)	1(0.90%)	20(18.70%)	33(30.80%)	00.00%)	4239.70%)
	30 to 60	3(1.60%)	0(0.00%)	20(11.00%)	91(50.00%)	42.20%)	7440.20%)
	60 and above	0(0.00%)	0(0.00%)	7(43.80%)	5(31.20%)	00.00%)	425.60%)

Source: Field survey.

(Figures in parentheses represent percentages).

An analysis of the responses from the colonies clearly suggests that MCP neglected colonies during its spraying activity.

The analysis on the basis of gender suggested that 1.4 per cent males said that the MCP undertook spraying activities once in month, 0. 3 per cent said the frequency was once in three months, 16.1 per cent opined that the frequency was once in six months, 41.8 per cent expressed that the frequency was once in a year, 1. 4 per cent called it to be more than a year while 39.24 per cent said MCP did not initiate such activities at all. In case of female respondents, 68.3 per cent opined that the frequency was once in a year, while 41.7 per cent opined that MCP did not initiate spraying activities at all.

Employment wise, around 1.1 per cent employed said that MCP undertook spraying activities once in a month, 14.5 per cent stated the frequency as once in six months, 48.2 per cent as once in a year, 1.5 per cent as more than a year while 38.3 stated MCP did not initiate it at all. About 1.6 per cent private employees remarked that the frequency was once in month, 16.4 per cent as once in six months, 57.2 per cent as more than a year, while 24.6 per cent stated that MCP did not initiate such activities at all. In case of unemployed, 2.3 per cent said that MCP undertook spraying activities once in a month, 2.3 per cent stated the frequency as once in three months, 20.5 per cent opined the frequency as once in six months, while 29.5 per cent as more than a year while 45.4 stated MCP did not initiate such activities at all.

The analysis on the basis of education shows that1.35 per cent below matric answered that the frequency was once in a year, and 47. 29 per cent opined that it was once in a year, 1.35 per cent rated it as more than a year, while 0.50 per cent reported MCP did not initiate such activities at all. In case of above matric, 1.7 per cent said the frequency was once in a month, 0.4 per cent as once in three months, 19.9 per cent as once in six months, 40.7 per cent opined once in a year, 1.3 per cent as more than a year while 35.6 per cent stated MCP did not initiate spraying activities at all.

On the basis of income, out of the total respondents having no income, 2.2 per cent said the frequency was once in a month, 2.2 per cent as once in three months, 23.9 per cent as once in six months, 30.4 per cent as once in a year, and 41.3 per cent opined MCP did not undertake spraying activities at all. 1.2 per cent respondents having income between Rs 5,000 to Rs 20,000 said the frequency was once in a month, 14.8 per cent as once in six months, 45.30 per cent as once in a year, 1.6 per cent as more than a year while 37.1 per cent remarked MCP did not initiate spraying activities at all. Amongst the respondents having income of Rs 20,000 and above, 31.2 per cent expressed that the frequency was once in a year while 69.8 per cent opined that MCP did not initiate spraying activities at all.

On the basis of age, out of the total respondents having an age below 30 years, 0.9 per cent said that the frequency was once in a month, 0.9 per cent as once in three months, 18.7 per cent as once in six months, 30.8 per cent as once in a year, and 39.7 per cent opined MCP did not initiate spraying activities at all. Out of total respondents having an age between 30 to 60 years, 1.6 per cent reported the frequency was once in a month, 11 per cent as once in six months, 50 per cent said once in a year, 2.2 per cent said more than a year and 40.2 per cent opined MCP did not initiate it at all. Out of total respondents having an age 60-years and above, 43.8 per cent reported it as once in six months, 31.2 per cent as once in a year, and 25.6 per cent said that MCP did not initiate spraying activities at all.

(iv) Privatisation of Sanitation Work

Municipal Council, Panchkula provides sanitation services through contracting out. The responses of the citizens about whether they favour privatisation or not, were also sought and analysed on the basis of area, gender, employment, education, income and age in Table 6.15.

Table 6.15
Responses Regarding the Privatisation/Contracting out of Sanitation Work

		Yes	*No*	*No idea*
Area	Rural	0(0.00%)	72(90.00%)	8(10.00%)
	Urban	4(2.00%)	123(61.50%)	193(36.5%)
	Colony	0(0.00%)	24(96.00%)	1(4.00%)
Gender	Male	4(1.40%)	213(72.90%)	76(25.70%)
	Female	0(0.00%)	5(41.70%)	7(48.30%)
Employment	Employed	3(1.14%)	197(75.47%)	61(23.37%)
	Unemployed	1(2.30%)	22(50.00%)	16(47.70%)
Education	Below matric	0(0.00%)	66(89.18%)	7(10.82%)
	Matric and above	4(1.70%)	153(66.20%)	74(32.10%)
Income	No income	1(2.20%)	23(50.00%)	22(47.80%)
	Between Rs. 5000 to 20000	3(1.20%)	186(76.50%)	54(22.30%)
	Rs. 20000 and above	0(0.00%)	10(62.50%)	6(37.50%)
Age	Below30	1(0.90%)	70(65.40%)	36(33.70%)
	30 to 60	3(1.60%)	138(75.80%)	41(22.60%)
	60 and above	0(0.00%)	11(68.80%)	5(31.20%)

Source: Field survey
(Figures in parentheses represent percentages).

Out of rural respondents, 90 per cent opposed the privatisation of sanitation services and 10 per cent remained neutral. Out of the total urban respondents, two per cent favoured privatisation, whereas 61.5 per cent were against privatisation and 36.5 per cent remained neutral. From colonies, 96 per cent respondents were against privatisation and four per cent remained neutral.

The analysis of responses from rural areas and colonies put together, clearly suggests that most of the citizens were against privatisation of sanitation services.

The analysis on the basis of gender reveals that out of total males, 1.4 per cent favoured privatisation of sanitation services where as 72.9 per cent were against and 25.7 per cent remained neutral. In case of female respondents, no one favoured privatisation, around 41.7 per cent opposed privatisation and the remaining 48.3 per cent were neutral.

Employment wise, around 1.1 per cent employed favoured privatisation of sanitation services, whereas 75.4 per cent were against privatisation and 23.3 per cent remained neutral. In case of unemployed, two per cent favoured privatisation of sanitation services, whereas 50 per cent were against privatisation and 48 per cent remained neutral.

The analysis on the basis of education shows that 89.1 per cent illiterates were against privatisation of sanitation services and10.8 per cent remained neutral. About two per cent of above matric favoured privatisation where as 66 per cent were against privatisation and 32 per cent remained neutral.

On the basis of income, out of total respondents having no income, 2.2 per cent favoured privatisation of sanitation services, whereas 50 per cent were against privatisation and 47.8 per cent remained neutral. About 1.2 per cent of the respondents having income between Rs 5,000 to Rs 20,000, favoured privatisation, whereas 76.5 per cent were against privatisation and 22.30 per cent remained neutral. Out of the total respondents having income above Rs 20,000, 62.5 per cent were against privatisation whereas 37.5 per cent remained neutral.

On the basis of age, out of the total respondents having an age below 30 years, one per cent favoured privatisation of sanitation services, whereas 65 per cent were against privatisation and the remaining 34 per cent were neutral. Out of the total respondents having an age between 30 to 60 years, 1.6 per cent favoured privatisation, whereas 75.8 per cent were against privatisation, and 22.6 per cent remained neutral. Out of the total respondents having an age of 60 and above years, 68.8 per cent were against privatisation and 31.2 per cent remained neutral.

The respondents who were satisfied with the privatisation of sanitation services identified following reasons:

1. Privatisation leads to a faster delivery of service; 2. Privatisation brings out improvement in the quality of work; 3. Privatisation results in financial savings; 4. Privatisation increases proper supervision; 5. Privatisation results in better performance; 6. Privatisation improves economy, efficiency and effectiveness in services; 7. Privatisation promotes accountability; 8. Privatisation reduces corruption in service delivery; and 9. Privatisation helps in immediate handling of complaints.

The respondents who were not in agreement with privatisation of sanitation services opined that:

1. Privatization lacks accountability, supervision and control; 2. It promotes interest; 3. Privatisation serves rich clients better; 4. Government is best service provider; 5. Privatisation results into worse conditions of work and harassment of people; 6. Privatisation encourages corruption; 7. Citizens have to pay more taxes; and 8. No proper use of money.

Thus, on the basis of above analysis one can see that the citizens living within the jurisdiction of Municipal Council, Panchkula (MCP) were not satisfied with the sanitation (Garbage collection, cleanliness and spray activities) services being provided by the MCP, and a large number of respondents do not favoured privatisation of sanitation services of MCP.

The respondents who were not satisfied with the performance of Municipal Council, Panchkula in the field of sanitation services identified the following reasons:

1. Lack of time schedule in the collection of garbage.
2. Absence of trained workforce to handle garbage collection.
3. No provision of dustbins.
4. Carelessness of workers.
5. No proper transportation of garbage.

6.2.2. Street Lights

As mentioned earlier, street lights are other services covered in this study. Before analysing the responses of citizens, it is desirable to discuss the importance of street light services to the communities. Street lighting provides many community benefits mentioned as under:

(i) preventing night time personal injury accidents,
(ii) reducing street crime,
(iii) reducing the fear of street crime,
(iv) promoting sustainable transport, promoting public transport, cycling and walking,
(v) facilitating social inclusion by providing the freedom to walk along, and use streets after dark,
(vi) facilitating lifelong learning by providing after dark access to educational facilities,
(vii) assisting the emergency services to identify locations and carry out their duties,
(viii) without modern street lighting the time taken to attend an incident could be increased,

Panchkula being a modern city, the importance of street lights can naturally be emphasised. Keeping in view the significance of the functions of street light, in this study, responses of the citizens have been analysed on the basis of (i) Satisfaction and (ii) Whether they favour privatisation of street light services or not.

(i) Satisfaction: In case of street lights, out of 305 sample population, 25 per cent were satisfied, whereas the remaining 75 per cent expressed their dissatisfaction.

The level of satisfaction further has been examined on the basis of area, gender, employment, education, income and age of the respondents. The level of significance across these attributes of sample population has been examined by using ÷2.

Area

An area wise responses of citizens with regard to satisfaction with the provision of Street lights have been given in Table 6.16.

Table 6.16
Satisfaction with the Provision of Street lights (Area Wise)

		Satisfied	***Dissatisfied***
AREA	Rural	0(0.00%)	80100%
	Urban	75(37.5%)	125(62.5%)
	Colony	0(0.00%)	25(100%)

Source: Field survey
(Figures in parentheses represent percentages).

Out of the rural respondents, none was satisfied with street light services. Out of the total urban respondents, 37.5 per cent were satisfied while , 62.5 per cent were not satisfied. From colonies, again none of the respondents was satisfied with the street light services.

An analysis of responses from rural areas and colonies put together clearly suggests that the Municipal Council, Panchkula has failed to provide street light services to these marginalised areas.

Gender

The gender-wise responses of citizens with regard to satisfaction with the provision of Street Lights have been given in Table 6.17.

Table 6.17
Satisfaction with the Provision of Street Lights (Gender Wise)

		Satisfied	*Dissatisfied*
GENDER	Male	68(23.3%)	225(76.7%)
	Female	7(58.3%)	5(41.7%)

÷2 =7.6, df = 1, P > 0.05
(Figures in parentheses represent percentages).

The analysis on the basis of gender reveals that 23.3 per cent males expressed their satisfaction and in contrast 66.7 per cent were not satisfied with the provision of the Street Lights. In case of females 58.3 per cent expressed satisfaction while 41.7 per cent expressed dissatisfaction.

The chi square test value works out to be 7.6, which is significant at five per cent level and d.f=1. This indicates that the level of satisfaction is influenced by the gender.

Employment

The employment wise responses of the citizens with regard to satisfaction with the provision of Street lights have been given in Table 6.18.

Table 6.18
Satisfaction with the Provision of Street Lights (Employment Wise)

		Satisfied	*Dissatisfied*
EMPLOYMENT	Employed	56(21.4%)	205(78.5%)
	Unemployed	20(45.5%)	24(54.5%)

÷2 =11.6, df = 1, P > 0.05
(Figures in parentheses represent percentages).

Further employment wise, around 21.4 per cent employed were satisfied, while 78.5 per cent expressed dissatisfaction with the provision of street light services. In case of unemployed, 45.5 per cent opined satisfaction and 54.5 per cent were not satisfied.

The chi square test value works out to be11.6, which is significant at five per cent level and d.f=1.This shows that the level of satisfaction varies across employment.

Education

The education wise responses of citizens with regard to satisfaction with the provision of Street lights have been given in Table 6.19.

Table 6.19
Satisfaction with the Provision of Street Lights (Education Wise)

		Satisfied	*Dissatisfied*
EDUCATION	Below matric	4(5.4%)	70(94.5%)
	Matric and above	71(30.7%)	160(69.3%)

÷2 =19.4, df = 1, P > 0.05
(Figures in parentheses represent percentages).

The analysis on the basis of education shows that among below matric respondents, 5.4 per cent expressed their satisfaction while a whooping 94.5 per cent were not satisfied. In case of above matric, 30.7 per cent were satisfied, while the remaining 69.3 per cent were not satisfied.

The chi square test value works out to be 19.4, which is significant at five per cent level and d.f=1. This indicates that the level of satisfaction is influenced by the educational background of the respondents.

Income

The income wise responses of citizens with regard to satisfaction with the provision of Street lights have been given in Table 6.20.

Table 6.20
Satisfaction with the Provision of Street Lights (Income Wise)

		Satisfied	*Dissatisfied*
INCOME	No income	20(43.5%)	26(56.5%)
	Between Rs. 5000 to 20000	53(21.8%)	192(78.2%)
	Rs. 20000 and above	2(12.5%)	14(87.5%)

÷2 =11.1, df = 2, P > 0.05
(Figures in parentheses represent percentages).

On the basis of income, out of the total respondents having no income, 43.5 per cent were satisfied and 56.5 per cent were not satisfied with the provision of street light services. Furthermore, about 21.8 per cent of the respondents having income between Rs 5,000 to Rs. 20,000 were satisfied, whereas 78.2 per cent reported being dissatisfied. Out of the total respondents having income above Rs. 20,000 12.5 per cent were satisfied and 87.5 per cent were not satisfied.

The chi square test value works out to be 11.1, which is significant at 5 per cent level and d.f=2. This indicates that the level of satisfaction is influenced by income.

Age

The age-wise responses of citizens with regard to satisfaction with the provision of Street lights have been given in Table 6.21.

Table 6.21

Satisfaction with the Provision of Street Lights (Age Wise)

		Satisfied	*Dissatisfied*
AGE	Below30	33(30.8%)	74(69.2%)
	30 to 60	39(21.4%)	143(68.6%)
	60 and above	3(18.8%)	13(81.2%)

÷2 =3.5, df = 2, P > 0.05

(Figures in parentheses represent percentages).

On the basis of age, among the respondents having an age below 30 years, 30.8 per cent were satisfied with the provision of Street Light services, whereas 69.2 per cent were not satisfied. Out of the total respondents, having an age between 30 to 60 years, 21.4 per cent were satisfied while whooping 78.6 per cent were not satisfied. Out of the total respondents having an age of 60 years and above, 18.8 per cent opined satisfaction, while remaining 81.2 per cent opined sheer dissatisfaction.

The chi square test value works out to be 3.5, which is insignificant at five per cent level and d.f=2. This indicates that the level of satisfaction is not influenced by age.

The respondents who were not satisfied with provision of street light services by the MCP identified the following reasons:

a. Improper working ;
b. No proper maintenance;
c. Poor repair services; and
d. Sparking and accidents due to improper functioning of Street lights.

(ii) ***Privatisation of Street Light Works:-*** It is relevant to mention here that Municipal Council, Panchkula provides Street Light services through contracting out.The responses of the citizens about whether they favour privatisation or not, have been shown on the basis of area, gender, employment, education, income and age wise in Table 6.22.

Table 6.22

Responses Regarding the Privatization of the Maintenance of the Street Light Work

		Yes	*No*	*No idea*
Area	Rural	10(12.50%)	66(82.50%)	4(5.00%)

	Urban	38(19.00%)	139(69.50%)	23(11.50%)
	Colony	0(0.00%)	25(100.00%)	0(0.00%)
Gender	Male	47(16.10%)	224(76.40%)	22(7.50%)
	Female	1(8.30%)	7(58.30%)	4(33.30%)
Employment	Employed	40(15.32)	200(76.62%)	21(8.04%)
	Unemployed	8(18.20%)	30(68.20%)	6(13.60%)
Education	Below matric	6(8.10%)	64(86.04%)	4(5.40%)
	Matric and above	42(18.20%)	166(71.80%)	23(10.00%)
Income	No income	7(15.20%)	32(69.60%)	7(15.20%)
	Between Rs. 5000 to 20000	36(14.80%)	189(77.80%)	18(7.40%)
	Rs. 20000 and above	5(31.20%)	9(56.30%)	2(12.50%)
Age	Below30	16(15.00%)	74(69.10%)	17(15.90%)
	30 to 60	27(14.80%)	146(80.20%)	9(5.00%)
	60 and above	5(31.20%)	10(62.50%)	1(6.30%)

Source: Field survey.

(Figures in parentheses represent percentages).

In response to the question whether they thought that the maintenance of the streetlight should be privatized, the respondents gave their views, which are presented as under:

Out of rural respondents, 12.5 per cent favoured privatisation of maintenance of street light services while 82.5 per cent opposed privatisation and 5 per cent remained neutral. Out of the total urban respondents, 19 per cent favoured privatisation, whereas 69.5 per cent were against privatisation and 11.5 per cent remained neutral. From colonies , 100 per cent respondents were against privatisation.

The analysis on the basis of gender reveals that out of the total males, 16.1 per cent favoured privatisation of maintenance of street light services where as 76.4 per cent were against and the remaining 7.5 per cent remained neutral. In case of female respondents, 8.3 per cent favoured privatisation, around 58.3 per cent opposed it and remaining 33.3 per cent remained neutral.

Employment wise, around 15.3 per cent employed favoured privatisation of maintenance of street light services, whereas 76.6 per cent were against privatisation and 8.04 per cent remained neutral. In case of unemployed, 18.2 per cent favoured privatisation of sanitation services, whereas 68.2 per cent were against privatisation and 13.6 per cent remained neutral.

The analysis on the basis of education shows that 8.1 per cent below matric favoured privatisation, whereas 86.4 per cent were against privatisation of maintenance of street light services and 5.4 per cent remained neutral. About 18. 2 per cent of above matric favoured privatisation whereas 71.8 per cent were against privatisation while the remaining 10 per cent remained neutral.

On the basis of income, out of the total respondents having no income, 15.2 per cent favoured privatisation of street light services, whereas 69.6 per cent were against privatisation and 15.2 per cent remained neutral. About 14.8 per cent of the respondents having income between Rs 5,000 to Rs 20,000 favoured privatisation, whereas 77.8 per cent were against privatisation and 7.4 per cent remained neutral. Out of the total respondents having income above Rs 20,000 31.2 per cent favoured privatisation, whereas 56.3 per cent were against privatisation and 12.5 per cent remained neutral.

On the basis of age, out of the total respondents having an age below 30 years, 15 per cent favoured privatisation of maintenance of street light services, whereas 69.1 per cent were against privatisation and the remaining 15.9 per cent were neutral. Out of the total respondents having an age between 30 to 60 years, 14.8 per cent favoured privatisation, whereas 80.2 per cent were against privatistation, and five per cent remained neutral. Out of the total respondents having an age of 60 and above years, 31.2 per cent favoured privatisation, whereas 62.5 per cent were against privatisation and 6.3 per cent remained neutral. Finally, majority of respondents were of the opinion that maintenance of street lights should not be privatised in MCP jurisdiction.

The respondents who did not agree with the privatisation of street light services identified the following reasons: 1. Privatisation encourages corruption; 2. Rich customers get better treatment; 3. Privatisation lacks control; 4. Government is the best supplier of services; 5. It burden citizens with more taxes; and 6. No arrangement for proper handling of complaints or grievances.

The respondents who agreed with privatisation of street light services gave the following reasons:

1. Privatisation speeds up the completion of work;
2. Privatisation results in proper supervision.

6.2.3. Roads

As mentioned earlier, the next findings are concerned with the road services. Before analysing this, it is desirable to discuss the importance of road services for the community. Roads are the arteries of a city. Good roads are necessary for a smooth flow of traffic and prevention of accidents. Keeping in view the significance of the function of Roads in this study, the responses of citizens have been analysed on the basis of (i) Satisfaction regarding condition of roads; and (ii) Privatisation of Roads services.

(i) Satisfaction: In case of road services out of 305 sample population, 11 per cent were satisfied, whereas the remaining 89 per cent expressed their dissatisfaction.

The level of satisfaction further has been examined on the basis of area, gender, employment, education, income and age of the respondents. The level of significance across these attributes of sample population has been examined by using ÷2.

Area

The area-wise responses of the citizens with regard to satisfaction with the conditions of roads in their locality have been given in Table 6.23.

Table 6.23
Satisfaction with the Condition of Roads (Area-Wise)

		Satisfied	*Dissatisfied*
AREA	Rural	0	80 (100.00%)
	Urban	3316.50%	167 (83.50%)
	Colony	0	25) 100.00%)

Source: Field Survey
(Figures in parentheses represent percentages).

When the respondents were questioned about their satisfaction with the condition of roads in their locality, the responses were as under:

Out of the rural respondents, none was satisfied with the condition of roads. Out of the total urban respondents, 33 per cent were satisfied, while whooping 83.50 per cent were not satisfied. From colonies, again none of the respondents was satisfied with the condition of the roads.

The analysis of responses from rural area and colony put together clearly suggests that Municipal Council, Panchkula has failed to provide road services to these marginalised areas.

Gender

The gender wise responses of the citizens with regard to satisfaction with the conditions of roads in their locality have been given in Table 6.24.

Table 6.24
Satisfaction with the Condition of Roads (Gender-wise)

		Satisfied	*Dissatisfied*
GENDER	Male	29(9.90%)	264(90.10%)
	Female	4(33.30%)	8(66.70%)

÷2 =6.5, df = 1, P > 0.05
(Figures in parentheses represent percentages).

The analysis on the basis of gender reveals that 9.9 per cent males expressed their satisfaction, and in contrast 90.1 per cent were not satisfied with the condition of roads services. In case of females, 33.3 per cent were satisfied, while 66.7 per cent were not satisfied.

The chi square test value works out to be 6.5, which is significant at five per cent level and d.f=1.This indicates that the level of satisfaction is influenced by gender.

Employment

The employment wise responses of the citizens with regard to satisfaction with the conditions of roads in their locality have been given in Table 6.25.

Table 6.25
Satisfaction with the Condition of Roads (Employment-wise)

		Satisfied	*Dissatisfied*
EMPLOYMENT	Employed	26(9.96%)	235(90.03%)
	Unemployed	7(15.90%)	37(84.10%)

÷2 =1.3, df = 1, P > 0.05
(Figures in parentheses represent percentages).

Further Employment wise around 9.96 per cent of employed were satisfied, while 90.03 per cent expressed their dissatisfaction with the condition of roads services. In case of unemployed, 15.9 per cent opined satisfaction while 84.1 per cent opined their dissatisfaction.

The chi square test value works out to be 1.3, which is significant at five per cent level and d.f=1.This shows that the level of satisfaction varies across employment.

Education

The education wise responses of the citizens with regard to satisfaction with the conditions of roads in their locality have been given in Table 6.26.

Table 6.26
Satisfaction with the Condition of Roads (Education-wise)

		Satisfied	*Dissatisfied*
EDUCATION	Below matric	2(2.70%)	72 (97.29%)
	Matric and above	31(13.40%)	200(86.60%)

÷2 =6.67, df = 1, P > 0.05
(Figures in parentheses represent percentages).

The analysis on the basis of education shows that out of the total respondents who were below matric, 2.70 per cent were satisfied with the condition of roads services while a whooping 97.2 were dissatisfied. About 13.4 per cent of above matric, were satisfied, while the remaining 86.6 per cent were not satisfied.

The chi square test value works out to be 6.67, which is significant at five per cent level and d.f=1.This shows that the level of satisfaction is influenced by education.

Income

The income wise responses of the citizens with regard to satisfaction with the conditions of roads in their locality have been given in Table 6.27.

Table 6.27
Satisfaction with the Condition of Roads (Income-wise)

		Satisfied	*Dissatisfied*
INCOME	No income	7(15.20%)	39(84.80%)
	Between Rs. 5000 to 20000	26(10.70%)	217(89.30%)
	Rs. 20000 and above	0(0.00%)	16(100.00%)

÷2 =2.8, df = 2, P > 0.05
(Figures in parentheses represent percentages).

On the basis of income, out of the total respondents having no income, 15.2 per cent were satisfied, whereas 84.8 per cent reported being not satisfied with the condition of road services. About 10.7 per cent respondents are having income between Rs 5000 to Rs 20000, reported being satisfied while a major 89.3 per cent reported being not satisfied. Out of the total respondents having income above Rs 20000, none of the respondents was satisfied with the road services.

The chi square test value works out to be 2.8, which is insignificant at five per cent level and d.f=2.This shows that the level of satisfaction is not influenced by income.

Age

The age wise responses of the citizens with regard to satisfaction with the conditions of roads in their locality have been given in Table 6.28.

Table 6.28
Satisfaction with the Condition of Roads (Age-wise)

		Satisfied	*Dissatisfied*
AGE	Below 30	7(6.50%)	100(93.50%)
	30 to 60	19(10.40%)	163(89.60%)
	60 and above	7(43.80%)	9(56.20%)

÷2 =20.0, df = 2, P > 0.05
(Figures in parentheses represent percentages).

On the basis of age, out of the total respondents having an age below 30 years, 6.5 per cent were satisfied, while a majority of 93.5 per cent were not satisfied with the condition of roads services. Out of the total respondents having age between 30 to 60 years, 10.4 per cent were satisfied, and 89.6 per cent were not satisfied. Out of the total respondents having an age of 60 years and above, 43.8 per cent were satisfied, and 56.2 per cent were not satisfied.

The chi square test value works out to be 20.0, which is significant at five per cent level and d.f.=2. This shows that the level of satisfaction varies across age.

The respondents who were not satisfied with the performance of Municipal Council, Panchkula in the road services, identified the following reasons:

1) Poor condition of roads;
2) Accumulated water on roads;
3) No proper maintenance of roads;
4) Main entry of roads in worse conditions; and
5) No roads in some areas.

While making observations based on the conditions of roads in MCP jurisdiction, it is found that the roads are not in apretty bad shape. The condition of road in pitiable in both posh sectors as wellas other sectors. Villages have worse conditions. The condition of roads in colonies was even more pathetic. In a nutshell, MCP has failed to provide adequate road facilities resulting in citizens sheer dissatisfaction.

(ii) ***Privatisation of Road Services:*** It is relevant to mention that Municipal Council, Panchkula provides road services through contracting out, particularly road construction and maintenance. So the responses of the citizens about whether they favour privatisation or not have been solicited. The responses across area gender, employment, education, income and age wise have been shown in Table 6.29.

Table 6.29
Responses Regarding the Privatisation of the Maintenance of Roads

		Yes	*No*	*No idea*
Area	Rural	10(12.50%)	66(82.50%)	4(5.00%)
Area	Rural	8(10.00%)	68(85.00%)	4(5.00%)
	Urban	62(31.00%)	117(58.50%)	21(10.50%)
	Colony	1(4.00%)	24(96.00%)	0(0.00%)
Gender	Male	69(23.60%)	202(68.90%)	22(7.50%)
	Female	2(16.70%)	7(58.30%)	3(25.00%)
Employment	Employed	58(22.22%)	186(71.26%)	17(6.51%)
	Unemployed	13(29.50%)	23(52.30%)	8(18.20%)
Education	Below matric	7(9.45%)	64 (86.48%)	3(4.05%)
	Matric and above	64(27.70%)	145(62.80%)	22(9.50%)
Income	No income	13(28.30%)	24(52.20%)	9(19.60%)
	Between Rs. 5000 to 20000	52(21.40%)	176(72.40%)	15(6.20%)
	Rs. 20000 and above	6(37.50%)	9(56.20%)	1(6.20%)
Age	Below30	21(19.60%)	72(67.30%)	14(13.10%)
	30 to 60	44(24.20%)	128(70.30%)	10(5.50%)
	60 and above	6(37.50%)	9(56.20%)	1(6.20%)

Source: Field survey.
(Figures in parentheses represent percentages).

In response to the question, 'do you think maintenance of roads in your locality should be privatised', 10.0 per cent rural respondents favoured privatisation of road maintenance services while 85.0 per cent opposed it and five per cent remained neutral. Out of the total urban respondents, 31 per cent favoured privatisation, whereas 58.5 per cent were against privatisation and 10.5 per cent remained neutral. From colonies, about four per cent respondents were in favour, whereas 96 per cent were against privatisation.

The analysis on the basis of gender reveals that in case of male respondents, 23.6 per cent favoured privatisation of road maintenance services where as 68.9 per cent were against it and 7.5 per cent remained neutral. In case of female respondents, 16.7 per cent favoured privatisation, around 58.3 per cent opposed privatisation and the remaining 25.0 per cent were neutral.

Employment wise, around 22.22 per cent employed favoured privatisation of road services, whereas 71.26 per cent were against it and 6.51 per cent remained neutral. In case of unemployed, 29.5 per cent favoured privatisation of road maintenance services, 52.3 per cent were against it while 18.2 per cent remained neutral.

The analysis on the basis of education shows that among below matric, 9.4 per cent favour privatisation, where as 86.4 per cent were against privatisation of road services and 4.04 per cent remained neutral. About 27.7 per cent of above matric favoured it where as 62.8 per cent were against privatisation and 9.5 per cent remained neutral.

On the basis of income, 28.3 per cent of citizens belonging to no income category favoured privatisation of road maintenance services, whereas 52.2 per cent were against privatisation and 19.6 per cent remained neutral. About 21.4 per cent of the respondents having income between Rs 5,000 to Rs 20,000, favoured of privatisation, whereas 72.4 per cent were against it while 6.2 per cent remained neutral. Out of the total respondents having income above Rs 20,000, 37.5 per cent were in favour of privatisation, whereas 56.2 per cent against it and 6.2 per cent remained neutral.

On the basis of age, out of the total respondents having an age below 30 years, 19.6 per cent favoured privatisation of road maintenance services, whereas 67.3 per cent were against privatisation and remaining 13.1 per cent were neutral. Out of the total respondents having an age between 30 to 60 years, 24.2 per cent favoured privatisation, whereas 70.3 per cent were against it, while 5.5 per cent remained neutral. Out of the total respondents having an age of 60 and above years, 37.5 per cent favoured privatisation, whereas 56.2 per cent were against it and 6.2 per cent remained neutral. Ultimately, a majority of respondents were of the opinion that maintenance of road services should not be privatised in MCP jurisdiction.

The respondents who were in agreement with the privatisation of maintenance of road services cited the following reasons: 1. Privatisation will improve the quality of work; 2. Privatisation will help in completing work on a fast track; 3. Privatisation will free roads construction and maintenance from bureaucratic control; and 4. Privatisation will favour economy, efficiency and effectiveness.

The respondents who were not in agreement with the privatisation of maintenance of road services cited the following reasons:

(1) It will increase Tax burden;
(2) In will result in misuse of money;

(3) Contracting out may not ensure proper check and control on contractors ;
(4) Privatsation will result in Corruption;
(5) Government provide better services; and
(6) Quality of work done by contractor is usually poor.

6.2.4. Parks

The next discussion is concerned with the park services. Before analysing responses of the citizens, it is desirable to mention the need of parks for the community. Parks are green spaces; act as lungs of any living city; and are sources of fresh air. Parks also provide a place for people to stroll, exercise and play. For these very reasons, their regular maintenance is of utmost importance. Parks also add to the beauty of any city's landscape. The various flora in the park also provide shelter to various kinds of birds. All this is a visual delight. Keeping in view, the significance of the functioning of park services, in this study the responses of citizens have been analysed on the basis of: (i) Availability of the public parks; (ii) Proper landscape of the parks; (iii) Satisfaction with parks maintenance; and (iv) privatisation of the maintenance of parks.

(i) Availability of the Public Parks: Respondents were asked whether they had any public parks in their sector/locality. Their responses have been discussed on the basis of area, gender, employment, education, income and age wise in Table 6.30.

Table 6.30
Responses Regarding Availability of the Public Parks

		Available	*Not Available*
Area	Rural	80(100.00%)	0(0.00%)
	Urban	160(79.90%)	40(20.10%)
	Colony	0(0.00%)	25(100.00%)
Gender	Male	230(78.40%)	63(21.60%)
	Female	10(83.30%)	2(16.70%)
Employment	Employed	204(78.16%)	57(21.83%)
	Unemployed	36(81.80%)	8(18.20%)
Education	Below matric	41(55.40%)	33(44.59%)
	Matric and above	199(86.10%)	32(13.90%)
Income	No income	39(84.80%)	7(15.20%)
	Between Rs. 5000 to 20000	186(76.40%)	57(23.60%)
	Rs. 20000 and above	15(93.80%)	1(6.20%)
Age	Below30	81(75.70%)	26(24.30%)
	30 to 60	146(80.10%)	36(19.90%)
	60 and above	13(81.20%)	3(18.80%)

Source: Field Survey.
(Figures in parentheses represent percentages).

Out of total rural respondents, 100 per cent answered that there is availability of parks in their locality. Out of the total urban respondents, 79.9 per cent answered in positive while 20.1 per cent answered in negative. From the colonies, all of the respondents reported an absence of parks in their locality.

An analysis of the responses from colony clearly suggests that Municipal Council, Panchkula has failed to provide provision of park services in these marginalised areas.

The analysis on the basis of gender reveals that 78.4 per cent males, answered that parks were available while 21.6 per cent in contrast answered the parks were not available. In case of females, 83.3 per cent answered in positive, whereas 16.7 per cent answered in negative.

Employment wise, around 78.16 per cent of employed reported availability, while 21.83 per cent in contrast reported no availability of parks in their locality. In case of unemployed, 81.8 per cent reported availability and 18.2 per cent answered non availability of parks in their locality.

The analysis on the basis of education shows that 55.4 per cent below matric, answered in positive, while 44.59 per cent answered in negative. Furthermore, about 86.1 per cent of above matric answered in positive while 13.9 per cent answered not availability of parks in their locality.

On the basis of income, out of the total respondents having no income, 84.8 per cent reported availability while 15.2 per cent reported not availability. About 76.4 per cent respondents having income between Rs 5,000 to Rs 20,000, reported availability, and 23.6 per cent reported not availability. Out of the total respondents having income above Rs 20,000, 93.8 per cent reported availability while 6.2 per cent reported not availability of parks in their areas.

On the basis of age, out of the total respondents having an age below 30 years, 75.7 per cent answered in positive, and 24.3 per cent answered in negative. Out of the total respondents having an age between 30 to 60 years, 80.1 per cent answered in positive while 19.9 per cent answered in negative. Out of the total respondents having an age of 60 years and above, 81.2 per cent answered in positive while 18.8 per cent answered in negative about the availability of parks in their locality.

(ii) Proper Landscape of the Parks: Respondents were asked whether the park in their locality were properly landscaped.

Responses have been discussed on the basis of area, gender, employment, education, income and age wise in Table 6.31.

Table 6.31
Responses Regarding the Proper Landscape of the Park

		Properly landscaped	*Not properly landscaped*
Area	Rural	0(0.00%)	80(100.00%)
	Urban	126(78.75%)	34(11.25%)
	Colony	0(0.00%)	0(0.00%)
Gender	Male	120(52.20%)	110(47.80%)
	Female	6(60.00%)	4(40.00%)
Employment	Employed	102 (50.00%)	102(50.00%)
	Unemployed	25(69.40%)	11(30.60%)
Education	Below matric	11(26.82%)	30 (73.17%)
	Matric and above	116(58.30%)	83(41.70%)
Income	No income	27(69.20%)	12(30.80%)
	Between Rs. 5000 to 20000	90(48.40%)	96(51.60%)
	Rs. 20000 and above	10(66.70%)	5(33.30%)
Age	Below30	53(65.40%)	28(34.60%)
	30 to 60	65(44.50%)	81(55.50%)
	60 and above	9(69.20%)	4(30.80%)

Source: Field Survey.
(Figures in parentheses represent percentages).

Out of the total rural respondents, all the respondents stated that the parks in their locality were not landscaped. Out of the total urban respondents, 78.75 per cent stated that they were properly landscaped, whereas 11.25 per cent stated that they were not properly landscaped. From the colonies, none said that the park in their locality was landscaped.

The analysis on the basis of gender reveals that 52.20 per cent male stated that they were properly landscaped, whereas 47.80 per cent in contrast stated they were not properly landscaped. In case of females respondents, 60 per cent stated they were properly landscaped while 40 per cent stated they were not properly landscaped.

Employment wise, around 50 per cent employed stated that they were properly landscaped, while 50 per cent stated that they were not properly landscaped. In the case of unemployed respondents, 69.4 per cent stated that they were properly landscaped while 30.6 per cent stated that they were not properly landscaped.

The analysis on the basis of education shows that 26.8 per cent above matric respondents stated that they were properly landscaped, while 73.1 per cent stated that they were not properly landscaped. Furthermore, about 58.3 per cent above matric, stated that they were properly landscaped, while 41.7 per cent stated that they were not properly landscaped.

On the basis of income, out of the total respondents having no income, 69.2 per cent stated that they were properly landscaped and 30.8 per cent stated that they were not properly landscaped. About 48 per cent respondents having income between Rs 5,000 to Rs 20,000, stated that they were properly landscaped while 51.6 per cent stated that they were not properly landscaped. Out of the total respondents having income above Rs 20,000, 66.7 per cent stated that they were properly landscaped, while 33.3 per cent stated that they were not properly landscaped.

On the basis of age, out of the total respondents having an age below 30 years, 65.4 per cent stated that they were properly landscaped and 34.6 per cent stated that they were not properly landscaped to the question. Out of the total respondents having an age between 30 and 60 years, 44.5 per cent stated that they were properly landscaped whereas 55.5 per cent stated that they were not properly landscaped. Out of the total respondents having an age of 60 years and above, 69.2 per cent stated that they were properly landscaped while 30.8 per cent stated that they were not properly landscaped. Thus, it can be inferred from the responses that most of the respondents were of the opinion that the parks in their locality were not landscaped.

(iii) Satisfaction With Parks Maintenance: In case of satisfaction with the maintenance of the parks., out of 305 sample population, 31 per cent were satisfied whereas the remaining 69 per cent have expressed their dissatisfaction.

The level of satisfaction further has been examined on the basis of area, gender, employment, education, income and age of the respondents. The level of significance across these attributes of sample population has been examined by using ÷2.

Area

The area-wise responses of citizens with regard to satisfaction with the maintenance of parks in their locality have been given in Table 6.32.

Table 6.32
Satisfaction with Park Maintenance (Area-wise)

		Satisfied	*Dissatisfied*
Area	Rural	2(2.50%)	78(97.50%
	Urban	124(62.00%)	76(38.0%)
	Colony	0	25(100.00%)

Source: Field Survey.
(Figures in parentheses represent percentages)

Out of total rural respondents, 2.5 per cent were satisfied, and 97.5 per cent were not satisfied with the maintenance of parks undertaken by MCP in their area. Out of the total urban respondents, 62 per cent were satisfied, and 38 per cent were not satisfied. Whereas in case of colonies, none of the respondents was satisfied.

Gender

The gender wise responses of citizens with regard to satisfaction with the maintenance of parks in their locality have been given in Table 6.33.

Table 6.33
Satisfaction Park Maintenance (Gender-wise)

		Satisfied	*Dissatisfied*
GENDER	Male	119(40.80%)	173(59.2 %)
	Female	6(50.00%)	6(50.00%)

÷2 =0.4, df = 1, P > 0.05
(Figures in parentheses represent percentages).

The analysis on the basis of gender reveals that 40.8 per cent males expressed satisfaction, whereas 59.2 per cent in contrast were not satisfied with the maintenance of parks undertaken by MCP in their area. In case of female respondents the division across the level of satisfaction was even.

The chi square test value works out to be 0.4, which is insignificant at five per cent level and d.f=1.This shows that the level of satisfaction does not vary across gender.

Employment

The employment wise responses of citizens with regard to satisfaction with the maintenance of parks in their locality have been given in Table 6.34.

Table 6.34
Satisfaction with Park Maintenance (Employment-wise)

		Satisfied	*Dissatisfied*
EMPLOYMENT	Employed	101(38.69%)	161(61.30%)
	Unemployed	25(56.80%)	19(43.2%)

÷2 =5.10, df = 1, P > 0.05
(Figures in parentheses represent percentages).

Employment wise, around 38.6 per cent employed were satisfied, while 61.3 per cent expressed dissatisfaction with the maintenance of parks undertaken by MCP in their area. In case of unemployed, 56.8 per cent opined satisfaction, while 43 per cent were not satisfied.

The chi square test value works out to be 5.10, which is significant at five per cent level and d.f.=1. This shows, the level of satisfaction is influenced by employment.

Education

The education wise responses of citizens with regard to satisfaction with the maintenance of parks in their locality have been given in Table 6.35.

Table 6.35
Satisfaction with Park Maintenance (Education-wise)

		Satisfied	*Dissatisfied*
EDUCATION	Below matric	10(13.51%)	64(86.48%)
	Matric and above	116(50.20%)	115(49.8%)

÷2 =31.1, df = 1, P > 0.05
(Figures in parentheses represent percentages).

The analysis on the basis of education shows that 13.51 per cent below matric were satisfied, and remaining 86.48 per cent were not satisfied with the maintenance of parks undertaken by MCP in their area. About 50.2 per cent of above matric were satisfied, while the remaining 49.8 per cent were not satisfied.

The chi square test value works out to be 31.1, which is significant at five per cent level and d.f=1. This shows that the level of satisfaction is influenced by education.

Income

The income wise responses of citizens with regard to satisfaction with the maintenance of parks in their locality have been given in Table 6.36.

Table 6.36
Satisfaction with Park Maintenance (Income-wise)

		Satisfied	*Dissatisfied*
INCOME	No income	27(58.70%)	19(41.3%)
	Between Rs 5,000 to 20,000	89(36.60%)	154(63.40%)
	Rs 20,000 and above	10(62.50%)	6(37.5%)

÷2 =11.5, df = 2, P > 0.05
(Figures in parentheses represent percentages).

On the basis of income, out of the total respondents having no income, 58.7 per cent were satisfied, while 41.3 per cent, were not satisfied. About 36.6 per cent respondents having income between Rs 5,000 to Rs 20,000, reported being satisfied, while 63.4 per cent reported not being satisfied with the park maintenance undertaken by MCP in their area. Out of the total respondents having income above Rs 20000 62.5 per cent reported being satisfied, and 37.5 per cent reported not being satisfied.

The chi square test value works out to be 11.5, which is significant at five per cent level and d.f=2. This shows that the level of satisfaction is influenced by income.

Age

The age-wise responses of citizens with regard to satisfaction with the maintenance of parks in their locality have been given in Table 6.37.

Table 6.37
Satisfaction with Park Maintenance (Age-wise)

		Satisfied	*Dissatisfied*
AGE	Below30	53(49.50%)	54(50.5%)
	30 to 60	64(35.20%)	118(64.8%)
	60 and above	9(56.20%)	7(43.80%)

÷2 =12.6, df = 2, P > 0.05
(Figures in parentheses represent percentages).

On the basis of age, out of the total respondents having an age below 30 years, 49.5 per cent were satisfied, and 50.5 per cent were not satisfied with the maintenance of parks undertaken by MCP in their area. Out of the total respondents having an age between 30 to 60 years, 35.2 per cent were satisfied, and 64.8 per cent were not satisfied. Out of the total respondents having an age of 60 years and above, 56.3 per cent are satisfied, and 43.8 per cent were not satisfied.

The chi square test value works out to be12.6, which is significant at five per cent level and d.f.=2. This shows that the level of satisfaction varies across age.

The respondents, who were not satisfied with the performance of the Municipal Council Panchkula regarding maintenance of parks, identified the following reasons:

(1) Lack of maintenance;
(2) No fencing;
(3) Misuse of money ;
(4) Broken pavements;
(5) Lack of Gardeners;
(6) Dysfunctional Fountains;
(7) Absence of Security guards; and
(8) Lack of Playing equipments for children.

(iv) Privatisation of the Maintenance of Parks: It is relevant to mention here that Municipal Council, Panchkula provides park services through contracting out, regarding its construction and maintenance. So responses of the citizens about whether they favour privatisation or not have been discussed on the basis of area, gender, employment, education, income and age wise in Table 6.38.

Table 6.38
Responses Regarding Privatisation of the Maintenance of the Parks

		Yes	*No*	*No idea*
Area	Rural	8(10.00%)	68(85.00%)	4(5.00%)
	Urban	32(20.00%)	118(83.75%)	10(6.25%)
	Colony	0(0.00%)	0(100.00%)	0(0.00%)
Gender	Male	40(17.40%)	176(76.50%)	14(6.10%)
	Female	0(0.00%)	8(80.00%)	2(20.00%)
Employment	Employed	33(16.17%)	161(78.92%)	10(4.90%)
	Unemployed	7(19.40%)	24(66.70%)	5(13.90%)
Education	Below matric	3(7.31%)	35(85.36 %)	3(7.31%)
	Matric and above	37(18.60%)	151(75.90%)	11(5.50%)
Income	No income	7(18.00%)	26(66.60%)	6(15.40%)
	Between Rs. 5000 to 20000	30(16.10%)	147(79.10%)	9(4.80%)
	Rs. 20000 and above	3(20.00%)	12(80.00%)	0(0.00%)
Age	Below30	13(16.00%)	60(74%)	8(10%)
	30 to 60	24(16.40%)	116(79.50%)	6(4.10%)
	60 and above	3(23.10%)	9(69.20%)	1(7.70%)

Source: Field Survey
(Figures in parentheses represent percentages).

In response to the question whether the maintenance of the parks in their sector/locality should be privatised, the responses have been mentioned as under:

Out of rural respondents, 10 per cent favoured privatisation of maintenance of park services while whooping 85.0 per cent opposed it and five per cent remained neutral. Out of the total urban respondents, 20 per cent favoured privatisation, whereas 83.7 per cent were against it and 6.2 per cent remained neutral. From colonies, about 100 per cent respondents were against privatisation.

The analysis on the basis of gender reveals that out of the total male respondents, 17.4 per cent favoured privatisation of maintenance of park services where as 76.5 per cent were against it and 6.1 per cent remained neutral. In case of females respondents, none favoured privatisation, around 80 per cent opposed privatisation and remaining 20 per cent were neutral.

Further, Employment wise, around 33 per cent employed favoured privatisation of parks services, whereas 78.9 per cent were against it and 4.9 per cent remained neutral. In case of unemployed, 19.4 per cent favoured privatisation of maintenance of parks services, whereas 66.7 per cent were against it and 13.9 per cent remained neutral.

The analysis on the basis of education shows that 7.3 per cent below matric respondents favoured privatisation, whereas 85.3 per cent were against privatisation of maintenance of park services and 7.3 per cent remained neutral. About 18. 6 per cent of above matric favoured privatisation where as 75.9 per cent were against it and 5.5 per cent remained neutral.

On the basis of income, out of total respondents having no income, 18.0 per cent favoured privatisation of maintenance of park services, whereas 66.6 per cent were against it and 15.4 per cent remained neutral. Furthermore, About 16.1 per cent of the respondents having income between Rs 5,000 to Rs 20,000, favoured privatisation, whereas 79.1 per cent were against it and 4.8 per cent remained neutral. Out of the total respondents having income above Rs 20,000, 20 per cent favoured privatisation, whereas 80 per cent were against it.

On the basis of age, out of the total respondents having an age below 30 years, 16 per cent favoured privatisation of parks services, whereas 74 per cent were against it and the remaining 10 per cent were neutral. Out of the total respondents having an age between 30 to 60 years, 16.4 per cent favoured privatisation, whereas 79.5 per cent were against it, and 4.1 per cent remained neutral. Out of the total respondents having an age of 60 and above years, 23.1 per cent favoured privatisation, whereas 69.2 per cent were against it and 7.7 per cent remained neutral. Ultimately, a majority of respondents were of the opinion that the maintenance of park services should not be privatised in MCP jurisdiction.

The respondents who were not in agreement with the privatisation of parks services, argued that privatisation leads to: (i) more tax burden; (ii) Increase in government work; (iii) Lack of proper accountability; (iv) Less supervision and control; and (v) high incidences of corruption.

The respondents who agreed upon privatisation of park services opines that privatisation results in (i) good quality of work on a fast track, (ii) effective supervision, (iii) no corruption.

6.2.5. Fire Services

As mentioned earlier, the next findings are concerned with Fire services. Before analysing the responses of the citizens, it is desirable to mention importance of fire services for the community. High density of population and the nature of urban settlement have created such a situation in the urban areas where good fire brigade services is becoming the need of the hour. Cities in India present a picture of congested markets, large number of people living in very small area, slums, which are nothing but tinder boxes. Keeping in view the significance of the function of Fire services, the study has made on attempt to assess the level of satisfaction of the citizens with regard to Fire services in the Municipal Council, Panchkula limit.

Satisfaction with Fire Services: In case of fire services, out of 305 sample population, 58 per cent were satisfied, whereas the remaining 42 per cent have expressed their dissatisfaction.

The level of satisfaction further has been examined on the basis of area, gender, employment, education, income and age of the respondents. The level of significance across these attributes of sample population has been examined by using ÷2.

Area

The area-wise responses of citizens with regard to satisfaction with fire prevention\fire brigade services in their city have been given in Table 6.39.

Table 6.39
Satisfaction with Fire Prevention\Fire Brigade Service (Area-wise)

		Satisfied	*Dissatisfied*	*No Experience*
AREA	Rural	63(78.80%)	3(3.80%)	14(17.40%)
	Urban	113(56.50%)	68(34.00%)	19(9.50%)
	Colony	1(4.00%)	22(88.00%)	2(8.00%)

Source: Field Survey
(Figures in parentheses represent percentages).

Out of total rural respondents, 78.8 per cent were satisfied with fire prevention/fire brigade service in the city, 3.8 per cent were not satisfied and 17.4 per cent had no experience. Out of the total urban respondents, 56.5 per cent were satisfied, 34 per cent were not satisfied and 9.5 per cent had no experience. From the colony respondents, four per cent were satisfied, 88 per cent were not satisfied, and eight per cent had no experience.

Gender

The gender wise responses of citizens with regard to satisfaction with fire prevention\fire brigade service in their city have been given in Table 6.40.

Table 6.40
Satisfaction with Fire Prevention\Fire Brigade Service (Gender-wise)

		Satisfied	*Dissatisfied*	*No Experience*
GENDER	Male	166(56.80%)	93(31.50%)	34(11.60%)
	Female	10(83.30%)	1(8.30%)	1(8.40%)

÷2 =3.5, df = 2, P > 0.05
(Figures in parentheses represent percentages).

The analysis on the basis of gender reveals that 56.8 per cent males expressed their satisfaction with fire prevention\fire brigade service in the city, 31.5 per cent in contrast were not satisfied and 11.6 per cent had no experience. In case of females respondents, 83.3 per cent were satisfied, 8.3 per cent were not satisfied and 8.4 per cent had no experience.

The chi square test value works out to be 3.5, which is significant at five per cent level and d.f.=2.This shows that the level of satisfaction varies across gender.

Employment

The employment wise responses of citizens with regard to satisfaction with fire prevention\fire brigade service in their city have been given in Table 6.41.

Table 6.41
Satisfaction with Fire Prevention\Fire Brigade Service (Employment-wise)

		Satisfied	*Dissatisfied*	*No Experience*
EMPLOYMENT	Employed	155(59.38%)	75(28.13%)	31(11.87%)
	Unemployed	22(50.00%)	18(40.90%)	4(9.10%)

÷2 =2.6, df =2, P > 0.05
(Figures in parentheses represent percentages).

Further employment wise, around 59.3 per cent employed were satisfied with fire prevention\fire brigade service in their city, while remaining 28.1 per cent expressed their dissatisfaction and the remaining 11.8 per cent said that they had no experience. In case of unemployed, 50 per cent opined satisfaction, 40.9 per cent were not satisfied and 9.1 per cent had no experience.

The chi square test value works out to be 2.6, which is insignificant at five per cent level and d.f.=2. This shows that the level of satisfaction does not vary across employment.

Education

The education wise responses of citizens with regard to satisfaction with fire prevention\fire brigade service in their city have been given in Table 6.42.

Table 6.42
Satisfaction with Fire Prevention\Fire Brigade Service (Education-wise)

		Satisfied	*Dissatisfied*	*No Experience*
EDUCATION	Below matric	35(47.29%)	32(43.24%)	7(9.45%)
	Matric and above	142(61.50%)	61(26.40%)	28(12.10%)

÷2 =7.5, df =2, P > 0.05
(Figures in parentheses represent percentages).

The analysis on the basis of education shows that 47.2 per cent below matric were satisfied, 43.2 per cent were not satisfied with fire brigade service and 9.45 per cent had no experience. Around 61.5 per cent of above matric were satisfied, 26.4 per cent were not satisfied and the remaining 12.1 per cent had no experience.

The chi square test value works out to be 7.5, which is significant at five per cent level and d.f.=2. This suggests that level of education influences level of satisfaction.

Income

The income wise responses of citizens with regard to satisfaction with fire prevention\fire brigade service in their city have been given in Table 6.43.

Table 6.43
Satisfaction with Fire Prevention\Fire Brigade Service (Income-wise)

		Satisfied	*Dissatisfied*	*No Experience*
INCOME	No income	22(47.80 %)	20(43.50%)	4(8.70%)
	Between Rs. 5000 to 20000	146(60.10%)	68(28.00%)	29(11.90%)
	Rs. 20000 and above	9(56.20%)	5(31.30%)	2(12.50%)

÷2 =4.4, df =4, P > 0.05

(Figures in parentheses represent percentages).

On the basis of income, out of the total respondents having no income, 47.8 per cent were satisfied with fire prevention\fire brigade service in their city, 43.9 per cent were not satisfied, and the remaining 8.7 per cent had no experience. About 60.1 per cent respondents having income between Rs 5000 to Rs 20000, reported being satisfied, 28 per cent reported being not satisfied and the remaining 11.9 per cent had no experience. Out of the total respondents having income above Rs 20000, 56.2 per cent reported being satisfied, 31.3 per cent reported being not satisfied and the remaining 12.5 per cent had no experience.

The chi square test value works out to be 4.4, which is significant at five per cent level and d.f=4. This suggests that level of income influences level of satisfaction.

Age

The age wise responses of citizens with regard to satisfaction with fire prevention \fire brigade service in their city have been given in Table 6.44.

Table 6.44
Satisfaction with Fire Prevention\Fire Brigade Service (Age-wise)

		Satisfied	*Dissatisfied*	*No Experience*
AGE	Below30	52(48.60%)	45(42.10%)	10(9.30%)
	30 to 60	112(61.50%)	45(24.70%)	25(13.70%)
	60 and above	13(81.20%)	3(18.80%)	0(0.00%)

÷2 =13.9, df =4, P > 0.05

(Figures in parentheses represent percentages).

An analysis on the basis of age reveals that out of the total respondents having an age below 30 years, 48.6 per cent reported satisfaction with fire brigade service, 42.1 per cent reported dissatisfaction, while the remaining 9.3 per cent had no experience. Out of the total respondents having an age between 30 to 60 years, 61.5 per cent were satisfied, 24.7 per cent were not satisfied and the remaining 13.7 per cent had no experience. Out of the total respondents having an age of 60 years and above, 81.2 per cent were satisfied, while the remaining 18.8 per cent were not satisfied.

The chi square test value works out to be 13.9, which is insignificant at five per cent level and d.f=4. This shows that level of satisfaction is not influenced by age.

The respondents who were not satisfied with the performance of Municipal Council, Panchkula in the field of fire services, cited the following reasons:

1. Lack of staff;
2. Lack of infrastructure;
3. No timely response; and
4. Lack of trained personnel.

6.2.6 Complaint

The performance of Municipal Council, Panchkula from citizens perspective has also been analysed on the basis of the following:

(A) Lodging a complaint
(B) Problems faced in lodging a complaint
(C) Services for which a complaint may be filed
(D) Time consumed to redress a 'complaint

(A) Lodging of a Complaint: Respondents were asked whether they ever filed a complaint against the performance of Municipal Council, Panchkula. The responses have been discussed on the basis of area, gender, employment, education, income and age in Table 6.45.

Table 6.45
Responses Regarding Complaint Made against the Municipal Council, Panchkula

		Lodging Complaints	*Not Lodging Complaints*
Area	Rural	52(65.00%)	28(35.00%)
	Urban	87(43.50%)	113(56.50%)
	Colony	14(56.00%)	11(44.00%)
Gender	Male	150(51.40%)	142(48.60%)

	Female	3(25.00%)	9(75.00%
Employment	Employed	132(50.57%)	129(49.42%)
	Unemployed	21(47.70%)	23(52.30%)
Education	Below Matric	44(59.45%)	30(40.54%)
	Matric and above	109(47.20%)	122(52.80%)
Income	No Income	24(52.20%)	22(47.80%)
	Between Rs. 5000 to 20000	124(51.00%)	119(49.00%)
	Above Rs. 20000	5(31.20%)	11(68.80%)
Age	Below 30	56(52.30%)	51(47.70%)
	30 to 60	89(48.90%)	93(51.10%)
	60 and above	8(50.00%)	8(50.00%)

Source: Field Survey
(Figures in parentheses represent percentages).

Out of total rural respondents, 65 per cent responded that they had filed a complaint against the MCP, 35 per cent said that they hade not filed a complaint. Out of total urban respondents 43.5 per cent remarked having lodged a complaint, while 56.5 per cent remarked that they had not lodged a complaint. From colony respondents 56 per cent said they had lodged complaints, whereas 44 per cent had not.

The analysis on the basis of gender reveals that 51.4 per cent males had lodged a complaint, while 48.6 per cent had never lodged any. In case of females, 25 per cent remarked having lodged complaints and 75 per cent remarked never having done that.

Employment wise, around 50.5 per cent employed said that they had lodged complaints, 49.4 per cent said they had not lodged complaints. About 54.1 per cent unemployed reported that they had lodged complaints, 45.9 per cent reported that they had never lodged complaints. In case of unemployed, 47.7 per cent said that they had lodged complaints, 52.3 per cent said that they had not lodged complaints.

The analysis on the basis of education shows that 59.4 per cent below matric, reported lodging complaints, 44.5 per cent reported not lodging complaints. Around 47.2 per cent above matric, reported lodging complaints, 52.8 per cent reported in negative.

On the basis of income, out of total respondents, having no income, 52.2 per cent stated lodging complaints, 47.80 per cent stated not lodging complaints. About 51 per cent respondents having income between Rs 5,000 to Rs 20,000, reported lodging complaints, while 49 per cent reported in negative. Out of total respondents, having income above Rs 20,000, 31.2 per cent reported lodging complaints, while 68.8 per cent reported in negative.

On the basis of age, out of total respondents, having an age below 30 years, 52.3 per cent reported lodging complaints and 47.70 per cent reported in negative. Out of total respondents, having an age between 30-60 years 48.9 per cent reported lodging complaints while 51.10 per cent reported in negative. Out of total respondents, having an age 60 years and above, 50 per cent reported lodging complaints, 50 per cent reported negative.

(B) Problems Faced for Filing a Complaint: The Respondents were regarding the problems faced while filing complaints against Municipal Council, Panchkula. The responses have been discussed on the basis of area, gender, employment, education, income and age in Table 6.46.

Problems faced during the time of filing complaints:

1. Non availability of the concerned officials,
2. Rude behaviour,
3. Harassment,
4. All of the above,
5. None,

Table 6.46
Problems Faced During the Time of Filing Complaints

		1	*2*	*3*	*4*	*5*
Area	Rural	2	0	30	18	2
		(3.80%)	(0.00%)	(57.70%)	(23.10%)	(3.80%)
	Urban	2	2	42	19	22
		(2.30%)	(2.30%)	(48.30%)	(21.80%)	(25.30%)
	Colony	0	1	5	8	0
		(0.00%)	(7.15%)	(35.75%)	(57.15%)	(0.00%)
Gender	Male	4	3	76	44	23
		(2.70%)	(2.00%)	(50.70%)	(29.40%)	(15.30%)
	Female	0	0	1	1	1
		(0.00%)	(0.00%)	(33.33%)	(33.30%)	(33.33%)
Employment	Employed	4	3	62	42	28
		(2.07%)	(2.09%)	(46.96%)	(31.1%)	(21.2%)
	Unemployed	0	0	8	8	5
		(0.00%)	(0.00%)	(38.20%)	(38.00%)	(23.80%)
Education	Below	1	2	25	14	2
	Matric	(2.07%)	(4.54%)	(56.81%)	(31.81%)	(4.54%)
	Matric	3	1	53	30	22
	and above	(2.70%)	(0.90%)	(48.60%)	(27.40%)	(20.20%)
Income	No Income	0	0	10	9	5
		(0.00%)	(0.00%)	(41.70%)	(37.60%)	(20.90%)
	Between	4	3	64	35	18
	5000 to					

	20000	(3.30%)	(2.40%)	(51.60%)	(28.20%)	(14.50%)
	20000	0	0	3	1	1
	and above	(0.00%)	(0.00%)	(60.00%)	(20.00%)	(20.00%)
Age	Below 30	1	1	31	19	4
		(2.00%)	(2.00%)	(55.40%)	(34.00%)	(7.10%)
	30 to 60	3	2	46	23	15
		(3.40%)	(2.20%)	(51.70%)	(25.80%)	(16.80%)
	60 and	0	0	0	3	5
	above	(0.00%)	(0.00%)	(0.00%)	(37.5%)	(62.5%)

Source: Field Survey
(Figures in parentheses represent percentages).

Out of total rural respondents, 3.80 per cent faced problems like non-availability of the concerned officials; 57.70 per cent faced unnecessary harassment, 23.1 per cent faced non availability of the concerned officials, rude behaviour and unnecessary harassment while 30 per cent faced no problem.

Out of the total urban respondents, 2.3 per cent faced problems like non-availability of concerned officials; 2.3 per cent faced rude behaviour; 48.3 per cent faced unnecessary harassment; while 25.3 per cent faced no problem and 21.8 per cent faced non availability of the concerned officials, rude behaviour and unnecessary harassment. Out of the total colony respondents, 7.15 per cent faced rude behaviour, 35.75 per cent faced unnecessary harassment, and 57.15 per cent faced non-availability of the concerned officials, rude behaviour and unnecessary harassment while filling complaints against MCP services.

The analysis on the basis of gender reveals that 2.7 per cent male, faced problems like non-availability of the concerned officials; 2.0 per cent faced rude behaviour, 50.7 per cent faced unnecessary harassment; while 29.4 per cent faced non availability of the concerned officials, rude behaviour and unnecessary harassment whereas 15.30 per cent faced no problem. In case of female respondents, 33.3 per cent faced unnecessary harassment; 33.3 per cent faced no problem and 33.3 per cent faced non-availability of the concerned officials and rude behaviour and 33.3 per cent faced no problem while filing the complaint against MCP services.

Employment wise, around two per cent employed, faced problems like non-availability of the concerned officials; 2.09 per cent faced rude behaviour, 46.9 per cent faced unnecessary harassment; 31.2 per cent faced non availability of the concerned officials, rude behaviour and unnecessary harassment; where as 21.2 per cent faced no problem.

About 38.2 per cent unemployed faced unnecessary harassment; 38 per cent faced non availability of the concerned officials, rude behaviour and unnecessary harassment while 23.8 per cent faced no problem.

The analysis on the basis of education shows that 2.07 per cent below matric, faced non-availability of the concerned officials, 4.54 per cent faced rude behaviour 56.8 per cent faced unnecessary harassment, 31.8 per cent faced non availability of the concerned officials, rude behaviour and unnecessary harassment while filing the complaint against services while 4.54 per cent faced no problem. Furthermore, around 2.7 per cent of above matric, faced non-availability of the concerned officials; 0.9 per cent faced rude behaviour; 48.6 per cent faced unnecessary harassment; 27.4 per cent faced non-availability of the concerned officials, rude behaviour and unnecessary harassment; while 20.2 per cent faced no problem.

On the basis of income, out of the total respondents having no income, 41.7 per cent faced unnecessary harassment; 37.6 per cent faced non-availability of the concerned officials, rude behaviour and unnecessary harassment; while 20.2 per cent faced no problem.

About 3.3 per cent respondents having income between Rs 5000 to Rs 20000 faced non-availability of the concerned officials; 2.4 per cent rude behaviour; 51.6 per cent unnecessary harassment; 28.2 per cent faced non-availability of the concerned officials, rude behaviour and unnecessary harassment; while 14.5 per cent faced no problem. Out of the total respondents having income above Rs 20000, 60 per cent faced unnecessary harassment; 20 per cent faced non-availability of the concerned officials, rude behaviour and unnecessary harassment; while 20 per cent faced no problem.

On the basis of age, out of the total respondents having an age below 30 years, two per cent faced rude behaviour; two per cent faced unnecessary harassment; 55.4 per cent faced unnecessary harassment; 34 per cent faced non-availability of the concerned officials, rude behaviour and unnecessary harassment; 7.1 per cent faced no problem.

Out of the total respondents, having an age between 30 to 60 years, 3.4 per cent faced non-availability of the concerned officials; 2.2 per cent faced rude behaviour; 51.7 per cent unnecessary harassment; 25.8 per cent faced non-availability of the concerned officials, rude behaviour and unnecessary harassment; whereas 16.8 per cent faced no problem. Out of the total respondents having an age of 60 years and above, 37.5 per cent faced non-availability of the concerned officials, rude behaviour, and unnecessary harassment; and a whooping 62.5 per cent faced no problem.

(C) Services for which a Complaint was Filed: The respondents were asked the specific service against which they had filed the complaint in Municipal Council, Panchkula. The responses have been discussed on the basis of area, gender, employment, education, income and age wise in Table 6.47.

Table 6.47
Services for which the Complaint was Filed

		Roads	*Sanitation*	*Street Light*	*Parks*	*Fire Services*	*All the above*
Area	Rural	0(0.00%)	2(3.80%)	16(30.80%)	0(0.00%)	0(0.00%)	34(65.40%)
	Urban	11(12.60%)	15(17.20%)	26(29.20%)	1(0.50%)	1(1.10%)	33(28.00%)
	Colony	0(0.00%)	1(7.15%)	2(14.30%)	0(0.00%)	0(0.00%)	11(78.50%)
Gender	Male	11(7.30%)	18(12.00%)	44(29.20%)	1(0.70%)	1(0.70%)	73(49.00%)
	Female	0(0.00%)	0(0.00%)	1(33.33%)	0(0.00%)	0(0.00%)	2(66.60%)
Occupation	Employed	7(4.89%)	17(11.88%)	44(30.76%)	1(0.69%)	0	63(44.68%)
	Unemployed	4(19.25%)	1(4.80%)	1(4.80%)	0(0.00%)	1(4.80%)	14(64.20%)
Education	Below Matric	2(4.54%)	4(9.09%)	15(34.09%)	1(2.27%)	0	22(50.00%)
	Matric and above	9(8.25%)	14(12.85%)	29(26.60%)	0(0.00%)	1(0.95%)	56(51.4%)
Income	No Income	4(3.90%)	2(1.80%)	1(.9%)	0(0.00%)	1(.9%)	14(14.40%)
	Between Rs. 5000 to 20000	6(4.80%)	15(12.10%)	43(34.70%)	1(0.80%)	0(0.00%)	60(47.40%)
	Rs. 20000 and above	1(20%)	1(20%)	1(20%)	0(0.00%)	0(0.00%)	2(40.0%)
Age	Below 30	5(8.9%)	9(16.10%)	6(10.70%)	0(0.00%)	1(1.80%)	35(62.50%)
	30 to 60	5(5.60%)	9(10.15%)	33(37.10%)	1(1.15%)	0(0.00%)	41(46.0%)
	60 and above	1(12.5%)	0(0.00%)	5(62.5%)	0(0.00%)	0(0.00%)	2(25.0%)

Source: Field Survey
(Figures in parentheses represent percentages).

Out of total rural respondents, 30.8 per cent complained about street lights; 3.8 per cent complained about sanitation; 3.8 per cent about road, sanitation and street lights while 65.4 per cent complained about all. Out of the total urban respondents, 12.6 per cent complained about roads; 17.2 per cent about sanitation; 29.2 per cent complained about street lights; 1.1 per cent about parks; 1.1 per cent complained about fire services and 28 per cent about roads, sanitation, street lights, parks and fire services. From colony respondents, 7.15 per cent complained about sanitation; 14.30 per cent complained about street light whereas 78.5 per cent complained about all.

The analysis on the basis of gender reveals that 3.8 per cent males complained about roads; 7.30 per cent complained about sanitation; 12 per cent complained about street lights; .7 per cent c about parks; 7 per cent about fire services; while 49 per cent complained about all. In case of female respondents, 3.33 per cent complained about street lights; 33.33 per cent about roads, sanitation and street light; and 33.33 per cent complained about roads and sanitation and 66.66 per cent complained about all.

Employment wise, around 6.05 per cent employed complained about roads; 11.88 per cent about sanitation; 30.76 per cent about street lights; 0.69 per cent about parks, while 44.6 per cent about roads, sanitation, street lights, parks and fire services. In case of unemployed, 19.25 per cent complained about roads; 4.80 per cent complained about sanitation; 4.8 per cent about street light; 4.8 per cent about fire services and 64.20 per cent complained about all.

The analysis on the basis of education shows that below matric, 4.54 per cent complained about roads; 9.09 per cent about sanitation, 34.09 per cent about street lights, 2.27 per cent about parks while 50 per cent about roads sanitations, street lights, parks and fire services. Around 8.2 per cent above matric, complained about road; 12.8 per cent about sanitation; 26.6 per cent about street light; .9 per cent about fire services; and 51.3 per cent complained about all.

On the basis of income, out of the total respondents having no income, 3.9 per cent complained about roads; 1.8 per cent about sanitation; .9 per cent about street lights; .9 per cent about fire services while 14.4 per cent complained about roads, sanitation, street lights, parks and fire services. About 4.8 per cent respondents having income between Rs 5,000 to Rs 20,000, complained about roads; 12.1 per cent about sanitation; 34.7 per cent about street lights; eight per cent about parks whereas 47.4 per cent complained about roads, sanitation, street lights, parks and fire services. Out of the total respondents having income above Rs 20,000, 20 per cent complained about roads; 20 per cent complained about sanitation; 20 per cent complained about street light; and 40 per cent complained about all.

On the basis of age, out of the total respondents having an age below 30 years, 8.9 per cent complained about roads; 16.1 per cent about sanitation; 10.1 per cent about street lights; 1.8 per cent about fire services while 62.5 per cent complained about road sanitation, street lights, parks and fire services. Out of the total respondents having an age between 30 to 60 years, 5.6 per cent complained about roads; 10.1 per cent about sanitation; 37.1 per cent about parks; 1.1 about roads, sanitation and street lights whereas 46 per cent complained about roads, sanitation, street lights, parks and fire services. Out of the total respondents having an age of 60 years and above, 12.5 per cent complained about road, sanitation and street light; while 62.5 per cent complained about sanitation street light and 25 per cent complained about all.

(D) Time Consumed to Redress a Complaint: The respondents were asked that in case of complaints made by them in Municipal Council Panchkula, how long did it take for proper action and redressal of the problems. The responses have been discussed on the the basis of area, gender, employment, education, income and age wise in Table 6.48.

Table 6.48
Responses Regarding Time Taken to Take Action Against Complaint

		1-7days	*7-14 days*	*One month*	*Above onemonth*	*Not still*
Area	Rural	4(7.70%)	0(0.00%)	32(61.55%)	6(11.55%)	10(19.25%)
	Urban	12(13.00%)	4(4.60%)	17(19.55%)	1(1.15%)	53(60.95%)
	Colony	0(0.00%)	0(0.00%)	0(0.00%)	3(21.45%)	11(78.60%)
Gender	Male	16(10.70%)	4(2.70%)	46(30.70%)	10(6.70%)	74(49.35%)
	Female	0(0.00%)	0(0.00%)	3(100%)	0(0.00%)	0(0.00%)
Employment	Employed	15(10.48%)	4(2.09%)	46(32.16%)	8(5.59%)	59(41.25%)
	Unemployed	1(1.80%)	0(0.00%)	3(14.30%)	2(9.55%)	15(71.45%)
Education	Below matric	3(6.81%)	1(2.29%)	15(34.09%)	4(9.09%)	21(47.72%)
	Matric and above	13(11.95%)	3(2.75%)	34(31.20%)	6(5.50%)	53(48.65%)
Income	No income	1(4.20%)	0(0.00%)	3(12.5%)	2(8.35%)	18(75.0%)
	Between Rs. 5000 to 20000	15(36.30%)	4(3.25%)	44(35.50%)	7(5.65%)	54(43.55%)
	Rs. 20000 and above	0(0.00%)	0(0.00%)	2(40%)	1(20%)	2(40%)
Age	Below30	1(1.80%)	0(0.00%)	11(19.65%)	7(12.50%)	37(66.10%)
	30 to 60	11(12.35%)	4(4.50%)	35(39.35%)	3(3.40%)	36(40.45%)
	60 and above	4(50.00%)	0(0.00%)	3(37.5 %)	0(0.00%)	1(12.5%)

Source: Field Survey
(Figures in parentheses represent percentages).

Out of the total rural respondents, 7.70 per cent said that it took 1-7 days to redress the complaint; 61.55 per cent said that it took 1 month; 11.55 per cent said that it took over a month while 19.25 per cent said that it was still pending. Out of total urban respondents, 13.8 per cent said that it took 1-7 days; 4.60 per cent said it took 7-14 days; 19.55 per cent said that it took 1 month; 1.55 per cent said that it took over a month; while 60.95 per cent said that the complaint was still pending. Out of total colony respondents, 21.45 per cent said that it took above a month to redress the complaint, while 78.60 per cent said that it was still pending.

The analysis on the basis of gender reveals that 10.7 per cent males respondents opined that it took 1-7 days to redress the problem; 2.7 per cent stated that it took 7-14 days; 30.7 per cent said that it took 1 month; 6.7 per cent opined that it took above a month; while 49.35 per cent said that it was still pending. In case of females respondents, 100 per cent said that it took one month to redress the complaint.

Employment wise, around 10.48 per cent employed respondents replied that it took 1-7 days to redress the complaint; 2.79 per cent replied that it took 7-14 days; 32.16 per cent replied that it took 1 month; 5.59 per cent said it took above a month; while 41.25 per cent replied that it was still pending. In case of unemployed respondents, 1.8 per cent said that it took 1-7 days; 14.3 per cent stated that it took a month to redress the complaint; 9.55 per cent opined that it took above a month ;whereas 71.45 per cent state that it was still pending.

The analysis on the basis of education shows that 6.81 per cent of the below matric respondents replied that it took 1-7 days to redress the complaint; 2.29 per cent replied it took 7-14 days; 34.09 per cent replied that it took one month; 9.09 per cent replied that it took above a month to redress the complaint; while 47.12 per cent replied that complaints were still pending. Around 11.95 per cent above matric replied that that it took 1-7 days; 21.75 per cent replied that it took 7-14 days; 31.2 per cent replied that it took a month; 5.5 per cent said that it took above a month to redress the complaint; while 48.65 per cent replied that the complaints were still pending.

On the basis of income, out of the total respondents having no income, 8.35 per cent opined that it took 1-7 days to redress the complaint; 12.5 stated that it took one month; 8.35 per cent said it took above a month; while 75 per cent replied that the complaints were still pending. About 36.3 per cent of respondents having income between Rs 5,000 to Rs 20,000, 36.3 per cent said that it took 1-7 days; 3.25 per cent that it took

7-14 days; 35.5 per cent said that it took one month; 5.65 per cent stated that it took above a month; while 43.55 per cent said that the complaints were still pending. Out of total respondents having income above Rs 20,000, 40 per cent said that it took a month to redress the complaint; 20 per cent said that it took above a month to redress the complaint; whereas 40 per cent said that it was still pending. Out of total respondents who had income below Rs 5,000 to Rs 20,000, 36.3 per cent replied that it took 1-7 days; 3.25 per cent that it took 7-14 days; 35.5 per cent said that it took one month; 5.65 per cent said that it took above a month to redress the complaint; while 43.55 per cent opined that complaints were still pending.

Analysis on the basis of age reveals that out of the total respondents having an age below 30 years, 1.8 per cent replied that it took 1-7 days to redress the complaint; 19.65 per cent replied that it took one month; 12.5 per cent replied that it took above a month and 66.1 per cent replied that complaints were still pending. Out of the total respondents having an age between 30 to 60 years, 12.35 per cent stated that it took 1-7 days to redress the complaint; 4.5 per cent said that it took 7-14 days to redress the complaint; 39.35 per cent opined that it took 1 month t, 3.4 per cent said it took above a month to redress the complaint; while 40.45 per cent said that the complaints were still pending. Out of the total respondents having an age of 60 years and above, 50 per cent replied that it took 1-7 days; while 37.5 per cent replied that it took one month to redress the complaint; whereas 12.5 per cent replied that complaints were still pending.

Handling of Complaint Compared with Citizens Charter of MCP

According to Citizens Charter of MCP published on 15/08/2003 it is on obligation of MCP to redress the complaint for sanitation, road, street lights, parks and fire services.

Table 6.49
Handling of Complaint Compared with Citizens Charter of MCP

Services		*Nature of Complaints*	*Time for redressed of the complaints*
1. Sanitation	a.	Removal of Garbage	2 days
	b.	In sanitary Conditions	2 days
	c.	Stray dogs/ cattle	Same day
	d.	Dead animals	Immediate
	e.	Removal of rubbish Malba from public land	2 days
2. Roads	a.	Temporary filling of pot holes/ roads cuts	3 days
	b.	Patch repair	5 days

	c.	Construction of new roads	Two months
3. Street Lights	a.	Repair of street light	Two days
	b.	New arrangement	1 month
4. Parks	a.	Development of New parks	2 months
	b.	Grass cutting, pruning of hedges	1 week
	c.	Watering cleaning	2 days
5. Fire	a.	Fire calls	Immediately
	b.	Fire reports as per occurrence book	2 days

Source: Citizens Charter of MCP.

It has been found that the time taken by MCP in handling complaints has been much more than the time stipulated in the Citizens Charter for select services.

6.2.7 Overall Satisfaction Level of Citizens

The overall satisfaction level of the citizens regarding basic services provided by Municipal Council, Panchkula has been analysed on the basis of area, gender, employment, education, income and age as shown in Table 6.50 to 6.55.

Area

The area wise responses of citizens with regard to overall satisfaction with the performance of Municipal Council, Panchkula regarding quality of service delivery of select services have been depicted in Table 6.50.

Table 6.50
Satisfaction Level Regarding the Overall Performance of Municipal Council, Panchkula (Area-wise)

		Satisfied	*Dissatisfied*
AREA	Rural	0	80(100%)
	Urban	43(21.5%)	157(78.5%)
	Colony	0	25(100%)

(Figures in parentheses represent percentages).

The respondents were asked about their overall satisfaction level regarding the service delivery. Out of total rural respondents, none was satisfied with the overall performance of Municipal Council, Panchkula regarding quality of service delivery of select services. Out of the total urban respondents, 21.5 per cent were satisfied, while 78.5 per cent were not satisfied. From colony respondents, again none was satisfied.

An analysis of responses from rural areas and colony put together clearly suggests Municipal Council, Panchkula has failed to provide all the services with quality to these marginalised areas.

Gender

The gender wise responses of citizens with regard to the satisfaction with overall performance of Municipal Council, Panchkula regarding quality of service delivery of select services have been depicted in Table 6.51.

Table 6.51
Satisfaction Level Regarding the Overall Performance of Municipal Council, Panchkula (Gender-wise)

		Satisfied	*Dissatisfied*
GENDER	Male	37(12.7%)	255(87.3%)
	Female	6(50%)	6(50%)

÷2 =13.2, df = 1, P > 0.05
(Figures in parentheses represent percentages).

The analysis on the basis of gender reveals that 12.7 per cent males expressed their satisfaction while whooping 87.3 per cent in contrast were not satisfied with the overall performance of MCP regarding services provided by MCP. In case of female respondents, the division across level of overall satisfaction was even.

The chi square test value works out to be 13.2, which is significant at five per cent level and d.f=1. This suggests that satisfaction level is influenced by gender.

Employment

The employment wise responses of citizens with regard to satisfaction with overall performance of Municipal Council, Panchkula regarding quality of service delivery of select services have been depicted in Table 6.52.

Table 6.52
Satisfaction Level Regarding the Overall Performance of Municipal Council, Panchkula (Employment-wise)

		Satisfied	*Dissatisfied*
EMPLOYMENT	Employed	35 (13.4%)	226 (86.5%)
	Unemployed	8(18.2%)	36(81.8%)

÷2 =0.7, df = 1, P > 0.05
(Figures in parentheses represent percentages).

Employment wise, around 13.4 per cent employed expressed their satisfaction, while remaining 86.5 per cent expressed their dissatisfaction with the overall performance of MCP regarding services provided by MCP. In case of unemployed, 18.2 per cent opined satisfaction while a majority 81.8 per cent were not satisfied.

The chi square test value works out to be 0.7, which is significant at five per cent level and d.f=1. This suggests that level of satisfaction is influenced by employment.

Education

The education wise responses of citizens with regard to satisfaction with the overall performance of Municipal Council, Panchkula regarding quality of service delivery of select services have been depicted in Table 6.53.

Table 6.53
Satisfaction Level Regarding the Overall Performance of Municipal Council, Panchkula (Education-wise)

		Satisfied	*Dissatisfied*
EDUCATION	Below matric	5(6.7%)	69(93.2%)
	Matric and above	38(16.5%)	193(83.5%)

÷2 =4.3, df = 1, P > 0.05

(Figures in parentheses represent percentages).

The analysis on the basis of education shows that 6.7 per cent below matric were satisfied while 93.2 per cent dissatisfied. About 16.5 per cent of above matric were satisfied whereas remaining 83.5 per cent were not satisfied.

The Chi-square test value works out to be 4.3, which is significant at five per cent level and d.f=1.This suggests that the level of satisfaction varies across education.

Income

The income wise responses of citizens with regard to satisfaction overall performance of Municipal Council, Panchkula regarding quality of service delivery of select services have been depicted in Table 6.54.

Table 6.54
Satisfaction Level Regarding the Overall Performance of Municipal Council, Panchkula (Income-wise)

		Satisfied	*Dissatisfied*
INCOME	No income	8(17.4%)	38(82.6%)
	Between Rs 5000 to 20000	34(14.0%)	209(86.0%)
	Rs 20000 and above	1(6.3%)	15(93.8%)

÷2 =1.2, df = 2, P > 0.05

(Figures in parentheses represent percentages).

On the basis of income, out of the total respondents having no income, 17.4 per cent were satisfied while 82.6 per cent were not satisfied with the overall performance of MCP. About 14 per cent respondents having income between Rs 5,000 to Rs 20,000, reported being satisfied, and 86.0 per cent reported not being satisfied. Out of the total respondents having income above Rs 20,000, 6.3 per cent were satisfied and 93.7 per cent were not satisfied.

The chi square test value works out to be 1.2, which is insignificant at five per cent level and d.f=2. This suggests that the level of income does not influence level of satisfaction.

Age

The age wise responses of citizens with regard to overall satisfaction with the performance of Municipal Council, Panchkula regarding quality of service delivery of select services have been depicted in Table 6.55.

Table 6.55
Satisfaction Level Regarding the Overall Performance of Municipal Council, Panchkula (Age-wise)

		Satisfied	*Dissatisfied*
AGE	Below30	10(9.3%)	97(90.7%)
	30 to 60	25(13.7%)	157(86.3%)
	60 and above	8(50.0%)	8(50.0%)

÷2 =19.0, df = 2, P > 0.05

(Figures in parentheses represent percentages).

On the basis of age, out of the total respondents having an age below 30 years, 9.3 per cent were satisfied while a majority 90.7 per cent were not satisfied with the overall performance of MCP regarding services provided by it. Out of the total respondents having an age between 30 to 60 years, 13.7 per cent were satisfied while 86.3 per cent were not satisfied. Out of the total respondents having an age of 60 years and above, the division across the level of satisfaction was even.

The chi square test value works out to be 19.0, which is significant at five per cent level and d.f.=2. This suggests that level of satisfaction varies across age.

6.3 Status of Hypothesis

For evaluating the status of the Hypothesis 6: "Users of services of Municipal Council Panchkula are not satisfied with the quality of services", primary data have been used and main hypothesis has been split into the various sub-hypotheses such as: satisfaction of the citizens with the condition of 'roads'; 'sanitation'; 'street light'; 'parks'; and 'fire brigade services'. The major findings regarding satisfaction of citizens have been summarized in Matrix 4.

Matrix 4
Summing up the Testing of Hypothesis 6

Services and Sub-hypothesis	*Sources of Data*	*Analysis*	*Status of Sub hypothesis Y Valid N Invalid*
1. Sanitation a) Users are not satisfied with the provision of sanitation services	Primary Data	A. About 80 per cent of citizens are dissatisfied with Garbage collection. B. Around 75 per cent of citizens are dissatisfied with cleanliness	Y
2. Street Lights a) Users are not satisfied with the provision of street lights service	Primary Data	A. About 75 per cent of citizens are dissatisfied with the quality of street lights	Y
3. Roads a) Users are not satisfied with the quality of roads	Primary Data	A. Around 89 per cent of citizens are dissatisfied with the conditions of roads	Y
4. Parks a) Users are not satisfied with maintenance of parks	Primary Data	A. Around 59 per cent citizens are dissatisfied with the maintenance of parks.	Y
5. Fire Brigade services a) Users are not satisfied with the quality of fire brigade services	Primary Data	A. Around 58 per cent of citizens are satisfied with the fire prevention services.	N
6. Users are not satisfied with the overall quality of services	Primary Data	A. About 86 per cent of users are dissatisfied with the overall quality of services provided by MCP.	Y

Analysis of the sub hypotheses reveals that the main Hypothesis 6: "Users of services of MCP are not satisfied with the quality of services" stands validated.

Concluding Observations

The level of satisfaction of citizens regarding services is one of the known yardsticks to measure the performance of a municipality. The study found that the service-wise performance of MCP from the citizens perspective is not satisfactory. The citizens expressed their dissatisfaction on account of all the five services namely, sanitation, street light, road services, parks and fire brigade services. The level of dissatisfaction was particularly more severe in case of citizens residing in villages and colonies.

Thus, from citizens perspective the report card of the MCP does not score well.

7

Summary, Conclusion and Policy Prescriptions

The aim of this chapter is to summarize the major findings of the study and also to put forth recommendations for improving the performance of local self governance.

The chapter has been organized into four parts. Part I summarizes the rationale of the study. The review of literature; inadequacies of the earlier studies; the scope and period of study; objectives; hypothesis; and the research methodology have been mentioned in part II of the chapter. Thc part III of the chapter covers gist of the major findings. The last part of the chapter offers a set of policy prescriptions.

I RATIONALE OF THE STUDY

Local governments in India especially after the 73rd and 74th Constitutional Amendments have played a vital role in providing local services to the citizens in their jurisdictions. The last few decades have seen a massive expansion in the urban areas across the country. The expectations of citizens from the municipal governments in urban areas are rising with every passing day. Municipalities around the country are gearing up to meet these expectations. It is therefore, important to make an assessment about the performance of these bodies as well as to find out the perceptions of the citizens about the quality of services being provided to them. It is in this backdrop that the present study has been undertaken ,along with the issues and challenges of Urban Local Bodies .

II REVIEW OF LITERATURE

With a view to comprehend the various facets of the research problem and identify the limitations of the earlier studies, a review of several research papers, books and reports was undertaken.

INADEQUACIES OF EARLIER LITERATURE AND APPROACH FOR OVERCOMING THE INADEQUACIES

A review of literature reveals that most of the earlier studies focused only on one or two primary aspects of the urban local bodies at a time. For example the previous studies focused either on the structural the procedural or on the financial aspects but none of the earlier works has attempted to study the overall performance of the urban local bodies by focusing on delivery of municipal services from the citizens perspective. Furthermore, the previous studies did not make any attempt to assess the performance of the local government on the basis of the benchmarks set for service delivery.

The present study aims to evaluate the overall performance of the urban local body, namely Municipal Council, Panchkula by covering organizational, financial and physical aspects relating to select municipal services. In addition, the study also focuses on measuring the satisfaction level of the citizens towards the basic services being provided by Municipal Council, Panchkula. Besides these, the present study has also attempted to analyse the performance of MCP regarding service delivery on the basis of comparison with select benchmarks.

Scope of the Study

An urban local self government provides a number of services that have a direct impact on its citizens. The subject matter of the urban local self government since the 74th Constitutional Amendments has become so wide, complex and dynamic that it would have been most difficult to delve into the complete study of all the services being provided by an urban local self government. The present study therefore, due to time and resource constraints has confined itself only to sanitation, roads, parks, streetlights and fire brigade services being provided by Municipal Council, Panchkula.

Time Period of Study

The MCP was established in 2001 and, almost a decade has passed since its inception. Therefore, the study period covered a decade of MCP functioning i.e. 2001 to 2010.

OBJECTIVES OF THE STUDY

The objectives of the study are to:

1. examine the organizational structure of Municipal Council, Panchkula;
2. study the Personnel Administration of the Municipal Council, Panchkula;
3. review how efficiently the Municipal Council Panchkula is managing its finances;
4. analyze the physical performance of Municipal Council, Panchkula;
5. examine the level of satisfaction of citizens regarding basic services; and
6. suggest policy prescriptions for improving the performance of Municipal Council, Panchkula.

HYPOTHESES OF THE STUDY

In the present study, an attempt has been made to test the following hypotheses

1. The organizational structure of Municipal Council, Panchkula is not conducive to performance.
2. The employees of Municipal Council, Panchkula are dissatisfied with the personnel policy of the Council.
3. The Municipal Council, Panchkula does not manage its financial resources properly.
4. The sources of income of MCP are inadequate resulting in its overdependence upon grants in aid.
5. The physical performance of Municipal Council Panchkula is not satisfactory.
6. Users of services of Municipal Council Panchkula are not satisfied with the quality of services.

RESEARCH METHODOLOGY

The study is based on both primary as well as secondary data. The primary data was collected from 305 respondents spread over urban, rural and slum areas, through a structured questionnaire. The breakup of the respondents include 200 from the urban areas, 80 from the rural areas and 25 from the slum areas which were chosen by means of simple random sampling. Amongst the urban areas, sectors in the city were grouped into three categories on the basis of the level of prosperity: (i) posh area; (ii) other sector; and (iii) village and colony. One sector from each was selected. On the other hand, villages were included in the sample on the basis of distance i.e. one village each in close proximity to Municipal Council, Panchkula and one Village each at maximum distance. In the case of colonies, the biggest slum in the municipal area, namely, Rajiv Colony was included in the sample for study.

The objective for collecting primary data in this regard was to assess the users satisfaction about the quality of services provided by the MCP. In addition to the questionnaire, pictorial depictions, content analysis of news reports; the primary data was also collected from 79 employees of MCP (58 permanent and 21 contractual) to assess their level of satisfaction regarding the personnel policy of MCP.

In addition, various officials of MCP viz, President, former President and 16 Councilors (present and former) were also interviewed. The observation method was also used to supplement the data collected through various tools as mentioned above.

The secondary data was collected from various sources which included Audit and Annual Reports of MCP, Citizens Charter, Municipal Act of Haryana 1973 and the official documents related to sanitation, parks, fire brigades, streetlight and roads of MCP. The secondary data was also collected from the official documents of the Directorate of Urban Local Bodies Haryana, the Directorate of Local Bodies Audit and the Office of State Finance Commission, Haryana. The assessment of the physical performance of MCP with regard to select services has been undertaken by comparing the existing position of MCP regarding these services vis-à-vis the select parameters for the provision of these services.

The data thus collected, was analysed after classification, coding, editing, and tabulation by using SPSS package, and interpreted to test the hypotheses. Chi square was also used to check the association between selected variables.

III MAJOR FINDINGS

The major findings of the study along with the status of hypotheses have been presented chapter-wise as under.

A. General Findings

It has been found in the study that the Government has constituted several committees & commissions time to time to get recommendations for the improvement in Local Bodies. Despite plethora of recommendations made by them, the situation has not improved, due to the indifference of the state governments, lack of political will to initiate reforms and enforce the recommendations.

The rural population of India is urbanising and approximately one third of total population (377 million, 31.16.%) lives in 7935 Cities. In Solid Waste Management Sector, the door to door collection or house hold coverage is found to be 48 percent collection efficiency, 75 percent and scientific fill around 8 percent. Thus, even after more than a decade of formulation of Solid Waste Management Rules compliance of the same by cities found to be poor.

Other Inadequate access to infrastructure is a key constraint to the development of the cities. The cities and towns in India are visibly deficient in the level of infrastructural development and in provisioning of quality services, thus, the abysmal state of service delivery in the urban areas India lags far behind in terms of ensuring coverage, accessibility, quality, reliability and effectiveness of major public services.

Moreover, It has also been found in the study that to improve urban water supply and signification services, there is a need to constitute core teams in UBLs for each of the four sectors for formulating and implementing service delivery projects and an urgent need for states to establish and institutionalize the frame work with support from (MOUD) and other technical agencies.

Further, number of population residing in urban areas has increased from 2.58 crore in 1901 to 37.7 crore in 2011. Increase in population of class-1 cities (cities with 1,00,000 population) during 2001-2011 from 394 to 468 house, 264.9 million persons constituting 70% of total population, 53 Million plus cities and density of Urban population is 382/sq.km. This proportion has increased considerably as compared to 2001 census.

The study is also stressed upon the effective procedure for Solid Waste Management may be done through maintaining of waste hierarchy namely, Reduce, Reuse, Recycle and Recovery. However, in India, under this approach focus is generally on the last phase, i.e Recovery of resources and as a result, leading to poor states of Solid Waste Management. Kanpur PPP Model and Role of Informal sector initiative as a Muskan Jyoti initiative started in a small segment of Lucknow city were good start in a big and small Urban Settlement. In solid waste management, they suggest that for greater efficiency in public service provision, with the effect being to dilute rather than eliminate public ownership.

It has also raised in the study that in recent years, public service provisions are made through various forms of corporatization, public-public collaboration, public private partnership and contracting with the aim is to increase cooperation between public and private sector.

The municipality has to play multiple role at the same time as purchaser, local regulator and shareholder, which may cause conflicts of interest especially in the areas of water, waste and transportation sectors.

It brings out from the study that the Local Self Government in India is the most prominent and eye-opening factor is a conspicuous mismatch between sources of revenue and devolved functions.

Although, with 74th the Constitutional Amendment various, supportive provisions have been made for enhancement of urban local bodies but still several challenges are being faced by these institutions in the area of devolution of power, funds and functions.

The study also reveals that in India an half of our population will have been living in Urban Centre within next three decades and it may also make complexity for the Urban Governance. The purpose of understanding the dynamic of Urban Governance in the changed Scenario, State has been taking a backseat in terms of providing number of Urban Services to the citizen's earlier and remaining occupied by the private sector but also widens about the steps that have been taken place on the basis of Philosophy, the State would play the role not only as an instrument but also promoter, facilitator and include itself in only core areas of the affairs and many times the competitor in the service market as well and Economic pressure grouping .But ,this process presents very perplexing pictures of contrast and complexities in one and other ways. Moreover, other issues like, how government may be made participatory, transparent and accountable which may allocate developmental resources in appropriate manner and show responsiveness, consensus orientation, equity, effectiveness, efficiency and strategic vision with the quality of Governance.

The study depicts that it is glaring that neither the domain governments nor outside donor agencies have any faith and belief in the local urban bodies and they still rely on their own implementing agencies and bureaucratic machinery. So, this does not indicate well for the future of the Urban governance. On the basis of this, he beats the drum for if the charity is to begin at home, we shall have to create certain confidence levels, not only within the system as to these agencies, but also amongst the functionaries of these bodies as to their abilities to handle their affairs at these levels. He also presumes, beginning of this charity will as a challenge of 'democratic consolidation' process for India .

It is also highlighted in the study that according to 74th amendment, there were 18 matters given to the urban local body.

But only a small number of matters have actually been developed in most of states and ultimately it defeated the very purpose of the Act.

On the bases of the study the various major important findings have been given in the matrix below:

Matrix 1. General Issues & Challenges of Urban Local Bodies & Its Implication

Source	*Findings*
Issues & Challenges of Urban Local Bodies from various related literature	Inadequate level of empowerment of Urban Local Bodies, lack of personnel with appropriate skill sets, Inadequate skill sets of personnel already deployed. Apart from this presently numerous issues of Urban Governance i.e. devolution of power, funds and functions, maintaining coordination with others related departments and Ministry particularly Centre as well as State Government, dilemma of autonomy, capacity building, how developed the confidence upon these institutions, are they capable in their affairs, how secure transparency, accountability through adopting of e-governance concept, explore new concepts and practices for generating finances for urban local self government. One of the important methods is being adopted recently as 'Pooled Finance Development Fund Scheme' and secure participation of citizens and other agencies (like NGOs, civil societies and academia) in better policy formulation and implementation. For the purpose of understanding the dynamics of Urban Governance in the changed Scenario State has been taking a backseat in terms of providing number of Urban Services to the citizen's earlier and remaining occupied by the private sector. The steps have been taken place on the basis of Philosophy the State would play the role as a not only instrument but also promoter, facilitator and include itself in only core areas of the affairs and many times the competitor in the services market as well and Economic pressure complexities in one and other ways

and new methods and technique like Public Private Partnership, contracting out, as recent development Public Public collaboration.

The 58th round survey of NSSO conducted in 2002

Slum population is increasing day by day and figured about 8 million urban house folds lives in slums.

The MoHUPA committee

estimated the slum population to be 9.30 crore in 2011 and 10.46 crore in 2017

MGI Report (2010)

estimated that there will be sharp deterioration in the quality of urban services in the Indian cities by 2030, and this projection has been made keeping the view of current trends approaches of the city Governance.

Census 2011

classified the towns primarily in two categories i.e. statutory and census towns and these census towns do not enjoy statutory municipal status and as statutory. Therefore, they are largely unregulated, lying outside the municipal governance and Tax net; Bereft of basic civic services and amenities as well as serve as potential sites for unplanned and slum-type growth. there was a only 6.37% increase in statutory towns between 2001-2011 and huge 185.90 % increase in Census towns, there were 1362 Census Towns in 2001 and it increased to 3894 in 2011. From this, it may be observed that policy was made for 242 but 2532 are expected to get benefit for this.

The first time India added more people to cities (91 million) than rural (90.4 million) areas. The decadal population growth rate for urban India is quite high compared to rural India (12.2%) leading to over congestion and heavy pressure on urban infrastructure and amenities.

Analysis of Census (2011) and NSS Data, 54th Round survey 1998-99 & 65th Round Survey 2008-09 Data on Current Service Levels- All India and States

Only 80% of house hold having access to safe drinking water and 62 percentage of house hold having tap water from treated source, percentage of garbage collected disposed off daily in Urban areas are merely 70% to 90% in big cities and less than 50% in small cities share of Urban roads in total road network is only 9.0% and 92.7 % of households having access to electricity against the 100% Bench marks.

The Ministry of Urban Development	has brought out the Handbook of Service Delivery Bench Marking which is prescribed universal service delivery benchmarks for some urban services
The 12the Plan (2012-17)	called for spectral reforms in this for critical sectors in a big way and it has emphasized the principle of Simultaneous and Integrated Service Provision (SISP) approach for covering road map to implementing service level benchmarks and suggested a method to formulating and implement state and city sanitation plans as per National Urban Sanitation Policy for solid waste management and also, prepare implementable PPP Policy for cities.
the 13th Finance Commission	Has made it mandatory to adopt the service level benchmarks by Urban Local Bodies across the country. The 13th finance commission has also endorsed the indicators and made it mandatory for all the states to issue a gazette notification on current service levels and fix the largest for improvement on annual basis. The main sources of increase in income of all the categories of municipal bodies because of grants-in-aid not due to raising of revenue from their own resources.
High Powered Expert Committee (HPEC) Report-2011	It has brought out only 21 percent of the waste water generated is treated, less than 30 percent of solid waste is segregated and scientific disposal of water is almost never practiced.
A Pilot Exercise of MoUD in selected 28 cities and around 1500 ULBs	To assess the current service level in them against these bench marks. The data give prominence to significant gaps in service delivery and the need for improving the performance of the sector in the coming year.
Advisory Note of the MoUD (2012) on "Improving Urban water supply and sanitation services: The key principle of service delivery"	favours key role of local bodies in the area of sanitation and water supply for service provision, operation and maintenance either directly or by engaging PPPs, through establishment of appropriate institutional and organizational framework. It also suggests that state should set up regulatory mechanism as an independent agency for setting

	standards, monitoring performance, and adjusting tariffs, etc.
The 12th Plan Working Group on Industrial and Urban water supply and sanitation	the planning commission has favoured to build capacity of municipal officials and engineers to implement innovative and emerging technologies and approaches.
ARC-II (Sixth Report)	The committee has recommended the creation of new deliberation house at the State level Legislative Council for Local Bodies at the district level District Council. Further, new institution on namely, separate Standing Committee for examination of Audit Report for entire local bodies in the State and Audit Committee for each district in particular state.
AIMC-2007 at Chandigarh	Various methods were highlighted in the conference for improvement of working conditions of urban local bodies, such as: Bus Rapid Transit System, Role of Local Self government in the way of governance, And emphasis on larger public institutional alongwith matrix/ structure, Prof. B.S. Ghuman, who has participated in conference stresses State Government should be forced for devolution of powers. Other amenities have given weightage for great participation of women in local bodies. It also highlighted the various issues like; how to make city gender friendly, greening the city, proper solid waste management an answer to global warming, adopting E-Governance, increasing colonies & migrant population, development of urban infrastructure, Public- Private Partnership and bench marking through TWINNING.
AIMC-2012 at Bathinda	Conference suggested contour of Policy and genuine certain facts in the tune of method and technology, which may be helpful in development in Urban Local Bodies.
The World Bank Report-2014	According to The World Bank Report-2014, Punjab (India) provides Water Supply 85%, Sewerage Cover 65% and with 65 % of Sewerage Treatment Plant Capacity of its urban

	population and it is merely 54.7% and 50.49% and 58% respectively for all India level. Thus, the report gives prominence to Punjab as a top leading State in India for providing some of urban amenities such as, water supply sewerage and having sewerage treatment plant.
14th Finance Commission Report and Urban Local Bodies (2015)	The Commission has proposed grants in aid of revenues of States for revenue deficit local bodies and disaster management under article 275 of the Constitution of India. It has put up that local bodies **should be required to spend the grants only on the basic services within the functions assigned to them and for the distribution of grants to states for local bodies 2011 population to be taken in consideration** with weightage 90% for population and 10 % for on the basis of area. The purpose grants will be divided into two parts for rural bodies and urban local bodies on the bases of urban and rural population and worked out a total grant of Rs.2,87,436/- crore for the period of 2015-2020 for local bodies and it has been categoried as a basic grant and performance grant in the ratio of 80:20 with respect to Municipalities. It is weighty to mention here that the government has accepted above recommendations.
3rd State Finance Commission Haryana- 2008	emphasized and put up social audit for effecting transparency in the functioning of institutions, facilitates public activities, works or programmes being undertaken by Local Bodies for their timely completion, costs, achievements and quality of works and for maintaining of roads correctly. With warranty the quality of works, plugging leakages in the system and reduces manipulation. Capacity building and empowerment of the various stakeholders of local bodies i.e. elected representatives, functionaries and civil societies and empowerment of citizens and secure e-community

participation were others remarkable enjoinder of the commission.

The commission has observed that the data base of local bodies is very precious. There is no reliable mechanism for collection of data at any level i.e. local body, departmental and government level. So, it suggested that there should be creation of effective and appropriate database.

B. Organizational Structure and Functioning

The organizational structure of MCP has been divided into 2 wings the Deliberative wing and the Executive wing. The Deliberative Wings includes the councilors while The Executive Wing comprises of several branches. The major findings with regard to their organization and functioning are summed as under:

The study found that the MCP comprises of the Deliberative wing and the Executive Wing. However, it has not constituted any sub-committee which could have played an important role in improving its effectiveness and functioning of MCP. Further, the study found that there is a lack of proper coordination between its different branches impacting its performance. In terms of task allocation, the study reveals that no proper rationale has been used. Some branches of the MCP have been over burdened in contrast to others which have been allocated only few tasks. Besides, the structure has no in-built mechanisms for proper supervision.

Unfair means while electing the President in the Council are galore. Democracy does not exist in letter and spirit, when it comes to the electing a President or the Council. The Judiciary has also taken cognizance of it. Manier times, The President has been removed from his post during his tenure by the Government. In some cases even the court has ruled that the removal of President by the Government is illegal and ordered his reinstatement of the President.

The study reveals that the scheduled meetings of Council are not conducted according to the given stipulated time. The interval between the two meetings is generally large. Between the years 2001-2010 on an average only 3 meetings were held. The absence of the President is one of the reasons for the irregular conduction of the meetings. There is a provision in the Haryana Municipal Act, 1973 that if the President and the Vice President are not available, then the councilors can elect one amongst themselves as a chairman. But this provision has been violated due to political motive and a lack of clearly defined procedure. Another reason is a lack of quorum for the meeting which is 1/10 of the total members. The councilors do not have much interest in attending the meetings and hence, the quorum suffers.

Honorarium of members is also not adequate and it is another major factor affecting the functioning of the Council.

The Council has not constituted any sub-committees for carrying out its responsibilities; this affects its working in terms of economy, effectiveness and efficiency. It is relevant to mention here that the Haryana Municipal Act, 1973 has provisions for constituting the sub-committees for Municipal Council, Panchkula.

The Engineering branch is over burdened as it has to perform a large number of functions dealing with parks, roads, and works regarding the passing of maps. Besides, there is no separate branch of MCP for catering to the park services.

Another finding of the study was that in some cases, the resolutions passed by the Council are manipulated by the Executive wing at the time of implementation. For example it has been found that, the executive wing sometimes draws extra money from the municipal funds than the sanctioned amount.

It is also found in the study that due to shortage of employees, the MCP has a larger span of control in its organizational structure.

The study reveals that there was no separate public relations branch of MCP to handle the grievances of citizens and to provide citizen centric inputs.

Testing of Hypothesis 1:

The analysis of the secondary data was used to check the status of Hypothesis 1: "The organizational structure of Municipal Council, Panchkula is not conducive to performance".

According to S K Bhatacharya[1], an organizational structure having the following features is conducive for performance:

i) Effective task allocation.
ii) Proper coordination.
iii) Proper supervision.
iv) Formation of smaller task groups.

As mentioned above, in order to be conducive to performance, an organizational structure should have effective task allocation. In case of MCP, it has been found that some of the branches have been allocated work disproportionate to their capacity to perform. For example, the Engineering Branch of MCP has to not only look after the large area relating to roads (405 kilometers) in the MCP jurisdiction, but also perform tasks related to the all around development and maintenance of around 200 parks.

Secondly, proper coordination is another significant determinant for the conducive performance of any organization. The study shows that in MCP, there are cases of lack of coordination between The Deliberative Wing and the Executive Wing as well as between different branches of the MCP. For example, during the interview the Councilors clearly opined that the policies formulated by the Deliberative Wing are not executed properly by the MCP staff and, due to weak coordination between both the wings. Further, the study showed a lack of coordination between the Accounts Branch and The Engineering Branch with regard to payments to the contractors, particularly to the Park Development Societies.

The literature also shows that for a conducive performance, the structure should facilitate supervision. In case of supervision, the study reveals that in MCP, there is a lack of proper supervision on the part of the Council due to an inadequate number of Sanitary Inspectors and Junior Engineers for Sanitation and Electrical Branches, respectively. In the case of sanitation services, the areas under MCP jurisdiction have been divided into 2 sanitary zones but in MCP a post of Sanitary Inspector is lying vacant. Further, only 2 Saffai Darogas have to supervise a large area i.e. 39.5 square kilometer area covering1,90,000 population. For street lights, one Junior Engineer has to look after as many as 10,000 street light points.

The formation of smaller task groups or sub-committees results in good organizational performance. The study suggests that MCP has failed to set-up sub-committees or smaller task groups. It is relevant to mention here that the Haryana Municipal Act, 1973 authorizes urban local governments to constitute sub committees for effective functioning in different fields. MCP has not implemented this provision of the Act.

Thus, an evaluation of MCP on the basis of above mentioned parameters suggests that the existing organizational structure of MCP is at variance with the organizational structure's conducive performance. In the light of this the hypothesis 1, namely, "The organizational structure of Municipal Council Panchkula is not conducive to performance" **stands validated.**

C. Personnel Administration

The personnel administration of the MCP suffers on many accounts.

A shortage of staff is the major impediment in the way of performance of MCP. About 44.2% of posts in MCP are lying vacant in its various wings. The present staff is not in a position to deliver time bound services to the citizens and thus the performance of MCP gets adversely affected.

There is no proper system of classification for the employees of MCP. A discussion with the employees revealed that they do not know about their positions/ranks in the classification.

For long the MCP has not recruited new staff. The Recruitment Rules are very old; and thus, the qualifications required for particular posts are not as per requirements of the present job scenario.

Frequent transfers at the senior levels of MCP have been noticed. A long gap has been observed in filling the posts which got vacated due to transfers. This affects the working of MCP adversely.

No appropriate policy of deputation has been adopted by MCP for filling the vacant posts through deputation.

The capacity building of the employees suffers the most in MCP. No separate institute for providing training to the employees of the Municipalities including MCP, has been set up in Haryana. The Higher officials of the MCP are imparted training at Haryana Institute of Public Administration (HIPA). However, there is no provision for training the lower level employees in MCP. The employees learn their job responsibilities through a hit- and- trial basis. It was found during study that only one employee i.e. an Accountant got training between the years 2001 and 2010.

The study shows that the promotional avenues for the lower level employees are very few. This affects their morale adversely.

In cases of indiscipline in MCP, the disciplinary actions are taken in rare cases. Even in those cases, the employees try to use political and other influences to escape the disciplinary proceedings.

Testing of Hypothesis 2:

The analysis of both primary and secondary data was used to check the status of Hypothesis 2: "The employees of Municipal Council Panchkula are dissatisfied with the personnel policy of the Council". This hypothesis has been split into sub-hypotheses, covering areas such as recruitment policy; classification system; pay scale policy; training system; promotion system; leave system; fringe benefit system; disciplinary action; service conditions; management employees relation; and working hours.

More than half of the total permanent employees reported that they were not satisfied with the personnel policy of the MCP. In the case of Contractual employees, 100 percent reported dissatisfaction about recruitment policy, working hours, pay scale policy, leave system and service conditions. The major findings have been summarized in the Matrix below:

Matrix 2. Summing the Testing of Hypothesis 2

Sr. No.	*Sub-hypothesis*	*Sources of data*	*Analysis*	*Status of Sub-hypothesis Y Valid N Invalid*
1.	The Employees of MCP are not satisfied with the recruitment Policy	Primary	**1.Permanent employees:** About 48% employees are dissatisfied with the recruitment policy while 22 per cent were indifferent	No conclusion can be drawn
			2.Contractual employees: About 90% employees are dissatisfied and very few are indifferent towards the recruitment policy	Y
2.	The Employees of MCP are not satisfied with the classification system	Primary	Permanent employees: About 66per cent employees are dissatisfied with the classification policy	Y
3.	The Employees of MCP are not satisfied with the pay scale Policy	Primary	1.Permanent employees: About 80 per cent employees are dissatisfied with the pay scale policy	Y
			2.Contractual employees: All the contractual employees are dissatisfied with the pay scale policy	Y
4.	The Employees of MCP are not satisfied with the training Policy	Primary	Permanent employees: About 71 per cent employees are dissatisfied with the	N

		training policy	
5. The Employees of MCP are not satisfied with the transfer Policy	Primary	Permanent employees: About 73 per cent employees are dissatisfied with the transfer policy	Y
6. The Employees of MCP are not satisfied with the promotion Policy	Primary	Permanent employees: About 62 per cent employees are dissatisfied with the promotion policy	Y
7. The Employees of MCP are not satisfied with the leave system	Primary	1.Permanent employees: About 81 per cent employees are dissatisfied with the leave system 2.Contractual employees: All the contractual employees are dissatisfied with the leave system	Y Y
8. The Employees of MCP are not satisfied with the fringe benefits system	Primary	1.Permanent employees: About 78 per cent employees are dissatisfied with the fringe benefits system	Y
9. The Employees of MCP are not satisfied with the disciplinary action	Primary	1.Permanent employees: About 63 per cent employees are dissatisfied with the disciplinary action system 2.Contractual employees: About 71 per cent employees are dissatisfied and only 29 per cent are indifferent with the disciplinary action system	Y Y
10. The Employees of MCP are not satisfied with the service conditions	Primary	1.Permanent employees: About 84 per cent employees are	Y

		dissatisfied with the service conditions 2.Contractual employees: All the contractual employees are dissatisfied with the service conditions	Y
11. The Employees of MCP are not satisfied with the management employees relation	Primary	1.Permanent employees: About 71 per cent employees are dissatisfied with the management employees relation 2.Contractual employees: About 53 per cent employees are dissatisfied with the management employees relation	Y Y
12. The Employees of MCP are not satisfied with the Working hours	Primary	Contractual employees: All the contractual employees are dissatisfied with the Working hours	Y

Thus, on the basis of the above analysis of sub hypotheses, the Hypothesis 2: "The employees of Municipal Council Panchkula are dissatisfied with the personnel policy of the Council" is **accepted.**

D. Financial Administration

The findings of the study regarding the financial administration reveal that though, the budget of the MCP is passed regularly, but it is not implemented in stipulated time mainly because the permission is not granted timely by the State Government through District administration. This leads to spending of lesser money vis-à-vis allocated in the budget and finally, results in the poor performance of MCP.

The study also shows that the income of MCP between 2001-2010 has fluctuated.

It has also been found that the area of obligatory taxes is constrained by the policies of the state government. Another revealing finding is the huge gap between the estimated and the actual income both, in cases of major and minor sources of income of MCP. The State government has got special powers regarding taxation through Municipal Act of Haryana. Sometimes these powers are misused in terms of tax modification, under considerations other than merit.

In this way the concentration of power in the hands of the state government to allow the raising of resources through taxation adversely affects the fiscal health of MCP.

The study reports that the grants-in aid are not a major source of income of MCP. Their share was merely 2.20 per cent of the total income between 2001 to 2010. Further, the State Finance Commissions are not set up on a regular basis as stipulated in the Act, as a result, MCP received its share of grants only for one year despite the recommendations covered for a time period of five years.

Another finding of the study is that the non developmental expenditure consumes the maximum revenue and as a result the development work of the city suffers majorly.

The study shows that there was clear imbalance in expenditure of select services. For instance, if Rs.100 were spent on the five basic services of MCP between 2001 to 2010 then Rs.57.53 were allocated for roads, Rs. 12.88 for sanitation, Rs. 13.65 for Parks, Rs. 4.95 for street lights and Rs. 1.60 for fire brigade implying thereby, that the distribution of resources of these services were not in adequate proportion.

There is no proper system of maintenance of accounts in MCP.

Further, the audit objections are not properly cleared by the MCP. There is lack of proper coordination between the Audit and Accounts branch of MCP.

Testing of Hypotheses 3 & 4

The analysis of both primary and secondary data was used to check the status of Hypothesis 3: "The Municipal Council, Panchkula does not manage its financial resources properly" and Hypothesis 4 "The sources of income of Municipal Council Panchkula are inadequate resulting in its over dependence upon grants-in-aid".

Matrix 3. Summing the Testing of Hypothesis 3 and 4

Hypothesis	*Sub-hypothesis*	*Sources of data*	*Analysis*	*Status of Sub-hypothesis Y Valid N Invalid*
Hypothesis 3: The Municipal	I. The MCP does not	Secondary data	The data about major and minor	Y

Council, Panchkula does not manage its financial resources properly	prepare budget estimates properly, especially in case of taxes.	heads of income from taxes shows a huge variation between the budgeted estimates and actual income, thereby reflecting a lack of undertaking of scientific exercise to estimate revenue from taxes and also indicating a poor tax compliance. This trend is particularly visible in case of the development work wherein on an average only 22.53 per cent of the estimated taxes were actually realized between 2001 and 2009. In case of minor heads, the actual income from fire tax, interest on investments, rent of shops and electricity duty has always been much higher than the budgeted estimates. For example, between the years 2001-09, the income from the fire tax, interest on investments, rent of shops and electricity duty as percentage of budgeted estimates was 3481 percent, 280 percent, 135 percent and 104.9 percent respectively. In case of road cut charges, tehbazari

		malba and composition fees, it was 1513 percent, 228 percent and 172 percent of the budgeted estimates respectively.	
II. Non developmental expenditure maximum revenue and in the process, the development of the city suffered	Secondary data	The ratio of development expenditure to the non-development expenditure has been low. The average of development expenditure as a percentage of non-development for the years 2001 to 2010 was only 8.2%, 25.5%, 36.5%, 26.2%, 24.7%, 21.80%, 20.82%, 18.30% and 17.08% respectively.	Y
III. There is an imbalance expenditure on select services by MCP.	Secondary data	There is an imbalance in expenditure on select service delivered by MCP. For example, over the years the expenditure on roads has been larger than that on other services like sanitation, parks, street lights and services. The expenditure on road as a percentage of development expenditure for the years from 2001 to 2010 was 60.5%, 13.40%, 15.09%, 4.87%, 1.79%, respectively. If Rs. 100 were spent between 2001 to 2010 for select	Y

		services, Rs 57.53 were allocated for road, Rs 12.88 for sanitation, Rs 13.65 for Parks, Rs 4.95 for street light and Rs 1.60 for fire brigade.	
Hypothesis 4: The source of income of MCP are inadequate resulting in its over dependence upon grants -in-aid	Secondary data	The contribution of grants-in-aid received by the MCP as a percentage of its total income is only 2.9% (average of the period 2001-2009). During the period 2001-2004, The contribution of grants-in-aid received by the MCP as a percentage of its total income is only 2.9% (average of the period 2001-2009). During the period 2001-2004, MCP did not receive granst-in-aid.	N

Thus, on the basis of the above analysis of sub hypothesis, the Hypothesis 3: "The Municipal Council Panchkula does not manage its financial resources properly" **stands validated** and Hypothesis 4: "The sources of income of Municipal Council Panchkula are inadequate resulting in its over dependence upon grants-in-aid" gets **rejected**.

E. Physical Performance

The physical performance of the MCP is not satisfactory. Many factors are contributing towards poor performance of MCP on the basis of certain physical indicators. The status of physical performance of MCP has been studied as under:

Testing of Hypothesis 5

For evaluating the status of the Hypothesis 5: "The physical performance of Municipal Council Panchkula in not satisfactory", the results have been summarized in the Matrix.

Matrix 4. Summing up the Status of Hypothesis 5

Sub-hypothesis *data*	*Source of*	*Analysis* *hypothesis* *Y Valid* *N Invalid*	*Status of Sub-*
(i) Physical performance of MCP with regard to sanitation services is not satisfactory due to a drastic decline over time in physical equipment per thousand population, inadequate manpower, lack of modern waste management methods and deviation of provision of sanitation services from the prescribed benchmarks	Primary and Secondary data	• In 2001 MCP had 290 equipment which increased marginally to 292 in 2010. Equipment per 1000 population suggests that the same declined drastically from 193 to 153 between 2001 and 2010. • Further it was found that no practice of segregation of waste, recycling and incineration of waste was adopted by the MCP. • Pictorial depictions indicate worse conditions of sanitation services, specifically in villages and colonies. • Sanitation services are not extended to 30 percent of the population. • Collection of waste was 50 % of the total. • Disposal of waste 70% against the standards of 100%. • The number of Disposal Bins was 1/1373 population against the norm of 1/75. • The number of sanitary workers was 1.54 per thousand population against the benchmark of 2.8.	Y
(ii) Physical performance of MCP with regard to road services is not satisfactory on account of lack of inadequate manpower, physical equipment, poor	Primary and secondary data	• The Engineering Branch has only 3 employees against the requirement of 20 employees. • The existing staff of Engineering Branch is mainly non-technical and cannot ensure compliance of terms	

maintenance of roads, improper monitoring of the contractual work and provision of road services not according to the benchmarks		and conditions of the contracts. • Between 2001 to 2010, only 186 km roads were repaired and maintained. • MCP has no equipment of its own for road services. It mainly depends upon equipment of contractors which are many time made available slowly. • District Administration Reports and Urban Estate Department Reports of Haryana were very critical of road services. • Pictorial depictions indicate very bad conditions of roads in MCP jurisdiction. • In MCP, there are only 2.11 km roads per thousand population against the prescribed benchmark of 11.09 km roads. The roads cover only 70% of the population.	Y
(iii) The Physical performance of MCP in terms of Street light services is not satisfactory owing to inadequate physical equipment, shortage of employees, negligence by MCP, the provision of services not in consonance with increase in population, poor monitoring and standard of street light services not being as per the prescribed standards.	Primary and secondary data	• The Electrical Branch has only 2 employees against the requirement against the requirement of 58 employees. • Further the existing staff of the Engineering Branch is mainly non technical and cannot ensure compliance of terms and conditions of the contracts. • The number of street lights was 8607 in 2001 which increased only which increased only to 8763 in 2010 thus, adding only 156 street lights. • Street lights per of thousand population clearly suggest that MCP has failed to provide street	

		lights in tune with the growing population. • Street lights per thousand were only 44.75 in 2001 which declined drastically to 21.68 in 2010. • Between 2001 to 2010 the physical equipment with Electrical Branch remained three only. • Pictorial depiction indicates very bad conditions of Street light in MCP jurisdiction. • Distance between two poles was not as per the benchmarks. The distance between two poles should be 28 meters, whereas, in case of MCP, the distance is of 35 meters. • The number of contractual workers was 13 in 2001, which increased only to 21 in 2010. During this period, the population of Panchkula increased manifolds. • The performance of MCP on account of street lights is not satisfactory as per the report of District Administration and Urban Estate Department of Haryana.	Y
(iv) The Physical performance of MCP in regard to services is not satisfactory due to insufficient physical equipment, absence of up gradation and modernization, inadequate manpower and provision of fire services not being in consonance with the	Primary and secondary data	• The number of contractual employee was 20 in 2001, which decreased to 17 in 2010. During this period, the population of Panchkula increased manifolds. • Between 2001 to 2010, the physical equipment with Fire Branch increased from 5 to 7 only. MCP could not upgrade and modernize its physical equipment	

benchmarks prescribed by National Disaster Management Authority		according to the present demands of fire situation. • The prescribed norms are 4 fire tenders, 2 water tenders. Against these MCP has only 2 fire tenders and 2 water tenders.	
(v) The Physical performance of MCP terms of park services is not satisfactory owing to an inadequate provision of parks viz-a-viz population, absence of physical equipment, non-monitoring of the works of Parks Development Society, deprivation of parks services for the resident of colonies and slums, and absence of services in relation to prescribed standard.	Primary and secondary data	• MCP has no separate personnel for catering to parks services. This function is looked after by itsEngineering Branch. • Further the existing staff of the Engineering Branch mainly consists of non technical staff and cannot ensure compliance of terms and conditions of the contracts. • Only 78 parks were developed and maintained against the requirement of 204 parks. • MCP has no physical equipments for providing adequate park services to residents. • Pictorial depictions indicate worse conditions of parks in MCP jurisdiction. • In case of villages and colonies, there are no parks. MCP has only one park for 250 meters areas against the prescribed benchmarks of 2 for same area. • No proper physical infrastructure in parks as per the prescribed benchmarks. • Urban Estate Department of Haryana found irregularities in development of parks and inferior quality of park in MCP jurisdiction.	Y

An analysis of the sub hypotheses reveals that the Hypothesis 5: "The physical performance of Municipal Council Panchkula is not satisfactory" **stands validated**.

F. CITIZENS' SATISFACTION

The performance of MCP from the citizens perspective is also not satisfactory. Citizens in villages and colonies are more dissatisfied vis-à-vis those from posh sectors. A brief account of the performance of MCP from citizens' perspective is as under:

In case of Sanitation, it is observed that the colonies are totally neglected. Though, posh areas are more cleaner than other areas, but a large number of citizens of MCP are not satisfied with the sanitation services being provided.

In case of street lighting also most of the citizens are not satisfied. There is no provision of street lighting in villages and colonies.

As far as the parks are concerned that there is no provision of parks in colonies and rural areas. As far as the urban areas are concerned, the parks are not well maintained and this has resulted in dissatisfaction of citizens of Panchkula.

Fire brigade services are also poor. In most of the cases, the services are not provided promptly.

In case of Road services, most of the people are dissatisfied. Rural areas and colonies are totally neglected as some parts in these areas donot have roads at all. In urban areas, the citizens complained about the poor maintenance of roads.

The Citizens also have grievances regarding the handling of complaints promptly.

Testing of Hypothesis 6

For evaluating the status of the Hypothesis 6: "Users of services of Municipal Council Panchkula are not satisfied with the quality of services", primary data has been used and main hypothesis has been split into various sub-hypotheses such as: satisfaction of the citizens with the condition of 'roads'; 'sanitation'; 'street light'; 'parks'; and 'fire brigade services'. The major findings regarding the satisfaction of citizens have been summarized in Matrix.

Matrix 5. Summing up the Testing of Hypothesis 6

Services and Sub-hypothesis	*Sources of Data*	*Analysis*	*Status of Sub-hypothesis Y Valid N Invalid*
1. Sanitation a) Users are not	Primary Data	A. About 80 % of citizens are dissatisfied with	

satisfied with the provision of sanitation services		the garbage collection.	
		B. Around 75% of citizens are dissatisfied with cleanliness.	Y
2. Street Lights a) Users are not satisfied with the provision of street lights services	Primary Data	A. About 75 % of citizens are dissatisfied with the quality of street lights.	Y
3. Roads a) Users are not satisfied with the quality of roads	Primary Data	A. About 89 % of citizens are dissatisfied with the conditions of roads.	Y
4. Parks a) Users are not satisfied with the maintenance of parks	Primary Data	A. About 59 % of citizens are dissatisfied with the park maintenance.	Y
5. Fire Brigade services a) Users are not satisfied with the quality of fire brigade services	Primary Data	A. About 59 % of citizens are dissatisfied with the fire prevention services.	Y
6. Users are not satisfied with the overall quality of services	Primary Data	A. About 86 % of users are dissatisfied with the overall quality of services being provided by MCP.	Y

An analysis of the sub hypotheses reveals that the main Hypothesis 6: "Users of services of Municipal Council Panchkula are not satisfied with the quality of services" **stands validated.**

IV POLICY PRESCRIPTIONS

Based on the findings of the study, a number of policy prescriptions have been suggested. The policy prescriptions cover facets such as organizational structure and functioning of MCP, personal administration, financial administration and physical performance.

A. Organisational Structure and Functioning of MCP

The literature especially Bhattacharya (1989) reveals that the organisation structures are conducive to performance which have proper coordination, effective tasks allocations, proper supervision, and forms smaller task groups. Following policy prescriptions have been made covering these aspects of organizational structure of MCP.

(i) Proper Coordination

The present study reveals a lack of coordination between the Deliberative and the Executive Wings on one hand and among various branches of MCP on the other hand. It is therefore suggested, that better coordination be ensured between different wings as well as within branches of MCP for improving its overall performance.

(ii) Effective Task Allocation

The study reveals that MCP has failed to effectively allocate of the tasks to its different branches and in the process, some branches have been over-burdened. It is suggested that rational task allocation be done for the various branches of MCP taking into account their mandate, important functions, budget and manpower.

(iii) Proper Supervision

The study showed that the performance of MCP suffered due to ineffective supervision. In the light of this, it is suggested that MCP should appoint more supervisory staff for ensuring better performance.

(iv) Smaller Task Groups

The formation of smaller task groups are seen as an effective means of carrying out activities by the administrative organizations. The study found that in MCP, no such effort has been made. It is relevant to mention here that despite the provision in the Haryana Municipal Act 1973 to create sub-committees for effective functioning, the MCP has not set up the sub committees. It is suggested that MCP should set up need based sub-committees as per the Act. This initiative will certainly help in improving the performance of MCP.

(v) Regular Meetings

The study reveals that in MCP on an average, only 3-4 meetings are held. It is suggested that 12 meetings of MCP as per statutory provisions should be held each year.

(vi) Public Relations Branch

In the light of the study, it is recommended that there should be Public Relations Branch in MCP. This branch should act as a liaison office between MCP and citizens. The suggestions received from the citizens should regularly be conveyed by this branch to MCP for improving its functioning.

(vii) Grievance Redressal Machinery

The study clearly suggests that the citizens are not satisfied with the provision and quality of services. MCP does not follow a declared time frame work in attending and disposing of the citizens complaints. It is recommended that MCP, should activate its grievance redressal machinery for winning over the confidence of its citizens.

B. Personnel Administration

The study clearly suggests that MCP has not paid adequate attention to personnel administration. This has resulted in poor performance of MCP. For improving various aspects of personnel administration, the study has suggested the following recommendations:

(i) Recruitment of Staff on Priority Basis

A grain shortage of staff adversely affects the service delivery of any organisation. In case of MCP, shortage of staff is a norm, not an exception. The acute shortage of staff has emerged as a stumbling block in the performance of MCP. It is strongly recommended that MCP should a launch recruitment drive immediately, so that the problem or shortage of staff is solved and the confidence of public towards service delivery is restored.

(ii) Modification of Recruitment Rules

Improvement in the eligibility conditions for recruitment for better performance of governance is must . The employees should possess educational qualifications corresponding to the nature of functions to be performed. In the present, context there is a strong need for well qualified man power particularly, in the light of quality- centric development. The study revealed that the eligibility conditions of recruitment in case of MCP, which are governed by HMIRC, 1988 rules, lay down have relatively become out dated. It is therefore, suggested that the eligibility conditions for recruitment be improved in tune with the need of the service delivery as per the expectations of the citizens.

(iii) Capacity Building of Existing Staff

In the light of the changing landscape of organisations and expectations of citizens, it is essential to equip the staff with the latest developments. MCP has failed in this regard. It is suggested that its staff may be trained regularly to upgrade their working.

There should be a separate Training Institute for imparting training to the municipal employees. The course contents of the trainings should reflect the realities of the of present day municipal administration. The MCP must make efforts to train its lower categories of employees as well to improve the delivery of services in the field.

(iv) Expediting Disciplinary Action

It has been found that MCP is very lenient with respect to its disciplinary action. This practice sends wrong signals. It is therefore, suggested that strict disciplinary action must be taken against erring officials and penalty imposed should be carried out without any fear or prejudice.

(v) Transparent Transfer Policy

In MCP, several concerns were shown by its employees regarding the non-transparent and arbitrary transfer policy. In the light of this, it is suggested that the transfer decisions about the employees of MCP should be undertaken in an open and transparent manner and frequent transfers should be avoided. This would help in raising the morale of the employees and enable them to concentrate on the work.

C. Financial Administration

Financial administration is another casuality in MCP. This specialized area of public policy has not been steered as per the cannons of public financial administration. For improving the fiscal health of MCP, a couple of policy prescriptions have been made.

(i) Effective Tax Estimation

Tax administration plays a pivotal role in the financial administration. This area, however, is not scientifically handled by MCP. For example, there is a glaring gap between the tax estimates and the actual tax revenue. This considerable gap suggests that both, the procedure for estimating tax revenue and tax compliance need to be improved considerably. This qualitative change in the budgetary exercise will help in bring stability in the revenue of MCP.

(ii) Balanced Development Expenditure

At present the maximum resources are eaten up by the non-developmental heads and subsequently development becomes the victims. MCP should make efforts to ensure that there is an adequate and balanced allocation of resources under every head especially, the heads covering developmental works.

(iii) Statutory Time Frame for Passing of Budget

The study suggests that the budget of the MCP is often approved late by the District administration and thus a lot of money during the financial year remain unspent. It is therefore suggested that there should be a statutory time- frame within which the District Administration must approve the budget of the MCP so to enable the MCP to implement its programmes as per the stipulated time frame.

(iv) More Obligatory Taxes

The area of obligatory taxes of MCP should be enlarged so as to make it financially self sufficient. The state Government must ensure that any tax exemptions for any category of persons /bodies should not be governed by political considerations. While taking such decisions, the financial health of MCP should be the only criterion.

(v) Constitution of State Finance Commission within Stipulated Time Frame

It has been found that Haryana Government does not constitute the State Finance Commission well within time framework. It is recommended that the State Government should constitute Finance Commission on time, so that the MCP can receive its grants on time.

(vi) Proper Audit and Account System

There should be a proper system of record keeping of the accounts of MCP. A mechanism should be evolved whereby reply to audit objections is filed in time and in case of delay a system of imposing fine/penalty on the erring official should be imposed. This is necessary to check the wastage of public money. There should be a proper co-ordination between the Audit and Accounts branches for efficient utilization of funds.

D. Physical Performance

For improving the physical performance of MCP the following policy recommendations have been identified:

(i) Better Contract Agreement System

MCP provides many services through contracting out mode. Therefore, the contract agreement plays a significant role towards the delivery of services. It is suggested that the contract should be designed in a scientific manner. Each term and condition of the contract be designed in such manner that the violations should automatically result in a levying of penalty. It should also be ensured in contract agreement that no contractor, should be allowed to leave the contract midway.

(ii) Regular Inspection of Road Works

It has been found in the study that the material used for road construction and maintenance is of substandard quality. In the light of this, it is suggested that the materials used by contractors should be as per the norms of Public Works Department (PWD). This quality can be ensured only if there is proper and regular supervision. Regular inspection of roads after construction should also become a normal feature of MCP.

(iii) Monitoring of Park Development Society (PDS)

The study has mentioned that the maintenance of parks have been contracted out by Municipal Council Panchkula (MCP) to PDS. The working of PDS is not up to the mark mainly due to poor monitoring and supervision system. It is thus, suggested that an inspection team be constituted for ensuring compliance of the contract with PDSs.

(iv) More Funds for Basic Services

There has been a large scale development and growth of areas under Municipal Council Panchkula. The increasing population has created a pressure on the existing infrastructure. It is suggested that the MCP needs to invest heavily in the maintenance as well as expansion of the basic services particularly-streetlights, park and fire services to cope with the increasing pressure of growing population.

(v) Improvement in Physical Equipment

Inadequate physical equipment results in the poor performance of MCP. It is therefore, suggested that the physical equipment related to maintenance and working of MCP should be increased as per the expansion in the population being served by MCP. For instance, sanitation, fire brigade, and street light services need addition in terms of their physical equipments every year.

(vi) Use of Modern Technology

For improved sanitation services, modern methods like segregation of waste, recycling and incineration of waste be used. Like wise fire services, modern technology like advanced ladders and foam water tenders must be used.

(vii) Improve Basic Services

MCP must give special attention to the provision of sanitation services for the entire city in general, and the colonies and rural areas in particular. There should be a provision of street lights and parks in colonies and rural areas. The maintenance of street lighting should be a priority in the urban areas/sectors of the city. The provision of fire brigade services in MCP jurisdiction must be prompt in consonance with the saying, 'A stich in time saves nine'.

(viii) General Suggestions

1) There are several issues & challenges of Urban Local Bodies in India. Keeping the issues and challenges of those bodies, while making the policy for urban development and ensure effective implementation with assistance of these bodies as well.
2) The Government had established various committees and commissions for giving the recommendations for the improvement of Local Bodies. But these recommendations had not been implemented by the government heartily. Appropriate actions and measures base on these suggestions are needed to be taken. Further, Public Public Collaborations in service delivery as a alternative of privatization is desired.
3) Regulation of census city through Municipal Act and Regulation of State Government and bring them in the jurisdiction of Urban Local Government which ultimately may enhance the receipts of respective authority and quality of services will also be raised by curving the leakage.

REFERENCES

1. Bhattacharya, S. K. *op. cit.*

Bibliography

Books

Argal, R., *Municipal Government in India,* Agarwal Press, Allahabad, 1967.

Arora, Ramesh K. and Goyal, Rajni, *Indian Administration: Institutions and Issues*, Wishwa Parkashan, New Delhi, 1977.

Avasthi, A. and Narain, Lakshmi, *Municipal Administration in India*, Agarwal, Agra, 1980.

Basu, D. D., *Introduction to the Constitution of India,* Wadhawa and Company Law Publishers, Agra, 2003.

Bhatia, D. H. L., *Public Finance*, Vikas Publishing House, Alahabad, 2008.

Bhattacharya, S. K. *Achieving Managerial Excellence Insight from Indian Organization*, Macmilan India Ltd., New Delhi, 1989

Bhayana, Sahib Singh, *Local Government in India*, New Academic, Jalandhar, 1989.

Chandran, E., *Public Administration Part-I*, Cosomos Bookhire, Gurgaon.

Charles, Adrian, R., *Governing Urban America*, Charles Press McGraw-Hill, book Company, 1977.

Cox III, Raymond W., Buck, Suan J., Morgan, Betty N., Public Administration in Theory and Practice, Pearson Education, Delhi, 2005.

Dhaliwal, S. S, *Municipal Administration*, Deep and Deep, New Delhi, 1990.

Dutt, R. K., *Survey of Local Government in India Including Punjab and Haryana,* Malhotra Book Depot, Jalandhar City, 1978.

Etzioni, Amitai, *Modern Organisation*, N. J. Prentice-Hall, New Delhi, 1964.

Fadia, B. L., *Public Administration*, Sahitya Bhawan Publication, Agra, 2008.

Finer, Herman, *Theory and Practice of Modern Government*, Hereditary Holt and Company, New York, 1949.

Gladden, E. N., *The Civil Services, its Problems and Future*, Staples Press, London, 1945.

Goel, S. L., *Personnel Administration and Management*, Sterling Publishers, New Delhi, 1993.

Horn, Charles-T, *Accounting for Management Control: An Introduction*, Prentice-hall of India, New Delhi, 1976.

Humes, Samuel and Martin, Eileen M., *The Structure of Local Government through out of the World,* The haguemartinus Nijhoff, Netherlands, 1956.

Hussain, M., *Role of Municipal Councilor: A Case Study of Chitoor Municipality, The Universe of Public Administration*, Associated Publishing House, New Delhi, 1993.

Jackson, R. M., *The Machinery of Local Government*, Macmillan and Co., New York, 1959.

Khanka, S. S., *Organisational Behaviour (Test and Cases)*, S. Chand and Company, 2004.

Khanna, Ratan Lal, *Power, Function, Duty: Local Government in Punjab*, The English Book Shop-Book Seller and Publishers, Chandigarh, 1994.

Koontz, Harold and Wihrich, Heinz, *Essential of Management,* Tata McGraw Hill Publishing Company, New Delhi, 2001.

Maddic, Henary, *Democracy, Decentralization and Development*, Asia Publishing House, Bombay, 1963.

Maheshwari, S. R., *Local Government in India*, Laxmi Narain, Agra, 2012.

Mamoria, C. B. and Gankar, S. V, *Personnel Management*, Himalya Publishing House, Mumbai, 2007.

Marsheil, L., *Development Teaching*, New York, 1949.

Marx, F. M. (Ed.), *Elements of Public Administration*, Prentice Hall of India, New Delhi, 1968.

Mohanty, Bijoyini, *Municipal System in India: Citizen's Involvement*, Ashish Publishing House, New Delhi, 1993.

Nigro, Felix, *Public Administration Readings and Documents*, Rinehart and Co-Inc., New York, 1951.

Paul, Pigours and Myers, Charles A., *Personnel Administration-A Point of View and Method*, McGraw Hill, New York, 1965.

Robson, William A., *Great Cities of the World*, George Allen and Unwin, London, 1972.

Sachdeva, P., Municipal Administration: The Punjab Scenario, Associated Publishing House, New Delhi.

Sachdeva, Pradeep, *Urban Local Government and Administration in India*, Kitab Mahal, Allahabad, 1993.

Sharma, Mahadeo Prasad, *Local Self Government and Finance in Utter Pradesh*, Kitab Mahal, Allahabad, 1954.

Singh, Partap, *Urban Government in India*, Upkar Publishing House, New Delhi, 1978.

Singh, Sahib and Singh, Swinder, *Local Government in India*, New Academic, New Delhi, 2000.

Stahl, Glen, O., *Public Personnel Administration*, Harper and Row Publishers, New York, 1966.

Torpey, William G., *Personnel Management*, D. Van Nostrand, New York, 1953.

White, L. D., *Introduction to the Study of Public Administration*, McMillan, New York, 1955.

White, L. D., *Introduction to the Study Public Administration*, Eurasia Publishing House Delhi, 1968.

Willoughby, W. F. *Principal of Public Administration*, New York, 1964.

Journals

Alok, V.N. "Share of Local Governments in the Union Divisible Pool: An Option Before the 13th Finance Commission", *Indian Journal of Public Administration*, Vol. LV, No.1, January-March, 2009.

Ammons, David N., William C. Riven Bark. "Factors influencing the use of performance data to improve Municipal services Evidence from the North Carolina Benchmarking project", *Public Administration Review*, March-April, 2008.

Bagchi, Kanak Kanti and Taran Kumar Ghosh, "Finance of Panchayats in West Bengal-New Areas of Resource Mobilisation", *Indian Journal of Public Administration*, Vol. L, No.3, July-September, 2004.

Chatterjee, Biswajit and Dilip Kumar Ghosh, "Globalisation and Decentralised Governance Reflection on Panchayats in India", *Indian Journal of Public Administration*, Vol. XLIX. No.2, April- June, 2003.

Coe, Charles K., "Preventing Local Government Fiscal Crises: - Emerging Best Practices", *Public Administrative Review*, July-August, 2008.

Col, Jeanne-Marie, "Managing Disasters: The Role of local Government", *Public Administration Review*, December 2007, Special Issue.

Datta, Abhijit, "National Level Municipal Training in India: Need Reorientation", *Indian Journal of Public Administration*, Vol. XXXIX No.4, October-December 1993.

Dubey, A.K. "Relevance of Rural Development in the Context of Urbanisation", *Indian Journal of Public Administration*, Jan- Mar, 2000.

Dubey, P.K. "Strengthening Urban Local Bodies in Chhatishgarh", *Nagarlok*, Vol. XXXVIII, No.2, April-June, 2006.

Garnett, James L. Justin Marlowe, Sanjay K Pandey, "Penetrating the performance predicament: Communication as a Mediator or moderator of organizational culture's impact on public organizational performance", *Public Administration Review*, March-April, 2008.

Ghuman, B.S. and A. Mehta, "Privatisation of Public Services by Urban Local Governments in India: A Case Study of Municipal Council, Panchkula", *Nagarlok,* Vol. XLII, No. 1, Jan- March, 2010.

Gnaneshwar, V. "State Finance Commission and Urban Local Bodies in India: An Assessment of their Recommendation", *Indian Journal of Public Administration*, Jan-March, 2003.

Handley, Donna Milam, "Strengthening the inter governmental grant system- Long tern Lessons for the federal – Local relationship", *Public Administration Review*, Jan-Feb, 2008.

Heikkila, Tanya "Citizen Involvement and Performance Management in Special Purpose Governments, Kimberley Roussin", *Public Administration Review*, March-April, 2007.

H-Svara, James, Strengthing, "Local Government Leadership and Performance: Reexamining and updating the winter commission Goals", *Public Administration Review*, Dec. 2008,

Kundu, R.K. "Urban local bodies and SFC in Haryana: Some Observation", *Nagarlok*, Vol-XXXIX, No. 1, Jan-Mar, 2008.

Luthra, Ashwani, "Public-Private Partnership: A Tool for integrated urban Development – An Urban affairs quarterly", *Indian Journal of Public Administration*, Vol. XXXVIII, No, 2, April – June, 2006.

Malik, Lokendra and Kaur, Avneet, "Urban Governance in India: An Analysis", *Nagarlok*, Vol. XLV, No. 3, July-Sept, 2013.

Malik, Lokendra, "Solid Waste Management and Sustainable cities in India: A critique" *Indian Journal of Public administration*" VOL. XLII, No.4, Oct- Dec 2010.

Meena, Manna Lal, "Urban Governance in India: Urbanisation, Initiatives, Challenges and Futuristic Perspective", *Nagarlok,* Vol. XLIV, No. 2, April-June, 2012.

Misra, G. "Public and private partnership", *Quarterly Journal of Local Self Government*, LXVII No.2, 1995.

Nahvi, G.L. "Municipal Administration in Sri Nagar (J&K) A Review", *Indian Journal of Public Administration*, Vol. XLIX. No.2 April-June, 2003.

Palnitkar, Sneha "Public–private partnerships for urban service delivery system with special reference to solid waste management", *Local Government Quarterly*, July-Sept, 2007.

Ranjan, Sanjeev "Service Level Benchmarking : an initiative of the Ministry of Urban Development", Government of India ,", *Nagarlok* ,Vol. XLII, No.1, Jan- March 2010.

Reddy, M. Gopinath and N. Sreedevi, "Local Finances in Andhara Pradesh: A Situational Analysis", *Indian Journal of Public Administration*, Vol.4, No.3, July-Sept, 2004.

Sangwan, Randhir Singh "Urabanization in Haryana: The Emerging Trends", *Nagarlok*, Vol. XL April-June, 2008.

Sarda, A, "Financial Management for Decentralised Governance", *Indian Journal of Public Administration*, Vol. XLIX, No.4, Oct-Dec. 2003, pp. 693-710.

Sharma, Ashok and Sodhi, Inderjeet Singh, "Civil Society and the Governance of Local Bodies: Issues and Challenges", *Nagarlok,* Vol. XXXIX, No.2, April-June, 2007.

Singh, Gurgant and Gill, Rajbans, "Status of Reforms in Urban Governance in India: An Overview", *Nagarlok*, Vol. XLV, No. 2, Apr-Jun, 2013.

Singh, Rajesh "Performance Impediments In Government: Some Suggestion For Reforms", *Indian Journal Of Public Administration*, Vol. LV, No.2, April-June, 2009.

Singh,Mohinder "Transparency in Functions : Vital for Gram Panchayats", *Indian Journal of Public Administration*, Vol. YLIX, No.4, Oct-Dec, 2003.

Sodhi, Inderjeet Singh, "Evolution and Development of Local Government in Tanzania Issues and Challenges", *Nagarlok*, Vol. XLV, No. 2, Apr-June, 2013.

Tyagi, A.R. "Administrative Training: A Theoretical Postulate", International Review of Administrative Science, Vol. XI, No. 2, 1974, p.157.

Vyasuly, Vinod. "The Functioning of Local Government in Federal System", *Local Government quarterly*, Jan-Mar, 2009.

Wichowsky, Amber, Donald P. Moynihan, "Availability Administrative Modernization in German", *Public Administration Review*, Sept-Oct, 2008.

Reports

Government of India, *"Report of Local Finance Enquiry Committee"*, Vol. II, New Delhi, 1951.

Government of India, *"Report of Taxation Enquiry Commission"*, Vol. II, New Delhi, 1955.

Government of India, *"Report of Committee on Training of Municipal Employees"*, New Delhi, 1963.

Government of India, *"Report of Committee on Service Condition of Employees"*, New Delhi, 1968.

Government of India, Ministry of Works and Housing, *"Report of the Committee on Budgetary Reform in Municipal Administration"*, New Delhi, 1974.

Government of India, *"Rural Urban Relationship Committee Report"*, Volume 1, 1978.

Government of India, *"Report of National Commission on Urbanization"*, New Delhi, 1988.

Government of Haryana, *1st State Finance Commission Report*, 1997.

Thesis

Khem Singh, *"Organisation and Working of Municipal Corporation Shimla"*, Unpublished Thesis, Department of Public Administration, Panjab University, Chandigarh, 1990.

News Papers

Singh, Sukhbir, "Mayors: Looking Beyond Ceremonial Role", *The Tribune*, Nov. 27, 2010, p. 13.

Acts and Rules

Haryana Municipal Act, 1973, Punjab Law Agency, Chandigarh,

Haryana Municipal Safai Majdoor Service Rules, 1976.

Haryana Municipal Services, H.M.S I.R.C.S. Rules, 1982.

Municipal Council, Panchkula, Audit's Inspection Note, 2005-06.

ANNEXURE - I

Contractual Agreement of Sanitation Services

1. The sanitary agencies should be responsible for the cleaning of towns, streets and drainage of the allocated areas/ its zonal jurisdiction and in cleaning process collected waste material, silt and every type of waste material should be put in an area authorized by Municipal Council, Panchkula.
2. The ratio of workers should be 2 against 1000 population in Council jurisdiction.
3. Municipal Council should appoint separate employees for cleaning, pick up of waste material, capturing stray animals and in addition to this other special employees be employed for cleaning squad. The Trollies used for carrying purposes should be of closed type. Further, one refuse collector and one dumper is to be provided by Council and for this driver and other employees are to be provided by the contractors. The appointed drivers should have driving license for driving these vehicles.
4. Agencies should clean the silt from drainage system/drainages within 5 days after the commencement of the contract and the silt taken out is to be disposed properly and this whole process is to be completed within stipulated time period. In this process, it is the estimated that 5 tractor trolliess are required.
5. Community toilets and fire brigade offices should be cleaned twice a day and the materials used in this like phenyl, acid, soap, washing powder, deodorant should be of good quality.
6. All *safai* workers have to be in uniform.
7. Cleaning system should be of such type by which people are satisfied.
8. Whenever, a VIP person arrives or public function is organized, cleaning facilities should be completed /well maintained.

9. Cleaning process in Municipal Council jurisdiction also includes the proper disposal of small dead animals like cat, dog, pig, rat and birds. All this is to be done by *safai* workers.
10. Waste-disposal should be undertaken in a systematic manner. It be poured into proper garbage bins meant for this purpose and these garbage bins be dumped daily into proper place. In these places lime and bleaching powder should be sprayed and waste material should be in closed chamber for transport to dumping grounds.
11. All Cleaning work is to be compulsorily done on Sunday and on gazetted holidays also.
12. For public grievances there should be made a proper authority, whose function would be to see public problems. It has to be opened regularly from 6.00 A.M. to 6.00 P.M., and made functional on all Sundays and public holidays. All complaints should be handled and solved within stipulated time period i.e. 24 hours.
13. Safai workers would also do the job of cleaning the waste generated by public from their kitchen, gardens, like grass, cut branches of trees and dry leaves.
14. Cleaning is to be done in all parks, open plots, foot paths, all roads, and waste near curved roads properly. Road crossings and market parking is also included in this. And all cleaning process is to be done in morning and evening also.
15. Material used in this process is to be provided to the sanitation workers e.g. brooms, spade, cutting swords and masks, gloves, hand pulled rickshaw and Rehris.
16. Dust deposited on road sides and dividers is to be dusted regularly. Bushes and congress grass is to be swept properly and regularly.
17. Cleaning timing in summer would be 6.00 a.m. to 11 a.m. and 2.00 p.m. to 5.00 p.m. and in winter timing should be 7.00 a.m. to 12.00 p.m. and 2.00 p.m. to 5.00 p.m.. Working hours are to be constant of 8 hours in summer and winter.
18. Waste material collected which is fire prone/flammable, cannot be burned.
19. In every sector market, a notice board be put in proper place which reflects where to contact for complaints.
20. No employee should be absent so that sweeping process get affected.

ANNEXURE-II

Contractual Agreement of Road Services

1) The road works must be completed within stipulated period. For example for construction of new roads, the stipulated period is two months.
2) The work is to be executed as per the norms of the Measurement Work-4; approved D.N.I.IT and the work order.
3) The agencies have to do the work strictly as per specifications and further during the inspection of work/testing of samples, if any deficiency in the specifications is noticed, the agency 'personally' will be responsible. Moreover, the agency will bear the losses personally without any excuses.
4) If there is any addition or alteration in the work, the agency has to do the work on same terms, condition and rates.

ANNEXURE-III

Contractual Agreement of Street light Services

1. Agency will provide all the necessary material required for the maintenance of existing points such as lamps/sodium lamps/ tube rods/ chokes/ starters/ igniters etc.
2. Agency will provide sufficient skilled labour – Mechanical Lift Ladders, Tool Kits and required safety measure instruments at its own level.
3. Supervisors employed by the Agency must be technically qualified. In each sector /village, the agency shall employ 2 full time supervisors with mobile communication system and shall give their contact numbers, to Municipal Council, Panchkula..
4. Maintenance materials of standard make like Philips/ Bajaj / GE/ Crompton/ Osram will be used by the agency. The chokes will also be used of copper instead of Aluminium.
5. Intensity of lamps should not be less than 85% of the rated lumen output.

6. Intensity of lamps should remain "ON" in case of non-functioning of street light points.
7. The agency shall have to rectify the unlit street light points within 48 hours on the receipt of the complaint.
8. Agency will be responsible for switching "ON/OFF" the street light system and maintain scheduled timings fixed by the competent authority. In case the agency fails to switch off the lights in time, it will be liable to pay the difference of energy calculated on the basis of connected load for the period of default or Rs. 5/- per point per hour, whichever is higher will be charged.
9. Agency will not remove any installed material from the site of work and handover the same to the J.E. (Electrical) of the Municipal Council, Panchkula.
10. Service lanes will be provided with ACSR conductor given by the Municipal Council and PVC insulated/PVC sheathed wire/ cable of good quality duly ISI marked shall be provided by the contractor.
11. Agency shall make provision for opening offices at two places within the municipal area and one in M.C. office with telephone facilities where public can contact and lodge their complaints. One full time qualified employee in each office will have to be deputed by the contractual agency. The said office will remain open with attendant from 6.00 am to 12.00 midnight including all Saturdays, Sundays and all other gazette holidays.
12. Numbering of street light points shall be done by the Agency as per MC coding system and detailed report shall be submitted by the agency within seven days from the date of commencement of contract to M.C. Panchkula at its own cost.
13. The main connection of street light points will be shown to the Agency only before the start of work by JE concerned of MC, Panchkula and written confirmation in this regard will be submitted by the Agency before the commencement of work.
14. The Agency will submit daily compliance report of all complaints attended during the day at 4.45 p.m. to Executive Office/ Secretary/J.E. (Electrical).
15. The Agency shall get checked all material to be replaced from the JE concerned before replacement.
16. The Agency will be bound to get the signatures of the owner of the house after getting the street light repaired in front of his house.

ANNEXURE-IV

Contractual Agreement of Park Services

1. There should be Mali and Saffai workers employed in every park.
2. The Agency will be responsible for bordering the parks providing grilles, establishing proper gates at entrance of the parks, well painted, street lights and foot paths are also requirements.
3. There should be proper arrangement for flowering seeds and tools used in gardening.
4. Inside the park, there should be proper watering of flower beds, rose and other plants should be planted and also to green grass.
5. Parks should be proper fenced by iron grill, with sitting arrangement.
6. Peace of silence is to be maintained in parks.

ANNEXURE-V

QUESTIONNAIRE FOR CITIZENS

Q1. How long you have been staying here?
- (i) 10 years and above ☐
- (ii) Between 5 – 10 years ☐
- (iii) Between 1- 5 years ☐
- (iv) Any other ☐

Q2. Who is your councilor? ____________________

SANITATION

Q3. Who is responsible for providing sanitation services in your locality?
- (i) Municipal Council Panchkula
- (ii) Contractor
- (iii) Any other Agency (Specify)

Q4. How many times roads/streets are swept / cleaned in your area?
(i) Daily
(ii) One in a week
(iii) Twice in a week
(iv) Thrice in a week
(v) Any other

Q5. Are you satisfied with the cleanliness in your locality?
(i) Yes (ii) No
If No, give the reason.
____
____
____

Q6. Who is responsible for collection of garbage in your locality?
(i) Municipal Council Panchkula
(ii) Contractor
(iii) Any other Agency (Specify)

Q7. Are you satisfied with the system of collection of garbage from your area?
(i) Yes (ii) No
If No, state reason.
____
____
____

Q8. What does the Municipal Council initiates spraying of your area?
(i) Yes (ii) No
If yes, How often?
(i) Once in a month
(ii) Once in three months
(iii) Once in six months
(iv) Once in a year
(v) Any other (Specify)

Q9. Are you satisfied with this frequency?
(i) Yes (ii) No
If No, state reason.
____
____
____

Q.10 Do you think sanitation work should be privatized?
(i) Yes (ii) No
If Yes, specify the reasons.

____

____

____

If No, specify the reasons.

____

____

____

ROADS

Q.11 Who is responsible for providing and maintaining the roads in your locality?
(i) Municipal Council Panchkula
(ii) Contractor
(iii) Any other Agency (specify)

Q12. Are you satisfied with the condition of roads in your locality?
(i) Yes (ii) No
If No, specify the reasons.

____

____

____

Q13. Do you think maintenance of roads in your locality should be privatized?
(i) Yes (ii) No
If Yes, specify the reasons.

____

____

____

If No, specify the reasons.

____

____

____

STREET LIGHTS

Q14. Who is responsible for the provision of street lights in your locality?
(i) Municipal Council Panchkula
(ii) Contractor (iii) Any other Agency (Specify)

Q15. Are you satisfied with the provision of street lighting in your locality?
(i) Yes (ii) No
If No, give reasons.
____
____
____

Q16. Do you think maintenance of the street light work should be privatized ?
(i) Yes (ii) No
If Yes, specify the reasons.
____
____
____
If No, specify the reasons.
____
____
____

PARK

Q.17 Do you have any park in your sector/locality?
(i) Yes (ii) No

Q18. Who is responsible for the provision and maintenance of parks in your area?
(i) Municipal Council Panchkula
(ii) Contractor
(iii) Any other agency (specify)

Q19. If yes, is it properly landscaped and maintained?
(i) Yes (ii) No

Q20. Are you satisfied with its maintenance
(i) Yes (ii) No

If No, specify the reasons.
____
____
____

Q21. Do you think maintenance of parks work should be privatized?
(i) Yes (ii) No
If Yes, specify the reasons.

____
____
____

If No, specify the reasons.

____
____
____

FIRE SERVICE

Q22. Who is responsible for the provision of fire-fighting services in your locality?
(i) Municipal Council Panchkula
(ii) Contractor
(iii) Any other agency (specify)

Q23. Are you satisfied with fire prevention / fire brigage service in your city?
(i) Yes (ii) No
If No, give reasons.

____
____
____

Q24. Have you ever made any complaint to Municipal Council regarding these services?
(i) Yes (ii) No
If yes, for which of the following services did you make the complaint.
(i) Roads
(ii) Sanitation
(iii) Street Lights
(iv) Parks
(v) Fire Service
(vi) All the Above

Q25. Have you faced any problems while filing complaints?
(i) Non availability of the concerned officials
(ii) Rude behaviour
(iii) Unnecessary harassment
(iv) All of the above
(v) None

Q26. In case of complaints made by you, to the authorities, how long does it take for them to actually take action and remove the problems?

(i) Same Day ☐

(ii) 1- 7 days ☐

(iii) 7 – 14 days ☐

(iv) One month ☐

(v) Any other ☐

Q27. What is your over all satisfaction level regarding the service delivery by Municipal Council Panchkula?

(i) Highly Dissatisfied

(ii) Dissatisfied

(iii) Neutral

(iv) Satisfied

(v) Highly satisfied

PERSONAL DETAILS

Name :

____

Address :

____

____

Ward No.

____

____

Occupation

____

____

Education

____

Salary

____

Age

____

Gender. ☐ Male ☐ Female

Date: Time

ANNEXURE-VI

QUESTIONNAIRE FOR THE EMPLOYEES OF MCP

1. Name and Contact No. :

....

2. Education :

....

3. Age :

....

4. Department/Branch :

....

5. Designation :

....

6. Job Description :

....

7. Work experience in the organization
   (a) Less than 2 years ☐
   (b) 2 years to 5 years ☐
   (c) 5 years to 10 years ☐
   (d) More than 10 years ☐
8. How did you come to the present job?
   (a) Through Newspaper Advertisement ☐
   (b) Through Employment Exchange ☐
   (c) Through Interview ☐

(d) Through Deputation ☐
(e) Through any other source (specify) ☐

Please tick (Ö) the relevant response indicating your level of satisfaction with regard to the following aspects of personnel policy of Municipal Council, Panchkula

Sr. No.	Aspects of Personnel Policy	High Satisfied	Satisfied	In-different	Dis-satisfied	Highly Dis-satisfied
9	Recruitment Policy					
10.	Classification system					
11.	Pay scale Policy					
12.	Training Policy					
13.	Transfer Policy					
14.	Promotion Policy					
15	Leave System					
16	Allowance / Fringe Benefits					
17	Disciplinary Action System					
18	Service Conditions					
19	Management & Employee Relations					

ANNEXURE-VII

Questionnaire for the Municipal Councilors

Name & Contract No.: ....

Address : ....

Ward No : ....

Councilor since : ....

1. The powers provided to Municipal Councilors are adequate to perform the functions of Municipal Administration ?

   Yes/No

2. Do you think Municipal Council, Panchkula needs more autonomy in working ?

   Yes/No

3. What you have done for the provision of roads?

   ____

   ____

4. What your have done for improving the quality of roads ?

____

5. What you have done for the provision of street lights ?

____

6. What you have done for improving the quality of street lights ?

____

7. What you have done for the provision of sanitation ?

____

8. What you have done for improving the quality of sanitation ?

____

9. What you have done for the provision of Fire Services ?

____

10. What you have done for the improving quality of Fire Services ?

____

11. What you have done for the provision of Parks?

____

12. What you have done for improving the quality of parks ?

____

13. Do you think Municipal Council, Panchkula has adequate financial resources ?

Yes/No

14. In your opinion, are finances properly utilized by Municipal Council, Panchkula ?

Yes/No

15. Do you think there is adequate staff to run Municipal Council, Panchkula ?

Yes/No

16. Do you think co-opted members (MLAs and MPs) are helpful in working of Municipal Council, Panchkula ?

Yes/No

If no what are the problems ?

....

17. What are the challenges being faced by you as the elected representative of the municipal Council, Panchkula ?

18. What are the problems being faced by you as the elected representative of the Municipal Council, Panchkula ?

19. Any suggestions for improving the services provided by Municipal Council

Index

R

U

V

W

Z